Mosaic 1

GRAMMAR

Patricia K. Werner

Lou Spaventa

McGraw Hill

Mosaic 1 Grammar, Silver Edition

Published by McGraw-Hill ESL/ELT, a business unit of The McGraw-Hill Companies, Inc., 1221 Avenue of the Americas, New York, NY 10020. Copyright © 2007 by The McGraw-Hill Companies, Inc. All rights reserved. No part of this publication may be reproduced or distributed in any form or by any means, or stored in a database or retrieval system, without the prior written consent of The McGraw-Hill Companies, Inc., including, but not limited to, in any network or other electronic storage or transmission, or broadcast for distance learning.

ISBN 13: 978-0-07-340641-1
ISBN 10: 0-07-3406414
1 2 3 4 5 6 7 8 9 10 VNH 11 10 09 08 07 06

Editorial director: Erik Gundersen
Series editor: Valerie Kelemen
Developmental editor: Susannah MacKay, Jennifer Bixby
Production manager: Juanita Thompson
Production coordinator: Lakshmi Balasubramanian
Cover designer: Robin Locke Monda
Interior designer: Nesbitt Graphics, Inc.
Photo researcher: Photoquick Research

The credits section for this book begins on page 472 and is considered an extension of the copyright page.

Cover photo: David Samuel Robbins/Corbis

The McGraw-Hill Companies

A Special Thank You

The Interactions/Mosaic Silver Edition team wishes to thank our extended team: teachers, students, administrators, and teacher trainers, all of whom contributed invaluably to the making of this edition.

Macarena Aguilar, **North Harris College**, Houston, Texas ▪ Mohamad Al-Alam, **Imam Mohammad University**, Riyadh, Saudi Arabia ▪ Faisal M. Al Mohanna Abaalkhail, **King Saud University**, Riyadh, Saudi Arabia; Amal Al-Toaimy, **Women's College, Prince Sultan University**, Riyadh, Saudi Arabia ▪ Douglas Arroliga, **Ave Maria University**, Managua, Nicaragua ▪ Fairlie Atkinson, **Sungkyunkwan University**, Seoul, Korea ▪ Jose R. Bahamonde, **Miami-Dade Community College**, Miami, Florida ▪ John Ball, **Universidad de las Americas**, Mexico City, Mexico ▪ Steven Bell, **Universidad la Salle**, Mexico City, Mexico ▪ Damian Benstead, **Sungkyunkwan University**, Seoul, Korea ▪ Paul Cameron, **National Chengchi University**, Taipei, Taiwan R.O.C. ▪ Sun Chang, **Soongsil University**, Seoul, Korea ▪ Grace Chao, **Soochow University**, Taipei, Taiwan R.O.C. ▪ Chien Ping Chen, **Hua Fan University**, Taipei, Taiwan R.O.C. ▪ Selma Chen, **Chihlee Institute of Technology**, Taipei, Taiwan R.O.C. ▪ Sylvia Chiu, **Soochow University**, Taipei, Taiwan R.O.C. ▪ Mary Colonna, **Columbia University**, New York, New York ▪ Lee Culver, **Miami-Dade Community College,** Miami, Florida ▪ Joy Durighello, **City College of San Francisco**, San Francisco, California ▪ Isabel Del Valle, **ULATINA**, San Jose, Costa Rica ▪ Linda Emerson, **Sogang University**, Seoul, Korea ▪ Esther Entin, **Miami-Dade Community College**, Miami, Florida ▪ Glenn Farrier, **Gakushuin Women's College**, Tokyo, Japan ▪ Su Wei Feng, Taipei, Taiwan R.O.C. ▪ Judith Garcia, **Miami-Dade Community College**, Miami, Florida ▪ Maxine Gillway, **United Arab Emirates University**, Al Ain, United Arab Emirates ▪ Colin Gullberg, **Soochow University**, Taipei, Taiwan R.O.C. ▪ Natasha Haugnes, **Academy of Art University**, San Francisco, California ▪ Barbara Hockman, **City College of San Francisco**, San Francisco, California ▪ Jinyoung Hong, **Sogang University**, Seoul, Korea ▪ Sherry Hsieh, **Christ's College**, Taipei, Taiwan R.O.C. ▪ Yu-shen Hsu, **Soochow University**, Taipei, Taiwan R.O.C. ▪ Cheung Kai-Chong, **Shih-Shin University**, Taipei, Taiwan R.O.C. ▪ Leslie Kanberg, **City College of San Francisco**, San Francisco, California ▪ Gregory Keech, **City College of San Francisco**, San Francisco, California ▪ Susan Kelly, **Sogang University**, Seoul, Korea ▪ Myoungsuk Kim, **Soongsil University**, Seoul, Korea ▪ Youngsuk Kim, **Soongsil University**, Seoul, Korea ▪ Roy Langdon, **Sungkyunkwan University**, Seoul, Korea ▪ Rocio Lara, **University of Costa Rica**, San Jose, Costa Rica ▪ Insung Lee, **Soongsil University**, Seoul, Korea ▪ Andy Leung, **National Tsing Hua University**, Taipei, Taiwan R.O.C. ▪ Elisa Li Chan, **University of Costa Rica**, San Jose, Costa Rica ▪ Elizabeth Lorenzo, **Universidad Internacional de las Americas**, San Jose, Costa Rica ▪

Cheryl Magnant, **Sungkyunkwan University**, Seoul, Korea ▪ Narciso Maldonado Iuit, **Escuela Tecnica Electricista**, Mexico City, Mexico ▪ Shaun Manning, **Hankuk University of Foreign Studies**, Seoul, Korea ▪ Yoshiko Matsubayashi, **Tokyo International University**, Saitama, Japan ▪ Scott Miles, **Sogang University**, Seoul, Korea ▪ William Mooney, **Chinese Culture University**, Taipei, Taiwan R.O.C. ▪ Jeff Moore, **Sungkyunkwan University**, Seoul, Korea ▪ Mavelin de Moreno, **Lehnsen Roosevelt School**, Guatemala City, Guatemala ▪ Ahmed Motala, **University of Sharjah**, Sharjah, United Arab Emirates ▪ Carlos Navarro, **University of Costa Rica**, San Jose, Costa Rica ▪ Dan Neal, **Chih Chien University**, Taipei, Taiwan R.O.C. ▪ Margarita Novo, **University of Costa Rica**, San Jose, Costa Rica ▪ Karen O'Neill, **San Jose State University**, San Jose, California ▪ Linda O'Roke, **City College of San Francisco**, San Francisco, California ▪ Martha Padilla, **Colegio de Bachilleres de Sinaloa,** Culiacan, Mexico ▪ Allen Quesada, **University of Costa Rica**, San Jose, Costa Rica ▪ Jim Rogge, **Broward Community College**, Ft. Lauderdale, Florida ▪ Marge Ryder, **City College of San Francisco**, San Francisco, California ▪ Gerardo Salas, **University of Costa Rica**, San Jose, Costa Rica ▪ Shigeo Sato, **Tamagawa University**, Tokyo, Japan ▪ Lynn Schneider, **City College of San Francisco**, San Francisco, California ▪ Devan Scoble, **Sungkyunkwan University**, Seoul, Korea ▪ Maryjane Scott, **Soongsil University**, Seoul, Korea ▪ Ghaida Shaban, **Makassed Philanthropic School**, Beirut, Lebanon ▪ Maha Shalok, **Makassed Philanthropic School**, Beirut, Lebanon ▪ John Shannon, **University of Sharjah**, Sharjah, United Arab Emirates ▪ Elsa Sheng, **National Technology College of Taipei**, Taipei, Taiwan R.O.C. ▪ Ye-Wei Sheng, **National Taipei College of Business**, Taipei, Taiwan R.O.C. ▪ Emilia Sobaja, **University of Costa Rica**, San Jose, Costa Rica ▪ You-Souk Yoon, **Sungkyunkwan University**, Seoul, Korea ▪ Shanda Stromfield, **San Jose State University**, San Jose, California ▪ Richard Swingle, **Kansai Gaidai College**, Osaka, Japan ▪ Carol Sung, **Christ's College**, Taipei, Taiwan R.O.C. ▪ Jeng-Yih Tim Hsu, **National Kaohsiung First University of Science and Technology**, Kaohsiung, Taiwan R.O.C. ▪ Shinichiro Torikai, **Rikkyo University**, Tokyo, Japan ▪ Sungsoon Wang, **Sogang University**, Seoul, Korea ▪ Kathleen Wolf, **City College of San Francisco**, San Francisco, California ▪ Sean Wray, **Waseda University International**, Tokyo, Japan ▪ Belinda Yanda, **Academy of Art University**, San Francisco, California ▪ Su Huei Yang, **National Taipei College of Business**, Taipei, Taiwan R.O.C. ▪ Tzu Yun Yu, **Chungyu Institute of Technology**, Taipei, Taiwan R.O.C.

Table of Contents

Welcome to Interactions/Mosaic Silver Edition x

Scope and Sequence xvi

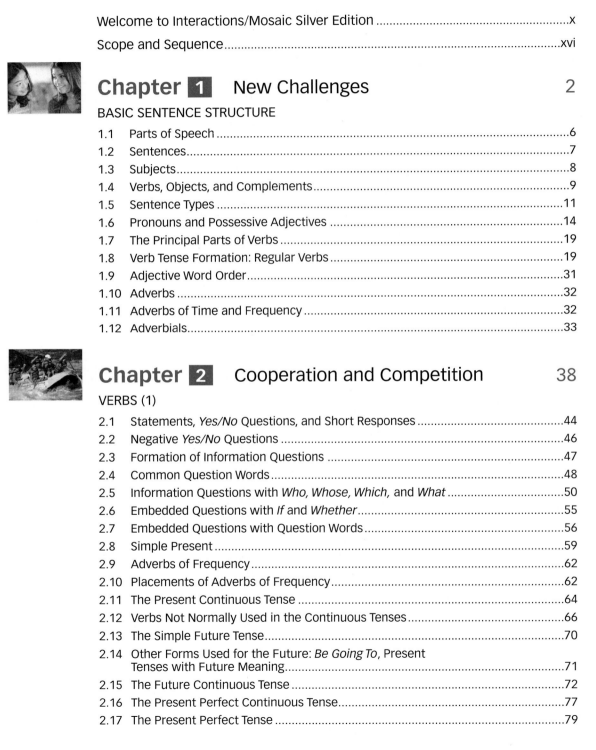

Chapter 1 New Challenges 2

BASIC SENTENCE STRUCTURE

1.1 Parts of Speech 6
1.2 Sentences...7
1.3 Subjects...8
1.4 Verbs, Objects, and Complements.....................................9
1.5 Sentence Types 11
1.6 Pronouns and Possessive Adjectives 14
1.7 The Principal Parts of Verbs 19
1.8 Verb Tense Formation: Regular Verbs 19
1.9 Adjective Word Order..31
1.10 Adverbs 32
1.11 Adverbs of Time and Frequency 32
1.12 Adverbials...33

Chapter 2 Cooperation and Competition 38

VERBS (1)

2.1 Statements, *Yes/No* Questions, and Short Responses 44
2.2 Negative *Yes/No* Questions 46
2.3 Formation of Information Questions 47
2.4 Common Question Words...48
2.5 Information Questions with *Who, Whose, Which,* and *What* 50
2.6 Embedded Questions with *If* and *Whether*...................55
2.7 Embedded Questions with Question Words 56
2.8 Simple Present 59
2.9 Adverbs of Frequency 62
2.10 Placements of Adverbs of Frequency...............................62
2.11 The Present Continuous Tense 64
2.12 Verbs Not Normally Used in the Continuous Tenses...........66
2.13 The Simple Future Tense..70
2.14 Other Forms Used for the Future: *Be Going To,* Present Tenses with Future Meaning................................71
2.15 The Future Continuous Tense 72
2.16 The Present Perfect Continuous Tense..............................77
2.17 The Present Perfect Tense 79

Chapter 3   Relationships   84

VERBS (2)

3.1   The Simple Past Tense 88
3.2   The Past Continuous Tense 94
3.3   *When* and *While* 96
3.4   The Present Perfect Tense 101
3.5   *Already*, *(Not) Ever, Just, Never, Recently, Still*, and *(Not) Yet* 103
3.6   The Habitual Past: *Would* and *Used To* 107
3.7   The Future in the Past: *Was/Were Going To* 108
3.8   The Past Perfect Tense 113
3.9   The Simple Past versus the Past Perfect Tense 114
3.10   The Past Perfect Continuous Tense 115
3.11   The Future Perfect and Future Perfect Continuous Tenses 116
3.12   Quotations versus Reported Speech 119
3.13   Verb Changes with Reported Speech 119
3.14   Changes in Pronouns, Adjectives, and Adverbials with Reported Speech 121
3.15   *Say* versus *Tell* 123

Chapter 4   Health and Leisure   130

MODAL AUXILIARIES AND RELATED STRUCTURES

4.1   Modal Auxiliaries 134
4.2   Expressing Present and Past Ability 134
4.3   *Should* and *Ought to* to Express Expectation 137
4.4   Requesting Action: *Would, Could, Can*, and *Will* 141
4.5   Requesting Action: *Would you mind . . .* 141
4.6   Requesting Permission: *May, Could*, and *Can* 142
4.7   Requesting Permission: *Would you mind if I . . .* 143
4.8   Expressing Preference: *Would like (prefer)* 144
4.9   Expressing Present Need or Lack of Need: *Must (not), Have to* 151
4.10   Expressing Past Need or Lack of Need: *Had to* 154
4.11   Expressing Advice: *Had better, Should*, and *Ought to* 155
4.12   Expressing Advice About the Past (Action Not Taken): *Should (not) Have, Ought (not)* 158
4.13   Expressing Present and Past Possibility 161
4.14   Expressing Probability with *Must* and *Must Have* 164
4.15   Changes in Modal Auxiliaries with Reported Speech 171
4.16   Commands, Modal Auxiliaries, and Reported Speech 172
4.17   Reduction of Requests for Action and for Permission 174
4.18   Reduction of Embedded Questions 175

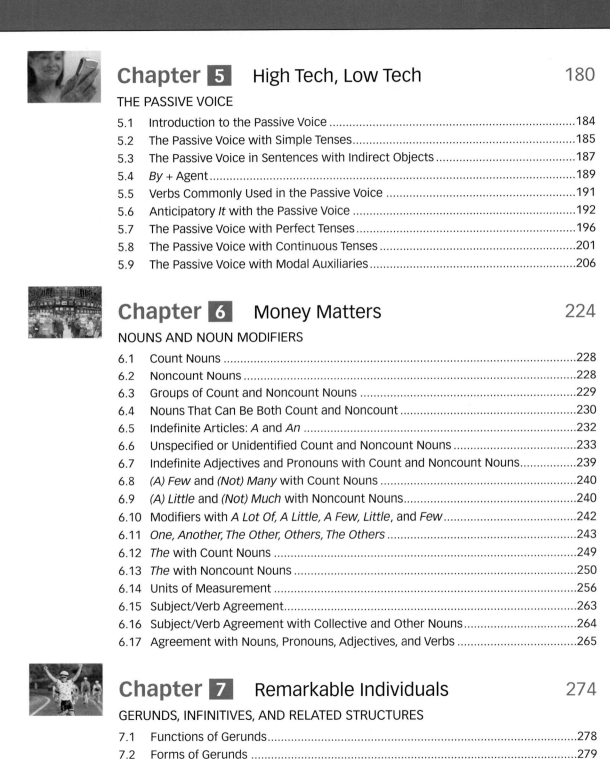

Chapter 5   High Tech, Low Tech   180

THE PASSIVE VOICE

5.1   Introduction to the Passive Voice 184
5.2   The Passive Voice with Simple Tenses..185
5.3   The Passive Voice in Sentences with Indirect Objects 187
5.4   *By* + Agent...189
5.5   Verbs Commonly Used in the Passive Voice 191
5.6   Anticipatory *It* with the Passive Voice 192
5.7   The Passive Voice with Perfect Tenses..196
5.8   The Passive Voice with Continuous Tenses 201
5.9   The Passive Voice with Modal Auxiliaries 206

Chapter 6   Money Matters   224

NOUNS AND NOUN MODIFIERS

6.1   Count Nouns 228
6.2   Noncount Nouns 228
6.3   Groups of Count and Noncount Nouns 229
6.4   Nouns That Can Be Both Count and Noncount 230
6.5   Indefinite Articles: *A* and *An* 232
6.6   Unspecified or Unidentified Count and Noncount Nouns 233
6.7   Indefinite Adjectives and Pronouns with Count and Noncount Nouns.............239
6.8   *(A) Few* and *(Not) Many* with Count Nouns 240
6.9   *(A) Little* and *(Not) Much* with Noncount Nouns..............................240
6.10 Modifiers with *A Lot Of, A Little, A Few, Little*, and *Few* 242
6.11 *One, Another, The Other, Others, The Others* 243
6.12 *The* with Count Nouns 249
6.13 *The* with Noncount Nouns 250
6.14 Units of Measurement 256
6.15 Subject/Verb Agreement...263
6.16 Subject/Verb Agreement with Collective and Other Nouns..................264
6.17 Agreement with Nouns, Pronouns, Adjectives, and Verbs 265

Chapter 7   Remarkable Individuals   274

GERUNDS, INFINITIVES, AND RELATED STRUCTURES

7.1   Functions of Gerunds..278
7.2   Forms of Gerunds 279
7.3   Use of Possessives and Pronouns with Gerunds 279

7.4   Gerunds Following Prepositions 281

7.5   Common Expressions with *To* That Are Often Followed by Gerunds....................282

7.6   Functions of Infinitives...286

7.7   Forms of Infinitives..287

7.8   Adjectives and/or Nouns + Infinitives..289

7.9   Adverbs + Infinitives 290

7.10 Verbs Followed by Either Gerunds or Infinitives..................................292

7.11 Parallel Structure with Gerunds and Infinitives 293

7.12 Verbs and Verb Phrases Commonly Followed by Gerunds 297

7.13 Verbs and Verb Phrases Commonly Followed by Infinitives 298

7.14 Verbs That May Be Followed by a (Pro)Noun Object Before an Infinitive 300

7.15 Verbs That Must Be Followed by a (Pro)Noun Object Before an Infinitive...........300

7.16 Verbs Followed by Gerunds or Infinitives, Depending on the
Use of Noun or Pronoun Object..308

7.17 Verbs That Change Meaning Depending on the Use of Infinitives or Gerunds 312

7.18 *Help, Let*, and *Make*..317

7.19 *Have* 318

7.20 *Get* and *Need* 318

7.21 Verbs of Perception...321

7.22 Present and Past Participles Used as Adjectives.................................322

Chapter 8   Creativity   330

COMPOUND AND COMPLEX SENTENCES; CLAUSES OF TIME AND CONDITION

8.1   Review of Sentence Types 334

8.2   Coordinating Conjunctions: *And, But, For, Or, So, Yet* 337

8.3   Coordinating Conjunction: *Nor* 337

8.4   Transitions 338

8.5   Habitual Activities 344

8.6   Present Activities 344

8.7   Past and Present Activities 344

8.8   Clauses of Condition: Present Time or Unspecified Time......................347

8.9   Clauses of Time: Past Time with the Simple Past and Past Perfect Tenses..........352

8.10 Adverbs with Time Clauses...352

8.11 *After, Before, By*, and *Until* as Prepositions 353

8.12 Clauses of Time and Condition: Past Time with the Simple
Past and Past Continuous...361

8.13 Clauses of Time: Future Time..369

8.14 Clauses of Condition: Future Time...371

8.15 Sentence Problems: Fragments, Comma Splices, and Run-Ons 374

Chapter 9 Human Behavior 382

ADJECTIVE CLAUSES

9.1 Adjective Clauses 387
9.2 Clauses with *That*: Replacement of Subjects 391
9.3 Clauses with *That*: Replacement of Objects of Verbs............................392
9.4 Clauses with *When* or *Where*: Replacement of Adverbials of Time or Place........393
9.5 Restrictive versus Nonrestrictive Clauses 398
9.6 The Same Clause as Restrictive or Nonrestrictive 398
9.7 Clauses with *Who* or *Which*: Replacement of Subjects..........................399
9.8 Clauses with *Whose*: Replacement of Possessives................................402
9.9 Clauses with *Whom* or *Which*: Replacement of Objects of Verbs.................407
9.10 Clauses with *Whom* and *Which*: Replacement of Objects of Prepositions..........409
9.11 Appositives..414
9.12 Past Participial Phrases...415
9.13 Present Participial Phrases 416
9.14 Agreement with Adjective Phrases and Clauses....................................418

Chapter 10 Crime and Punishment 422

HOPE, WISH, AND CONDITIONAL SENTENCES

10.1 *Hope* and *Wish* 426
10.2 The Subjunctive Mood with *Wish* 427
10.3 *Otherwise* 432
10.4 Imaginary Conditionals: Present or Unspecified Time...........................433
10.5 Perfect Modal Auxiliaries 437
10.6 Perfect Modal Auxiliaries and Past Advice 439
10.7 Imaginary Conditionals: Past Time...443
10.8 Imaginary Conditionals: Past-to-Present Time.....................................444

Appendix 1   460
Irregular Verbs

Appendix 2   462
Spelling Rules and Irregular Noun Plurals

Appendix 3   464
The with Proper Nouns

Appendix 4   466
Formation of Statements and Questions

Appendix 5   468
Modal Auxilaries and Related Structures

Appendix 6   470
Summary of Gerunds and Infinitives

Skills Index   473

Welcome to Interactions/Mosaic Silver Edition

Interactions/Mosaic **Silver Edition** is a fully-integrated, 18-book academic skills series. Language proficiencies are articulated from the beginning through advanced levels <u>within</u> each of the four language skill strands. Chapter themes articulate <u>across</u> the four skill strands to systematically recycle content, vocabulary, and grammar.

NEW to the Silver Edition of *Interactions/Mosaic Grammar:*

- **World's most popular and comprehensive academic skills series**—thoroughly updated for today's global learners
- **Redesigned Grammar Charts**—numbered sequentially, formatted consistently, and indexed systematically—provide lifelong reference value
- **Carefully refined scope and sequence** responds to teacher recommendations for building the most logical continuum of grammar topics within and across books
- **Enhanced focus on global content** honors the diversity of *Interactions/Mosaic* students from each region of the world
- **New Self-Assessment Logs** encourage students to evaluate their learning
- **New "Best Practices" approach** promotes excellence in language teaching

Interactions/Mosaic Best Practices

Our Interactions/Mosaic Silver Edition team has produced an edition that focuses on Best Practices, principles that contribute to excellent language teaching and learning. Our team of writers, editors, and teacher consultants has identified the following six interconnected Best Practices:

Making Use of Academic Content

Materials and tasks based on academic content and experiences give learning real purpose. Students explore real world issues, discuss academic topics, and study content-based and thematic materials.

Organizing Information

Students learn to organize thoughts and notes through a variety of graphic organizers that accommodate diverse learning and thinking styles.

Scaffolding Instruction

A scaffold is a physical structure that facilitates construction of a building. Similarly, scaffolding instruction is a tool used to facilitate language learning in the form of predictable and flexible tasks. Some examples include oral or written modeling by the teacher or students, placing information in a larger framework, and reinterpretation.

Activating Prior Knowledge

Students can better understand new spoken or written material when they connect to the content. Activating prior knowledge allows students to tap into what they already know, building on this knowledge, and stirring a curiosity for more knowledge.

Interacting with Others

Activities that promote human interaction in pair work, small group work, and whole class activities present opportunities for real world contact and real world use of language.

Cultivating Critical Thinking

Strategies for critical thinking are taught explicitly. Students learn tools that promote critical thinking skills crucial to success in the academic world.

Highlights of Mosaic 1 Grammar

Compelling instructional photos strengthen the educational experience.

Activating Prior Knowledge Questions and topical quotes stimulate interest, activate prior knowledge, and launch the topic of the unit.

Chapter

7

Remarkable Individuals

Connecting to the Topic

1. What does it mean to be remarkable?
2. Are remarkable people always successful people?
3. Does true success always involve achieving something remarkable?

In This Chapter

Gerunds, Infinitives, and Related Structures

Part 1 Introduction to Gerunds
Part 2 Introduction to Infinitives
Part 3 Verbs Followed by Gerunds; Verbs Followed by Infinitives
Part 4 Verbs Followed by Either Gerunds or Infinitives
Part 5 Special Uses of Other Verb Forms

"People become really quite remarkable when they start thinking that they can do things. When they believe in themselves they have the first secret of success."

—Norman Vincent Peale
U.S. clergyman and motivational speaker (1898–1993)

Interacting with Others
Group and pair work create situations for students to use the grammar they are learning.

Making Use of Academic Content
Academic topics provide context for the grammar.

Connecting to the Topic

1. Do you practice a formal religion?
2. Can you name the major religions of the world?
3. Which religion are you the most knowledgeable about? The least knowledgeable?

Introduction

In this chapter, you will study the forms and uses of verbs in the passive voice. You will notice that the time frame of a passive verb may be the same as that of an active verb, but the focus of the passive sentence is quite different. As you study the chapter, pay careful attention to the focus of the passive constructions.

Reading Read the following passage. It introduces the chapter theme, "High Tech, Low Tech," and raises some of the topics and issues you will cover in the chapter.

Old and New Technology

Old inventions are not necessarily eliminated by new ones. After all, people did not stop riding bicycles after the car was invented. Thus, older inventions may be replaced, but they seldom disappear because new roles are created for them. Some of the best examples of this are from the field of long-distance communication.

Until the 19th century, communication had been limited by distance and time. Then came a series of amazing inventions that extended the range of human communication. Each of these inventions was expected to replace existing technology. For example, when the telephone was invented in 1876, it was feared that letters would become obsolete. When television was introduced in the 1940s, many people predicted the "death" of radio. And as television became more popular, people worried that it would lead to the "death" of books and reading. But it is clear that these predictions were wrong. The older technologies—letters, books, and the radio—have not disappeared. Instead, their roles have been changed by the appearance of new technology. Television, together with the automobile, has provided a new role for the radio. Both television and the radio have created new roles for the newspaper. And all of these have affected the book.

The technology of the 21st century is progressing rapidly. With the availability and affordability of the personal computer, more and more households are wired to the World Wide Web on the Internet. This puts the individual in contact with people and information that can be located anywhere in the world. As a result, communication today is both more global and more personal than ever before.

At the same time, the inventions of one and two centuries before still play important roles in the daily life of millions of people all over the world. The telephone and the television, in their new forms, such as the cell phone and PDAs, are still with us. And, oh yes, that most ancient technology, the book, is still with us, too.

Redesigned grammar charts—
numbered sequentially, formatted
consistently, and indexed systematically—
provide lifelong reference value.

Leisure Time and Your Health

How important is leisure time? How important is it to relax? Taking time to relax could one day save your life. In our fast-paced lives, it's almost impossible to avoid stress, but if we keep the stress inside, we may cause ourselves physical and psychological problems.

Stress is anything that puts an extra demand on us. We encounter stress at school, at work, and at home. What happens when we feel stress? Our body responds to stress by "mobilizing its defenses." Blood pressure rises and muscles get ready to act. If our tension is not relieved, it may start a series of reactions, both physical and psychological.

What can we do? According to Hans Seyle of the University of Montreal, the effects of stress depend not on what happens to us, but on the way we react. We can learn to relax in the face of stress. Through sports, games, hobbies and other leisure time activities, we can learn healthy ways of releasing stress instead of carrying it with us hour after hour, day after day.

Discussing Ideas Discuss the questions.

Do you take time to relax each day? What types of things do you do to relax?

Grammar Structures and Practice

A. Expressing Present and Past Possibility

In affirmative and negative statements, *may (have)*, *might (have)*, and *could (have)* express possibility. All mean "possibly" or "perhaps."

4.13	**Expressing Present and Past Possibility**		
Meanings	Structures	Explanations	Examples
Present Possibility	*may (not)* *might (not)* + simple *could (not)* form	*May*, *might*, and *could* express present possibility. *May* is not used with questions with this meaning.	He **may be** the youngest competitor. He **might win** if he keeps going this fast. He **might finish** the race first. **Could** he **win**?
Past Possibility	*may (not) have* *might (not) have* + past *could (not) have* participle	In rapid speech, *may have* is pronounced /mayuv/, *might have* is pronounced /mituv/, and *could have* is pronounced /cudduv/.	Jim **may have fallen** over something. He **might have hurt** himself. He **couldn't have hurt** himself very badly. He's getting up.

---

4 **Practice** You are at the seashore with your friend. There are lots of people in the water and on the shore. There are also fish and marine mammals. You and your friend are looking out to sea. You are trying to identify the figures that you see moving about in and on the water. Use *may, might* or *could (have)* to guess what you are looking at.

Example There's something flying right over the water. It has a large bill.
It might be a pelican.

1. There's something inside that seashell. It's moving. It has claws.
2. It looks like there's a person standing on a board with a sail.
3. Something just jumped out of the water and back in. It was really big.
4. I see a black pipe just above the surface of the water. I also see rubber fins.
5. Those two swimmers out there have wet suits and some tanks on their backs. They have spears too.
6. There's a girl paddling out to that wave on her surfboard.
7. There were two surfers before that wave crashed. Now I only see one.
8. There are a lot of birds around that boat.
9. Some people seem to be digging in the sand.
10. That swimmer out there is holding onto the buoy.

B. Expressing Probability with *Must* and *Must Have*

In affirmative and negative statements, *must* and *must have* express probability. Both mean "probably."

■ *May* is not used in this meaning.
■ In rapid speech, *must have* is pronounced /mustuv/.

4.14	**Expressing Probability with *Must* and *Must Have***		
Meanings	Structures	Examples
Present Probability	*must (not)* + simple form	You **must** like board games if you like Monopoly. You **must** be holding a Get Out of Jail Free card. You **must not** be worried about landing in jail.
Past Probability	*must (not) have* + past participle	You **must have** been happy to win the game. You **must have** been holding more than one Get Out of Jail Free card. You **must not have** worried about landing in jail.

2 Practice Complete the second sentence in each pair with either an active or passive gerund. Use the example as a model.

Example Our children like being read books. We like
<u>reading books to our children</u>.

1. We enjoy reading stories to our children. Our children enjoy _____

2. Our children enjoy being sung to. We enjoy _____

3. Our children like being given gifts. We like _____

4. We like inviting friends to our house. Our friends like _____

5. Our children enjoy being played with. We enjoy _____

6. Our children like being helped. We like _____.

7. We enjoy including our friends. Our friends enjoy _____

8. We like telling stories to each other. Each of us likes _____

9. We enjoy applauding a good speaker. A good speaker enjoys _____

10. We enjoy calling our family on holidays. Our family enjoys _____

11. We like sending our family cards and letters. Our family likes _____

12. People enjoy being praised for a doing a good job. We enjoy _____

3 Practice Doing a good job at something usually involves enjoying what you are doing. What do you enjoy doing? Here are ideas from a "work aptitude inventory." These inventories help young people make choices about jobs and careers. Which activities do you enjoy? Which don't you enjoy? Make at least 10 sentences with active gerunds after the verb *enjoy* or *like*. Use these ideas and add some of your own.

Example *I enjoy building things like furniture and model ships and planes.*

- build things
- care for animals or plants
- cook and bake
- design or draw things
- fix machines
- help people with medical problems
- plan and organize
- read alone
- read to children
- solve problems
- teach people how to do things
- travel
- use a computer
- work with numbers
- work with people

Using What You've Learned

6 Taking an Inventory What food do you have at home? What personal care or cleaning products do you have? Choose two different cupboards or closets in your home. One should have food and cooking items. The other should have cleaning or personal care items. Make a list of the contents of each. Bring your lists to class and share your information with your classmates.

7 Comparing Prices How well do you know grocery prices? Check your budgeting ability. First, make a list of at least 10 items that you need to buy. Your list should include food and household items. Use specific units of measurement in your list, and write down what you believe each item costs. Then work with a partner. Do not let your partner see your estimated prices. Your partner should write down estimates for your list, while you write down estimates for your partner's list. Finally, go to a grocery store and check the prices. Report back to the class on how accurate you were. You can use the following chart to help you.

Item	My Cost Estimate	Partner's Cost Estimate	Actual Store Price
1			
2			
3			
4			
5			
6			
7			
8			
9			
10			

Scope and Sequence

Chapter	Grammar Structures	Grammar in Context
1 New Challenges Page 2	**Basic Sentence Structure** **Part 1** Parts of Speech and Sentence Structure **Part 2** Nouns and Pronouns **Part 3** Verbs and Verb Tense Formation **Part 4** The Verb Tense System **Part 5** Word Order	Studying a new language and culture Adjusting to and living in another culture Ideas of time, space, and order across cultures
2 Cooperation and Competition Page 38	**Verbs (1)** **Part 1** Auxiliary Verbs and Questions **Part 2** Embedded Questions **Part 3** The Simple Present and Present Continuous Tenses **Part 4** *Will* and *Be Going To* **Part 5** The Present Perfect Continuous and Present Perfect Tenses	Cooperation or competition in education The student-teacher relationship Dealing with exams and grades Sports and teamwork Cooperation and competition on the job
3 Relationships Page 84	**Verbs (2)** **Part 1** Past Verb Forms: The Simple Past Tense; The Past Continuous Tense **Part 2** The Present Perfect Tense with Unspecified Past Time **Part 3** Past Verb Forms: The Habitual Past; The Future in the Past **Part 4** The Past and Future Prefect Tenses **Part 5** Reported Speech	Families and birth order Sibling rivalry Adoptive children Family memories Household duties and chores Rural families The urbanization of America Immigrant families

Scope and Sequence

Chapter	Grammar Structures	Grammar in Context
4 **Health and Leisure** **Page 130**	**Modal Auxiliaries and Related Structures** **Part 1** Modal Auxiliaries and Related Structures of Ability and Expectation **Part 2** Modal Auxiliaries of Request, Permission, and Preference **Part 3** Modal Auxiliaries and Related Structures of Need and Advice **Part 4** Modal Auxiliaries of Possibility and Probability **Part 5** Modal Auxiliaries and Reported Speech	Health and well-being Leisure time and healthy activities Physical fitness Medical emergencies and first aid
5 **High Tech, Low Tech** **Page 180**	**The Passive Voice** **Part 1** The Passive Voice with Simple Tenses **Part 2** The Passive Voice with Perfect Tenses **Part 3** The Passive Voice with Continuous Tenses **Part 4** The Passive Voice with Modal Auxiliaries **Part 5** Review of Chapters 1–5	Old and new technology Telephones, computers, and electronics Transportation Robotics
6 **Money Matters** **Page 224**	**Nouns and Noun Modifiers** **Part 1** Count Versus Noncount Nouns **Part 2** Indefinite Adjectives and Pronouns **Part 3** The Definite Article **Part 4** Units of Measurement **Part 5** Agreement	The global economy Definitions of wealth Economics and organizational systems Banking and investment World resources Food resources and eating habits

Chapter	Grammar Structures	Grammar in Context
7 **Remarkable Individuals** Page 274	**Gerunds, Infinitives, and Related Structures** Part 1 Introduction to Gerunds Part 2 Introduction to Infinitives Part 3 Verbs Followed by Gerunds or Infinitives Part 4 Verbs Followed by Either Gerunds or Infinitives Part 5 Special Uses of Other Verb Forms	Remarkable humanitarians Remarkable athletes Remarkable explorers and scientists
8 **Creativity** Page 330	**Compound and Complex Sentences; Adverb Clauses** Part 1 Compound Sentences Part 2 Adverb Clauses: Unspecified or Present Time Part 3 Adverb Clauses: Past (1) Part 4 Adverb Clauses: Past (2) Part 5 Adverb Clauses: Future Time	The creative urge Definitions of creativity Creative artists, musicians, and scientists Creative activities Creativity in business
9 **Human Behavior** Page 382	**Adjective Clauses** Part 1 Introduction to Adjective Clauses Part 2 Clauses with *That, When,* and *Where* Part 3 Restrictive and Nonrestrictive Clauses Part 4 Clauses with *Whom* and *Which*: Replacement of Objects Part 5 Clause-to-Phrase Reduction	Religion and human behavior Hinduism Buddhism Judaism Christianity Islam
10 **Crime and Punishment** Page 422	***Hope, Wish,* and Conditional Sentences** Part 1 *Hope* and *Wish* Part 2 Conditional Sentences: Present or Unspecified Time Part 3 Perfect Modal Auxiliaries Part 4 Conditional Sentences: Past and Past-to-Present Time Part 5 Review of Chapters 6–10	Crime in U.S. society Violent crime and prison time Victims of crime Non-violent crimes Crimes against the environment Making positive changes

Author Acknowledgements

To the shining stars in my life:
Alfonso, Alex, Martin, Camila, Tito, and Lucas

1

New Challenges

In This Chapter

Basic Sentence Structure

Part 1 Parts of Speech and Sentence Structure
Part 2 Nouns and Pronouns
Part 3 Verbs and Verb Tense Formation
Part 4 The Verb Tense System
Part 5 Word Order

"Everything must have a beginning.**"**

—Proverb

Connecting to the Topic

1. Have you spent time in the past or are you presently spending time in another country or culture?

2. How was or is that experience for you?

3. What was challenging about the beginning of your experience?

Chapter 1 is a review chapter. It covers some basic structures and grammatical terms. It also looks at some special challenges involved in learning a new language and adjusting to life in a new culture.

Reading Read the following passage. It introduces the chapter theme, "New Challenges," and raises some of the topics and issues you will cover in the chapter.

Studying a New Language and Culture

Learning to communicate in another language can be very difficult and frustrating, but it can also be one of the most rewarding experiences of your life. Being able to communicate in another language will open doors for you to experience a world of new people, places, and ideas. It will offer you a look at cultures from every part of the earth. And if you have the opportunity to live in another culture, the experience will show you many things—above all, about your own culture. It will reveal cultural similarities and differences that you had never noticed in the past. Within a short time in another culture, you will find that you begin to learn a great deal about yourself and your own country and culture.

5

 Discussing Ideas Get to know your class by finding out a little about your classmates. Talk with three classmates to gather the information in the following chart. You can write the information in the chart, or you can use a piece of paper.
Use some of these questions and create others.

What's your name?   Do you speak another language?
Where are you from?   Are you interested in sports?
What do you like to do in your free time? Why are you studying English?
What . . . ?   Where . . . ?
Who . . . ?   When . . . ?
How many . . . ?   Why . . . ?

Name	Hometown and Native Language	Family	Interests (Sports, Hobbies, etc.)	Something Special

Previewing the Passage Discuss the question.

You are going to read a passage by a student from Switzerland who spent time studying English in the United States. What effects do you think this experience may have had on him?

Reading Read the passage.

How My American Stay Affected Me

When I left Switzerland, my life changed completely. I had not known what I should expect or how I would be affected in education, sophistication, and personality through my stay in the United States. Coming from a small town and not having traveled outside of my state, I was not exactly what people would call a sophisticated man. Now I believe that I am a little more aware. Not only 5
did I learn about the United States, but I also learned tremendously about other fascinating cultures. Most of all, I learned to understand and to accept other cultures. Living in a new country and learning about new cultures has been, I believe, the most important experience in my life.

—Daniel Pfister 10

 Discussing Ideas Write three things you expected before beginning your English studies. Then choose a partner. Take turns discussing your expectations. Have your experiences been different from your expectations? If so, how?

Grammar Structures and Practice

A. Parts of Speech

Every sentence in English is made up of basic building blocks, the parts of speech. You should be familiar with these: adjective, adverb, article, conjunction, noun, preposition, pronoun, and verb.

1.1 Parts of Speech

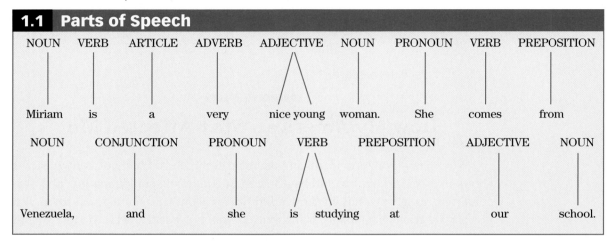

NOUN	VERB	ARTICLE	ADVERB	ADJECTIVE	NOUN	PRONOUN	VERB	PREPOSITION
Miriam	is	a	very	nice young	woman.	She	comes	from

NOUN	CONJUNCTION	PRONOUN	VERB	PREPOSITION	ADJECTIVE	NOUN
Venezuela,	and	she	is studying	at	our	school.

---

1 **Practice** Identify the part of speech of each italicized word.

Example   My name is *Daniel*.

1. *I* am *from* Switzerland.

2. I am *studying* English.

3. My class *has* students *from many different countries*.

4. Hau is *an interesting new student* who sits *next to me now*.

5. *He* is from Vietnam.

6. Ayeh is from *the* Middle East, *and* Bedi is from *Africa*.

7. *Gabriela came* to *this* school *because she* wants to *improve* her writing.

8. *Everyone is trying very hard* to improve in English.

B. Types of Sentences

A sentence is a group of words that expresses a complete idea.
- There are four kinds of sentences:

  ○ questions   ○ exclamations
  ○ statements   ○ commands

■ Each kind of sentence includes at least one subject and one verb. In commands, the subject is understood but not said or written.

1.2 Sentences

Structures	Explanations	Examples
Questions	A question asks for information or for a yes or no.	What is your name? Are you a student?
Statements	A statement gives information or opinions.	My name is Miriam. That's a beautiful name.
Exclamations	An exclamation expresses surprise, pleasure, or other emotions.	What a lovely name you have! We won the World Cup!
Commands	A command tells what to do. The subject "you" is understood.	(you) Tell me about yourself. Have a seat, please.

2 **Practice** Tell whether these sentences are questions, statements, exclamations, or commands. Identify the part of speech of each italicized word.

         noun verb

Examples My *name is* Daniel. (statement)

       pronoun

What's *yours*? *(question)*

1. *My* name *is* Ruben.

2. Tell *me* your *last* name.

3. If *you* really *want* to know, it's Taboada.

4. What an *unusual* name you *have*!

5. Are you *from Mexico*?

6. I've *always* wanted to go there, *but* I've never *had the opportunity*.

7. Mexico is *a large, beautiful* country *with* a variety *of* climates and landscapes.

8. The *capital* is Mexico City, *and its other* important cities *are* Veracruz and Guadalajara.

9. Were the *Aztec* Indians *an* ancient *or a relatively new* civilization?

10. How *unique their* civilization was!

C. Subjects

Every sentence has a subject. In commands, the subject "you" or "we" is understood. In a sentence, the subject is normally the most important word.
- Person
- Place
- Thing
- Event
- Idea

Subjects can take several forms:
- Nouns
- Pronouns
- Phrases
- Clauses

1.3 Subjects

Structures	Explanations	Examples
Noun or Pronoun	A noun names a person, place, thing, or idea. Pronouns replace nouns.	**Miriam** comes from Venezuela. **She** is from Caracas.
Phrase	A phrase is a group of related words. Infinitive (*to* + simple form) or gerund (*-ing* form) phrases can be used as subjects. These and other verb forms are covered in Chapter 7.	**Many Venezuelan students** are studying in the United States. **To study in the United States** can be expensive. **Studying in the United States** can be expensive.
Clause	A clause is a group of related words that includes a subject and a verb. Dependent clauses are covered in Chapters 8 to 10.	**How long they stay in the United States** depends on many things.

---

3 **Practice** Find the subjects in the following sentences. Underline each subject.

Example Every year, <u>thousands of foreign students</u> begin university studies in North America.

1. Most international students have studied some English before coming to an English-speaking country.

2. Many already read and write English fairly well.

3. A major difficulty for all new students, however, is to understand and speak English.

4. Making phone calls or understanding directions can be difficult.

5. Many Americans use a lot of slang.

6. What can be very difficult is to understand slang.

7. Different age groups use different kinds of slang.

8. In the United States, each part of the country also has variations in vocabulary and pronunciation.

9. Nevertheless, after the first few weeks in the United States, most new students will notice tremendous improvement.

10. All of a sudden, English becomes a lot clearer and easier!

D. Verbs, Objects, and Complements

Some verbs tell what the subject does. These verbs can be transitive or intransitive.
- Intransitive verbs do not have objects.
- Transitive verbs must have objects.

Other verbs are linking verbs.
- Linking verbs connect the subject to the complement.
- A complement is a noun, pronoun, adjective, phrase, verb form, phrase, or clause that describes the subject.
- Common linking verbs include *be, appear, become, feel, get* (when it means *become*), *look, seem, smell, sound,* and *taste*. The chart gives some examples.

1.4 Verbs, Objects, and Complements

Structures	Explanations	Examples
Intransitive Verbs	An intransitive verb is complete without an object.	Miriam **travels** often.
Transitive Verbs and Objects	A transitive verb *must* have an object. It is incomplete without one.	When she travels, she always **buys** souvenirs.
Direct Object	Direct objects answer the questions *who(m)?* or *what?*	She bought her daughter **a sweater.**
Indirect Object	Indirect objects answer the questions *to/for who(m)?* or *what?*	She bought **her daughter** a sweater.
Linking Verbs and Complements	Linking verbs are followed by complements: information that describes the subject. Remember that adverbs cannot be used as complements after linking verbs. Example: CORRECT: *He seems happy.* INCORRECT: *He seems happily.*	Miriam **is** a lawyer. She **seems** happy with her work. It **appears** to be a very interesting job.

4 **Practice** Find the verbs in the following sentences. Underline each verb. If the sentence has an object or complement, circle it.

Example Learning a new language <u>is</u> (difficult.)

1. It is difficult to learn a new language, but the experience can be very enjoyable.

2. When you speak another language, you can communicate with people from many places.

3. Thousands of languages exist in the world.

4. Speaking another language will open many new doors for you.

5. Since Daniel came to the United States, he has experienced many new people, places, and ideas.

6. During his studies, he has met people from cultures from every part of the earth.

7. While Daniel has been learning about other cultures, he's been learning more about his own.

8. The experience of looking at other cultures can show you a great deal about your own culture.

9. Think about some of the similarities and differences across cultures.

10. People who can experience life in another country are very fortunate.

E. Sentence Types

Sentences can be simple, compound, complex, or a combination of compound and complex.

1.5 Sentence Types

Structures	Explanations	Examples
Simple	A simple sentence has at least one subject and one verb. A simple sentence can have a compound subject. A simple sentence can have a compound verb.	Sukariati arrived from Indonesia last week. Sukariati's sister and brother are living here now. Her cousin wanted to come, too, but couldn't.
Compound	Compound sentences are sentences joined by a comma and a conjunction: *and, but, for, nor, or, so,* or *yet.*	Sukariati began her classes yesterday, and she likes them a lot.
Complex	Complex sentences are sentences joined by connecting words such as *who, that, because, after, while,* and so on. These are covered in Chapters 8 to 10.	Muljati, who is originally from Jakarta, has lived in the United States for some time. She chose to live in California because she liked the climate.

5 **Practice** Label the subject(s) and verb(s) in each of the following sentences. Tell whether the sentences are simple, compound, or complex. If the sentence is compound or complex, circle the connecting word.

Examples Have you met Kunio Takahashi? *simple sentence*

Kunio is one of the most interesting people (whom) I have met here. *complex sentence*

1. My friend Kunio is from Tokyo, Japan.

2. He has studied English in Canada for a year, and now he hopes to study veterinary science.

3. Because Kunio wants to study both English and veterinary science, he has applied to schools in Canada and Australia.

4. Is he working on an undergraduate or a graduate degree?

5. Kunio already has his bachelor's degree.

6. He will get his master's degree, and then he will begin a doctoral program.

7. What did he study as an undergraduate?

8. I'm not really sure.

9. Why don't you ask him when you see him again?

10. He's so busy enjoying Canadian life that I never see him!

 6 **Practice** Get into groups and reread the passage "How My American Stay Affected Me" on page 5. Find the subject(s) and verb(s) in each sentence. Then choose one or two sentences and label the parts of speech in each.

Using What You've Learned

 7 **Describing Similarities and Differences Across Cultures** If you have lived or are living outside your native region or country, think about some of the differences you have encountered. Can you think of several things that have surprised you? Perhaps they surprised you because they're different from what you are used to. Or, perhaps they surprised you because they're very similar to what you are used to. Write a short paragraph describing your experiences. Then share your ideas in small groups or with the class. If you have never traveled outside your native region or country, imagine what the experience might be like.

Example   *When I moved to Argentina from Colombia, I noticed many differences even though both countries are in South America and both are Spanish-speaking. First, a major difference was the food and times for eating. Argentines eat dinner very late . . . .*

Part 2 | Nouns and Pronouns

Setting the Context

Previewing the Passage Discuss the questions.

Can you think of a situation when you learned something completely new about yourself? What happened? What did you learn about yourself?

Reading Read the paragraph.

New Cultures

Years of study have convinced me that the real job is not to understand foreign culture but to understand our own. I am also sure that all you ever get from studying foreign culture is a token[1] understanding. The ultimate reason for such study is to learn more about your own system. The best reason for experiencing foreign ways is to generate a sense of vitality and awareness—an interest in life that can come only when you live through the shock of contrast and difference. 5

---

[1] *token* superficial, not in-depth
Source: *The Silent Language* (Edward T. Hall)

Discussing Ideas Discuss the questions.

This passage has some difficult language, but its message is fairly simple. Can you give the main idea of this passage? What does Hall think we learn when we experience another culture? Do we learn a great deal about the other culture? Or can we learn a great deal about ourselves?

Grammar Structures and Practice

A. Pronouns and Possessive Adjectives

There are five categories of pronouns and adjectives that are very similar to each other. It is important to know the difference between these categories.

1.6 Pronouns and Possessive Adjectives

Structure	Singular					Plural		
	First Person	Second Person	Third Person			First Person	Second Person	Third Person
Subject Pronouns	I	you	he	she	it	we	you	they
Object Pronouns	me	you	him	her	it	us	you	them
Possessive Adjectives	my	your	his	her	its	our	your	their
Possessive Pronouns	mine	yours	his	hers	its	ours	yours	theirs
Reflexive Pronouns	myself	yourself	himself	herself	itself	ourselves	yourselves	themselves

1 **Practice** Work alone or with a partner. Underline all pronouns and possessive adjectives in these sentences.

Example Ruben moved to Australia so that <u>he</u> could study English.

1. Ruben had a little trouble speaking in his second language, English.

2. After a few months, he gained both confidence and fluency.

3. I wish it had been the same for me.

4. Sometimes I ask myself if I will ever learn a second language well.

5. Gary started studying Korean a year after me, but his Korean is much more fluent than mine.

6. When we meet, Gary says, "Wow! Your language has really improved."

7. "My Korean will never sound like yours," I tell him.

8. "Nonsense! People learn at their own speed," Gary tells me.

9. "You are just better at language than I am. Admit it."

10. "Well, neither one of us will ever sound like a real Korean. Our Korean will sound a lot alike in the end, but it will never sound like theirs—true Korean."

2 **Practice** Complete the following sentences by using appropriate pronoun and adjective forms.

Example When we communicate, each of _____*us*_____ speaks two distinct languages.

1. We express _____ with _____ bodies as well as with _____ words.

2. People's movements often communicate more than _____ words.

3. Each culture has _____ own body language.

4. Arabs often move very close when _____ want to communicate.

5. A Japanese woman will tilt _____ head to the side when _____ is confused or puzzled.

6. Germans may feel uncomfortable when someone stands or sits close to _____ .

7. When an American businessperson is doing business, _____ tries to keep eye contact with _____ client.

8. You can learn more about _____ own body language by observing _____ as _____ talk with others.

3 **Practice** Complete the following passage by using appropriate pronoun and adjective forms.

Living on Her Own

When Maria went from the Philippines to Australia to study, _____*she*_____ learned many new things. Most of all, she learned new things about _____*herself*_____ .

In Australia, Maria lived on _____ own. Before then, $\frac{1}{}$

_____ had never lived by _____ , so there were $\frac{2}{}$ $\frac{3}{}$

many new things for _____ to do. _____ had to $\frac{4}{}$ $\frac{5}{}$

cook for _____, and _____ had to do
             6   7

_____ laundry, too. Maria had to learn about grocery shopping
        8

and banking, too. _____ had to manage _____
               9   10

money by _____. All of this was outside of classes.
          11

    In _____ classes, Maria met students from many parts of
           12

the world. Kyung Hee and Sung were from Korea. _____ were
                             13

very nice to Maria and helped _____ a lot. Roberto was from
                      14

Chile, and _____ helped Maria, too. Roberto had a car, and
            15

_____ offered to take Maria to the grocery store to buy food.
      16

_____ was too far to walk to the store, so getting a ride from
      17

Roberto helped Maria a lot. Bedi was a nice man from Africa, and

_____ had been in Australia for several months.
      18

_____ was very familiar with the town and the customs, so
      19

_____ could explain things to Maria and the others.
      20

    Maria really liked Sydney, Australia, with _____ beautiful
                         21

buildings and parks. She met many Australians and enjoyed _____
                                       22

very much. _____ laughed and joked a lot, and Maria some-
            23

times had difficulties understanding _____. Maria was also un-
                        24

comfortable at times because _____ was accustomed to being
                    25

much more formal. Sometimes _____ was hard for Maria to
                   26

relax and feel comfortable around the easy-going Australians.

▲ The Sydney Opera House in Australia

Using What You've Learned

4 **Describing Your Own Culture** Edward Hall wrote, "Culture hides much more than it reveals. Strangely enough, what it hides, it hides most effectively from its own members." Without experiencing other cultures, it's hard to see what makes our own culture different or special. We think our way of doing things is the way it's done everywhere.

Think about your own culture. What is something special or different or notable, something that makes your culture different from others? Think about work or free time. Think about how individuals behave—for example, men's behavior or women's behavior. Think about food or money or daily life and routines. Think about religion or celebrations. Choose one special thing about your culture and try to describe it in a short composition. How and why is it important? Then share your story with your classmates.

Example   *One of the most special things about life in Brazil is music. Music is everywhere, and music and dancing play important roles in every aspect of life. Brazil wouldn't be Brazil without music. It's in every Brazilian's heart and soul . . . .*

Setting the Context

 Previewing the Passage Discuss the questions.

What is culture? How much does our culture influence us?

Reading Edward Hall says that the most basic and obvious parts of our culture are often the parts that influence us the most. As you read the following passage, try to decide what he means by this. What are some of the most basic parts of your culture? Do they influence you a great deal?

What Is Culture?

Cultures are extraordinarily complex, much more so than TV sets, automobiles, or possibly even human physiology. So how does one go about learning the underlying structure of culture? Looking at any of the basic systems in a culture is a good place to start—business, marriage and the family, social organization—any will do. 5

Culture is humanity's medium; there is not one aspect of human life that is not touched and altered by culture. This means personality, how people express themselves (including shows of emotion), the way they drink, how they move, how problems are solved, how their cities are planned and laid out, how transportation systems are organized and function, as well as how economic and 10 government systems are put together and function. However, it is frequently the most obvious and taken-for-granted and therefore the least studied aspects of culture that influence behavior in the deepest and most subtle ways.

Source: *Beyond Culture* (Edward T. Hall)

 Discussing Ideas In the first paragraph, Hall gives three examples of basic cultural systems: business, marriage and the family, and social organization. Discuss one of these examples (or one of your own) with another classmate. Compare two cultures in the areas of business, marriage, the family, and so on. What do you think is the biggest difference between these two cultures?

Grammar Structures and Practice

A. Verbs: Principal Parts and Regular Verb Tense Formation

All tenses and verb constructions are formed from the five principal forms of the verbs.

1.7 The Principal Parts of Verbs

Infinitive	Simple Form	Past Form	Past Participle	Present Participle
to walk	walk	walked	walked	walking
to play	play	played	played	playing
to run	run	ran	run	running
to write	write	wrote	written	writing
to be	be	was / were	been	being
to do	do	did	done	doing
to have	have	had	had	having

Note: The modal auxiliaries—*can, could, may, might, must, ought to, shall, should, will,* and *would*—are not included here because each has only one form, the simple form. (See Chapter 4.)

Regular verb tense formation involves one of four forms: the simple form, past form, past participle, or present participle.

1.8 Verb Tense Formation: Regular Verbs

Structures	Explanations	Examples		
Simple Form	The simple form is used to form commands, the simple present tense, and the simple future tense.	COMMANDS Stand! Be seated!	SIMPLE PRESENT I walk. She walks.	SIMPLE FUTURE I will walk. She will walk.
Past Form	The past form is used for the simple past tense. Regular verbs are the simple form + *-ed.*	REGULAR VERBS I walked. She walked.		
Past Participle	The past participle is used to form the present, past, and future perfect tenses and all passive voice forms.	PRESENT PERFECT I have walked. She has walked.	PAST PERFECT I had walked. She had walked.	FUTURE PERFECT I will have walked. She will have walked.
Present Participle	The present participle is used with the verb *be* to form all continuous tenses.	PRESENT CONTINUOUS I am resting. She is resting. We are resting. PRESENT PERFECT CONTINUOUS I have been resting. She has been resting.	PAST CONTINUOUS I was resting. She was resting. We were resting. PAST PERFECT CONTINUOUS I had been resting. She had been resting.	FUTURE CONTINUOUS I will be resting. She will be resting. We will be resting. FUTURE PERFECT CONTINUOUS I will have been resting. She will have been resting.

Pronunciation Notes

The -s ending is pronounced three ways, according to the ending of the verb.

Examples

- /iz/ after -ch, -sh, -s, -x, and -z endings — teaches, washes, kisses, boxes, buzzes
- /s/ after voiceless endings: p, t, k, or f — stops, hits, looks, laughs
- /z/ after voiced consonant endings — calls listens, plays, sounds, runs

The -ed ending is pronounced three ways, according to the ending of the verb.

- /id/ after -d and -t endings — needed, insisted, waited, wanted
- /t/ after voiceless endings — boxed, helped, looked, watched, washed
- /d/ after voiced endings — carried, breathed, called, climbed, played, listened

---

1 **Practice** Change the following sentences to the singular. Add *a* or *an* and change pronouns when necessary. Use *his* or *her* instead of *their*. If you do this activity orally, give the spelling of the singular verbs. Notice the different ways the -s ending is pronounced.

Example Children begin to learn about culture at an early age.

A child begins to learn about culture at an early age.

1. Children pick up cultural rules quickly.

2. Children rely on their parents.

3. Children watch and imitate their parents.

4. Parents convey a great deal nonverbally, as well as with words.

5. Children also pay attention to their close relatives, such as grandparents, aunts, or uncles.

6. Children learn their society's rules of time, distance, and order.

7. For example, American parents teach children promptness.

8. If children miss the bus, they get to school late.

9. Eventually, the children try to be on time.

10. At first, children usually do things in the same ways as their loved ones.

11. As children grow older, their peer groups become very important to them.

12. Children start to imitate their peers more and more.

2 **Practice** Fill in the blanks with the past tense of the verbs in parentheses to complete the sentences. If you do this activity orally, give the spelling of each past tense form. Notice the different ways the -ed ending is pronounced.

Example Margaret Mead _____*lived*_____ (live) with the Manus tribe in the South Pacific.

1. Margaret Mead _____ (study) island people in the South Pacific.

2. She first _____ (visit) the isolated Manus tribe in 1928.

3. The Manus _____ (agree) to let her live among them.

4. They _____ (permit) her to record their day-to-day life.

5. The isolation of the Manus tribe _____ (stop) with World War II.

6. The United States government _____ (ship) supplies and soldiers through these islands during World War II.

7. This contact with another culture _____ (affect) every aspect of Manus life.

8. After the arrival of U.S. soldiers, incredible changes _____ (occur) on the islands.

9. Margaret Mead _____ (travel) to the islands again in 1953 and _____ (observe) many changes.

10. She _____ (notice) that the Manus _____ (dress) in Western clothes, _____ (cook) Western food, and _____ (carry) transistor radios.

▲ Margaret Mead

3 Practice Complete the sentences by filling in the blanks with the present continuous tense of the verbs in parentheses. If you do this activity orally, give the spelling of each present participle.

Example Social scientists _____*are trying*_____ (try) to understand the effect of television on culture.

1. Today, social scientists _____ (study) the influence of American television and movies in foreign countries.

2. Many believe that television and movies _____ (cause) cultural change.

3. Television stations around the world _____ (carry) programs, movies, and commercials from the United States.

4. Changes _____ (happen) worldwide because of the mass media.

5. Some people believe that TV and movies _____ (create) a world culture.

6. Through the mass media, people everywhere _____ (get) regular "lessons" in American culture and values from other countries.

7. Some countries _____ (control) the number of American programs on local stations.

8. Other countries _____ (begin) to monitor all foreign influences because they feel these influences _____ (threaten) their own culture.

9. Several countries _____ (monitor) radio, television, and films.

10. However, few countries _____ (succeed) in controlling the media, especially the Internet.

B. Verb Tense Formation: Irregular Verbs

Irregular verbs appear often in both spoken and written English. You should know the forms of these verbs *without* consciously thinking about them. The following exercises give you a brief review of some of the more common ones, and Chapters 2 and 3 include more practices.

Note: See Appendix 1 on pages 460–461 for a complete list of irregular forms.

4 Practice Complete the story by filling in the blanks with the past tense of the verbs in parentheses. If you do this activity orally, give the spelling and pronunciation of each verb.

Adjusting to a New Culture

When I _____*left*_____ Brazil to live in the States, I _____
        (leave)   1 (know)

I would probably experience "culture shock," but I really _____
                                                            2 (have)

no idea what culture shock actually _____.
                                        3 (be)

I _____through several different stages during my stay, and
    4 (go)

for a long time I _____ that these stages _____
                    5 (feel)   6 (be)

unique to me. Finally, I _____ to discuss my feelings with other
                          7 (begin)

foreign   students,   and   I   _____   that   our   "stages"
                                        8 (see)

_____ along similar lines. At first, we all _____
    9 (run)   10 (feel)

thrilled about everything "new." Then, problems _____—with
                                                    11 (arise)

transportation, money, housing, and so on. All of us _____ at
                                                        12 (say)

that point we suddenly _____ exhausted and frustrated-with
                        13 (become)

the language, the people, with everything. I almost _____
                                                        14 (go)

home! Luckily, I didn't because things _____ better in a short
                                        15 (get)

time. Soon, I _____that I _____ people better. I
                16 (find)   17 (understand)

_____ more and more used to my new way of life, and this
    18 (grow)

helped me relax. I _____ a lot of nice people, and I
                    19 (meet)

_____ some very good friends after that first "crisis." Later
    20 (make)

_____ a second crisis, though, and finally real "adjustment."
    21 (come)

Well, I still haven't gone back to Brazil. . . .

5 Practice Fill in the blanks with the past participles of the verbs in parentheses. If you do this activity orally, give the spelling and pronunciation of each verb.

Returning to Your Own Culture

People who have _____*spent*_____ time in other cultures often talk
(spend)

about "reverse culture shock." If you have _____ your country
1 (leave)

for more than a short tourist trip and then have _____ back
2 (go)

home, you may have _____ it. What is "reverse culture shock"?
3 (feel)

Well, imagine the following: you've _____ adjusted to a new
4 (become)

culture, and you've _____ to enjoy life in it. You've
5 (grow)

_____ new friends and have _____ a great
6 (make)   7 (have)

variety of new experiences. Then it's time to leave, and you're sad, but you're

also very excited about going home. Arriving home is "wonderful"—seeing all

the friends and relatives you hadn't _____, eating all the special
8 (see)

foods you hadn't _____, reading the newspapers you hadn't
9 (eat)

_____, hearing music you hadn't _____ in such
10 (read)   11 (hear)

a long time. But then, after you've _____ home for a few weeks,
12 (be)

perhaps, things may not seem so "wonderful." You may become critical of your

home country; you may not like certain things or ideas. Your city may have

changed, and people may have changed too. Or, perhaps in your eyes, you've

changed and they haven't changed at all.

This is the process of readjustment. It's a difficult period, and many people

experience it after the initial excitement of coming home has

_____ off. Fortunately, it doesn't usually last as long as adjust-
13 (wear)

ment to a new culture does.

Using What You've Learned

6 **Analyzing a Passage** In small groups, reread the passage "What Is Culture?" on page 18. First, discuss the ideas expressed in the passage and then analyze it. How many of the five different forms of verbs can you find? Underline them. Are all the verb forms used as verbs? Or do some function as other parts of speech?

7 **Discussing a Cartoon** In groups or as a class, read the following paragraph and discuss the questions after it.

Each Language Has Its Exceptions

At least 1,500 languages are spoken in the world, and some linguists estimate that as many as 8,000 languages may exist. Even though most languages seem very different, every known language seems to have exceptions to its "rules"!

1. What is wrong in the cartoon?

2. What exceptions or irregularities exist in your first language? Do there seem to be as many as in English? Why do you think English has so many "special cases"?

Part 4   The Verb Tense System

Setting the Context

Previewing the Passage Discuss the questions.

What differences have you noticed between the way people express time in English and in your first language?

Reading Read the paragraph.

Time

Time is a core system of cultural, social, and personal life. In fact, nothing occurs except in some kind of time frame. A complicating factor in intercultural relations is that each culture has its own time frames in which the patterns are unique. This means that to function effectively abroad it is just as necessary to learn the language of time as it is to learn the spoken language.

5

Source: *The Dance of Life (*Edward T. Hall)

FRANK AND ERNEST   By Bob Thaves

Madame LaZonga
☆ Tells You Your ☆
PAST, PRESENT
☆ and FUTURE!
←

NO THANKS, KNOWING
TWO TENSES IS
ENOUGH REALITY
FOR ME.

© 1988 by NEA. Inc THAVES 11-15

Discussing Ideas Discuss the questions.

Does your first language have a system of tenses? If so, is it similar to the English system? If not, how does your language express time? Can you give some examples?

Grammar Structures and Practice

A. The Tense System

Developing a sense of time in English, as well as a sense of order, is essential to your mastery of the language. The following exercises are designed to give a brief review of the tenses and their time frames *before* you study each tense in more detail. Verb tenses in English can express a variety of time frames:
- present
- past
- past to present
- present to future
- "timeless" (general present)

There are specific tenses for each. Note that each tense will be covered in detail in Chapters 2 and 3. The passive voice will be covered in Chapter 5. How the tenses interconnect in complex sentences will be covered in Chapters 8–10.

1 Practice Work with a partner. Underline the verbs in the following sentences. Tell the time frame that each expresses (past, present, past to present, or future). In sentences with two verbs, explain the relationship of the verbs by time (earlier, later, at the same time). Then indicate the tense of each.

past time   *past to present time*
(simple past)   *(present perfect)*

Example Emilda <u>was born</u> in Switzerland, but she <u>has spent</u> very little of her life there.

1. While Emilda was growing up, her parents moved frequently.

2. By the time she was 10, she had already lived in Europe, Africa, and the U.S.

3. She would speak French with her father, Italian with her mother, and English at school.

4. As a result, she speaks three languages fluently.

5. She's been living in Iowa for the last 10 years.

6. During this time, she has become accustomed to life in the United States, but she misses her family.

7. She is planning a trip to Europe to visit her parents.

8. She'll be leaving on September 20.

2 Practice The following passage is a story about an Iranian student's first few days in the United States. Complete the story by circling the appropriate verb form from the pair in parentheses. As you make each choice, try to decide why the other possibility is incorrect. The first one is done as an example.

The Restaurant

Before I (left / had left) for the United States, my father (was warning / had warned) me, "Every foreigner (has / is having) problems in a new country." But I (told / was telling) myself, "Ali, you (will have been / will be) different. You (don't have / won't have) problems in the United States. By the time you (arrive / arrived), you (will have learned / will be learning) enough English to understand everyone!" So I (made / have made) my preparations, and on January 2 I (flew / had been flying) to Boston.

Of course, I (have had / have) many problems since I (arrived / was arriving) in the United States. Some of the funniest ones (occurred / occur) during the

first few days after my arrival. English (was not / had not been) as easy as I
13

(think / had thought). But I (was making / made) a friend, and I
14   15

(was having / would have) a good time. During those first few days, the most
16

comical experience (was / was being) our first night out in a Boston restaurant.
17

My friend (spoke / was going to speak) no English, but I (thought / would think)
18   19

that I (knew / was knowing) a lot. Before we (went / have gone) to the
20   21

restaurant, we (had promised / used to promise) each other that we
22

(would speak / spoke) a lot of English. And we (were going to listen / listened)
23   24

carefully so that we (learned / would learn) a lot!
25

When we (arrived / were arriving) at the restaurant, we (sat / had sat) down,
26   27

and the waiter (was giving / gave) us menus. While I (was trying / had tried) to
28   29

read mine, my friend (was staring / used to stare) blankly at his. He
30

(understood / understands) nothing! The waiter (came / was going to come)
31   32

back, and we (ordered / were ordering). Still staring blankly, my friend
33

(pointed / would point) to the first three items on the menu. The waiter
34

(seemed / was seeming) surprised and (asked / was asking), "(Is / Will . . . be)
35   36   37

your friend sure?" I (was answering / answered), "My friend (will be / is) sure. I
38   39

(have / will have) the same." The waiter (was saying / said), "OK. If you
40   41

(want / are wanting) that, you
42

(have gotten / will get) that. Foreigners . . ."
43

(Imagine/ To imagine) our surprise when
44

the waiter (came / had come) back
45

with six dishes: two bowls of tomato soup,

two bowls of cream of mushroom

soup, and two bowls of clam chowder!

—Ali Mohammed Rooz-Behani

3 **Error Analysis** Many of the following sentences contain errors because the verb tenses and time expressions do not correspond. Discuss the sentences and suggest possible corrections. Put a check (√) next to sentences that are correct as they are. The first one is done as an example.

had studied *came*

Example After Andrea <u>studied</u> in Argentina, she <u>had come</u> to Canada.

1. Andrea was moving to Canada on August 20, 2005.

2. She has finished her studies in Argentina in 2004.

3. Andrea had been buying her ticket before the exchange rates changed.

4. Andrea said that she was going to stay in Canada for a year.

5. While she lived in Toronto, she was working on her master's degree.

6. She has received her degree three months ago.

7. Since she finished her degree, she travels around the country.

8. She wants to visit as many places as possible.

9. She is staying in Montreal since last week.

10. Next week, she will be leaving for South America.

Using What You've Learned

4 **Writing Your Autobiography** Briefly tell or write a short autobiography. Be sure to include any important events from the past and present, and any plans for the future. You may answer some of these questions: When and where were you born? Where did you live while you were growing up? Where did you go to school? What did you study? Have you ever worked? What are you doing now? What special hobbies or interests do you have? What are some of your plans for the future?

If you choose to tell your autobiography, work in small groups and take turns. Include information about past, present, and future events. When one person finishes, the other group members may ask questions if they have any.

If you choose to write your autobiography, write three paragraphs—one each for past, present, and future events. When you finish, exchange autobiographies with another classmate.

5 **Telling Stories** In small groups, take turns talking about your own experiences learning a new language or adjusting to life in a new culture. Share some of your stories—funny ones, sad ones, embarrassing ones, happy ones. Later, write your story and, if possible, make a class collection of "memorable moments" you have had.

Setting the Context

 Previewing the Passage In English, word order is important. The first noun in a sentence is usually the focus of that sentence. Take a look at the pictures and sentences below. In your opinion, which sentence captures the meaning of which picture? Discuss the question.

a. The cat caught the mouse.

b. The mouse caught the cat.

Reading Read the passage.

Order

The laws of order are those regularities that govern changes in meaning when order changes. "The cat caught the mouse" means something obviously different from "The mouse caught the cat." Order is used differently in different languages and cultures. While order is of major importance on the sentence level in English, this is not the case in some languages. 5

Order also has great importance in other parts of cultural systems besides language: order of birth, order of arrival, order in line to get tickets. Order applies to the courses of a meal. Consider what it would be like to start dinner with dessert, then switch to potatoes, hors d'oeuvre,[1] coffee, salad, and end with meat! 10

---

[1]*hors d'oeuvre* (French) appetizers, small snacks before a meal

Source: *The Silent Language* (Edward T. Hall)

Discussing Ideas Work in pairs or small groups. Take turns comparing your first language to English. Can you give some specific examples of how word order differs?

Grammar Structures and Practice

A. Adjectives

One or more adjectives can modify a noun. Usually, no more than three or four adjectives are used to describe the same noun. The chart gives examples of the usual order of some descriptive adjectives.

1.9	Adjective Word Order						
Number	**Quality or Characteristic**	**Size**	**Shape**	**Age**	**Color**	**Origin**	**Noun**
a	beautiful			new	green	Italian	suit
three		big	long		red		pencils
some	expensive			old		Oriental	carpets
five	different	small	round		gold		rings

1 **Practice** Add the adjectives in parentheses to the following sentences.

Example Learning a language is difficult. (new)
　　　　　Learning a new language is difficult.

1. When you study languages, you can learn about cultures. (other, foreign)

2. People can speak languages. (some, many, foreign)

3. John speaks languages. (four, different)

4. John has traveled to places. (distant, many)

5. He always carries a dictionary. (paperback, small)

6. Which of those students is Susan? (graduate, two, Canadian)

7. Susan is the one with long hair. (brown, curly)

8. She is wearing a suit. (green, jogging, dark)

B. Adverbs

Adverbs modify verbs and adjectives. Many adverbs are formed by adding -ly to related adjectives (quick ——→ quickly). In general, adverbs cannot come between a verb and a direct object.

1.10	Adverbs				
	Subject	**Verb**	**Object**	**Adverb**	**Adjective (Complement)**
Modifying Verbs	Our teacher They I	speaks answered drank	 the question the hot tea	**slowly.** **quickly.** **politely.**	
Modifying Adjectives	John The test Linda	is was seems		**very** **extremely** **terribly**	tired. difficult. unhappy.

Adverbs of time or frequency can appear at various points in a sentence.
- In sentences, adverbs come after the verb be or the first auxiliary verb, **or** before the main verb.
- In questions, adverbs usually come after the subject.
- Longer expressions come at the beginning or end of sentences.

1.11	Adverbs of Time and Frequency			
	Subject and Auxiliary Verb or _Be_	**Adverb**	**Main Verb (+ Object or Complement)**	**Adverb, Phrase, or Clause**
Adverbs of Time	Mr. Jones was Dr. Gill will I can		sick give the test see you	**yesterday.** **today.** **tomorrow.**
Adverbs of Frequency	We are The train I have Do you We can	**seldom** **almost always** **never** **usually**	late leaves been good study English study	to class. on time. at math. at home? at the library.

Note: See Chapters 2 and 3 for more information on adverbs of frequency and other time expressions.

C. Adverbials

Adverbials are words or groups of words that act like adverbs—that is, they modify verbs and adjectives. The chart gives some examples. Notice the word order of the different adverbials.

1.12	Adverbials						
Subject	Auxiliary Verb	Main Verb	Indirect Object	Direct Object	Adverbial of Direction/ Place	Adverbial of Manner	Adverbial of Frequency/ Time
The men		ride				on the bus	every day.
We		carried		our books	to school	in back-packs	this morning.
Bob		brought	me	those shoes	from Italy		last summer.
You	can	go			to work	by train	on weekdays.
I	couldn't	speak		Spanish		fluently	until this year.

2 **Practice** Add the information in parentheses to the following sentences.

Example Traveling is an amazing experience. (in foreign countries, always)
Traveling in foreign countries is always an amazing experience.

1. Travel can be tiring but rewarding. (very, extremely)

2. When people travel, they can have problems. (to foreign countries, sometimes)

3. The problem is the language. (most, difficult, often)

4. Travelers who don't speak the language have difficulties. (frequently, in foreign countries)

5. It is easier if you speak the language. (much, of the country, fluently)

6. If you don't speak the language, however, it is helpful to know some words and phrases. (fluently, extremely, useful)

7. Travel guides about foreign countries have sections that list words and phrases. (usually, special, important)

8. People in foreign countries are happy even if you only try to speak a few words. (almost always, very, of their language)

3 **Practice** Circle the correct word from each pair to complete the following paragraph. As you make each choice, think about why the other possibility is wrong. The first one is done as an example.

Distance and Communication

In interpersonal (communicate / communication), people in almost every culture recognize four (different / differently) distances: intimate, personal, (society / social), and public. Intimate distance occurs in a very (close / closely) relationship such as between a mother and a child. Personal distance lets good friends talk closely but (comfortable / comfortably). Social distance is used at parties or other gatherings. Public distance (concerns / concerning) more formal situations such as between a teacher and a student.

These (fourth / four) types of distance exist in all countries, but the amount of distance (usual / usually) depends on the culture. At a party, for example, a Canadian may sit several feet away from you, while (a / an) Arab may sit very near you. (Your / Yours) awareness of the other (culture / culture's) use of distance can often help you communicate better with (its / it's) people.

4 **Error Analysis** The following sentences have errors in word order. Find the errors and correct them, as in the example.

Example Many North Americans speak rapidly English.
Many North Americans speak English rapidly.

1. It is difficult often to understand Americans.

2. That Italian new student has with English some problems.

3. He went yesterday to a restaurant, but he couldn't understand the waiter.

4. The waiter spoke very rapidly English.

5. The student ate at the restaurant a hamburger.

6. He paid money too much.

7. The waiter realized this and returned immediately the money to the student.

8. Some people always are honest, but other people take frequently advantage of situations like that.

9. Problems with communication interpersonal can from speaking come, but they can come from also differences in body language.

10. The gesture Italian for "come here" looks exactly almost like the gesture North American for "good-bye."

 5 **Practice** Work with a partner. Make complete sentences by putting the following groups of words in correct order. The first word in each sentence is capitalized.

Example important / of / our / Our / part / bodies / an / are / language
Our bodies are an important part of our language.

1. expressions / often / Our / people / a / deal / facial / tell / great

2. contact / important / also / Gestures / are / eye / and

3. cultures / use / frequently / some / very / gestures / in / People

4. from / only / them / People / occasionally / North / use / America

5. look / people's / into / some / cultures / People / from / directly / other / eyes

6. Americans / other / not / keep / contact / North / with / constant / do / eye / people

6 **Describing a Visit to Another Country** The following paragraph is incomplete. Add your own descriptive words or phrases.

Visiting a(n) _____ country can be a(n) _____ experience. Sometimes there are _____ problems, especially with _____. People _____ have difficulties because _____. They may feel _____, or they may _____ _____ .

Using What You've Learned

7 **Understanding Body Language** Have you had any problems understanding the body language of people from other cultures? Have you misunderstood someone's gestures or facial expressions? Write a short paragraph about your experience. Include as much description as you can. When you finish writing, exchange papers with another student. How were your experiences similar or different?

 8 **Observing People** Follow these steps to test your skill at reading body language.

1. With a partner, visit a place where you can observe people. Choose two or more people in a group to watch. Stay far enough away that you cannot hear the people's conversation and try not to let them know you are watching. Notice their physical appearance and body language—their gestures, facial expressions, posture, their physical distance from each other, and so on. What can you guess about the people?

2. Each partner should complete a chart like the one below. (Add more information if you like.) After you have finished, compare your charts. Are your guesses the same?

	Person 1	Person 2	Person 3
Male or female			
Approximate age			
Occupation			
Level of education			
Current mood (sad, happy, angry, and so on)			
General personality type (talkative, shy, stubborn, and so on)			
What is the relationship of this person to the other(s)?			
Why did you make these guesses? What gave you clues?			

3. In class, discuss your experiences. How many different kinds of body language did you notice? Did people interpret this body language the same way?

9 **Role-Playing Difficult Situations** In pairs or small groups, role-play one or more of the following situations. As you talk, try to give as much description as possible: shape, size, color, height, weight, and so on.

1. You've just arrived at an international airport in the United States. You have been waiting at the baggage claim for your luggage, but nothing has arrived. Go to the baggage claim counter and describe your luggage and the contents in detail.

2. You are at an international airport in Canada. You are supposed to meet the sister of your friend and drive her into the city. You can't find anyone who looks like her. Talk to the airline personnel and ask for help. Describe your friend's sister in detail.

3. You left your jacket at a shopping mall, and you are trying to find it. You have gone to the lost and found desk to ask for help. Describe your jacket in detail.

4. You bought a car soon after arriving in Australia. You parked it downtown while you were shopping. Your car has been stolen. You have gone to the police for help. Describe your car and all the things that were in it in detail.

10 **Creating Jumbled Sentences** Write two or three sentences. Your sentences don't have to be long, but they should use as many descriptive words as possible. For example, "Late yesterday afternoon, I bought a fascinating new English grammar book." Or "On most weekends, I usually stay up extremely late at night." Give your sentences to your teacher to correct. Then, print each corrected sentence neatly on a piece of paper. Cut apart each sentence into words, and put the words for each sentence in a separate envelope. Finally, work in pairs or groups. Trade "cut up" sentences and then try to reassemble the sentences in correct order.

Self-Assessment Log

Each of the following statements describes the grammar you learned in this chapter. Read the statements, then check the box that describes how well you understand each structure.

	Needs Improvement	Good	Great
I can identify the parts of speech in English.	❏	❏	❏
I can identify subjects and verbs in sentences.	❏	❏	❏
I can identify a variety of verb tenses and time frames.	❏	❏	❏
I can use a variety of nouns, pronouns, adjectives, and adverbs in speaking and in writing.	❏	❏	❏
I can use a variety of verb tenses in speaking and writing.	❏	❏	❏

Cooperation and Competition

In This Chapter

Verbs (1)

Part 1 Auxiliary Verbs and Questions
Part 2 Embedded Questions
Part 3 The Simple Present and Present Continuous Tenses
Part 4 *Will* and *Be Going To*
Part 5 The Present Perfect Continuous and Present Perfect Tenses

"Many hands make light work, but too many cooks can spoil the broth!**"**

—Proverb

Connecting to the Topic

1 This traditional proverb in English talks about the idea of working together and helping one another. When is it good to work together?

2 When can "help" be a bad thing?

3 Which sports depend on cooperation? Which sports are based on competition?

Chapter 2 reviews uses of the auxiliary verbs *be, do,* and *have* and covers several present and future verb tenses. More information on tenses is in Chapter 3, and modal auxiliaries are covered in Chapter 4. Some of this chapter is review, and you may not need to study everything in detail.

Reading Read the following passage. It introduces the chapter theme, "Cooperation and Competition," along with information and issues you will cover in the chapter.

Cooperation versus Competition

What is competition? What does it mean to compete? According to the dictionary, competition is the attempt to outdo someone else, to be better or achieve more than someone else. Most living things, including humans, seem to have an inborn trait[1] that pushes them to compete. This is probably connected to the instinct for survival.

5

What is cooperation, then? What does it mean to cooperate? Is cooperation of any use to humans? The dictionary tells us that cooperation is the process of working together for a common purpose or goal. That is, people are willing to work together, and they have basically the same purpose in mind. Like competitiveness, cooperativeness also seems to come at birth because all living things perform better and achieve more when working together. Do you doubt this? Just look at a colony of ants or a flock of geese during migration.

10

---

[1]*trait* characteristic or quality

When is it good to cooperate, and when is it good to compete? Does the answer to this depend on the area or circumstances? For example, is competition more important in sports? Or does it depend on the specific sport, for example? 15

In school, do students perform better in a competitive environment or in a cooperative one? Within families, is competition amongst brothers and sisters normal and natural? Can families function without at least some cooperation? If so, how?

For centuries, researchers, educators, and psychologists and philosophers 20 have been trying to answer questions like these, but so far no one is completely sure. We don't really know whether one is more useful or more important than the other. In general, humans appear to be both competitive and cooperative, but the happiest humans seem to achieve a good balance between the two.

Discussing Ideas Discuss the questions.

What do you think? Are humans naturally competitive? Cooperative? Do you think this is true for both males and females? When is competition important? When is cooperation important?

Part 1 Auxiliary Verbs and Questions

Setting the Context

Previewing the Passage Discuss the questions.

In the schools you're most familiar with, do students usually work together? Is it common to do projects in groups? Or, does each student generally work alone?

▲ Assignments may require students to work cooperatively or independently.

Reading Read the passage.

Cooperation or Competition in Education—Which One Works?

Do students benefit from getting along well with their classmates? Are group efforts and group projects generally effective? Is it better for all students to work independently? Or is it best to compete for grades or honors? What happens to young people when the pressure to achieve in school is very strong? What happens when there is no pressure—no tests, no grades? 5

Researchers around the world have looked at these questions. What can the researchers tell us? First, they see three different types of interaction in classrooms. That is, students generally interact in three ways: they compete to see "who is best," they work independently, or they work cooperatively, where the success of the group depends on the success of each member. 10

In many parts of the world, cooperative learning is widely used, but in the U.S., competition continues to be the most common model. Competition begins even before a child in the U.S. starts school, and it grows stronger through grade school and high school. Many researchers view the end of U.S. high school as being one of the most competitive times in a child's life. 15

Is this model effective? How well do students learn in U.S. high schools? Many say that U.S. high schools are the "weakest part" of the U.S. education system, so perhaps the competitive model does not work very well.

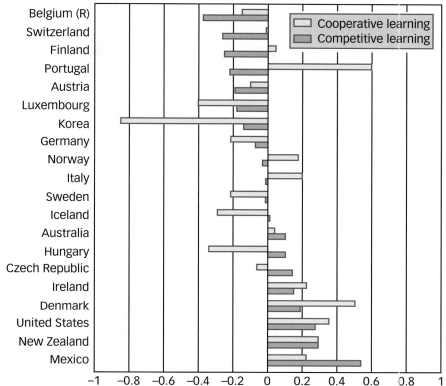

Competitive and cooperative learning index in OECD (Organisation for Economic Co-operation and Development) member countries, 2000

Legend: Cooperative learning, Competitive learning

Countries (top to bottom): Belgium (R), Switzerland, Finland, Portugal, Austria, Luxembourg, Korea, Germany, Norway, Italy, Sweden, Iceland, Australia, Hungary, Czech Republic, Ireland, Denmark, United States, New Zealand, Mexico

X-axis: −1, −0.8, −0.6, −0.4, −0.2, 0, 0.2, 0.4, 0.6, 0.8, 1

Note: OECD average is 0. Positive figures refer to values above OECD average, negative figures to those below.

Source: *Knowledge and Skills for Life, 2001*

Discussing Ideas Reread the questions in the first paragraph. Many studies on competitive learning versus cooperative learning have tried to answer these questions. What do you think?

Grammar Structures and Practice

A. Statements, *Yes/No* Questions, and Short Responses

The formation of statements, questions, and short responses follows two different patterns in English:

- With *do*
- With *be, have,* and modal auxiliaries

(continued)

2.1 Statements, *Yes/No* Questions, and Short Responses

Structures	Explanations	Examples	
Do	The simple present and past tenses use forms of *do* in questions, negatives, short responses, and tag questions. The verb *have* follows the same patterns when it is a main verb in these tenses.	**Affirmative Statements** We study a lot. Maria has a lot to do.	**Negative Statements** They don't study a lot. He doesn't have a lot to do.
		***Yes/No* Questions** Do you study a lot? Does he have a lot to do?	**Possible Responses** Yes, I do. No, I don't. Yes, he does. No, he doesn't.
Be, Have, and Modal Auxiliaries	Sentences with continuous and perfect tenses, modal auxiliaries, and the verb *be* as a main verb all follow the same patterns for formation of questions, negatives, short responses, and tag questions.	**Affirmative Statements** We are studying. Maria can help us. Tomas has left.	**Negative Statements** They aren't studying now. Ming can't help us. Ali hasn't left yet.
		***Yes/No* Questions** Are you studying now? Can Leah help? Has Alfred left?	**Possible Responses** Yes, I am. No, I'm not. Yes, she can. No, she can't. Yes, he has. No, he hasn't.

1 **Practice** Many Americans use incomplete questions in conversation. Form complete questions from the following by adding auxiliary verbs and subjects.

Examples Working hard?
Are you working hard?
Study until late last night?
Did you study until late last night?
Gotten any sleep?
Have you gotten any sleep?

▲ Working hard?

1. Doing OK today?
2. Get any sleep last night?
3. Work late last night?
4. Have a lot of homework today?
5. Writing a paper for history class now?
6. Need some ideas for your paper?
7. Finished writing it?
8. Already entered it on the computer?
9. Printed it yet?
10. Want me to proofread it?
11. Have to hand it in today?

12. Going to campus soon?

13. Your roommate already leave?

14. Your roommate say when he was coming back with the car?

15. Want a ride?

16. Ready to leave now?

 2 **Practice** Working in pairs, make short conversations using the information in parentheses in items 1 to 5. After you have completed this the first time, change roles or work with a new partner to practice it again.

Example A: I saw Tomoko last night.
            Have you seen her recently? (see her/recently)
        B: No, *I haven't. Is she still studying biology?* (still/study biology)
        A: No, *she isn't. She's studying botany now.* (botany)
        B: *Do you have her phone number? I'd like to call her.* (phone number/call)
        A: Sorry, I don't.

1. A: I ran into Professor Sommer yesterday.

        _____ (see him/recently)

    B: No, _____ (still/teaching beginning German)

    A: No, _____ (German literature)

    B: _____ (schedule/make an appointment with him)

    A: Sorry, _____

2. A: I saw Brenda the other day.

        _____ (run into her/recently)

    B: No, _____ (still/study accounting)

    A: No, _____ (finance)

    B: _____ (email address/send her a message)

    A: Sorry, _____

3. A: I got a card from your old roommate yesterday.

        _____ (hear from him (her)/recently)

    B: No, _____ (still/go to the University of Massachusetts)

    A: No, _____ (Boston College)

    B: _____ (address/write)

    A: Sorry, _____

4. A: I had lunch with Tony last week.

_____ (talk to him/recently)

B: No, _____ (still/take classes at the community college)

A: No, _____ (work at a bank)

B: _____ (phone number/call)

A: Sorry, _____

5. A: I saw Miki this morning.

_____ (call her/recently)

B: No, _____ (still/write textbooks)

A: No, _____ (novels)

B: _____ (address/visit)

A: Sorry, _____

B. Negative *Yes/No* Questions

Negative *yes/no* questions often show a speaker's expectations or beliefs.
- A negative question can mean the speaker hopes for a *yes* answer but realizes a *no* answer is also possible.
- If the speaker is sure of a *no* answer, he or she can ask a negative question to show anger or surprise.
- Note that contractions must be used in negative questions.

2.2 Negative *Yes/No* Questions	
Uses	**Examples**
Asking for Information	Teacher: "You look confused. **Didn't you study?**" Student: "Yes, I did, but I didn't understand the homework."
Showing Surprise or Anger	Teacher: "You made a lot of mistakes on the test. **Didn't you study?**" Student: "No, I didn't. I'm sorry."

3 Practice Change the following questions to negative questions. Then work in pairs and take turns asking and answering the questions. As you practice, vary the tone of your voice. Ask some of the questions to get information, and ask other questions to show surprise or anger.

Example Are you going to the library?
      A: Aren't you going to the library? (surprised)
      B: Well, no, I'm not. I'm too tired.

1. Are you going to study tonight?

2. Are your roommates going to study tonight?

3. Did you buy your books?

4. Did Miki buy her books?

5. Have you finished your work?

6. Has Anni finished her work?

7. Are you reviewing for the quiz?

8. Are your friends reviewing for the test?

9. Have you turned in your assignment?

10. Can you go with us to the party?

11. Can your roommates go with us?

12. Can Miki go with us?

C. Information Questions

Information questions ask *when? where? why? how? how often*? and so on. As in *yes/no* questions, an auxiliary verb normally precedes the subject in information questions.

2.3	**Formation of Information Questions**		
Question Word	**Auxiliary Verb (+ Negative)**	**Subject + Verb**	
When	do did	you have class today? you have class last semester?	
Where	will are have had	you take classes? you going to take classes? you taken classes? you taken classes before enrolling here?	
Why	are weren't	you late? you on time yesterday?	

Common question words include *when, where, why, how, what,* and many combinations with *how* or *what.*

(continued)

2.4 Common Question Words

Question Words	Meaning	Question Words	Meaning
How	asks about manner	**What color (size, shape, and so on)**	asks for specific details
How . . . like	asks for an opinion	**What time**	asks for a specific time
How cold (fast, old, and so on)	asks for a description*	**When**	asks about time (specific or general)
How far	asks about distance	**Where**	asks about place
How long	asks about length of time	**Which book (city, one, person, and so on)**	asks about a specific person, place, and so on
How many	asks about quantity (count nouns)	**Who(m)**	asks about people
How much	asks about quantity (noncount nouns)	**Whose**	asks about ownership or possession
How often	asks about frequency	**Why**	asks for reasons
What	asks about things	**Why . . . not**	gives suggestions
What . . . (look) like	asks for a description*		

*Note: *What does he look like?* asks for a physical description. *What is he like?* asks about qualities or characteristics (*funny, nice, serious,* and so on). *What does he like?* asks about preferences. *(Does he like soccer? Baseball?)*

---

4 **Practice** Complete the following questions by adding appropriate question words or phrases.

Example _____Why_____ are you leaving?
Because I have to study.

1. A: _____ did you leave home this morning?

B: At 8:30.

2. A: _____ did you get to school today?

B: By bus.

3. A: _____ did you take?

B: The express bus.

4. A: _____ are you going later?

B: To the library.

5. A: _____ don't you study at home?

    B: Because it's too noisy.

6. A: _____ roommates do you have?

    B: Three.

7. A: _____ do your roommates make noise?

    B: Almost every night.

8. A: _____ do you live with?

    B: Two Americans and one foreign student.

9. A: _____ do you pay for rent?

    B: $200 a month.

10. A: _____ is your apartment like?

    B: It's large, but it's old.

11. A: _____ is it to campus from there?

    B: Three blocks.

12. A: _____ does it take to get there?

    B: About fifteen minutes.

5 **Rapid Oral Practice** Write short questions for the following answers. Some answers can have more than one question. Then work in pairs. Take turns asking and answering the questions.

Example A: _____ *When?* _____

         B: At 3:00.

1. A: _____   B: On Monday.

2. A: _____   B: At the library.

3. A: _____   B: Ann and Mary.

4. A: _____   B: For two semesters.

5. A: _____   B: Mary's.

6. A: _____   B: Three times a week.

7. A: _____   B: 10:00.

8. A: _____   B: The red one.

9. A: _____   B: Four hours.

10. A: _____   B: Fifty miles per hour.

11. A: _____   B: Because I want to.

12. A: _____   B: Size 12.

13. A: _____   B: That one.

14. A: _____   B: Twenty-two years old.

15. A: _____   B: English class.

D. Information Questions with *Who, Whose, Which,* and *What*

In some information questions, the question word replaces part or all of the subject. Auxiliary verbs are *not* used, and the order of the subject and verb does *not* change.

2.5	Information Questions with *Who, Whose, Which,* and *What*	
Structures	**Explanations**	**Examples**
Who	*Who* is used only with people. It normally takes a singular verb even if the answer is plural.	**Who** teaches that class? Dr. Johnson. **Who** teaches that class? Dr. Johnson and two teaching assistants.
Whose	*Whose* replaces a possessive noun or pronoun.	**Whose** class has a lot of reading? Dr. Johnson's class.
Which	*Which* can be used with or without a noun. It normally refers to a small set of people, places, or things familiar to the speaker.	**Which art class** has the most work? **Which** (one) has the most work? Art 210.
What	*What* is generally more informal than *which*, and it usually refers to a larger set of people, places, or things unfamiliar to the speaker.	**What** makes the class so difficult? The amount of homework.

6 **Practice** Complete the following questions by using *who, what, which,* or *whose.*

Example   A: _____*Who*_____ is your roommate this semester?

         B: I have three. Miki, Mary, and Anni. One is from Canada, one is from Spain, and one is from Poland.

1. A: _____ is the Canadian?
     B: Mary is.

2. A: _____ roommate is from Spain?
     B: Anni is.

3. A: _____ is the most difficult thing about foreign roommates?
     B: The problems with language. We speak four different ones.

4. A: _____ accent gives you the most difficulty?
     B: Miki's accent. It's very strong.

5. A: _____ roommate brought that great CD player?
     B: Anni did.

6. A: _____ kinds of music do you listen to?

B: Miki likes rock music, but Anni likes Latin jazz and salsa.

7. A: _____ buys the most CDs?

B: Miki does.

8. A: _____ CD is your favorite?

B: Right now, I like the Dave Matthews CD a lot. But last week, it was Carlos Santana.

9. A: _____ mother came to visit last week?

B: Miki's mother, Bakka.

10. A: _____ did Bakka say about the rock music?

B: She doesn't like it. She likes classical music better.

Cultural Note

A roommate is someone who shares a dormitory (dorm) room or an apartment with you. Generally, roommates share expenses, like rent and utilities such as electricity and gas. Sharing housing is very common among young people in the United States, and most universities are surrounded by relatively low-cost student dormitories and apartments.

 7 Practice Create information questions for these answers. Have your teacher check your questions if necessary. Then, in pairs, alternate asking the questions and giving these answers.

Example A: *How often do you study at the library?*

B: I usually study there once or twice a week.

1. A: _____

B: In the evening, from about 7:00 to 9:00.

2. A: _____

B: I walk.

3. A: _____

B: Because it's quieter than my apartment.

4. A: Oh, you have an apartment. _____

B: About five blocks from here.

5. A: I'm looking for an apartment too. _____

B: Well, our apartment rents for $800 a month.

6. A: Eight hundred dollars a month? _____

B: I have three roommates. Two of my roommates, Miki and Anni, are here right now.

7. A: _____

B: She's the one with brown hair and a red dress.

8. A: _____

B: She usually rides her bike.

9. A: _____

B: My other roommate is tall and slim.

10. A: _____

B: Oh, it's *my* watch beeping. Sorry.

11. A: _____

B: It's almost 9:00 o'clock.

12. A: _____

B: I set my alarm because it's so quiet here at the library that I sometimes fall asleep!

8 **Error Analysis** Many of the following sentences contain errors in formal, written English. Circle each error and correct it, or indicate that the sentence contains no errors.

Example   Why (he didn't) come to the party?

   Correction: *Why didn't he come to the party?*

   Why didn't they come to the party? *(Correct)*

1. Do I haves to do all the homework for tomorrow?

2. Does he has the right directions to get here?

3. Which sweater did she buy?

4. Who did call you?

5. Where he is studying now?

6. Why you don't come to visit us more often?

7. Whose car are you driving?

8. Whose dictionary you are using?

9. Who told you that story?

10. Did not she mail the package?

11. Where you have classes?

12. Whose book this is?

13. Where you got this?

14. Did not you study economics?

15. How long time does it take you to get to school?

Using What You've Learned

 9 **Understanding Cartoons** Read the following cartoon, "Real Life Adventures." What is happening in it? Can you understand the general idea even though none of the questions in the cartoon is complete? After reading the cartoon, work in pairs. Write a dialogue for the cartoon using complete questions and statements instead of the shortened forms.

There's always more wrong with your car than you thought.

Setting the Context

▲ In the U.S., most teachers address students by their first names.

 Previewing the Passage Discuss the question.

In your country or culture, what is the typical way to address a teacher?

Reading Read the passage.

The Student-Teacher Relationship

From culture to culture, the student-teacher relationship can be very different. In many cultures, the relationship is formal. Students always use titles such as *Professor* or *Doctor* when addressing a teacher. They never use first names. Interaction is very polite. For example, when a student asks a teacher about a test, the question might be something like this, "Excuse me, please, Dr. Vera-mani. Could you tell me whether we will have a test in the near future?"

In the U.S. and Canada, the student-teacher relationship is often less formal. Some teachers allow students to call them by first name, for example, *John*, instead of *Mr. Nelson* or *Professor Nelson* or *Dr. Nelson*. So, instead of some-

5

thing like: "Dr. Nelson, could you please tell me when our term paper is due? I   10
would like to know when I should hand it in?," you might hear this: "Hey, John. I
can't remember the due date on our next paper. When do you want it?"

Informality is most common at the university level in the United States. The
university level is also where cooperation among students and faculty is perhaps the strongest. Students work with faculty members on projects and papers   15
or in labs and clinics. The success of the work depends on the collaboration of
the group. With the emphasis on the group, stronger, less formal, and more personal relationships tend to develop.

 Discussing Ideas Discuss the questions.

In your culture, how do students and teachers interact? Is the relationship usually
formal? Has this changed in recent years?

Grammar Structures and Practice

A. Introduction to Embedded Questions

Embedded, or indirect, questions are generally very polite in English. They involve
putting one question "inside" a statement or another question. The following expressions are frequently used before an embedded question:

- Could you tell me...?
- Can you tell me...?
- Do you know...?
- I would like to know...
- I wonder...

B. Embedded Questions with *If* and *Whether*

Yes/no questions may be changed to noun clauses by using *if* or *whether (or not)* to introduce them.

- *Whether* is preferred in formal English. It also implies choice among alternatives
  rather than a strict *yes/no* decision.
- Remember that the subject must come before the verb in the noun clause.

2.6 Embedded Questions with *If* and *Whether*	
Yes/No Questions	**Embedded Questions**
Is Mr. Brown here now?	Do you know if Mr. Brown is here now?
Does he have office hours now?	Could you tell me if he has office hours now?
Should I wait for him?	I would like to know whether (or not) I should wait for him.

1 Practice Politely ask your teacher for more information about your English course. Change the following direct questions to embedded questions. Be sure to use correct word order. Begin with the following: *Could you tell me...? I would like to know ...*

Example Will there be any homework this week?

I would like to know whether (if) there will be any homework this week.

1. Do I need to attend every class?

2. Will there be a final test in this class?

3. Do I have to take a proficiency exam?

4. Is it necessary to study for the proficiency exam?

5. Have I completed all my assignments so far?

6. Am I missing any work?

7. Could I talk to you about my progress?

8. Am I going to pass this course?

9. Will we have any research assignments?

10. Does anyone have an extra dictionary?

C. Embedded Questions with Question Words

Information questions may also be changed to embedded questions.

- Question words such as *when, why, what,* and *who(m)* are used to introduce these embedded questions.
- When the question is embedded, the subject must come before the verb, as it does in statements.

2.7 Embedded Questions with Question Words	
Information Questions	**Embedded Questions**
When does Mr. Brown teach today?	Could you tell me when Mr. Brown teaches today?
Where is Mr. Brown's class?	I'd like to know where Mr. Brown's class is.
How long has he taught here?	Can you tell me how long he has taught here?
Why might he be late?	Do you know why he might be late?

2 Practice Imagine that you have to write a term paper for a class. Again, politely ask for information by changing the following to embedded questions. Be sure to use correct word order. Begin your new sentences with the following: *Could you tell me...? I would like to know... I wonder... I don't know....*

Example   When is the term paper due?
Could you tell me when the term paper is due?

1. How long should the paper be?
2. How much should I write?
3. How many sources do I need to use?
4. What kinds of sources are acceptable? Magazines, websites, books?
5. Where can I get information on the topic?
6. Which section of the library should I check?
7. When could I discuss this with you?
8. Where is there a computer lab open late at night?
9. How many drafts do you usually do on your papers?
10. Who will edit the first draft of my essay?
11. How are you grading the papers? A, B, C, or Pass / Fail?
12. When are you going to return our papers?

Using What You've Learned

3 Meet the Press! Role-play interviews with several people who are important figures in your school, your community, your city, or your region. Choose a variety of public figures, for example, your teacher, the president or director of your school, an important athlete, a local politician, a famous musician or actor, and so on. One person can role-play the public figure, while other students are in "the press corps." Each member of the press must ask at least one question. Try to begin your questions with the following:

Could you tell me...?

Can you tell me...?

Do you know...?

I would like to know...

I wonder...

Setting the Context

Previewing the Passage Discuss the questions.

What sport are these players playing? What do you know about the sport?

Reading Read the passage.

Sports and Teamwork

Soccer is the most popular sport on earth. People everywhere watch it, talk about it, play it, and even live and die for it every single day. In fact, at this moment, someone somewhere is watching a soccer game. That means 22 other people are playing it right now. For those particular 23 people, and millions of others worldwide, soccer is the best of both cooperation and competition. 5

In soccer, team cooperation is key. Every player can touch the ball, and all players have to work together to move the ball up and down the field. A good pass or a good corner kick goes directly to another player. A penalty affects the whole team. Teams may have stars, such as Pelé or Maradona, but every person on the team is vital. 10

Competition among teams is ferocious, however. Both the players and the fans are incredibly loyal to their own team and wildly against other teams. While the team is playing a game on the field, the fans are screaming and yelling and even threatening and fighting the opposition. Many stadiums are like war zones. Players and referees enter with armed guards, and police patrol the 15 stands to stop fights. Injuries and even deaths can occur in soccer, but these are most often off the playing field, not on it.

Discussing Ideas Discuss the questions.

Do you play soccer? Do you have a favorite team? What is the team like? What are the fans like?

Grammar Structures and Practice

A. The Simple Present Tense

The simple present tense often refers to actions or situations that do not change frequently or quickly.

- This tense is used to describe habits or routines, to express opinions, or to make general statements of fact.
- The simple present can also be used to refer to the future.

2.8 Simple Present		
Uses	**Examples**	**Time Expressions**
Facts	Alan and Lu **are** professors at the university. Alan **works** in the physics department. Lu **teaches** music.	
Habits or Routines	Lu **has** classes every day. Alan **doesn't have** classes on Friday.	*every day (week, month, year)* *always, generally, sometimes*
Opinions	**Do** they **enjoy** their work? Lu **enjoys** her classes very much. Alan **doesn't like** to teach.	*as a rule* *in general*
Reference to the Future	Next year, Alan **has** a sabbatical. He **doesn't teach** next year.	*next week (month, year)*

1 **Review** Give the *he* or *she* form (third person singular) of the following verbs in the present tense. Then list them according to the way the *-s* ending sounds in each: *s* (walks), *z* (runs), or *ez* (watches).

Example study *studies (-z sound)*

1. carry

2. establish

3. reply

4. watch

5. go

6. employ

7. laugh

8. bet

9. worry

10. box

11. fly

12. do

13. collect

14. argue

15. stay

2 Practice Form complete sentences from the following cues. Use the simple present tense and pay attention to the spelling and pronunciation of the *-s* endings.

Examples be a soccer player
Omar is a soccer player.

go to a Canadian university
He goes to a Canadian university.

1. be Lebanese

2. come from Beirut, Lebanon

3. have an American roommate

4. enjoy several hobbies

5. like music and cooking

6. do a lot of sports, like soccer, tennis, and swimming

7. watch a lot of TV

8. stay out late sometimes

9. not like cafeteria food very much

10. not go to the cafeteria very often

11. go to movies once or twice a week

12. study at the library now and then

13. play soccer almost every day

14. not be a very good student

15. miss his family

3 Practice Now tell about yourself. Answer the following in complete sentences using the simple present tense. Then, in pairs, take turns asking each other these questions.

1. What are three facts about yourself?

2. What are three things that you like (to do)?

3. What are two things that you don't like (to do)?

4. What are three things that you do every day?

5. What are two things that you do not do every day?

4 **Practice** Look at the picture of a soccer practice. Teams everywhere practice and have coaches who help them. What does a coach do? Make statements about coaching from the following cues, and then add three original sentences. Use *a coach, a player, he,* or *she* in your statements.

Example   work with the players on the team
　　　　A coach works with the players on the team.

1. teach the players

2. demonstrate new moves

3. give advice

4. set rules

5. make schedules for practices and games

6. watch the players

7. look for mistakes

8. try to find ways to improve performance

9. try alternatives

10. record game statistics

B. Adverbs of Frequency

Expressions such as the following are frequently used with the simple present tense to describe habits or routines. Many of these also appear with verbs in the present and past perfect tenses.

2.9 Adverbs of Frequency

Adverbs of Frequency		Other Time Expressions
always	100%	*all the time, without fail*
almost always	↑	*as a rule, on a regular basis*
usually, normally, typically,		*by and large*
commonly, generally		*in general*
often, frequently		*generally*
sometimes		*at times, from time to time*
occasionally		*(every) now and then*
seldom		*(every) now and again*
rarely		*off and on*
hardly ever		*once in a (great) while*
almost never	↓	
never	0%	

The placement of adverbs of frequency depends on the structure of the sentence.

2.10 Placements of Adverbs of Frequency

Uses	Explanations	Examples
In Statements with One Verb	Adverbs of frequency and many one-word adverbs can be placed before the main verb of a sentence.	We **usually** have games on Tuesdays and Fridays. I **always** enjoy a good game. I **almost never** miss a game.
In Statements with Auxiliary Verbs and *Be* as the Main Verb	Adverbs of frequency usually follow. auxiliary verbs and *be* used as a main verb	Our games are **generally** interesting. We have **occasionally** missed a game.
In Questions and Negatives	*Ever*, meaning "at any time," is often used in questions and negatives.	Are you **ever** late for practice? He isn't **ever** late for games. Do you **usually** get to practice on time?
Longer Expressions with Verbs in All Tenses	Longer time expressions are normally placed at the beginning or the end of a sentence.	**As a rule,** we get to the stadium early. I am late **every now and then.**

5 **Practice** Look at the schedule for the soccer team below. Answer the following questions in complete sentences.

1. When does the team have games?

2. How many times a week does the team play games?

3. How often does the team practice?

4. Which days does the team practice?

5. How long does the team practice each session?

6. Are the practices always the same length?

7. When does the team clean the locker room?

8. When does the team do laundry?

9. When do the players wash uniforms?

10. What do players do on Saturdays? What do they do on Sundays?

Schedule for the Soccer Team						
Monday	**Tuesday**	**Wednesday**	**Thursday**	**Friday**	**Saturday**	**Sunday**
6:30–8 A.M. • Practice	No practice	6:30–8 A.M. • Practice	6:30–8 A.M. • Practice	No practice	8–10:00 A.M. • Practice	No practice
• Classes	8:30–3:30 • Classes				10–Noon • Do laundry (wash uniforms)	All Day • Call home • Do homework • Visit family
4–7 P.M. • Practice		4–7 P.M. • Practice		5:00 P.M. • Game	• Clean the locker room	• Spend time with friends
5:30 P.M. • Game			5:30 P.M. • Play games	Evening • Relax • Study	Afternoon • Call home • Do homework • Visit families	

 6 **Practice** In pairs, take turns asking and answering these questions. Then add a few original questions. Give complete answers.

1. What is something that you always do every morning?

2. What is something that you never eat for breakfast?

3. What is something that you seldom wear?

4. Who is someone that you occasionally write to?

5. Who is someone that you hardly ever see now?

6. How often do you watch TV or listen to the radio?

7. How often do you call home? Call your friends?

8. How often do you use a computer? Do you have email? How often do you email your friends or family?

9. How often do you go out at night?

10. How often do you go out on weekends? What do you do? When do you do that?

C. The Present Continuous Tense

The present continuous tense describes actions or situations in progress at the moment of speaking.

- This includes activities that are happening right now and current activities of a general nature.
- In some cases, the present continuous tense can also refer to the future.
- As a rule, the present continuous tense is used for activities that are temporary rather than permanent.

2.11	The Present Continuous Tense	
Uses	**Examples**	**Time Expressions**
Activities at the Moment of Speaking	Sandy **is studying** in the other room right now. Jim **is working** on the computer. I'm **proofreading** the report.	*now, right now* *at the moment, today, still*
Current Activities	Sandy **is majoring** in economics. She **isn't taking** many courses this semester.	*nowadays* *these days*
Reference to the Future	Sandy **isn't taking** classes next semester. **Is** she **going** to Europe instead?	Expressions with *this (this morning, this week, this year)*

Note: See Appendix 2 on pages 462–463 for spelling rules for the *-ing* ending.

7 **Review** Write the *-ing* form of the following verbs, making any necessary spelling changes.

Example sit *sitting*

1. study

2. occur

3. travel

4. insist

5. write

6. open

7. plan

8. happen

9. begin

10. change

11. swim

12. heat

8 **Practice** Make complete sentences from the following cues. Use the present continuous tense and pay attention to the spelling of the *-ing* endings.

Example not study right now
Pierre's not studying right now.

play tennis again
He's playing tennis again.

▲ Pierre's playing tennis again.

1. have fun in the United States

2. get a lot of exercise this semester

3. play tennis tonight and tomorrow night

4. not study very much

5. not do very well in school

6. fail one course

7. enjoy himself

8. plan to study more next week

9 **Practice** Now tell about yourself. Answer the following in complete sentences using the present continuous tense. Then, in pairs, take turns asking each other these questions.

1. What are three things that you are doing right now?

2. What are two things that you are not doing now?

3. What are two things that you are doing this quarter (semester)?

4. What are three things that you are not doing this quarter (semester)?

D. Verbs Not Normally Used in the Continuous Tenses

These verbs are seldom used in the continuous tenses, *except* in certain idiomatic uses or in descriptions of a definite action.

2.12 Verbs Not Normally Used in the Continuous Tenses

	Verbs		Explanations	Examples
Feelings or Thoughts	appreciate be believe consider* dislike hate know like love mean*	mind miss need prefer recognize remember think* understand want*	These verbs are rarely used in a continuous tense. The verbs with an asterisk (*), however, sometimes appear in the present perfect continuous tense. The verbs *think* and *consider* occasionally appear in the present continuous tense.	He **doesn't understand** the problem. We **need** to talk about it. I **think** that is a good idea. We **prefer** to talk later. *Compare:* We **have been considering** another possibility. I **am thinking** about several other possibilities now.
Perceptions	appear hear* look see*	seem smell sound taste	These verbs sometimes appear in a continuous tense in the description of a specific action or in certain idioms.	This apple **looks** good. It **tastes** delicious. *Compare:* I'm **looking** at the apple now. I **am tasting** the apple now.
Possession	belong to cost have*	own possess	These verbs almost never appear in continuous tenses, except for the verb *have*. In idiomatic use, *be having* has several meanings, including "be experiencing" or "be eating, drinking."	We **own** a car. It **belongs** to my brother and me. He **has** the car today. *Compare:* He's **having** a great time. I'm **having** dinner with him tonight.

10 **Practice** Complete the passage with present forms of the verbs in parentheses. Include negatives and adverbs when indicated. The first one is done as an example.

Promoting Cooperation and Competition

Manchester United _____*is working*_____ with UNICEF, the United Nations Children's Fund, on a program called Sport for Development. This partnership _____ little, but it _____ a tremendous

1 (cost) 2 (have)

impact on children. The program _____ healthy development

3 (promote)

of children and _____ important lessons in respect, leadership,

4 (teach)

cooperation, and equality. Children everywhere _____ posi-
5 (respond)
tively. They _____ their favorite soccer players and
6 (love)
_____ very willing to learn from them.
7 (be)

Each year, through "United for UNICEF," the soccer club
_____ millions of dollars for charity for children. In addition to
8 (raise)
money, Manchester United _____ its sports expertise. The
9 (contribute)
team _____ coaching materials and _____
10 (create)   11 (do)
publicity for "Soccerwise," which _____ good citizenship.
12 (promote)

Now, Manchester United team members _____ active in
13 (be / also)
programs with children. Players who _____ to the team
14 (belong)
_____ in sports tournaments and clinics in countries where
15 (participate)
UNICEF _____. But it _____ just the soccer
16 (work)   17 (not be)
players. Manchester United board members, employees, and even fans
_____ support to UNICEF's work, too.
18 (give / now)

According to Sir Alex Ferguson, Manchester United Manager and UNICEF
Goodwill Ambassador, "We at Manchester United _____ in a
19 (be)
position to give something back to society and I _____ we
20 (believe / firmly)
_____ a responsibility to do so. It _____ in-
21 (have)   22 (be)
spiring to see our players using their international profile to deliver important
social messages to children worldwide."

Using What You've Learned

11 **Talking About Schedules and Routines** Read Practice 6 on page 63 again.
In pairs or small groups, discuss the differences in your personal habits based on the
questions in the activity. For example, what kinds of things do you do every morning?
Think about your daily life here compared to that in your home country. Or think about
your life today compared to two years ago. How are your personal habits different?
What other differences have you noticed between your personal life then and now?

12 **Describing Lifestyles** In pairs or in small groups, learn a little more about lifestyles in your classmates' cultures. Take turns describing some of the following.

1. a typical grandmother or grandfather in your culture
2. a typical teenager in your culture
3. a typical weekday for a typical family
4. a typical weekend
5. a typical holiday or special event such as a wedding
6. a typical house or apartment

As you share your ideas, be sure to include information or opinions about changes that are taking place in your culture.

Part 4 | *Will* and *Be Going To*

Setting the Context

 Previewing the Passage Discuss the questions.

What will our world be like the future? What kind of families will our children and our children's children have? What kinds of jobs will we have?

Reading Read the passage and the graph that follows.

Jobs in the 21st Century

What will our world be like in 2050? Will families be smaller? Will people change jobs and careers frequently? Will there be more elderly people?

Around the world, people are living longer and staying healthier. People in economically rich societies are having fewer children. For example, in the United States in 1980, people over age 65 made up only 11.3 percent of the total population. In 2050 they will make up over 22 percent. In the 1950s average families had 4.8 children. Now the average family has less than 1. 5

The aging population in the U.S. is going to affect the job market a great deal. Health and entertainment industries will need many more workers to provide services for older Americans. Jobs in education, especially adult education, will be increasing, too, as these older Americans are probably going to go back to school again and again. 10

With fewer children, who will fill the jobs of the future? Will job competition decrease, while competition for workers increases? That will depend a 15 great deal on immigration, especially if U.S. citizens have fewer children.

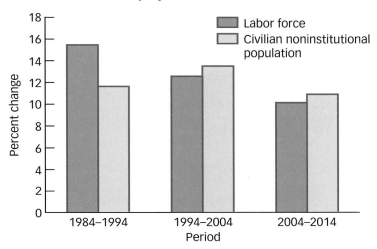

Percent change in the population and labor force, 1984–1994, 1994–2004, and projected 2004–2014

Source: *U.S. Bureau of Labor Statistics*

Discussing Ideas Discuss the questions.

Do you think that the trend toward an older population is also happening in other countries that you are familiar with? Why or why not?

A. The Simple Future Tense

The simple future tense expresses intentions. It can also be used to express offers and promises, predictions, and requests.

2.13 The Simple Future Tense		
Uses	**Examples**	**Time Expressions**
Intentions	**I'll try** to be home early tonight.	*this afternoon (evening)*
Offers and Promises	**I'll help** you with the housework in a little while. Thanks. Then I **will make** you a special dinner!	*later* *in a while*
Predictions	With your help, we**'ll finish** by 10:00.	*tonight, tomorrow, next week* *in the future, in September, in*
Requests	**Will** you **promise** to help?	*2050,* and so on

1 **Practice** The following are predictions that researchers have made about the future in the United States. Add *will* to form complete sentences. Then discuss whether these predictions may be true for other countries also.

Example divorce rates in the U.S. / remain high
Divorce rates in the U.S. will remain high.

1. Fifty percent of marriages / end in court

2. A majority of people / marry more than once during their lives

3. Some couples / get divorced and remarried three or four times

4. More and more marriages / be interracial or intercultural

5. In general, couples / have fewer children

6. Immigrants / fill many jobs of the future

7. People / change jobs and careers several times during their lifetime

8. "Aging" students / fill university classrooms

9. Universities / offer a wide variety of courses for older people

10. Many people / earn four or five different college degrees

11. Many of today's jobs / disappear

12. New jobs and new fields / develop

B. Other Forms Used for the Future

Other forms may be used to express future meaning, including *be going to* and the present tenses.

2.14 Other Forms Used for the Future: *Be Going To*, Present Tenses with Future Meaning

Structures	Explanations	Examples
be going to	*Going to* is often used to express specific future plans or intentions. It is used frequently in conversation and is often pronounced *gonna* or *gunna*. In some cases, *will* and *going to* are interchangeable, but *will* is preferred in formal English.	I'm **going to be** home no later than 7:00. What **are** we **going to have** for dinner? When **are** you **going to get** home?
Present Continuous and the Simple Present	Both the present continuous and the the simple present can be used to express future time. Normally a time expression or the context indicates that the action or situation is in the future. Verbs of movement such as *go*, *come*, *arrive*, and *leave* are often used in present tenses, even when they have future meanings.	I **am serving** dinner at 7:30. The guests **are coming** around 7:00. Dinner **is** at 7:30. We **leave** for the movie at 9:00.

 2 Practice In pairs, take turns asking and answering the following questions.

1. Will you see your family (boyfriend, girlfriend, best friend) soon?

2. When are you going to call them (him, her) next?

3. Will the call be long distance?

4. Will it be expensive?

5. When are you going to write your next letter (or email) to your family or a good friend?

6. Are you emailing someone after class?

7. What will you write about?

8. Is anyone coming to visit you soon?

9. When will the guests arrive?

10. What are you planning to do with them?

3 Practice Complete the passage with future forms of the verbs in parentheses. The first one is done as an example.

Changes in Work Life and Home Life

Technology has already changed the world of work, and in the near future improvements such as video conferencing and faster Internet access

<u>*are going to make*</u> it even easier for people to work from their homes.
(make)

In general, people _____ less tied to an office. Work
1 (be)

_____ a more international focus and _____
2 (have)   3 (need)

round-the-clock attention. Therefore, it _____ even more
4 (become)

difficult to separate work and home life.

Changes in the nature of work combined with changes in the workforce

_____ about major changes in company policies. Because
5 (bring)

women now are nearly half of the workforce, corporations already depend

more on female workers. Because of this, opportunities for females to advance

_____, and company policies _____ more
6 (increase)   7 (become)

"family friendly."

In the future, gender inequality _____. With more and more
8 (disappear / hopefully)

women in fields once dominated by men, the gap between male and female

wages _____. When this happens, power balances
9 (close)

_____ not only at the office, but also in the home. When both
10 (change)

sexes have equivalent jobs and paychecks, it _____ the woman
11 (not be / always)

who works "the second shift" of housework after hours or who stays home

when a child is sick. In addition, women _____ child custody in
12 (not receive)

a divorce as often as they do now.

C. The Future Continuous Tense

The future continuous tense normally refers to actions that will be in progress, often at a specified time, in the future.

2.15	The Future Continuous Tense		
Uses	**Examples**	**Time Expressions**	
Actions in Progresss in the Future	Can you imagine! At this time tomorrow we**'ll be landing** in London! Yes, but at the same time next week, we**'ll be flying** home.	*at this time next week (month,* and so on) *at that time (at 3:00,* and so on) *the day after tomorrow* *a week (year) from today*	

4 Practice The future continuous tense often gives a friendlier and more conversational feeling than the simple future does. Change the following sentences to the future continuous.

Example I'll see you.

I'll be seeing you.

1. We'll see you later this evening.
2. Will you go to the party tomorrow night?
3. They'll arrive in town the day after tomorrow.
4. I'll call you soon.
5. Deb will fax me the forms shortly.
6. He won't come home for dinner tonight.
7. When will we have our next exam?
8. Will Kim join us for dinner?
9. Judy will write us soon.
10. Brad will get his test results soon.
11. Kerri will meet us at the lecture hall.
12. Terry will let us know when he can leave.
13. They will wait for us outside the theater.
14. I'll look for you at the game.
15. When will you get together with Bill?

5 Practice Complete the following in your own words, using the future continuous. Give as many sentences as you can for each.

Example Right now I am sitting in class. At this time tomorrow . . .

I'll be studying at the library. I'll be working on . . .

1. Right now I am living . . . (with my parents / in an apartment). A month from now . . .
2. This session I am going to . . . (name of school). Next session . . .
3. This session I am taking English. Next session . . .
4. Right now I am studying grammar. At this time tomorrow . . .
5. Today I'm wearing . . . Tomorrow . . .
6. Tonight I'm . . . Tomorrow night . . .
7. This year I'm . . . Next year . . .
8. These days I'm . . . but soon . . .

6 **Practice** In pairs, take turns asking and answering the following questions. Give as much information as you can for each answer.

Example What will you be doing the day after tomorrow?
I will probably be studying for a test. I'll be reviewing my notes for chemistry, and I'll . . .

1. What will you be doing at this time tomorrow?
2. What will you be doing at this time on Saturday?
3. What will you be studying a month from now?
4. Will you still be going to school six months from now?
5. Will you be working a year from now?
6. Where will you be living a year from now?
7. Who will you be living with a year from now?
8. Will you be using English a year from now?

Using What You've Learned

7 **Role-Playing** In pairs or small groups, role-play the following scenes.

1. Imagine you are talking to your boyfriend or girlfriend.

   a. Make him or her an offer.

   b. Make him or her a promise.

   c. Make a prediction.

2. Imagine you are talking to your father or mother.

   a. Make him or her a promise.

   b. Make a request of him or her.

3. Imagine you are talking to your teenage son or daughter.

   a. Make a request of him or her.

   b. Make a prediction.

4. Imagine you are talking to an investor in your new company.

   a. Tell him / her your plans for your company's expansion.

   b. Tell him / her why he / she will make a lot of money by investing in your company.

5. Imagine you are the leader of a new nation. You are giving a televised speech to your citizens.

   a. Make three positive promises about the future.

   b. Make three negative promises about the future.

8 Predicting the Future What do you think life will be like in the 21st century? What do you hope you will be doing? Where will you be living? Will you have gotten married? Will you have children? Grandchildren? Will you still be in the same career?

Use a timeline like this to make notes about your ideal future. Write your ideas above the time you expect them to come true.

now   in 10 years   in 20 years   in 30 years

Then, in small groups, discuss your plans and dreams using the timeline you have made. Be sure to consider changes that will be occurring in the world around you—politically, economically, and technologically. After you have finished, you may want to choose one member of the group to give a brief summary of your discussion to the class.

Part 5 | The Present Perfect Continuous and the Present Perfect Tenses

Setting the Context

Previewing the Passage Discuss the question.

Grading is very competitive in U.S. schools and universities. Many grades are based on tests. What kinds of tests are you familiar with?

Reading Read the passage.

Dealing with Exams and Grades

Competition is strong at most U.S. universities, and international students have to learn about tests and grading very quickly in order to get a good start. Most schools have foreign student advisors who meet with international students periodically to see "how things are going." They help answer questions or solve problems the foreign students may have. The following is one of a series 5 of brief orientation talks for foreign students:

"Good morning, everyone. It's nice to see you again. Well . . . uh, let me get started. Up to now, we've been dealing with lots of basic needs—registering, finding housing, buying books, and so on. But you've all lived here for a while now and you've begun to learn about 'the system,' so it's time to talk about some upcoming realities—exams.

"Many of your instructors have been giving quizzes since classes started. Quizzes are much shorter and simpler than exams, right? You can expect two major exams in most of your courses: a midterm and a final exam.

"The two most common types of exams are objective tests and essay tests. Objective tests have traditionally been true/false or multiple choice. Individual instructors may use other types of questions, though. Essay tests involve writing paragraphs or short essays about a topic. In some cases, your instructor may tell you the topics in advance, or if you're lucky, they might give you a choice of topics to write about.

"Any questions so far? Not yet? Well then, let's take a look at some sample exams. . . ."

 Discussing Ideas Discuss the questions.

What is the difference between quizzes and exams? What kinds of exams are common in U.S. and Canadian universities?

Grammar Structures and Practice

A. The Present Perfect Continuous Tense

The present perfect continuous tense describes actions or situations that developed in the past and that have continued up to the moment of speaking.
- This tense often implies that the action or situation will continue in the future.
- Without time expressions, the present perfect continuous refers to a general activity.
- With time expressions such as the following, this tense stresses the length or duration of the activity.

2.16 The Present Perfect Continuous Tense

Examples	Time Expressions
How long **have** you **been studying** English? **I've been studying** English for six years. My brother **has** also **been taking** English since he was in high school. Lately, he **has been complaining** about his classes.	*for* + period of time *since* + beginning time *all morning (day, week,* and so on) *lately, recently* *so far, to date, up to now, until now* *How long...?*

 1 **Practice** In pairs, ask and answer questions based on the following cues, using the example as a model.

Example computer/interesting/learn to program in BASIC

A: How has your computer class been going? What have you been doing in it?

B: It's an interesting class. During the last few days we've been learning to program in BASIC.

1. psychology / interesting / do experiments with rats

2. economics / confusing / study World Bank policies

3. German / hard / memorize irregular verbs

4. physics / interesting / learn about Isaac Newton

5. botany / enjoyable / plan a field trip

6. statistics / boring / calculate probabilities

7. Chinese history / informative / read about the Cultural Revolution

8. grammar / fascinating / review verb tenses

 2 **Practice** In pairs, take turns asking questions and responding to them. Using the following cues and the example as a model, form questions with *How long . . .*? and answers with *for* or *since*. You may give long or short answers.

Example work on that report / early this morning

A: You look tired! How long have you been working on that report?

B: Too long! I've been working on it since early this morning.

1. study / 6:30 A.M.

2. research that term paper / three days

3. do homework / midnight

4. practice your presentation / early this morning

5. memorize German verbs / more than two hours

6. type that report / late last night

7. calculate those statistics / dinnertime

8. review English grammar / over six hours!

3 **Practice** In pairs, take turns asking questions and responding to them. Form logical questions using *How long . . . ?*

Example A: You're still in school!
         How long have you been working on your degree?
         B: I've been working on my master's degree for about three years.

1. A: I didn't know that you were a jogger.

          _____

      B: Well, I've been running about three years. I run two miles each day.

2. A: I didn't know that you moved.

          _____

      B: We've been living in Cambridge for two months.

3. A: It's still raining! What a shame. I come to Boston, and the weather is terrible.

          _____

      B: For almost a week.

4. A: I didn't know that you could play the guitar.

          _____

      B: A long time. Since I was in elementary school.

5. A: Did you know that Alfonso is an expert in karate? He has his black belt.
      B: You're kidding! I never would have guessed.

          _____

6. A: Did you know that I'm writing a book? I'm almost finished with it.
      B: Really? That's great!

          _____

      A: I've been working on it for about five years.

B. The Present Perfect Tense

The present perfect tense can also describe actions or situations that developed in the past and that have continued up to the moment of speaking.

- This tense implies that the action or situation will continue in the future.
- A time expression is used to give this meaning with verbs such as *begin, expect, hope, live, study, teach, wait,* and *work.*
- This use of the present perfect tense also occurs frequently with verbs not normally used in the continuous tenses such as *consider, mean, think,* and *want.* See p. 000 for a full list.
- See Chapter 3 for a different use of the present perfect tense.

2.17 The Present Perfect Tense

Examples	Time Expressions
We've **worked** hard for several weeks.	*for* + period of time
I've **studied** a lot since the beginning of the semester.	*since* + beginning time
Our teacher **hasn't taught** here for very long.	*all morning (day, week,* and so on)
We **haven't understood** everything in class.	*lately, recently*
The class **has seemed** difficult.	*so far, to date, up to now, until now*
How long **has** he **taught** here?	*How long . . . ?*

4 **Practice** Reread the passage "Dealing with Exams and Grades" on pages 75–76. Answer the following questions:

1. What tenses are used in line 3 of the second paragraph? What time frames are expressed? What time expressions are used?

2. What tense is used in the first sentence of the third paragraph? What is the time frame? What time expression is used? Compare this time expression to the one in line 3 of the second paragraph. How are the expressions different in terms of meaning and structure?

5 **Practice** Answer the following questions in your own words. Use *for, since,* or other time expressions in your answers.

1. How long have you been in this country?

2. How long have you lived in this city?

3. How long have you studied English?

4. Have you understood everything in your classes so far?

5. Up to now, which class has seemed the most difficult?

6 Practice Complete the following email with present perfect or present perfect continuous forms of the verbs in parentheses. Use contractions when possible. Mark all cases where both forms are possible and try to explain any difference in meaning between the two tenses. The first one has been done as an example.

From: Emily Church
Date: 10/4/05
To: Susan Weir
Cc:
Subject: Hi from the office!

Dear Susan:

I _'ve meant or 've been meaning_ to write you for weeks, but I
        (mean)

_____ much time! My classes _____ much
    1 (not have)   2 (seem)

more difficult this semester, and I _____ able to do anything
                                                3 (be/not)

else but study. I _____ dropping one course, but so far I
                          4 (consider)

_____ which one. To be honest, I _____ all
    5 (not decide)   6 (enjoy/really)

my classes up to now, and I _____ the work. It's funny... I
                                 7 (not mind)

_____ science courses, but this semester, I _____
    8 (hate/always)   9 (begin)

to change my mind. Physics class _____ my best class. We
                                   10 (be)

_____ Newtonian physics for the past few weeks, and I
    11 (study)

_____ many interesting things. Of course, I _____
    12 (learn)   13 (not understand)

everything, but my teaching assistant _____ me extra help. I
                                      14 (give)

_____ that a lot. Perhaps that's one reason why my attitude
    15 (appreciate)

---

about science _____.
16 (change)

Along other lines, things _____ fine here. And, how
17 (be)

_____ you _____? How _____
18 (do)   19 (do)   20 (go)

things _____? I _____ of you a lot. Please
21   22 (think)

give my best to everyone.

Love to all!

Emily

Using What You've Learned

7 **Researching Colleges and Universities** Visit your student advisor, your local library, or search the Internet to get information on a school or university that interests you. On the Internet, you can use "college search" or "university search" on a variety of search engines. You can find out about academic studies, or you can look into other types of programs such as vocational/technical, adult education, or university extension programs. The school can be located in your own area or in another part of the country.

Using the information you gather, prepare a brief report for your classmates. Be sure to include the following information:

- Admission requirements
- Tuition and other costs
- Starting dates and length of program
- Description of course(s) or major(s)

Testing is a major feature of academic life. Two basic types of tests exist: subjective and objective. Subjective questions can have a variety of answers, but objective questions have only one correct answer. Throughout this book, you will have short practice exams. In each, you will find reminders about common problems or hints on how to answer. Use these practice exams to help you find structures or ideas that you don't understand well or need to study more.

The following are examples of some of the types of questions asked on objective tests.

True/False Write *T* for true statements and *F* for false statements.

1. ___*T*___ The simple present tense is used to express facts, opinions, and habits.

2. _____ The present perfect tense is used with actions at a specific time in the past.

3. _____ The present perfect continuous tense is almost always used with nonaction verbs like *understand* and *seem*.

Correct/Incorrect Write *C* for correct statements and *I* for incorrect statements.

4. ___*I*___ John is appearing to be angry.

5. _____ This is unusual because he generally seems quite happily.

6. _____ I think John feels upset today.

Cloze Complete the following by adding the correct word(s).

7. How _____*many*_____ people did you invite to the party?

8. _____ book is that on the table? It's Mary's.

9. _____ time did the class begin?

Multiple Choice Mark the correct completion for the following.

10. We _____ your help.

   Ⓐ appreciate really   Ⓒ really are appreciating

   Ⓑ are really appreciating   ⒹＤ really appreciate

11. She _____ here since she was eight years old.

   Ⓐ lives   Ⓒ has lived

   Ⓑ has living   Ⓓ has live

12. Alex _____ up at 6:45 every morning.

    (A) is getting   (C) get

    (B) has been get   (D) gets

Error Analysis Circle the letter below the word(s) containing an error.

13. Since the mid-1980s, the number of international students <u>who</u> <u>are studying</u>
                                                  A   B

engineering <u>has</u> <u>been declined</u> somewhat.
           C   Ⓓ

14. In many countries, young people do not buy <u>generally</u> their own apartments
                                                   A

<u>because</u> the cost of housing is high and because parents <u>prefer</u> their children
    B   C

<u>to stay</u> at home.
  D

15. Margaret Mead began <u>first</u> <u>her</u> studies of people from <u>different</u> islands in <u>the</u>
                             A   B   C   D

South Pacific in 1928.

Self-Assessment Log

Each of the following statements describes the grammar you learned in this chapter. Read the statements; then check the box that describes how well you understand each structure.

	Needs Improvement	Good	Great
I can use *yes/no* questions appropriately.	❑	❑	❑
I can use information questions appropriately.	❑	❑	❑
I can use embedded questions appropriately.	❑	❑	❑
I can use present tenses appropriately.	❑	❑	❑
I can use future verb forms appropriately.	❑	❑	❑
I can take a test that has a variety of question formats.	❑	❑	❑

Relationships

In This Chapter

Verbs (2)

Part 1 Past Verb Forms: The Simple Past Tense; The Past Continuous Tense

Part 2 The Present Perfect Tense with Unspecified Past Time

Part 3 Past Verb Forms: The Habitual Past; The Future in the Past

Part 4 The Past and Future Perfect Tenses

Part 5 Reported Speech

"Family faces are magic mirrors. Looking at people who belong to us, we see the past, present, and future.**"**

—Gail Lumet Buckley
U.S. journalist (1937–)

Connecting to the Topic

1 What is your family of origin like?

2 Do you have brothers and sisters?

3 Do you have your own family now? A spouse? Children?

Introduction

In this chapter you will learn about other families and have opportunities to describe your own as you continue to study verb tenses. This chapter covers the past and future tenses and gives you more information on the present perfect tense. It also covers the expressions *used to, would,* and *was/were going to*. Some of this chapter will be a review for you, and you may not need to study everything in detail.

Reading Read the following passage. It introduces the chapter theme, "Relationships," and raises some of the topics and issues you will cover in the chapter.

Families

Exactly what is a family? Until about 50 years ago, the traditional American family consisted of a working husband, a wife at home, and two or more children. Responsibilities were clearly divided in the American nuclear family. While the husband was earning a living, the wife was caring for the home and raising the children. Of course, there were exceptions, but this concept of the family was the general rule until the 1960s. 5

Since the 1960s, however, the family has become more diverse, fragile, and changeable. Americans have accepted differing concepts of families, including single-parent, blended, two-paycheck, interracial, childless, and commuter families. 10

Some critics believe that the American family has suffered greatly because of all the changes in society. According to these critics, the family had been much stronger before it began to struggle with issues such as divorce, working mothers, gay couples, and unmarried relationships. Today's strongest critics feel that the traditional nuclear family will become rare in the 21st century. 15

Nationwide, however, most Americans believe that the family is going to survive. In fact, almost all major surveys in recent years have found that the American family is as strong as it has ever been. For most Americans, the family continues to provide their deepest source of satisfaction and meaning in life. Thus, although today's family is different from what it used to be, it seems to be thriving. 20

Discussing Ideas Discuss the question.

Think about a culture you know. Do you think there is a "typical" family in this culture?

Setting the Context

 Previewing the Passage Discuss the questions.

What made you the way you are? Some people believe your position in your family is a major factor. Do you agree?

Reading Read the passage.

Where Do You Fit?

Are you the oldest or youngest child? Are you in the middle or an only child? Many psychologists believe that your position in your family helped to shape you and your relationship to others. As a newborn, you quickly developed a relationship with your parents and later, while you were growing, you formed relationships with your siblings. According to psychologists, your birth order affected how your parents and your brothers and sisters reacted to you and treated you. That is, you and they behaved in certain ways depending on your position in the family. All of this strongly influenced your development, and in turn, influences you as an adult: what you think about yourself now and how you react to and treat others.

5

10

 Discussing Ideas Discuss the questions.

Think about your own family. Do you believe your birth order affected you and your brothers and sisters? In what ways?

Grammar Structures and Practice

A. The Simple Past Tense

The simple past tense describes actions or situations that began and ended in the past.
- Adverbs of frequency (*usually, often,* etc.) and sequence expressions (*first, then,* etc.) are frequently used with this tense.
- Adverbs of frequency normally come before the verb.
- Sequence expressions often begin or end sentences.

3.1 The Simple Past Tense

Uses	Examples	Time Expressions
Past Actions	Martin **grew up** in the country. Later, he **lived** in a small town. When **did** he **move** to the city? He **bought** a farm two years ago.	*ago, two weeks ago, a month ago today in the past, in 1995, in March often, sometimes, rarely first, then, later, finally, last*
Past Situations or Conditions	He **didn't like** life in a large city. He always **preferred** the country.	

Note: See Appendix 1 pages 460–461 for a list of irregular verbs.

Spelling Rules for *-ed* Endings

Ending	Rule	Examples
-y	If the simple form of a verb ends in -y after a consonant, change the -y to -i and add -ed.	carry/carried study/studied marry/married try/tried
Vowel + Consonant in One-syllable Verb	If the simple form of a one-syllable verb ends in one consonant after a vowel, double the last consonant (except *x*) and add -ed. Note: The letters *w* and *y* at the end of words are vowels, not consonants. Do not double them.	knit/knitted bow/bowed plan/planned play/played rob/robbed row/rowed stop/stopped stay/stayed
Stressed syllable	If the simple form of a verb ends in an accented (stressed) syllable, follow the preceding rule for one final consonant after one vowel.	occur/occurred permit/permitted prefer/preferred submit/submitted
-e	If the simple form of a verb ends in -e, add only -d.	tie/tied like/liked
All other verbs	Add -ed to the simple form of all other regular verbs.	ask/asked belong/belonged need/needed want/wanted

Pronunciation Notes for -ed Endings

Ending	Sound	Examples		
After -d and -t endings	/id/	exited knitted	needed persisted	waded wanted
After voiceless endings	/t/	cooked danced	hopped talked	washed watched
After voiced endings	/d/	argued listened	lived loaned	played sewed

1 **Practice** Quickly reread the passage "Where Do You Fit?" on page 87. Underline all the regular verbs in the simple past tense. Then group the verbs here according to the pronunciation of the -ed ending.

/t/	/d/	/id/
helped	_____	_____
_____	_____	_____
_____	_____	_____

2 **Review** Add -ed to the following verbs, making any necessary spelling changes. Pronounce the past forms aloud, emphasizing the various pronunciations of the -ed ending. List them according to pronunciation: /t/ (washed), /d/ (changed), /id/ (waited).

Example carry *carried (-d sound)*

1. need
2. study
3. insist
4. rob
5. travel
6. paint
7. hope
8. agree
9. permit
10. wrap
11. occur
12. stop
13. cry
14. play
15. clean
16. worry

3 Practice Complete the passage with the simple past form of the verbs in parentheses. Include adverbs when indicated, and pay careful attention to spelling. The first one is done as an example.

The First Born

Lily _____was_____ Bob and Dorothy's first child. When Dorothy
(be)

_____ pregnant, the couple immediately _____
1 (become)   2 (begin)

to prepare for the baby. They _____ shopping for baby furni-
3 (go)

ture and _____ toys and playthings. Dorothy _____
4 (buy)   5 (make)

little clothes and blankets. And when Baby Lily _____ into the
6 (come / finally)

world, the happy parents _____ in love with their precious
7 (fall)

child. They _____ pictures of Baby Lily's first smile, step, and
8 (take)

birthday party. At bedtime, they _____ and _____
9 (sit)   10 (hold)

her and _____ her little stories and _____ her
11 (tell)   12 (read)

books and _____ her lullabies. They _____ up
13 (sing)   14 (wake)

in an instant if they _____ her cry during the night. They
15 (hear)

_____ letters and _____ cards to friends and
16 (write)   17 (send)

relatives detailing every little thing Lily _____. In fact, her
18 (do)

parents _____ Lily their complete attention. That is, until her
19 (give)

sister, Cathy, _____ born two years later.
20 (be)

4 Practice Complete the passage with the simple past form of the verbs in parentheses. Include adverbs when indicated, and pay careful attention to spelling. The first one is done as an example.

Youngest Children

Jane _____was_____ the youngest of Dorothy and Bob's children. Be-
(be)

cause of her special position as the "baby of the family," Jane

_____ lots of attention. Her mother _____ her
1 (get / always)   2 (carry)

often, her father _____ her on his lap, and her brothers and
3 (hold)

sisters _____ turns watching her. All the neighborhood
4 (take)

children _____ with her and _____ her games
          5 (play)   6 (teach)
and songs and stories. Everyone _____ her.
                                  7 (spoil)

As parents, Dorothy and Bob _____ more relaxed and ex-
                             8 (be)
perienced by that time, so they _____ so much about every
                                 9 (not worry)
sniffle and whimper. Because of this, Jane _____ up in a freer,
                                            10 (grow)
more easygoing environment with fewer rules. Jane's parents
_____ her to do many things at a younger age, but at the same
  11 (permit)
time, they _____ as much help from her. This
             12 (not demand)
_____ problems between Jane and her siblings. Her older sister
  13 (cause / often)
said, "When I _____ her age, I _____ the
                14 (be)   15 (clean)
house, I _____ the dishes, I _____ the floor, I
           16 (wash)   17 (sweep)
_____ the bathtub, and I _____ clothes." These
  18 (scrub)   19 (iron)
_____ common complaints in their household.
  20 (be)

Jane _____ all the characteristics of youngest children. She
       21 (develop)
_____ an optimist and _____ good things from
  22 (become)   23 (expect)
life. She _____ rules _____ for other people,
            24 (think / frequently)   25 (be)
though—not for her. Sometimes, she _____ her own intellect
                                      26 (doubt)
and _____ to other people for help or advice. Of all the siblings,
      27 (go)
Jane _____ the most lighthearted and playful.
       28 (be)

5 Practice Complete the passage with the simple past form of the verb in parentheses. Include adverbs where indicated, and pay careful attention to spelling and pronunciation. The first one is done as an example.

▲ Mary and Daisy

Twins

Mary and Daisy _____were_____ born only moments apart. The
(be)

twin girls _____ both great similarities and great differences
1 (show)

from the moment of birth. Mary and Daisy _____ about the
2 (weigh)

same at birth. They _____ about the same amount, and they
3 (eat)

_____ similar sleep patterns, and they _____
4 (have)   5 (cry)

at about the same time. But that's where many of the similarities

_____. As babies, Mary _____ attention, but
6 (end)   7 (want / always)

Daisy _____ sitting or lying quietly. Mary _____
8 (enjoy)   9 (need)

to move a lot and play, but Daisy _____ to be held. Mary
10 (prefer)

_____ on being active. Daisy _____ happiest in
11 (insist)   12 (seem / usually)

quiet times. At birth, Mary and Daisy _____ many characteris-
13 (share)

tics, but the two girls _____ very different personalities.
14 (develop)

6 Practice Complete the passage with the simple past form of the verb in parentheses. Include adverbs where indicated, and pay careful attention to spelling and pronunciation. The first one is done as an example.

▲ Camila

International Adoptive Children

Camila _____was_____ found when she _____ about
           (be)   1 (be)

two-and-a-half years old. Soldiers _____ her alone in an area of
                                         2 (find)

intense fighting. She _____ pneumonia and other infections,
                                  3 (have)

and she _____ dead. The soldiers _____ her to
             4 (be / almost)   5 (take)

a public hospital, and there, she _____ better. Camila
                                  6 (get / slowly)

_____ many weeks in the hospital, and from there, she
     7 (spend)

_____ to a public orphanage. A government agency
     8 (go / first)

_____ a foster home for her, and Camila _____
     9 (locate)   10 (move)

there for about six months.

During Camila's stay with the foster family, the government agency

_____ hard to learn about her family. The agency
     11 (try)

_____ pictures of Camila on local TV, and it
     12 (broadcast)

_____ posters with her picture all around the area. No one
     13 (put)

_____ forward to get Camila, though. Finally, the agency
     14 (come)

_____ her for adoption. Dozens of international families were
     15 (offer)

waiting for children like Camila. They _____ to adopt a child to
                                     16 (want)

love and care for. Perhaps they _____ able to have children of
                              17 (be / not)

their own, but they _____ to create families with adoptive children.
               18 (hope)

Camila _____ her third set of parents and her new family a
     19 (get)

few years ago. At the same time, other children orphaned in the fighting

_____ new families. Families from all over the world
　　20 (gain)

_____ their houses and their hearts. Children with no parents,
　　21 (open)

with nothing, _____ a place to live and grow.
　　　　　　　22 (find)

　　　Today, these children, and many others around the world like them, have a

future. Perhaps they would have survived, and survived well, in their home

surroundings. But disease, civil war, and other catastrophes _____
　　　　　　　　　　　　　　　　　　　　　　　　　　　　　　　　　　　23 (face)

them then. Their futures _____ doubtful then. Today, however,
　　　　　　　　　　　　24 (be)

with their adoptive families, they have the opportunity to grow and shine.

B. The Past Continuous Tense

The past continuous tense describes actions in progress in the recent past (a few
moments before the moment of speaking) or at a specific time in the past. The past
continuous is often used to describe or "set" a scene.

3.2 **The Past Continuous Tense**		
Uses	**Examples**	**Time Expressions**
Events in the Recent Past	Mary, we **were** just **looking** for you. Oh! You startled me! I **was taking** a short nap.	*a few minutes ago* *a few moments ago* *at that time* *just* *still* *then*
Events at a Specific Time in the Past	A year ago now, we **were living** in Boston. At that time, I **was still working** at the bank, and my wife **was taking** classes.	
Description of a Scene	It was a beautiful summer evening. We **were** all **sitting** and **talking** on the front porch. Dad **was playing** the guitar, the boys **were singing,** and I **was watching** the stars.	

Note: See page 66 for a list of verbs not normally used in the continuous tenses. See Appendix 2 on pages
462–463 for spelling rules for verbs with *-ing* endings.

---

7 **Practice** Use the past continuous tense to answer the following questions in
complete sentences.

　1. What were you doing two hours ago?

　2. Where were you living a year ago?

　3. What were you doing when you decided to come to this school?

　4. What were you thinking about a moment ago?

5. What was your classmate, _____, doing a few minutes ago?

6. What were you doing the day before yesterday?

7. What was your teacher doing at this time yesterday?

8. What were you studying two weeks ago?

8 **Practice** These passages describe scenes from the past. Complete them with the past continuous forms of the verbs in parentheses. Pay attention to the spelling of the -ing endings. The first one is done as an example.

1. I have a special memory of Christmas when I was five years old. My aunts, uncles, and cousins ___*were visiting*___ us. I _____ my
   (visit)   1 (wear)
   beautiful new red dress. We _____around the Christmas
                                2 (sit)
   tree, and everyone _____ Christmas presents. I
                        3 (open)
   _____ one big present near the corner of the room. Then
   4 (look at)
   my mother took me over to that present. It was for me! It was the most
   beautiful dollhouse I had ever seen!

2. I have a special childhood memory of a summer night when I was seven or
   eight. My mom and dad and my sisters _____ on the front
                                          1 (sit)
   porch. The sun _____, and the sky _____
                    2 (set)   3 (become)
   red and golden. My sisters _____ on the porch swing, and
                               4 (swing)
   my mother _____ in her rocking chair. Our dog
                5 (rock)
   _____ on the steps. My father _____ his
   6 (lie)   7 (play)
   guitar and _____. Everyone _____ to him.
                8 (sing)   9 (listen)
   He loved to sing, and he had a wonderful voice. I felt so happy and peaceful
   and secure. That night is one of my best memories.

C. *When* and *While*

When and *while* are frequently used to connect two past actions. Chapter 8 includes more information on these connecting words.

3.3	*When* and *While*	
Structures	**Explanations**	**Examples**
while	*While* may connect two past continuous actions that were occurring at the same time.	He was watching TV **while** I was doing the dishes.
when or while	*When* or *while* may connect a simple past and past continuous action—*while* + the action in progress or *when* + the action that interrupted it.	John was talking to the man at the door **when** his mother phoned. **While** John was talking to the man at the door, his mother phoned.
when	*When* may connect two simple past actions; *when* comes before the action that happened first.	**When** the doorbell rang, John answered it.

9 **Practice** Complete the passages with the simple past or past continuous forms of the verbs in parentheses. The first one is done as an example.

This morning everything went wrong at the Peterson household.

1. I _____*wanted*_____ to get up early this morning, but I _____
  (want)   1 (forget)

to set the alarm. So I _____. When I _____
                        2 (oversleep)   3 (get)

up,   my   brother   _____   a   long   shower.   So   I
                          4 (take)

_____ to wait for a long time. While I _____
  5 (have)   6 (ride)

my bike to school, I _____ a flat tire. I _____
                       7 (get)   8 (miss)

my first class, and I _____ late for my second class. It
                              9 (be)

_____ a good morning.
  10 (not be)

2. I _____woke_____ up very early this morning and _____
(wake)   1 (leave)

the house while everyone else _____. I
2 (sleep / still)

_____ the bus at 6:45 in order to get to work early. I
3 (catch)

_____ the newspaper on the bus, and I
4 (read)

_____ attention to the traffic when suddenly a car
5 (not pay)

_____ a red light and _____ the bus on my
6 (run)   7 (hit)

side. When the car _____ into us, I _____ off
8 (crash)   9 (fall)

my seat, _____ my head, and _____ my arm.
10 (cut)   11 (break)

What a day!

10 **Practice** Using the simple past and past continuous tenses with *when* and *while*, tell a story using the following information.

Example *This morning everything went wrong for Dave Peterson, too. At 8:35 A.M., Dave woke up late. He took a two-minute shower. While he was getting out of the shower, . . .*

8:35 A.M.	wakes up late
8:36–8:38 A.M.	takes a shower
8:39 A.M.	gets out of the shower
8:39 A.M.	falls on the floor
8:39–8:40 A.M.	shaves
8:40 A.M.	cuts his face
8:40 A.M.	throws the razor on the floor
8:41–8:42 A.M.	gets dressed

8:42 A.M.	tears a hole in his shirt
8:43 A.M.	finds a new shirt
8:44 A.M.	makes coffee
8:45 A.M.	pours the coffee
8:45 A.M.	spills coffee on his shirt
8:46–8:47 A.M.	looks for another clean shirt
8:47 A.M.	hears the doorbell
8:47 A.M.	runs to the door, but no one is there
8:48 A.M.	loses his temper
8:48 A.M.	goes back to the bedroom
8:50 A.M.	lies down and goes back to sleep

Using What You've Learned

 11 **Telling Stories from Childhood** Do you have a memory of a particular time in your childhood when you disobeyed your parents? What was the rule that you broke? Why did you do it? What happened to you? Use these questions to help you tell about that time.

1. How old were you?
2. Where were you living?
3. What did you do?
4. Why was this against your parents' rules?
5. How angry were your parents?
6. How did you feel?
7. Did you get punished? What was your punishment?
8. Did you ever break that rule again?
9. How do you feel about it now?
10. Would you do it again if you were a child?

12 Describing a Cartoon *The Family Circus* is a daily cartoon. Billy is the oldest child in the family. He has a bad habit of going places *indirectly.* Follow his path, telling step by step where he went and what he did. Use the simple past tense. Add articles and other words as needed.

Example *Billy got off the school bus. He got into a soccer game.*

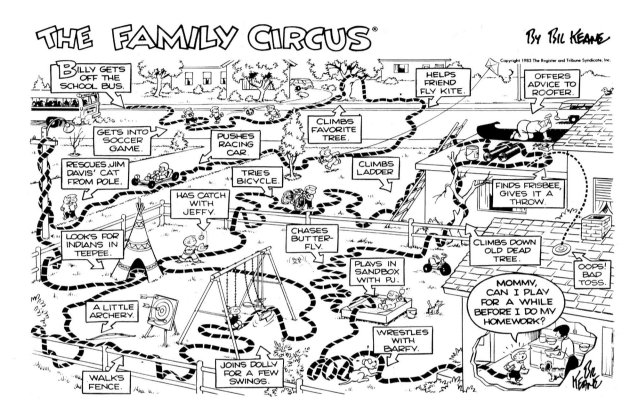

 13 Discussing Families The passage "Where Do You Fit?" on page 87 discusses birth order. Edward Hall's passage on page 31 in Chapter 1 also mentions that order of birth can be an important aspect of culture. Take some time to give your own perspectives on birth order.

First, get into groups according to birth order—that is, all students who are the oldest should work together, students who are the youngest together, only children together, and middle children together. If you are a twin or a triplet, move from group to group!

In your groups, take turns discussing what it was like to grow up as the oldest, youngest, second, and so on. Do you believe your order of birth is an important factor in your development? In your culture in general?

Setting the Context

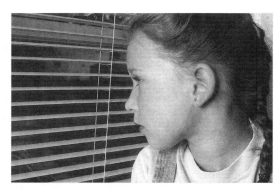

▲ Many children are home alone after school.

Previewing the Passage Discuss the questions.

These days, some school-age children come home to empty houses after school because both of their parents (or sole parent) are working. Do you know any children who do this?

Reading Read the passage.

Taking Care of Herself

Alicia Owens is eight years old. For the past two years, she has come home to an empty house. Her mother and her father work all day from 9 to 5. Alicia returns home from school by 3 o'clock. Alicia's mother, Laurie, calls her from work at 3:15. Alicia has already made herself a cup of cocoa and is sitting in front of the TV set when her mother calls. She asks if everything is all right. 5
Alicia always says, "Yes, Mom."

Alicia is not allowed to invite her friends to her house when her parents are not home. Sometimes she receives invitations to play at a classmate's home after school. However, she cannot accept them unless either her mother or father knows where she is. As a result, Alicia has spent a lot of afternoons alone 10
in her house, usually watching TV or playing on the computer. By the time her parents arrive, she has also finished her homework, and she has set the table for dinner. Sometimes she has even done laundry and started preparing dinner. All

by herself.

When Alicia was born, her mother took maternity leave and stayed at home. But when Alicia was six months old, her mother brought her to the home of a child-care worker who took care of the very young. When Alicia was two and a half, she began attending preschool. Although Alicia is just eight years old, she has attended school for nearly six years. In that time, she has learned to take care of herself. She can dress herself, make herself snacks, get in and out of her house, answer the phone, and take messages.

Discussing Ideas Discuss the questions.

In your culture, at what age, generally, do children begin staying home alone? Who takes care of the children if the parents are working or away?

Grammar Structures and Practice

A. The Present Perfect Tense

Chapter 2 included information on use of the present perfect tense in a past-to-present time frame. It has a more common use, however.

- The present perfect tense frequently refers to an event that happened (or did not happen) at an unknown or unspecified time in the past.
- The present perfect also refers to repeated past actions. No specific time is given with these statements. When a specific past time is used, the verb is in the past tense.

3.4 The Present Perfect Tense

Uses	Examples	Time Expressions
Events at Unspecified Times in the Past	**Have** you ever **gone** to Austria? I **haven't** ever **been** there. I**'ve visited** Germany, though. *Compare:* I **went** there last year.	*already* *ever* *recently* *still*
Repeated Actions at Unspecified Times in the Past	How many times **have** you **visited** your sister? I**'ve been** there five times. We**'ve called** her twice this month. *Compare:* We **called** her last week.	*yet* *(how) many times*

Note: See Appendix 1 pages 460–461 for a list of irregular past participles and Appendix 2 pages 462–463 for spelling rules for the *-ed* ending of regular past participles.

1 **Practice** Reread the passage "Taking Care of Herself" on pages 100–101. Underline the verbs in simple past and present perfect and circle time expressions.

2 **Practice** In Chapter 2, you learned about past-to-present meaning. Now in Chapter 3, you are learning about past meaning. Read the following pairs of sentences. In each pair, one sentence has a past meaning (a completed action) and one has a past-to-present meaning (still in progress). Write P (past) or P-T-P (past-to-present) for each.

Example: _____P_____ a. I've been in New York.

_____P-T-P_____ b. I've been in New York since Friday.

1. _____ a. I've lived in Boston.

_____ b. I've lived in Boston for ten years.

2. _____ a. We've been making some changes.

_____ b. We've made some changes.

3. _____ a. She's worked in that law firm since June.

_____ b. She's worked in that law firm.

4. _____ a. I've studied for the test.

_____ b. I've been studying for the test.

5. _____ a. Ling has been playing soccer on Fridays.

_____ b. Ling has played soccer.

6. _____ a. Our family has visited Paris.

_____ b. Our family has been visiting Paris every summer for the past ten years.

7. _____ a. They've been trying to call Billie.

_____ b. They've tried to call Billie.

8. _____ a. Bruce hasn't spoken to Deb.

_____ b. Bruce hasn't been speaking to Deb.

9. _____ a. Gabriel has taught algebra.

_____ b. Gabriel has taught algebra since 1988.

10. _____ a. Judy's read that book.

_____ b. Judy's been reading that book.

B. *Already, (Not) Ever, Just, Never, Recently, Still,* and *(Not) Yet* with the Present Perfect Tense

The adverbs *already, (not) ever, just, never, recently, still,* and *(not) yet* are frequently used with the perfect tenses. Here is information on the present perfect tense, and information on the past and future perfect tenses is in Part 4 of this chapter.

3.5 Already, (Not) Ever, Just, Never, Recently, Still, and (Not) Yet

Structure	Explanations	Examples
Questions	*Ever* must come before the past participle. *Already* can be used before the past participle or at the end of the sentence. *Yet* is generally used at the end of the sentence.	Have you **ever** read that book? Have you **already** read the book? Have you read it **already?** Have you read it **yet?**
Affirmative Statements	*Already* and *just* come before the past participle. *Recently* can come at the end of the sentence or before the past participle. It is sometimes used to begin the sentence.	I've **already** read it. I've **just** read it. I've read it **recently.** I've **recently** read it.
Negative Statements	*Never* generally comes before the past participle. *Not ever* must come before the past participle. *Still* must come before *have* or *has*. *Yet* is generally used at the end of the sentence.	I have **never** read it. I have**n't ever** read it. I **still** haven't read it. I haven't read it **yet.**

---

3 **Practice** Go around the class in a chain, asking and answering questions about the following.

Example meet a movie star

A: Have you ever met a movie star?

B: Yes, I have. I met Cameron Diaz once! She gave me her autograph.

1. be in a hurricane (earthquake, or other natural disaster)
2. lose your wallet
3. buy a car
4. have an accident
5. get a speeding ticket
6. have a flat tire
7. read a novel in English
8. be on television
9. design a website
10. fall asleep in a class
11. play chess
12. find a buried treasure
13. fly a small plane
14. ride a camel
15. take the TOEFL test

4 **Practice** In pairs, take turns making statements and responses. Complete each conversation by adding a sentence that uses *already*. Change nouns to pronouns when appropriate.

Example A: Don't start the washing machine! I haven't put all my clothes in yet.
B: Sorry! I've already started it.

1. Don't put the broom away. I haven't swept the floor yet. Sorry! . . .

2. Don't walk in the kitchen. The floor hasn't dried yet. Sorry! . . .

3. Don't wax the floor. I haven't washed it yet. Sorry! . . .

4. Don't mail those bills! I haven't signed the checks yet. Sorry! . . .

5. Don't throw the newspaper away! Your father hasn't read it yet. Sorry! . . .

6. Don't start painting the walls. I haven't washed them yet. Sorry! . . .

7. Don't turn off the computer! I haven't checked my email yet. Sorry! . . .

8. Don't go food shopping yet! I haven't told you what I need. Sorry! . . .

5 **Practice** Complete the passage with the present perfect form of the verbs in parentheses. Use *still . . . not* or *not . . . yet* when indicated.

Procrastinators

My friend Larry is always procrastinating. For example, he
___*has lived*___ in his apartment for a year now, but he _____
(live)   1 (not buy / still)

any furniture. He _____ to study at the university for a long time,
2 (want)

but he _____. His hair _____ so long he can barely
3 (not register / yet)   4 (grow)

see, but he _____ it cut. He _____ books he bor-
5 (not get / still)   6 (keep)

rowed from me for over three months, and he _____ them. I
7 (not return / still)

_____ several messages for him on his answering machine, and he
8 (leave)

_____ me back. I know what he will say when I finally talk to him.
9 (not call / yet)

"Tomorrow, I'll do it tomorrow." Those are his favorite words.

6 **"Find Someone Who"** Play a game of "Find Someone Who." This is a two-part game.

1. On a piece of paper, write three things that you have done: "I've climbed a mountain," "I've been to India," and so on. Do not show this to your classmates. Your teacher will collect the papers and make a class list of statements to distribute another day.

2. Your teacher will distribute the list. Walk around the room and ask your classmates, "Have you . . . ?" When you find the person who has done something on the list, ask him or her to sign your paper. The first student who gets signatures for each item wins the game.

7 **To-Do Lists** Are you a procrastinator? Have you written to your friends or family lately? Have you been to the language lab? Have you done your laundry yet? You still haven't paid your rent? List five things that you planned to do during the past month but still haven't done. Then, in small groups, compare your lists. How many of you are true procrastinators?

Part 3 · Past Verb Forms: The Habitual Past; The Future in the Past

Setting the Context

Previewing the Passage The next passage is a childhood story from a great storyteller, Al Monom. Think about your childhood. Discuss the questions.

Was there a storyteller in your family? Was storytelling an important part of family gatherings?

The Old Days

My Pa used to play the violin. Us children[1] would gather around the potbelly stove in the kitchen during those long, freezing-cold winter nights in Wisconsin, and we would be glued to the sounds of that old violin. My Pa made that violin sing.

That violin gave us our best entertainment because my Pa used to play for dances around the county. We would get so excited when he told us that we were going to go to a dance. About one Saturday night a month, he would hitch the horses, pack the entire family into the wagon, and take us off to the dance. Now that was real excitement!

I still have that violin. It has got to be at least 150 years old now. I've played it on and off through the years, and others have picked it from time to time. But nobody has made it sing the way Pa used to.

—Al Monom, age 87, Middleton, Wisconsin

---

[1]*us children* colloquial for "we children"

Discussing Ideas Discuss the question.

Al Monom grew up a long time ago, and his childhood was very different from childhood today. Think about children growing up now. For a child, how is life different today from what it used to be 50, 60, or 70 years ago?

Grammar Structures and Practice

A. The Habitual Past: *Would* and *Used To*

Would and *used* to are used to describe habitual actions in the past.

3.6	The Habitual Past: *Would* and *Used To*	
Uses	**Explanations**	**Examples**
Repeated Actions in the Past	Both *would* + simple form and *used to* + simple form are used to describe actions in the past that were repeated on a regular basis.	When I was a child, my family **would travel** in the West every summer. We **used to visit** the Teton Mountains every year.
Continuous Actions or Situations in the Past	For situations and continuous actions in the past, only *used to* is possible; *would* cannot be used.	My father **used to live** near the mountains. (not: *would live*) He used to work as a forest ranger. (not: *would work*)
Past Actions or Situations That No Longer Exist	*Used to* can also refer to actions or situations in the past that no longer exist.	Campsites **used to be** free; now you have to pay to camp. (not: *would be*)

Note: Do not confuse the constructions *used to* + simple form and *be used to* + gerund, which means "be accustomed to." Compare: *I used to get up early. (I don't anymore.) I am used to getting up early. (I frequently get up early, and it doesn't bother me.)*

---

1 **Practice** Underline all uses of *would* and *used to* in "The Old Days" on page 106. Then substitute simple past verbs in each case. Does the meaning change?

2 **Practice** Using *would* in a sentence can give a nostalgic, almost poetic, feeling to the words. Add *would* to these sentences, making any necessary changes. Then discuss the differences in meaning between the original and the new sentences.

Example My grandfather often spent hours reading.
My grandfather would often spend hours reading.

1. On Sundays, my grandfather often sat in his old rocking chair.

2. He smoked his pipe.

3. He read for hours and hours.

4. Sometimes he stopped reading for a while.

5. He took out his old mandolin.

6. He played songs for us.

7. He sang lovely melodies to us.

8. He held us on his lap in the big old rocking chair.

3 **Practice** Using *would* or *used to,* change the following sentences from the simple past tense to the habitual past. Note any cases where *would* cannot be used.

Example We lived in a small town.
> *We used to live in a small town. (Would cannot be used.)*

1. Our family had a television, but we seldom watched it.

2. We always found other ways to pass the time.

3. All of the children in the neighborhood were friends.

4. In the summer, we always played games, rode our bicycles, and went swimming.

5. All of us liked to swim.

6. In autumn, we always made big piles of leaves to jump in.

7. In winter, we skated and skied all the time.

8. We built snow slides through the backyards and went down them on sleds every day after school.

9. Finally springtime came after months of winter.

10. We waited for summer to arrive again.

B. The Future in the Past: *Was/Were Going To*

Was/were going to + verb is used to describe past intentions. In many cases, the action was not completed.

3.7 The Future in the Past: *Was/Were Going To*	
Uses	**Examples**
Past Intentions (Action Completed)	I said I **was going to get** an "A" in English, and I did. Last summer, our family **was going to visit** friends in Colorado. We did.
Past Intentions (Action Not Completed)	Last summer, we **were going to visit** friends in Colorado, but we didn't have enough time.

 4 **Practice** In pairs, use the following cues to ask and answer questions.

Example clean your room
> A: Have you cleaned your room yet?
> B: I was going to clean it a while ago, but I didn't have time.
>   OR
> I said I was going to clean it a while ago, and I did.

1. make your bed
2. sweep the floor
3. take the garbage out
4. pick your clothes up
5. do the laundry
6. iron your shirts
7. straighten your room up
8. do your homework

5 **Practice** Make sentences using *was/were going to.* Use the following cues and add ideas of your own.

Example Ann / make a cake / no sugar

Ann was going to make a cake, but she didn't have any sugar.

1. the man / use the pay phone / no coins
2. you / tell me a story / forget
3. her friends / visit her new apartment / get lost
4. the children / eat ice cream / melt
5. Bob / ride his bicycle / flat tire
6. José / play tennis / start raining
7. Dorothy / study in the library / too noisy
8. Craig and Gus / go swimming / too cold

Using What You've Learned

6 **Comparing the Past and the Present** Imagine the lives of the people listed on page 110. All have experienced major life changes. In pairs or small groups, create stories about each. Make original sentences with *used to* and *would* to compare their lives in the past with their lives today.

Example a couple with a new baby

Before their baby arrived, John and Susan used to do lots of things. They used to go to the movies often, but now it's more difficult because they need to get a babysitter. And, they would often go out for dinner, but they don't have as much money as they used to, so they eat at home a lot. Above all, they used to be able to sleep all night. Now they wake up every three hours.

1. a person who suddenly becomes famous

2. newlyweds

3. a freshman (first year student) at a university

4. a foreigner in a strange country

5. a newly elected president

6. a person beginning his or her first job

7. children of recently divorced parents

8. a person who wins the lottery

 7 **Telling Stories from Childhood** Your childhood may have been very different from those of your classmates. In small groups, choose a certain time period and take turns describing it in detail. You may want to tell about school vacations, or your first year in high school, or weekends when you were seven or eight years old. To get started, try to think of some of the funniest, most interesting, most awkward, or most memorable periods of your childhood. Then, after you have shared your story, write a short composition about it. As a class, you may want to put together a collection of childhood memories.

Examples

When we were children, our family used to go to the mountains for a month every summer. Our vacations were always in the mountains because my dad used to do a lot of climbing. On those vacations, we'd usually camp for most of the time. I'd share a tent with my two brothers. . . .

When I was a freshman in high school, I started going to dances. Our school used to have dances every Saturday night. They were terrible! All the boys would stand along one side of the room and all the girls along the other side. For the first hour or so, no one would dance. The girls would giggle and the boys would push and shove each other. . . .

8 **To-Do Lists** What did you learn about yourself in Activity 7 on page 105? Are you a procrastinator? Use your list from Activity 7 or make a new list of the important things you wanted to do during the past month. Then note whether you did each. If you did not, give a sentence explaining why. If you wish, make a chart like the one that follows.

Planned To Do	Done	Still Haven't Done	Why
write my brother		X	I was going to write a long letter telling about my life, but I got too busy.
balance my checkbook			
organize my apartment			

Setting the Context

▲ During the Depression, farmers left their land and moved to cities.

 Previewing the Passage Discuss the question.

All over the world, people have been moving from rural areas into the cities. What effects has this migration had?

Reading Read the passage.

The Urbanization of America

Like much of the world, the United States did not develop large urban centers until the 20th century. Before World War I, the majority of Americans had lived in rural areas or in small towns. In 1900, for example, over 40 percent of the U.S. population lived or worked on farms.

World War I and the Depression of the 1930s changed American life dramatically. By 1930, for example, the farm population had dropped to 30.1 percent. During the Depression, over three-quarters of a million farmers lost their land. As individuals and entire families moved to cities in search of work, urban areas grew tremendously. Today almost 80 percent of Americans live in metropolitan areas.

5

10

112 Chapter 3 ■■■

This migration from rural to urban areas has had a great impact on American society, just as it has in many parts of the world. In general, people in urban areas are more mobile and more independent, families are less stable, and friendships are often short-lived. Although cities may offer greater economic opportunities, they also present many difficulties in maintaining "the ties that bind": close, long-term relationships with family and friends.

15

Discussing Ideas Discuss the questions.

Is this pattern of rural-to-urban migration true in other countries you are familiar with? Why do people leave their rural homes? How does the move to a city affect them, their families, and their friends?

Grammar Structures and Practice

A. The Past Perfect Tense

The past perfect tense refers to an activity or situation completed *before* another event or time in the past. This tense may be used in a simple sentence, but it normally contrasts with the simple past in a compound or complex sentence.

3.8	The Past Perfect Tense		
Structures	**Examples**	**Time Expressions**	
Simple Sentences	Until 1932, the O'Keefes **had lived** on a farm. By the end of 1932, they **had** already **lost** their farm.	*already* *barely* *just* *no sooner* *rarely*	*recently* *still* *yet* *ever* *never*
Complex Sentences	Before the Depression began, the O'Keefes **had been** prosperous farmers. The children **had** just **begun** school when their parents lost the farm.	*after* *before* *by* *by the time (that)*	*until* *when*

Note: See Appendix 1 for a list of irregular past participles and Appendix 2 for spelling rules for the *-ed* ending.

Although the past perfect tense is often preferable in formal English, the simple past is frequently used instead of the past perfect in conversation. The meaning of the sentence must be clear, however. In sentences with *when*, the time difference in the two tenses can change the meaning of the sentence, for example.

(continued)

3.9 The Simple Past versus the Past Perfect Tense

Structures	Examples	Meaning
Simple Past + Simple Past	It **began** to rain **when I went** out.	The rain began at that time.
Past Perfect + Simple Past	It **had begun** to rain **when I went** out.	The rain had begun earlier.

1 **Practice** This activity tells the story of an immigrant family in the United States. Using *by* and the past perfect tense, form complete sentences from the cues that follow.

Example 1848 / John and Mary O'Keefe / leave Ireland
By 1848, John and Mary O'Keefe had left Ireland.

1. 1850 / the O'Keefes / start a farm in Wisconsin

2. 1852 / they / build a house

3. 1853 / they / clear several acres of land

4. 1854 / the O'Keefes and other families / construct a church and a school

5. 1880s / the O'Keefes / raise a family of 10 children

6. 1885 / their son John / marry Catherine

7. 1890 / Catherine / give birth to a daughter, Amanda

8. 1910 / Amanda / get married to Ed

9. 1920 / they / have a beautiful baby girl

10. 1950 / their daughter / begin her own family

2 **Practice** Complete the following sentences by using either the simple past or the past perfect tense of the verbs in parentheses, as in the example.

Example Before changing lifestyles _____*began*_____ (begin) to separate
modern families, several generations of the same family
___*had often lived*___ (life / often) together.

1. Until the automobile, the Depression, and the World Wars
_____ (bring) changes in U.S. society, American lifestyles
_____ (remain) constant for a century.

2. American society _____ (begin / already) to change when
World War II _____ (break out).

3. After rural families _____ (move) to the cities in search of
work, they _____ (create) new lives there instead of
returning to their farms.

4. Women _____ (work / rarely) outside the home before World War II _____ (produce) a labor shortage.

5. After women _____ (experience) the world of work, many _____ (find) it difficult to return to their traditional roles.

6. By the time that World War II _____ (come) to an end, the American way of life _____ (change) tremendously.

7. Soon after World War II _____ (ended), the great "Baby Boom" _____ (began).

8. By the early 1950s, many Americans _____ (move) to new homes in new suburbs near cities.

9. By then, hundreds of thousands of families _____ (bought) cars.

10. Telephones and televisions _____ (become / already) important parts of family life.

B. The Past Perfect Continuous Tense

The past perfect continuous tense, like the past perfect tense, is used to contrast an earlier and a later time in the past.
- This tense may be used instead of the past perfect tense to emphasize the continuous nature of the earlier activity.
- The past perfect continuous tense is seldom used in conversation but does appear in written English.

3.10 The Past Perfect Continuous Tense		
Structures	**Examples**	**Time Expressions**
Simple Sentences	Before the Depression, the O'Keefes **had been making** a decent living. Until the Depression, they **had been planning** to buy a larger farm.	*after* *before* *by* *by the time (that)* *until*
Complex Sentence	Before they lost their farm, the O'Keefes **had been making** a good living.	*already* *for* + a period

Note: See page 66 for a list of verbs not normally used in the continuous tenses. See Appendix 2 on pages 462–463 for spelling rules for the *-ing* ending.

3 **Practice** Using *by the time that* and *already,* combine the following pairs of sentences. Be sure to change verb tenses when necessary.

Example Women fought to get the vote for years.
The 19th Amendment was ratified in 1920.
Women had already been fighting to get the vote for years by the time that the 19th Amendment was ratified in 1920.

1. Serious economic problems affected world trade for several years.
The stock market crashed in 1929.

2. Farmers struggled to maintain their farms for several years.
The drought of 1935–36 began.

3. Blacks and other minorities tried for years to receive equality under the law.
Congress passed the Civil Rights Act in 1964.

4. Martin Luther King, Jr. worked for civil rights for more than a decade.
He received the Nobel Peace Prize in 1964.

5. The Soviet Union experimented with spacecraft for several years.
The United States began its space program.

6. Young Americans explored ways of working and helping abroad.
John F. Kennedy established the Peace Corps in 1961.

C. The Future Perfect and Future Perfect Continuous Tenses

These tenses refer to situations or actions that will have occurred *before* another event or time in the future. They appear in written English, but they are not used often in spoken English.

3.11 The Future Perfect and Future Perfect Continuous Tenses

Structures	Examples	Time Expressions
Future Perfect	By the end of this trip, we **will have traveled** over ten thousand miles.	*before* *by the time . . .* *by* + date or time *when*
Future Perfect Continuous	When you arrive, you **will have been flying** for more than 22 hours.	

4 **Practice** Change the following sentences to the future perfect tense. When possible, use *even, more,* or *even more* (for emphasis) in your new sentences.

Example   The role of women has changed greatly.

> *By 2030, the role of women will have changed even more.*
> Many women have gone back to school.
> *By 2030, even more women will have gone back to school.*

1. Families have become smaller.

2. Many couples have chosen to have children later in life.

3. The cost of living has increased.

4. Raising children has gotten more expensive.

5. The cost of a college education has grown higher.

6. Children have spent much time alone while their parents are working.

7. Many men have begun to do housework.

8. Many women have gone back to school.

9. Many women have started to work outside the home.

10. Two-income families have become common.

11. Many men and women have changed careers several times.

12. Distance education has provided many people with a way to study at home.

13. Many universities have started to offer degree programs with flexible schedules.

14. The Internet has provided many new ways of studying and learning.

15. Many companies have offered job retraining as new areas are created.

Using What You've Learned

5 **Describing Changes** The 20th century was a period of tremendous change worldwide: in work and careers, family life, education, medical care, transportation, eating habits, shopping, and entertainment, to name only a few areas. Choose one area of change as the topic for a short composition. First, describe the situation 25, 50, 75, or 100 years ago. Then, describe the situation today, making comparisons between the past and present. Finally, use your composition as the basis for a three-minute presentation to the class.

Example   *Life in Italy was very different 50 or 60 years ago. Until the age of television, most Italian families had spent their evenings together. They would talk, read, sing, or tell stories. . . .*

Setting the Context

 Previewing the Passage Discuss the questions.

Do you have brothers or sisters? Do you get along well with them? Which ones?

Reading Read the passage.

Sibling Rivalry: Growing Up and Growing Older

Sibling rivalry is a term in psychology for the competition between brothers and sisters. Since the beginning of time, brothers and sisters have argued and fought over matters great and small. What do siblings fight about and why?

According to researchers, many fights come from issues with jealousy and territory, but the full list of conflicts is unending! Brothers and sisters will fight about almost anything. For children, a fight is usually a matter of pride or honor, but for parents, it's a minefield[1]. How can parents ease the tensions coming from these rivalries? 5

One solution that has frequently worked for many families is teamwork. Siblings do something as a team. The children will prepare food together or build something together. Once the children have achieved goals together, they develop more of a bond. Doing household chores together is a way of promoting teamwork. This helps to make the rivalry less important, and it helps keep the house in good order! 10

---

[1] *minefield* figurative language for a very difficult and delicate situation

▲ Sibling teamwork can decrease rivalry.

Discussing Ideas Discuss the questions.

Can you think of other ways that parents can help reduce tension between brothers and sisters? What did your parents do?

Grammar Structures and Practice

A. Introduction to Reported Speech

There are different ways to explain something that someone said.
- Quotations are the exact words that someone says. They are used with quotation marks, and a comma often precedes or follows the quote.
- Reported speech gives the ideas, but *not necessarily* the exact words, of the original speaker or writer. Reported speech does not generally require commas or quotation marks.

3.12	Quotations versus Reported Speech
Quotation	**Reported Speech**
Someone said, "A brother shares childhood memories and grown-up dreams."	Someone once said that brothers shared (share) childhood memories and grown-up dreams.

To form a statement with reported speech, the verb tense must change.

3.13 Verb Changes with Reported Speech

Explanations	Quotation	Reported Speech
In reported speech, when the verb in the main clause (*Susan said*, etc.) is in the past, the verb in the noun clause is often shifted to one of the past tenses.	"Chris **is not** at home."	Susan said that Chris **wasn't** at home.
	"Chris **is** at work."	Susan said that Chris **was** at work.
	"He **has** a lot of work to do."	She mentioned that he **had** a lot of work to do.
In some cases, the shifts can be optional, especially if the information is still true at the moment of speaking. However, the changes must be consistent.	"**Has** he **finished** his work yet?"	Susan asked if (whether) he **had finished** his work yet.
	"**He's going to stay** until he finishes."	She added he **was going to stay** until he finished.
The use of *that* is also optional in these sentences	"He **was working** all day."	She remarked that he **had been working** all day.
	"When **did** he **come** home last night?"	She asked when he **had come** home last night.

1 Practice Change these sentences to reported speech. Begin your new statement with *The students*...or *The instructor*... Be sure to make all necessary changes in verb tenses.

Example Students: What is sibling rivalry?

The students *asked what sibling rivalry was (is).*

1. Sibling rivalry is the competition between brothers and sisters.

   The instructor _____

2. What do brothers and sisters fight about?

   The students _____

3. Why do brothers and sisters fight?

   The students _____

4. Since the beginning of time, siblings have argued and fought over just about anything.

   The instructor _____

5. Many fights come from issues with jealousy and territory.

   The instructor _____

6. One solution that has frequently worked for many families is teamwork.

   The instructor _____

7. The children will prepare food together or build something together.

   The instructor _____

8. Once the children have achieved goals together, they develop more of a bond.

   The instructor _____

B. Changes in Pronouns, Adjectives, and Adverbials with Reported Speech

In reported speech, pronouns, adjectives, and adverbs must also change. All changes in reported speech must be consistent.

3.14 Changes in Pronouns, Adjectives, and Adverbials with Reported Speech

Structures	Explanations	Quotations	Reported Speech
Pronouns	Pronouns are changed to show a change in speakers	Mary said, "I need **your** help." Mary asked, "Are **you** going to help?"	Mary said that **she** needed **my** (**our**) help. Mary asked if **I** was (we were) going to help.
Demonstrative Pronouns and Adjectives	The use of *this, that, these, those* depends on the time and place of the reported speech.	Mary said, "**This** is important." Mary said, "**These** papers are important."	Mary said **that** was important. Mary said that **those** papers were important.
Adverbs	*Now, then, here,* and *there* depends on the time and place of the reported speech.	Mary said, "I need them now." Mary said, "The papers are **here**."	She said that **she** needed them then. Mary said the papers were **there**.
Other Time Expressions	*Today, tomorrow,* and *yesterday* may also change according to the time of the reported speech.	She said, "I want more **tomorrow**." She said, "I needed this **yesterday**." (the following day)	She said **she** wanted more **the day after**. She said she needed it **the day before**. (the previous day)

---

2 Practice Families or friends who live together can often have problems. One of the best solutions to problems is to talk things over. In this conversation, five brothers, who share a house, are trying to resolve a common problem: housework. Retell the conversation in reported speech by completing the sentences on page 122. Be sure to use appropriate verb forms in your new sentences. Make any other necessary changes.

Steve: We're all brothers, and we're all good friends, but we've been having a lot of problems this week.

Tom: Well, in my opinion, the biggest problem is cleaning. Our house is a mess. Nobody cleaned this week or last week. We need to find a way to keep things cleaner.

Jon: I made a list of jobs to do. Which jobs does everyone want to do?

Ted: I like this idea! I like choosing my jobs.

Peter: I am going to be responsible for the kitchen area.

Tom: I am willing to do the living room, but we need a vacuum cleaner!

Steve: I'm going to check the newspaper. Look... Here's an ad for a good vacuum cleaner on sale.

Example Steve said that they *had been having a lot of problems lately.*

1. Steve remarked that they _____

2. However, he said _____

3. Tom felt the biggest problem _____

4. Moreover, he said _____

5. Tom added that nobody _____

6. Jon remarked that he _____

7. He asked _____

8. Ted exclaimed _____

9. Peter stated that he _____

10. Tom said that _____

11. Tom added that _____

12. Steve mentioned that he _____

13. Steve added that _____

C. *Say* versus *Tell*

Say and *tell* are used in different situations.

3.15	*Say* versus *Tell*	
Structure	**Explanations**	**Examples**
Say	In general, *say* is used when the listener is *not* mentioned.	Molly **said** that Max had to study. Max **said** that he would be home late.
Tell	*Tell* is used when the listener *is* mentioned. (We say something, but we tell *someone* something.)	Molly **told me** that she didn't feel well. Molly **told us** that she had a cold.

3 **Practice** Reread the conversation in Activity 2 on pages 121–122. Then complete the following with the past form of *say* or *tell*.

Example Steve _____*said*_____ that they'd been having a lot of problems lately.

1. Steve _____ his brothers that they were all good friends, but they had some problems.

2. Tom _____ his brothers that cleaning was their biggest problem.

3. Tom _____ that the house hadn't been cleaned in two weeks.

4. Jon _____ that he had made a list and they could each choose a job to do.

5. Ted _____ everyone that he liked the idea of choosing jobs.

6. Peter _____ that he was going to clean the kitchen.

7. Tom _____ everyone that he would take care of the living room.

8. Finally, Steve _____ the others that he would try to get a vacuum cleaner.

4 **Review** Complete the passage with appropriate present forms of the verbs in parentheses. Add adverbs when indicated. The first one is done as an example.

Sharing Responsibilities

Household chores _____*are usually*_____ boring. All of us in the Peterson

(be / usually)

household _____ busy schedules, so we _____

1 (have)   2 (try)

to share the chores. Our plan _____ out, though! For example,
3 (work / seldom)

our sons, Dan and Ed, _____ the dinner dishes, but tonight they
4 (do / usually)

_____ for exams. So guess who _____ the
5 (study)   6 (wash)

dishes tonight? Me! Our daughter, Sue, _____ care of the laundry,
7 (take / normally)

but she _____ friends out of town. So guess who
8 (visit)

_____ the laundry this week? Me! My husband and I
9 (do)

_____ cooking, as a rule, but he _____ with
10 (alternate)   11 (meet)

one of his most important clients this evening. So guess who

_____ dinner again? Me! I _____ doing all
12 (make)   13 (not mind)

these chores, and, in fact, I _____ housework. Time
14 (like / even)

_____ my problem, however. I _____ 35 hours
15 (be / always)   16 (work)

a week, and I _____ to stay late at my job. I
17 (have / often)

_____ that the family schedules _____ and
18 (understand)   19 (change)

that "someone" _____ to keep up the house. But I
20 (need)

_____ to be the "someone." It _____ easy to
21 (seem / almost always)   22 (not be)

have two full-time jobs!

5 **Review** The opening passage of this chapter is repeated below. First, complete
the passage with appropriate forms of the verbs in parentheses. Then, look back at page
86 and compare your choices with the original. The first one is done as an example.

Families

Exactly what_____*is*_____ a family? Until about 50 years ago, the
(be)

traditional American family _____ of a working husband, a
1 (consist)

wife at home, and two or more children. Responsibilities _____
2 (be)

clearly divided in the American nuclear family. While the husband

_____ a living, the wife _____ for the home
3 (earn)   4 (care)

and _____ the children. Of course, there were exceptions, but
5 (raise)

this concept of the family _____ the general rule until the
6 (be)

1960s.

Since the 1960s, however, the family _____ more diverse,
7 (become)
fragile, and changeable. Americans _____ differing concepts of
8 (accept)
families, including single parent, blended, two-paycheck, interracial, childless,
and commuter families. Some critics believe that the American family
_____ greatly because of all the changes in society. According
9 (suffer)
to these critics, the family _____ much stronger before it
10 (be)
_____ to struggle with issues such as divorce, working moth-
11 (begin)
ers, gay couples, and unmarried relationships. Today's strongest critics
_____ that the traditional nuclear family will become rare in
12 (feel)
the 21st century.

Nationwide, however, most Americans _____ that the fam-
13 (believe)
ily _____. In fact, almost all major surveys in recent years
14 (survive)
_____ that the American family is as strong as it has ever been.
15 (find)
For most Americans, the family _____ to provide their deepest
16 (continue)
source of satisfaction and meaning in life. Thus, although today's family
_____ different from what it _____ it seems to
17 (be)   18 (be)
be thriving.

6 **Review** Complete the following passage with appropriate past forms of the verbs
in parentheses. In some cases, more than one choice may be possible. Be prepared to
discuss your choices. The first two are done as examples.

Immigrant Families and the Great Depression

It _____was_____ 6:45 in the morning, and Katherine Nuss _____was going_____
(be)   (go)
out into the gray morning light. She _____ around the corner to
1 (walk)
the streetcar stop and _____ the journey to the great houses of
2 (begin)
High Street. The wages _____ low—$2 for a 12- or 13-hour day.
3 (be)
Some nights it _____ nearly nine o'clock by the time she
4 (be)
_____ from the trolley to her own home at 1020 West Mulberry
5 (trudge)

Street. Nevertheless, the work _____ money. While she
6 (mean)

_____ floors, _____ windows, _____
7 (scrub)   8 (wash)   9 (polish)

woodwork, and _____ meals for the rich families of
10 (cook)

Springfield, she _____ her children and _____
11 (support)   12 (keep)

the family together. In 1933, the economic situation _____
13 (get)

worse in her town, as in the rest of the nation. At that time, America

_____ close to the bottom of the Great Depression. Her hus-
14 (come)

band _____ disabled, and they _____ many
15 (be)   16 (have)

children to feed. So, Katherine Nuss _____ back to work. Once
17 (go)

again, she _____ houses, the same thing she _____
18 (clean)   19 (do)

as a teenage immigrant fresh off the boat from Europe. She

_____ houses for the wealthy families on the hill in order to
20 (clean)

keep her own family together.

Both she and her husband _____ the preciousness of fam-
21 (know)

ily because of their own hard experiences. Many years before, as children, both

_____ their own parents because of death or immigration to
22 (lose)

America. Both, as adults, _____ family as one of the highest
23 (place)

values of life.

Katherine _____ a little girl in Austria-Hungary when her
24 (be)

mother _____. Her father _____ her with rela-
25 (die)   26 (leave)

tives and _____ for America. Like millions of other immigrants,
27 (sail)

he _____ for his future in the New World.
28 (look)

Katherine _____ 14 years old when her father
29 (be)

_____ for her. She _____ at Ellis Island, New
30 (send)   31 (arrive)

York, in 1910—alone, frightened, and unable to speak a word of English. All she

_____ _____ a slip of paper with her father's
32 (have)   33 (be)

home address in Cincinnati.

Using What You've Learned

7 **Telling Folk Stories** Every culture has favorite folk stories. Many of these teach us lessons about life. Can you remember a folk story that you particularly liked as a child? In small groups, share some stories. You may want to write these stories and make a short collection of folktales from around the world.

Focus on Testing

Use of Verbs

Verb forms and tenses are frequently tested on standardized English proficiency exams. Review these commonly tested structures and check your understanding by completing the following sample items.

Remember that . . .

✓ All tenses should be formed correctly, and the tense should be appropriate for the time frame(s) of the sentence.

✓ Verbs of feeling, perception, and possession are not generally used in continuous tenses. Also, many of these verbs are linking verbs; adverbs cannot be used as complements after linking verbs.

✓ A singular verb is used with a singular subject, and plural verbs are used with plural subjects.

Part 1 Mark the correct completion for the following.

Example John ———————————— quite ill in the past few days.

    Ⓐ had became   Ⓒ has became

    Ⓑ had become   Ⓓ has become

1. Most major surveys in recent years ———————————— that Americans are satisfied with their family life.

    Ⓐ have find   Ⓒ has found

    Ⓑ find   Ⓓ have found

2. The Jacksons seem ———————————— with their decision to move.

    Ⓐ please   Ⓒ happily

    Ⓑ happy   Ⓓ pleasant

3. When Mary was younger, she ———————————— tennis much more than now.

    Ⓐ used to like   Ⓒ was liking

    Ⓑ would like   Ⓓ like

4. By 1924, over 12 million new Americans _____ the United States through Ellis Island.

- (A) had been entering
- (B) have entered
- (C) had entered
- (D) had been entered

5. George _____ it took him an hour to get there by bus.

- (A) said me
- (B) told
- (C) told that
- (D) said that

Part 2 Circle the letter below the word(s) containing an error.

Example An individual <u>may feel</u> <u>frustratedly</u> if she has difficulties in speaking
    A   B   Ⓒ

the language <u>where she is living</u>.
      D

1. <u>Long before</u> the Prime Minister <u>left</u> for Canada, she <u>had dicussing</u> the issue
   A   B   C

<u>in depth</u> with the entire cabinet.
 D

2. <u>By the time that</u> the report <u>is finished</u>, the committee <u>will have spending</u> over
   A   B   C

two months <u>working</u> on it.
    D

3. Ellen told <u>to me</u> that she <u>was going</u> <u>to help</u> me, but she couldn't.
     A B   C   D

4. <u>Since</u> the Depression <u>of the</u> 1930s, the farm population in the United States
  A   B

<u>have dropped</u> from around 30 percent <u>to less than</u> 4 percent.
  C   D

5. Soon after <u>the Sauters</u> <u>had arrived</u> in America, they <u>had started</u> <u>farming</u> in
     A   B   C   D

central Wisconsin.

Self-Assessment Log

Each of the following statements describes the grammar you learned in this chapter. Read the statements; then check the box that describes how well you understand each structure.

	Needs Improvement	Good	Great
I can use regular past verb forms.	❑	❑	❑
I can use irregular past verb forms.	❑	❑	❑
I can use a variety of past tenses appropriately.	❑	❑	❑
I can use present perfect and perfect continuous tenses appropriately.	❑	❑	❑
I can use past and future perfect tenses appropriately.	❑	❑	❑
I can use reported speech appropriately.	❑	❑	❑
I can take a test about verb forms and tenses.	❑	❑	❑

Chapter 4

Health and Leisure

In This Chapter

Modal Auxiliaries and Related Structures

Part 1 Modal Auxiliaries and Related Structures of Ability and Expectation

Part 2 Modal Auxiliaries of Request, Permission, and Preference

Part 3 Modal Auxiliaries and Related Structures of Need and Advice

Part 4 Modal Auxiliaries of Possibility and Probability

Part 5 Modal Auxiliaries and Reported Speech

“He who has health, has hope; and he who has hope, has everything.”

—Arabian proverb

Connecting to the Topic

1 Think about your current lifestyle. Is it a healthy one?

2 Do you get exercise and eat nutritious food?

3 Is there a lot of stress in your life?

Introduction

In this chapter, you'll look at health and leisure activities while studying the modal auxiliaries, as well as some structures related to them in usage. This chapter emphasizes the present forms, active voice. In Chapter 5, you will study the passive forms. In Chapter 10, you will review these and study the past forms in more detail.

Reading Read the following passage. It introduces the chapter theme, "Health and Leisure," and raises some of the topics and issues you will cover in the chapter.

How Healthy Are You?

Good health is not something you are able to buy at the drugstore, and you can't depend on getting it back with a quick visit to the doctor when you're sick, either. Keeping yourself healthy has to be your own responsibility. Mistreating your system by keeping bad habits, neglecting symptoms of illness, and ignoring common health rules can counteract the best medical care. 5

Nowadays, health specialists promote the idea of wellness for everybody. Wellness means achieving the best possible health within the limits of your body. One person may need many fewer calories than another, depending on metabolism. Some people might prefer a lot of easier exercise to more strenuous exercise. While one person enjoys playing 72 holes of golf a week, another 10 would rather three sweaty, competitive games of tennis.

Understanding the needs of your own body is the key. Everyone runs the risk of accidents, and no one can be sure of avoiding chronic disease. Nevertheless, poor diet, stress, a bad working environment, and carelessness can ruin good health. By changing your habits or the conditions surrounding you, you 15 can lower the risk or reduce the damage of disease.

Discussing Ideas Discuss the questions.

What do you do to stay healthy? What do people in your country do to try to stay physically fit?

Setting the Context

 Previewing the Passage Discuss the questions.

What is *physical fitness*? Can you describe a physically fit person?

Check off your answers to the following questions.

Are You Physically Fit?	Yes	No
Can you go through a busy day and feel good the next morning?		
Are you able to lift one half of your body weight?		
Can you bend and twist easily in all directions?		
Can you walk a mile in 15 minutes?		
Do you maintain your weight?		

After checking off your answers to the questions in the preceding chart, decide whether you are physically fit or you have to get into better shape.

▲ A couch potato

 Discussing Ideas In a small group, discuss the questions.

What is a "couch potato"? Do you know any couch potatoes? Are such people common in your culture? What is the common attitude toward physical fitness in your culture?

Grammar Structures and Practice

A. Introduction to Modal Auxiliaries

Modals are a group of words that modify the meaning of verbs.

- A modal has only one form for all persons of the verb, but it can have several meanings and time frames, depending on the context in which it is used.
- A complete list of the modals discussed in this chapter appears in Appendix 5 on pages 468–469; the list also includes related structures.

4.1 Modal Auxiliaries

Structures	Examples	Negative Contractions	
Statements	He **should get** more exercise.	can't	shouldn't
Questions	**Would** you **like** to go jogging?	couldn't	won't
Negatives	I **can't play** tennis today.	mustn't	wouldn't

Certain modals express present and past ability.

- With *can, could,* and *be able to,* affirmative and negative statements and questions all give the meaning of ability.
- In rapid speech, *can* is weakly stressed (*kin*). *Can't* is stressed more strongly.

4.2 Expressing Present and Past Ability

Meaning	Structures	Examples
Present Ability	*can (cannot)* + simple form *(not) be able to*	John **can** run five miles, but I **can't (cannot).** How many miles **are** you **able** to run?
Past Ability	*could (not)* + simple form *(not) be able to*	He **couldn't** run as fast as she **could.** I **wasn't able to** run because of the rain.

---

1 **Practice** It is often difficult to distinguish *can* and *can't* in rapid conversation. Of course, there is a tremendous difference in meaning! As your teacher rapidly reads the following sentences, circle *can* or *can't* according to what you hear.

Hint: Can has little stress, and *can't* is more clearly pronounced.

1. I (can / can't) swim a mile.

2. John (can / can't) run a mile.

3. I (can / can't) walk a mile.

4. She (can / can't) ski very well.

5. He (can / can't) jog 10 miles.

6. They (can / can't) skate very well.

7. I (can / can't) ride a bike.

8. I (can / can't) hear the difference between the two words!

9. He says he (can / can't) come.

10. I'm sure she thinks she (can / can't).

11. (Can / can't) you tell me the answer?

12. (Can / can't) you join us?

 2 **Practice** With a partner, take turns making statements. Choose one sentence in each pair, but don't tell which sentence you are choosing. Your partner should add a statement.

Example   a. I can surf.
    b. I can't surf.
    A: I can't surf.
    B: But I can. *OR* I can't either.

1. a. I can swim.
   b. I can't swim.

2. a. I can roller-blade.
   b. I can't roller-blade.

3. a. I can play the guitar.
   b. I can't play the guitar.

4. a. I can speak Arabic.
   b. I can't speak Arabic.

5. a. He can ride a bike.
   b. He can't ride a bike.

6. a. She can touch her toes.
   b. She can't touch her toes.

7. a. He can do a cartwheel.
   b. He can't do a cartwheel.

8. a. She can work tonight.
   b. She can't work tonight.

9. a. They can play piano.
   b. They can't play piano.

10. a. They can make pizza.
   b. They can't make pizza.

3 **Practice** Make a list of all the things that students in your class can do. Here are some suggestions: using a computer, rollerblading or doing other sports, playing musical instruments, speaking different languages, and so on. Then make a chart like the one on page 136 and check the boxes that apply to you. Finally, write at least eight sentences about your abilities.

Activity	Can Do Well	Can Do Pretty Well	Can't Do Very Well	Can't Do at All
1. swimming	X			
2.				
3.				
4.				
5.				
6.				
7.				
8.				

 4 **Practice** With a partner, take turns making statements and asking questions about the chart in Activity 3.

Example   A: I can swim pretty well. Can you?
B: I can, too.

 5 **Practice** Look at the chart you made for Activity 3 again. With your partner, compare your ability in each activity between the present and the past. What can you do now? What could you do when you were younger? Use these patterns:

When I was younger, I could (couldn't) . . .

Now that I'm older, I can . . .
I still can't . . .
I can't . . . anymore.

Example   When I was younger, I couldn't use a computer, but now I use a
computer every day!

6 **Practice** The chart on page 137 gives you the approximate calories you burn in sports and other activities. Use the information to form at least six sentences with *can*. Note that you must use the *-ing* form of a verb after *by*.

Example   *You (A person) can burn over 300 calories by walking briskly
for an hour.*

How Many Calories Can You Burn?

Food produces energy. One ounce of fat gives 267 calories of energy. A pound of fat is equivalent to 4,272 calories.

CALORIES BURNED PER HOUR	ACTIVITY
72–84	Sitting and talking
120–150	Walking at a slow pace
240–300	Doing housework (cleaning, mopping, scrubbing)
300–360	Walking briskly; playing doubles tennis; playing Ping-Pong (table tennis)
350–420	Bicycling; ice- or roller-skating
420–480	Playing singles tennis
480–600	Downhill skiing; jogging
600–650	Running (5.5 mph); bicycling (13 mph)
over 660	Running (6 or more mph); handball; squash; swimming (depends on strokes and style; excellent overall conditioner)

B. Expressing Expectation

Should and *ought to* can be used to express expectation.

- *Should* and *ought to* have two different meanings. One meaning is *will probably* (expectation). The other meaning of advice is covered later in this chapter.
- *Should* is more commonly used than *ought to*.
- In rapid speech, *ought to* sounds like /otta/.
- Negative questions with *should* are often used for emphasis.

4.3 *Should* and *Ought to* to Express Expectation

Structures	Examples
***Should (not)* + simple form**	He **should arrive** very soon.
	Shouldn't she **arrive** soon?
	This **shouldn't take** long to do.
***Ought (not) to* + simple form**	We **ought to be** finished soon.

7 Practice Form a group of three students. Take turns reading the statements on page 138 and creating new statements. The first student reads the statement from the text. The second student forms a sentence with *should,* and the third student uses *ought to* for the same sentence. As an alternative, write your new versions of the original statement, one with *should* and one with *ought to.*

Example We expect the doctor to arrive at any minute.

> A: We expect the doctor to arrive at any minute.
> B: The doctor should arrive at any minute.
> C: The doctor ought to arrive at any minute.

1. The doctor expects the exam to take only a few minutes.
2. She doesn't expect there to be any problems.
3. She expects to have plenty of time to answer questions.
4. The doctor expects your exam to be normal.
5. She doesn't expect you to need another checkup for at least a year.
6. You can expect your bill to arrive within a week.
7. We expect the insurance to cover most of your bill.
8. We don't expect to have any problems with your coverage.
9. The company doesn't expect insurance premiums to go up until next year.
10. The company expects premiums to increase within 18 months.

8 Practice Complete each item using one of the modal forms studied in this section: *be able to, can, could, ought to* or *should.*

Before

1. Before I began exercising at Ernie's Exercise Emporium, I _wasn't able to lose_ (not lose) weight, and I _____ (not find) any clothes that fit me well.

After

2. Now that my muscles are so big, I _____ (not find) anything to wear. Well, my instructor said that I _____ (to find) some clothes at "Miki's Muscle Shop for High Powered Females." They _____ (have) something that fits me!

Before

3. Before I began exercising at Ernie's Exercise Emporium, I _____ (not run), I _____ (not jog). I _____ (not walk), I _____ (not sit / even) without getting tired. I _____ (not do) anything!

After

4. Now I _____ (not do / still) anything! But the doctor says that I _____ (to leave) the hospital soon.

Using What You've Learned

9 **Talking About Health** Write a paragraph about physical fitness and staying healthy. Are you in good shape? Explain what you do every day or every week to stay in shape. Are you satisfied with what you currently do? Do you intend to make any changes? What can you do?

Setting the Context

 Previewing the Passage Discuss the questions.

How do you feel after studying all week? Are you exhausted? Or are you full of energy and ready to do things other than study?

Reading Read the passage.

Weekend Plans

Irma: I'm so glad it's Friday! What would you like to do this weekend? I'd like to get some exercise. How about tennis? Can you be ready in fifteen minutes? I've been studying all week, and I'm tired of sitting. Let's play a few matches.

Omar: Irma, I'm tired. Period. I don't feel like doing anything strenuous. I'd   5
rather stay home and watch movies. Could you stop by the Movie Center on your way here and rent five or six good movies?

Irma: Come on, Omar. I'd rather not watch movies again. I'd prefer to do something active. Would you like to play basketball instead of tennis?

Omar: No, Irma. I would prefer not to play basketball or tennis or any other   10
sport. I would like to relax.

Irma: Well, would you mind if I asked your roommate instead?

Omar: Now that you mention it, I wouldn't mind playing some tennis.

 Discussing Ideas Discuss the questions.

What do you think Irma will do? What do you think Omar will do? Does Omar want Irma to play tennis with Omar's roommate?

Grammar Structures and Practice

A. Requesting Action (1)

Requests often involve asking someone to do something. *Would, could, can,* and *will* are often used in these requests. *Please* is often added to any request.

4.4 Requesting Action: *Would, Could, Can,* and *Will*

Structures	Explanations	Examples
Would you *Could you*	*Could* and *would* are appropriate in most circumstances.	**Would you** call the theater for the movie schedule? **Could you** call the Granada Theater?
Can you	*Can* is informal, and it is used among friends.	**Can you** get us two tickets to the concert?
Will you *+ simple form . . . ?*	*Will* is somewhat rude in tone. It is used in urgent situations or among friends.	**Will you** find us three seats together up front?

Would you mind... is another way of requesting action.

4.5 Requesting Action: *Would you mind ...*

Structure	Explanations	Examples
Would you mind *+ gerund (verb + ing)?*	*Would you mind* . . . is polite and fairly formal. It is always followed by a gerund. A negative response means "I will." Informal answers are often affirmative, however.	**Would you mind** calling the theater for the movie schedule? No, not at all. (I will call.) **Would you mind** not going to that show? OK. (I won't go.)

Pronunciation Note

In rapid speech *can, could, will,* and *would* are seldom pronounced clearly.
Listen carefully as your teacher reads the following words:

Normal Speech	Rapid Speech	Normal Speech	Rapid Speech
Can you . . . ?	/ kenya /	Will you . . . ?	/ willya /
Can he . . . ?	/ keni /	Will he . . . ?	/ willi /
Could you . . . ?	/ kudja /	Would you . . . ?	/ wudja /
Could he . . . ?	/ kuddi /	Would he . . . ?	/ wuddi /

1 Practice Your teacher will read the following requests, but *not* in the order listed. Listen carefully and write down the form that you hear.

1. Could you help?
2. Could he help?
3. Would you help?
4. Wouldn't he help?

5. Can't you help?
6. Couldn't you help?
7. Can you help?
8. Wouldn't you help?

2 Practice In emergencies, we don't usually think about politeness, and we often use short commands. In most other situations, politeness is important, though. Change these short commands to polite requests for action by using *could, would,* or *would you mind.*

Example: Help me!
Could you help me, please?

1. Give me some information!
2. Explain this to me!
3. Tell me the meaning of this word!
4. Buy some tickets for the concert!
5. Make reservations for dinner at the Italian restaurant!
6. Rent a DVD for the weekend!
7. Give me directions to the soccer stadium!
8. Draw me a map to the tennis courts!

B. Requesting Permission (1)

Requests can also involve asking permission. *May, could,* and *can* are often used in these requests.

4.6	Requesting Permission: *May, Could,* and *Can*		
	Structures	**Explanations**	**Examples**
Formal Polite	*May I . . . ?* *Could I + simple form?*	Requests for permission to do something usually involve being polite and perhaps being formal. *May* and *could* are preferred in polite speech. *May* is more formal, and it is most often used in service situations, such as stores and restaurants.	**May I** help you? **Could I** talk with the manager, please?
Informal	*Can I + simple form?*	*Can* is very informal, but it is often used in conversation.	**Can I** see the fall schedule of games?

Would you mind if I ... is another polite and fairly formal way of requesting permission to do something.

4.7 Requesting Permission: *Would you mind if I...*

Structures	Explanations	Example
Would you mind if I + past form?	*Would you mind if I* . . . is always followed by the past tense of a second verb. A negative response means "It's all right. I don't mind."	**Would you mind if I** didn't go to the the game today? I'm tired. No. That's OK. I don't mind.

 3 Practice Imagine that you're at a restaurant. In pairs, take turns making and responding to requests for permission. Complete the following conversations by using *may, could,* or *can.* (Remember that *can* is informal and may not be appropriate for all situations.)

Example (see the manager)
   I'm sorry, but . . .
   A: May (Could) I see the manager?
   B: I'm sorry, but she's not available at the moment.

1. (have a table for two)
   Yes, of course . . .

2. (see a menu)
   Certainly, . . .

3. (change to a different table)
   Sure, . . .

4. (use the telephone)
   Sorry, but . . .

5. (pay by check)
   Certainly, . . .

6. (pay with a credit card)
   Sorry, but . . .

 4 Practice Make a chain around the class. Turn to the person next to you (your "neighbor") and make a request. Before you make your request, tell the class "who" you are addressing. Then make your request, and your neighbor will respond. Your neighbor then asks his or her neighbor, and so on, continuing the chain. After each, the class should decide if the form of the request was appropriate or not (for example, was the request polite enough? too polite?). Add other situations if necessary.

Example A: (*to my grandfather*) Grandpa, would you please let me use your car?
   B: Why of course! Would you like the Rolls Royce or the Mercedes?
   B: (*to a stranger*) Excuse me, sir. Could I . . . ?

1. You would like to borrow a pen from your classmate.

2. You would like to use your classmate's dictionary.

3. You would like to borrow your sister's (brother's, roommate's, father's, aunt's, grandfather's) car.

4. You need to use a telephone. Ask a stranger (your teacher, your friend, the school administrator, your roommate) for change for the pay phone.

5. You would like to use your sister's (brother's, roommate's, cousin's) favorite sweater (jacket, coat) for a special night out. Ask to borrow it from him or her.

6. You would like your roommate (brother, sister, friend, cousin) to lend you a bicycle. Ask him or her to lend it to you for a couple of days.

7. You need to talk with your advisor. Ask the assistant for an appointment.

8. You need to make a dentist appointment. Ask the receptionist for an appointment.

9. You need to get a prescription filled in a drug store. Ask the pharmacist (the cashier) to help you.

10. You don't have enough money for the rent and you desperately need to borrow $100. Ask your mother (father, roommate, best friend, boyfriend, girlfriend, classmate) to lend (or give) you the money.

D. Expressing Preference

Affirmative and negative statements and questions with *would like (prefer)* may express desires, preferences, or choices. The contracted form of *would* (*I'd,* etc.) is almost always used in conversational English.

4.8 Expressing Preference: *Would like (prefer)*

Structures	Explanations	Examples
I would (not) like **+ infinitive or noun** *Would you like* **+ infinitive or noun?** *Wouldn't you like* **+ infinitive or noun?**	*Would (not) like (prefer)* is followed by either a noun or the infinitive form of a verb.	I **would like** a window seat. No, I **would like (prefer)** to sit in the middle section. **Would you like** to see the new play? **Wouldn't you like (prefer)** to see the new play?
I would rather (not) **+ simple form or noun** *Would you rather (not)* **+ simple form or noun?** *Wouldn't you rather* **+ simple form or noun?**	*Would rather (not)* is followed by either a noun or the simple form of a verb.	**I'd rather not** go in the afternoon. **Would you rather** go in the morning or the afternoon? **Wouldn't** you **rather** go in the morning?

5 Practice Imagine that you have unlimited time and money. What would you like to do? Choose from the following list and add your own ideas. *Note:* For emphasis, you can say *I would really like to . . .* or *I would love to . . . .* Make at least eight sentences.

Example travel around the world
I would like (love) to travel around the world.

1. move to Paris
2. run a marathon
3. get a Ph.D
4. compete in the Olympics
5. buy a yacht
6. study art
7. learn yoga
8. play tennis everyday
9. go to a professional soccer game every weekend
10. take a placement exam five times
11. play a musical instrument well
12. study a lot more English grammar

▲ The Eiffel Tower in Paris, France

6 Practice Look at the list in Activity 5. Choose five things you wouldn't like to do. Then give an alternative for each.

Example travel around the world
I wouldn't like to travel around the world. I'd rather stay here and study grammar.
OR:
I'd rather not travel around the world. I'd much rather stay here and study grammar.

7 Practice Add appropriate words or phrases to complete the following conversation. The first two are done as examples.

▲ Purchasing tickets over the phone

Ticket Agent: Good afternoon. Total Ticket Sales. _____*Would*_____ you _____*mind*_____ holding for a minute? (click) Hello. Thank you for holding. _____1_____ _____2_____ help you?

Estela: Hello. I _____3_____ _____4_____ to purchase two tickets for the Jazz Ensemble on Saturday evening.

Ticket Agent: That concert is sold out for Saturday evening. _____5_____ you _____6_____ tickets for the Sunday afternoon concert?

Estela: No. I'd _____7_____ see her on Saturday evening. Is there a waiting list for tickets for that performance?

Ticket Agent: Yes, there is a standby list. Also, you can come to the theater on Saturday night to check for returned tickets. Would _____8_____ _____9_____ me to put on the list? Or, _____10_____ you _____11_____ come to the theater for standby tickets?

| Estela: | I _____ _____ not go to the |

Estela: I _____ _____ not go to the
12   13

theater if there's a chance I can't see the concert.

_____ you _____ just putting
14   15

me on the standby list.

Ticket Agent: Certainly. Your name is now on the list. You're the third on the

list. _____ I help you with other tickets?
16

Estela: No thanks. That's all I wanted. Let's hope there're two tickets

available.

Using What You've Learned

8 **Making Reservations and Buying Tickets** Have you been to a concert, a play, a sports event, or a restaurant recently? Will you go soon? In pairs, practice making telephone calls to purchase tickets or make reservations by phone for the following. First, create and write out your conversation. Then practice saying the dialogue.

1. three good seats for a concert or a sports event in the upcoming weeks

2. a reservation for a party of four at a nice restaurant this coming Saturday evening

3. six tickets for a play on Broadway in New York City

4. your choice

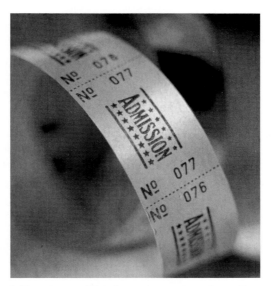

▲ Many types of tickets can be purchased over the phone by using a credit card.

9 Making Appointments Have you been to the doctor or dentist recently? Will you see one soon? In pairs, practice making telephone calls to arrange appointments. Role-play making appointments by phone for the following:

1. You want to make a dental appointment for a checkup. Call the dentist's office.

2. You have a bad toothache, and you would like to make an emergency appointment with the dentist. Call the dentist's office.

3. You want to make an appointment with your doctor for a yearly check-up. Call the doctor's office.

4. You have a high fever and you feel terrible. Call the doctor's office for an emergency appointment.

5. You were ill or injured a few weeks ago, and now you are better. Your doctor told you to return for a follow-up appointment. Call to make the appointment.

6. You are having problems seeing and perhaps you need (new) glasses. Call for an appointment to have your eyes checked.

10 Making Requests Work in pairs and role-play the following situations. Make the characters male or female, depending on each pair. As you role-play, think about how polite you should be when you make your requests.

1. You are in a movie theater watching an excellent new movie. The person next to you is a man (or woman) around 60 years old. He (She) keeps talking during the film. Ask him (or her) to be quiet.

2. You are waiting in line to buy tickets for a concert. Two people come to talk to the person in front of you and enter the line in front of you. Ask them to go to the back of the line.

3. This is your first time in a small neighborhood restaurant and bar where people seem friendly and most know each other. Someone nearby is smoking. Ask the person not to smoke.

4. You are at home and it is 1:30 A.M. Your neighbors are young, and many are college students. They often make noise, and tonight they are making a lot of noise. You have an important exam tomorrow, and you want to be able to sleep. Ask them to be quiet.

11 Making Plans Imagine that you have a friend visiting from out of town. Your friend is a good friend but very hard to please. He or she is very particular about what to do. Write an email/letter to your friend. Make at least five good suggestions of things to do. They may include suggestions on movies, restaurants, trips, classes, concerts, and so forth. Your "finicky" friend will respond.

Example A: Let's go out and see New York at night. Would you like to hear some jazz in Greenwich Village?

B: Jazz is boring. I'd rather stay here and do crossword puzzles.

A: Well, would you like to . . . ?

Part 3 | Modal Auxiliaries and Related Structures of Need and Advice

Setting the Context

 Previewing the Passage Discuss the questions.

Do you know what to do in a medical emergency? What are some of the basic steps to follow?

▲ An ambulance arrives at a hospital emergency entrance.

Medical Emergencies and First Aid

Medical emergencies happen all the time, so everyone ought to know the basic steps of first aid. If you don't know what to do in an emergency, you should contact your local Red Cross or Red Crescent. These organizations give guidelines and offer short courses on what to do in emergency situations.

1. RESCUE THE VICTIM
2. CALL FOR MEDICAL HELP
3. ARTIFICIAL RESPIRATION

 Discussing Ideas Discuss the questions.

Have you ever been in an emergency situation? Were you injured? Someone else? Share your experiences with your class.

Grammar Structures and Practice

A. Expressing Present Need or Lack of Need

Must and *have to* mean to need to do something.

4.9 Expressing Present Need or Lack of Need: *Must (not), Have to*

Meanings	Structures	Explanations	Examples
Present Need	*must (not)* + simple form *have to*	In affirmative statement and questions, *must (not)* and *have to* express need. *Must not* expresses a strong need not to do something. In rapid speech, *have to* and *has to* sound like *hafta* and *hasta.*	You **must** see a doctor about that cut on your hand. John **has to** go for a physical exam, so he can't play tennis today. You **must not** forget to go to the dentist for your checkup.
Present Lack of Need	*don't have to* + simple form *doesn't have to*	*Do/does not have to* refers to something that is *not* necessary to do. Its meaning is very different from *must not.*	I **don't have to** see the doctor because my fever went away.

1 **Practice** Change these commands to statements using *must / must not.*

Example Don't use electrical appliances in the water!
You must not use electrical appliances in the water!

1. Call a doctor right away!
2. Get an ambulance immediately!
3. Don't move!
4. Don't touch that!
5. Turn off the electricity!
6. Find someone to help!
7. Don't drink that!
8. Give me some bandages!

2 Practice Read the following guidelines for emergencies. Then complete the sentences below with *must not* or *don't / doesn't have to*.

The American Red Cross gives these guidelines to follow in emergency situations.
1. If necessary, rescue the victim as quickly and carefully as possible.
2. Call for medical help immediately.
3. Check to see if the victim is breathing, and give him or her artificial respiration if necessary.
4. Control severe bleeding.
5. If you suspect poisoning, immediately give a conscious victim water or milk to dilute[1] the poison. If you suspect a chemical poison, don't let the victim vomit. If the victim is unconscious or having convulsions,[2] however, do not give any fluids.
6. In an accident, do *not* move the victim unless absolutely necessary.
7. Always check for injuries *before* moving the victim, if possible.

───────────────
[1] *dilute* make thinner or weaker
[2] *convulsion* violent muscle contractions

Example If the victim has a neck injury, you _____*must not*_____ move him or her.

1. If you _____ make an emergency rescue, do not move the victim.

2. You _____ move a person with a neck or back injury unless absolutely necessary.

3. If your victim has swallowed a poison and is unconscious, you _____ give him or her anything to drink.

4. If your victim has swallowed a chemical poison, you _____ try to make her vomit.

5. You _____ try different remedies with a poison victim if you are not sure of the poison.

6. You _____ study first aid, but it may be helpful someday.

7. A person who knows first aid _____ call a doctor about every small accident.

8. In a true emergency, you _____ wait. Call a doctor immediately.

3 Practice Read the following medicine label. Then rephrase the instructions to tell what the user *must* or *must not* do. Make at least five statements.

Example *You must not use this medicine if the printed seal is not intact.*

USE ONLY IF PRINTED SEAL UNDER CAP IS INTACT.

Adult Dose: Use only as directed by your physician.

WARNINGS: Do not give this medicine to children under age 12. Keep this and all drugs out of the reach of children. In case of an overdose, contact a physician or a poison control center immediately. Do not use this product if you are pregnant or nursing a baby. Do not use this product while operating a vehicle or machinery. Consult your physician before using this product if you have any of the following conditions: heart problems, high blood pressure, asthma.

4 Practice An important part of first aid is knowing what is serious and what is not, what we must do versus what we don't have to do immediately. Use *must, must not,* or *don't / doesn't have to* to complete each set of sentences.

Examples a. This is very serious. We _____ *must* _____ hurry!

b. This is not very serious. We _____ *don't have to* _____ rush.

c. This is very serious. We _____ *must not* _____ wait any longer.

1. a. I _____ see a doctor because I'm feeling much better.

b. I really _____ see a doctor because I've been feeling worse every day.

c. I _____ wait any longer. I need to see a doctor because I'm very sick.

2. a. This accident is not very serious. We _____ call for an ambulance.

b. This accident has caused serious injuries. We _____ call for an ambulance.

c. This accident is serious. We _____ wait a moment longer.

3. a. There is no emergency. We _____ hurry with the victim.

b. There is an emergency. We _____ delay!

c. There is an emergency. We _____ get help for the victim immediately.

4. a. That car is going to explode. We _____ move the victim right away.

   b. That car is about to explode. We _____ wait. We need to rescue the victim.

   c. That car is not in danger. We _____ rescue the victim immediately.

5. a. The situation is under control, and everything will be OK. We _____ worry.

   b. The situation is serious, and everyone is nervous, but we _____ panic.

   c. This situation is very serious, so we _____ all remain calm.

B. Expressing Past Need or Lack of Need

Had to and *didn't have to* are used to talk about past needs. Note: *must* does not have this meaning in the past.

4.10	Expressing Past Need or Lack of Need: *Had to*		
Meanings	**Structures**	**Explanations**	**Examples**
Past Need	***had to +*** **simple form**	In affirmative statements and questions, *had to* implies that the action was completed.	I **had to** see a doctor for my sore throat. **Did** you **have to** buy antibiotics for your sore throat?
Past Lack of Need	***didn't have to*** **+ simple form**	In negative statements, *did not have to* refers to something that was not necessary to do.	I **didn't have to** take antibiotics because I had a virus. We **didn't have to** have medical exams. We had them last term.

5 **Practice** Imagine that you took a first aid class and practiced what to do in an emergency—a fire in an apartment. Tell what you *had to do* and *didn't have to do* by changing these commands to past tense statements.

Example Rescue the victims quickly and carefully.
We had to rescue the victims.

1. Call the fire department fast!

2. Get a doctor!

3. Check the victims carefully!

4. Don't worry about the cat! It already jumped out the window.

5. Give the child artificial respiration!

6. Don't worry about the dog! It wasn't inside.

7. Check the man for injuries!

8. Control the man's bleeding!

6 **Practice** Look at the picture on page 154 of the accident scene. Imagine that you were the first person to arrive at the scene when the accident occurred. You arrived before the emergency crews. Write ten statements about what you had to do and didn't have to do. Then, share these with a partner.

C. Expressing Advice

In affirmative and negative statements and questions, *had better, should,* and *ought to* all express advice.

4.11 Expressing Advice: *Had better, Should,* and *Ought to*		
Structures	**Explanations**	**Examples**
Should (not) + **simple form**	With *should,* the negative is most often used in contracted form: *shouldn't.* When *should not* is used, it gives more emphasis to the negative.	You **should** leave the building right now. You **shouldn't** hesitate. You **should not** take anything with you!
Ought (not) to + **simple form**	*Ought to* and *had better* are seldom used in questions. Likewise, the negative contraction, *oughtn't* is not common.	We **ought to** call the fire department. They **ought not to** go down the stairs.
Had better + **simple form**	*Had better* is commonly used in contracted form: *You'd better....* The negative form is *had better not....* In rapid speech, *had,* in *had better,* is not always pronounced. For example, *You'd better* often sounds like */ya bedder/. Ought to* sounds like */otta/.*	He**'d better** get some oxygen. She**'d better not** stay in the building.

7 Practice In pairs, take turns making the following statements and responding to them. Make suggestions from the phrases in parentheses or invent your own suggestions. Use *had better, ought to,* and *should.*

Example A: My knee has been swollen and sore since I played tennis.
(go to an orthopedist)
B: *You'd better go to an orthopedist.*

1. I've had a headache for several days. (call the doctor)

2. I've had a toothache since last week. (see a dentist)

3. I can't see well at night anymore. (have your eyes checked)

4. I can't get rid of this cold. (stay in bed for a few days)

5. None of my clothes fit anymore. (go on a diet)

6. I'm not doing well in my classes. (study more)

7. I don't understand the next assignment. (talk to the teacher about it)

8. I have a problem with my visa. (check on it right away)

8 Practice Test your understanding and your memory. Without looking back, write *T* (true) or *F* (false) next to the following statements. After you have finished, look back at Activity 2 on page 152 and check your answers.

1. _____ You should always call for help immediately.

2. _____ You should check to make sure the victim is breathing.

3. _____ If the victim is breathing, you ought to try artificial respiration.

4. _____ If you believe that the victim has swallowed a poison, you should give the person water or milk to dilute it.

5. _____ You shouldn't try to give liquids to someone who is unconscious.

6. _____ In any emergency, you should move the victim immediately.

7. _____ You should always check for injuries before you try to move a victim.

8. _____ The last thing you ought to do is call for medical help.

9 Practice Change the following from commands to affirmative or negative statements by using *should, ought to, had better, have to,* or *must.*

Example If someone feels faint:
Have the person lie flat with his head low. *OR* Make the person lower his head between his knees and breathe deeply.
If someone feels faint, you should have him lie flat. You must keep his head low. Or, you should make him put his head between his knees and breathe deeply.

1. If someone gets cut seriously:
   Try to stop the bleeding at once.
   Use a clean bandage to cover the wound.
   Do not remove the bandage when the bleeding stops.
   Try to raise the wound up high.

2. If you suspect a broken bone:
   Don't let the victim bend the surrounding joints (knee, ankle, elbow, and so on).
   Give first aid for shock.
   Don't touch an open wound.
   Cover the wound gently.

3. If you suspect a head injury:
   Keep the person quiet.
   If possible, do not move him or her.
   Loosen the clothing around his or her neck.
   Do not give the person any stimulants (coffee, and so on).

4. If someone gets burned (first- or second-degree burns):
   Apply cold water until the pain goes away.
   Dry the burned area very gently.
   Cover the burn with a bandage to protect it, if necessary.
   Do not break any blisters or remove any skin.

5. If someone is choking:
   Hit the person's back, between the shoulder blades, with the heel of your hand as quickly and forcefully as possible.
   OR:
   Stand behind the person and wrap your arms around the upper stomach.
   With your closed fist, press against the upper stomach or lower chest several times quickly (the Heimlich maneuver).

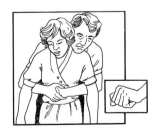

D. Expressing Advice About the Past (Action Not Taken)

In affirmative and negative statements questions, *should have* and *ought to have* give advice on past actions or situations. *Ought to have* is seldom used in questions, however.

4.12	Expressing Advice About the Past (Action Not Taken): *Should (not) Have, Ought (not)*	
Structures	**Explanations**	**Examples**
Should (not) have + past participle	Both *should have* and *ought to have* imply that the subject did not complete the action or take the advice. In rapid speech, these sound like /shudda/ and/ ottuv/.	You **should have** seen a doctor. **Should** I **have gone** to the nurse's office for a flu shot? We **ought to have** known that we'd catch colds in this rainy, chilly weather.
Ought (not) to have + past participle		

10 Practice In rapid conversation, it is often difficult to distinguish present and perfect modals. As your teacher reads the following sentences, circle the modal form (present or perfect) that you hear.

1. They (should come / should have come).

2. He (ought to set / ought to have set) a specific time.

3. She (should become / should have become) a doctor.

4. She (ought to quit / ought to have quit) her job.

5. It (should cost / should have cost) less.

6. We (shouldn't let / shouldn't have let) that happen.

7. He (ought to run / ought to have run) more often.

8. We (shouldn't shut / shouldn't have shut) all the windows.

9. That (shouldn't hurt / shouldn't have hurt) very much.

10. I (should buy / should have bought) some cough drops.

 11 Practice In pairs, respond to the following sentences with a statement using either *should have* or *ought to have*.

Example Jack studied first aid last semester.
     I should have studied it too, but I didn't.

1. Veronica went to the dentist last week.

2. Centa gave blood at the Red Cross.

3. Midori took a first aid class last quarter.

4. Ted checked his blood pressure this morning.

5. Futoshi had a checkup yesterday.

6. Nancy took Vitamin C this morning for her cold.

7. Carlos spent several hours reading his health insurance policy.

8. Ali studied for his anatomy exam last night.

12 **Practice** Veronica was the first to arrive at a car accident. She tried to help, but she panicked and did everything wrong. Use the information from Activity 2, page 152, and Activity 8, page 156, to help you tell what she *should (not) / ought (not) to have done.*

Example A young girl had a burn from an accident. Veronica washed the burn with hot water.
Veronica shouldn't have washed the burn with hot water. She should have applied cold water until the pain stopped.

1. One man started to faint. Veronica made him stand up quickly.

2. A woman had a head injury. Veronica had the woman walk around and drink several cups of coffee.

3. A boy had serious cuts. Veronica let the boy bleed for a few minutes. Then she covered the wound with a newspaper.

4. Another man had a broken arm. Veronica moved his elbow and shoulder to check them.

Using What You've Learned

13 **Using Your Common Sense** Think about the information on first aid that is given in this section. Then work in pairs or small groups and try to give "common sense" answers to the following questions.

Example If someone feels faint, why should you make the person lower his or her head and breathe deeply?
The person needs more oxygen going to his or her brain. Lowering his or her head will send more blood to the brain.

1. Should you try to move anyone who has had an accident? Why or why not?

2. Why should you check for injuries before moving a victim?

3. When should you move a victim? Try to give an example.

4. If someone has a serious cut, why should you raise the wound up high?

5. If someone is choking, where and why should you hit the person?

6. If someone has swallowed a chemical poison such as a cleaning fluid, why shouldn't you make the person try to vomit?

14 **Describing Folk Remedies** Around the world, many remedies exist for common problems and ailments. Such remedies are called folk remedies because they come from the wisdom of common people. Write a paragraph about a remedy for one of the following problems. Try to use *ought to, should,* and *have to* when possible as you discuss your cures.

indigestion	insomnia	heartburn
hiccups	a cold	a cramp in your leg
a rash	a toothache	stress
a headache	a stomachache	carsick or airsick

Part 4 | Modal Auxiliaries of Possibility and Probability

Setting the Context

▲ Rush-hour traffic

 Previewing the Passage Discuss the questions.

What is stress? What are some of the stressful things in your life each week?

Reading Read the passage.

Leisure Time and Your Health

How important is leisure time? How important is it to relax? Taking time to relax could one day save your life. In our fast-paced lives, it's almost impossible to avoid stress, but if we keep the stress inside, we may cause ourselves physical and psychological problems.

Stress is anything that puts an extra demand on us. We encounter stress at ⁵ school, at work, and at home. What happens when we feel stress? Our body responds to stress by "mobilizing its defenses." Blood pressure rises and muscles get ready to act. If our tension is not relieved, it may start a series of reactions, both physical and psychological.

What can we do? According to Hans Seyle of the University of Montreal, the ¹⁰ effects of stress depend not on what happens to us, but on the way we react. We can learn to relax in the face of stress. Through sports, games, hobbies and other leisure time activities, we can learn healthy ways of releasing stress instead of carrying it with us hour after hour, day after day.

Discussing Ideas Discuss the questions.

Do you take time to relax each day? What types of things do you do to relax?

Grammar Structures and Practice

A. Expressing Present and Past Possibility

In affirmative and negative statements, *may (have)*, *might (have)*, and *could (have)* express possibility. All mean "possibly" or "perhaps."

4.13	Expressing Present and Past Possibility		
Meanings	**Structures**	**Explanations**	**Examples**
Present Possibility	*may (not)* *might (not)* + simple *could (not)* form	*May, might,* and *could* express present possibility. *May* is not used with questions with this meaning.	He **may be** the youngest competitor. He **might win** if he keeps going this fast. He **might finish** the race first. **Could** he **win**?
Past Possibility	*may (not) have* *might (not) have* + past *could (not) have* participle	In rapid speech, *may have* is pronounced /mayuv/, *might have* is pronounced /mituv/, and *could have* is pronounced /cudduv/.	Jim **may have fallen** over something. He **might have hurt** himself. He **couldn't have hurt** himself very badly. He's getting up.

1 Practice Every day we face choices. Some are healthy and some are not. Here are some alternatives. Make sentences with *may, might,* and *could.* Use *or* as the connecting word.

Example eat some fruit/have an ice-cream cone

I might stay on my diet, or I might have an ice-cream cone.

1. exercise at the gym / watch TV
2. stay at home / hang out with friends
3. eat a banana / have some potato chips
4. try to fall asleep / watch another movie
5. mow the lawn / read the newspaper
6. spend the weekend studying / go out dancing
7. clean the room / play video games
8. take a walk / take a nap

2 Practice In the U.S. and Canada, there are many ways to spend your time actively. Some are expensive, but some cost little or nothing. Look at the list of activities on the next page, and add some of your own ideas. Then create at least eight sentences with *may, might,* and *could* to show possibilities. You can use these patterns:

I'd like to try (go) ..., but it's expensive, so I may (might, could) ... instead.

I would like to try (go) ...., but I don't have much money, so I ....

If I can afford it, I might ..., but if I can't, I may ....

Example *I'd really like to try ballooning, but it's an expensive hobby, so I might try hiking instead.*

High Cost		Low Cost or No Cost	
ballooning	scuba diving	backpacking	playing team sports
downhill skiing	skydiving	going to the beach	swimming
joining a fitness club	snowboarding	jogging	taking a walk
playing golf	waterskiing	hiking	visiting a park
sailing	windsurfing		

▲ Windsurfing

▲ Snowboarding

3 **Practice** Rephrase the following statements to use *may, might,* or *could have.*

Example Mary thinks she hurt herself when she went windsurfing.
Mary may (might) have hurt herself when she went windsurfing.

1. Bob thinks he left his surfboard at the beach.
2. I think his brother borrowed it.
3. Joan thinks Patrick was stranded on his board out in the water.
4. She thinks the wind stopped blowing.
5. Peter thinks they went windsurfing last week.
6. I think they went boogie boarding.
7. Bob thinks Alan hurt his head.
8. He thinks Alan got hit by somebody's board.
9. Michael thinks someone stole his windsurfing sail.
10. We think a friend found it and took it home.

4 **Practice** You are at the seashore with your friend. There are lots of people in the water and on the shore. There are also fish and marine mammals. You and your friend are looking out to sea. You are trying to identify the figures that you see moving about in and on the water. Use *may, might* or *could (have)* to guess what you are looking at.

Example There's something flying right over the water. It has a large bill.
It might be a pelican.

1. There's something inside that seashell. It's moving. It has claws.
2. It looks like there's a person standing on a board with a sail.
3. Something just jumped out of the water and back in. It was really big.
4. I see a black pipe just above the surface of the water. I also see rubber fins.
5. Those two swimmers out there have wet suits and some tanks on their backs. They have spears too.
6. There's a girl paddling out to that wave on her surfboard.
7. There were two surfers before that wave crashed. Now I only see one.
8. There are a lot of birds around that boat.
9. Some people seem to be digging in the sand.
10. That swimmer out there is holding onto the buoy.

B. Expressing Probability with *Must* and *Must Have*

In affirmative and negative statements, *must* and *must have* express probability. Both mean "probably."
- *May* is not used in this meaning.
- In rapid speech, *must have* is pronounced /mustuv/.

4.14	Expressing Probability with *Must* and *Must Have*	
Meanings	**Structures**	**Examples**
Present Probability	*must (not)* + simple form	You **must** like board games if you like Monopoly. You **must** be holding a Get Out of Jail Free card. You **must not** be worried about landing in jail.
Past Probability	*must (not) have* + past participle	You **must have** been happy to win the game. You **must have** been holding more than one Get Out of Jail Free card. You **must not have** worried about landing in jail.

5 Practice In pairs, take turns making statements and responses. Use *must* with the cues in parentheses to form your responses.

Example A: I am the chess champion of my school. (be pretty good)
   B: You must be pretty good.

1. I hear music coming out of Katie's room. (be listening to her new CD)
2. Fred likes poker and Monopoly. (like games of chance)
3. The kids put away the jigsaw puzzle. (finish it)
4. Dad didn't complete the crossword puzzle. (give up)
5. I see the card table is out and Mom's made her favorite dip. (be ready to play cards with her friends)
6. Johnny's name is at the top of the list on *Street Fighter.* (get the highest score)
7. The chessboard still has the pieces on it. (Bill and Bob . . . finish their match)
8. How strange! Mark is listening to the radio. (the television . . . be broken)
9. Lou had a big grin on his face when he got home from the poker game. (win)
10. Mike got a new computer game, but he returned it to the store today. (like it)

6 Practice In emotional situations, we often use *must feel* + adjective in a response to empathize with someone—to show that we understand. In pairs, take turns making statements with *must feel* + adjective. Choose appropriate adjectives for your responses. Use these words and statements, or create your own.

Positive Emotions	Negative Emotions	
ecstatic	angry	nervous
excited	awful	sad
happy	bored	scared
pleased	depressed	stressed
proud	exhausted	terrible
thrilled	frightened	upset
	frustrated	

Example A: I just won a Monopoly tournament! I'm the champ!
   B: You must feel ecstatic!

1. I just found out that I need to have a tooth pulled.
2. I just broke my surfboard on a rock. It was brand new.
3. I stayed up all night playing poker.
4. I just got some bad news from home.

5. I got a job teaching windsurfing.

6. I'm taking a scuba diving course beginning this weekend.

7. I just won a trophy in a surfing contest.

8. I was supposed to go up in a hot air balloon, but the weather is too bad to fly.

9. I just twisted my ankle skiing down that hill.

10. I can't see Alberto. He went body surfing in those huge waves.

 7 **Practice** In pairs, take turns making the following statements with *must have felt* + adjective.

Example A: I won six straight games of Monopoly from my brother. I'd never done
that before!
B: You must have felt great (good).

1. I fell off my surfboard and cut my leg on some coral.

2. I think I discovered a new star last night when I looked through my telescope.

3. I saw a pod of whales in the ocean yesterday.

4. I lost control of my windsurfer and started heading out to sea.

5. I am going on a long distance trip in a hot air balloon.

6. I lost every game of Monopoly that I played with my sister.

8 **Review** Complete the following with appropriate modal auxiliaries. Choose from the following: *can, could, may, might, should, would.* Add negatives when indicated. Note that more than one answer may be correct.

Something for Everyone

How _____ *can* _____ you stay physically active *and* enjoy yourself at the same time? Depending on where you live, there _____ *should* _____ be many possibilities. Some _____ be expensive, but others
1
_____ be low-cost or no-cost. Here are some ideas:
2

• _____ you like to try windsurfing, one of the hottest
3
and coolest sports around? Windsurfing is the sport for people who love the water but who _____ (not) get to the ocean regu-
4
larly. You _____ try it on a lake or a river or even a
5
pond. You _____ plan on spending three to six hours to
6

learn, and you _____ also plan on getting wet! Learning
        7
to windsurf usually means a lot of falls into the water.

- There are some things that you _____ do anywhere,
                                        8
  like observing birds. Bird watching is a pastime, even a competitive
  sport, for millions of people around the world. You
  _____ think that bird watching is only to find rare birds
          9
  in wild places, but it _____ be exciting to observe birds
                                10
  close to home, too. The sport is relaxing but rewarding for anyone who
  _____ like to spend time outdoors.
          11

- Some people _____ never imagine themselves standing
                      12
  in a basket and floating in the sky with only a small tank of gas as a
  power source, but others _____ love to try the exciting
                                    13
  sport of ballooning. For people who _____ like to
                                                14
  escape the work and worry on Earth, hot-air balloon
  _____ be just the right sport! They
          15
  _____ leave their troubles on the ground while they
          16
  float across the skies above.

- In the early 19th century, only the rich _____ afford to
                                                    17
  buy a bicycle because they were so expensive. Later, bicycles became
  more affordable, but most people _____ (not) dare to
                                            18
  ride one. The bicycle boom actually began many years later, in the late
  19th century. By 1899, one out of every six Americans
  _____ ride a bike. At that time, bicycle events and races
          19
  were some of the most popular activities in America. In fact, individuals
  and families _____ spend an entire weekend bicycling.
                      20
  Even the *New York Times* hired special reporters to cover races.

9 **Guessing About Each Other** Look around the room. Is anyone absent from class? Does anyone look particularly excited or happy? Does anyone look worried? Does anyone look as if he or she is not feeling well? Try to guess why.

Example   Jorge is not here.
He may be sick.
He might have gone away for a long weekend.
He must not have done his homework!

10 **Imagine Yourself a Hero** Your town is giving you a parade because you are a hero. You have done something very brave. Write a paragraph in which you describe what you must have done to become a hero.

11 **Talking About Activities** The chart on the next page shows the American Cancer Society's recommendations on exercise and physical activity. In pairs or small groups, read through the activities and discuss any new vocabulary. Add other activities, if you wish, and then try to make a weekly plan for yourself. Considering your age and your current situation, try to plan activities for the next several weeks. A month from now, report back to your class on what you could and couldn't do.

Adopt a physically active lifestyle!

Recommendations from the American Cancer Society:

- Adults should get at least 30 minutes or more of moderate exercise on five or more days of the week

- To reduce cancer risks, adults should try to do 45 minutes or more of moderate to vigorous activity on five or more days per week.

- Children and adolescents should get at least 60 minutes per day of moderate-to-vigorous physical activity for at least five days per week.

Examples of Moderate and Vigorous Physical Activities		
	Moderate Activities	**Vigorous Activities**
Exercise	Walking, dancing, leisurely bicycling, ice-skating or roller-skating, horseback riding, canoeing, yoga	Jogging or running, fast bicycling, circuit weight training, aerobic dance, martial arts, jump rope, swimming
Sports	Volleyball, golfing, softball, baseball, badminton, doubles tennis, downhill skiing	Soccer, field hockey or ice hockey, lacrosse, singles tennis, racquetball, basketball, cross-country
Home Activities	Mowing the lawn, general lawn and garden maintenance	Digging, carrying and hauling, masonry, carpentry
Occupational Activity	Walking and lifting as part of the job (custodial work, farming, auto or machine repair)	Heavy manual labor (forestry, construction, firefighting)

Setting the Context

 Previewing the Passage Discuss the questions.

What do we mean by "lifestyle?" What words can be used to describe a lifestyle?

Reading Read the passage.

A Healthier Lifestyle

Mario: You don't look very happy. What's wrong?

Pablo: Well, I went to the doctor for my annual medical check up, and I may have some health problems. My doctor said that I had to make some lifestyle changes.

Mario: What did the doctor tell you?

Pablo: He told me that I should change my diet and that I had to get more exercise. He urged me to exercise for an hour at least five times each week and to stop eating junk food. He said that I should eat more fruit and vegetables and I should avoid a lot of sugar and fat. If I don't, he said I might develop some serious problems.

Mario: Say, you shouldn't feel depressed about that! That's just a good, healthy lifestyle. You'll feel better and look better. So, you don't have serious health problems yet, right? A better lifestyle is prevention, right? So, hopefully you won't have problems later if you do what your doctor said.

Discussing Ideas Discuss the questions.

In your opinion, what is a healthy lifestyle? What do you do to have a healthy lifestyle and to prevent medical problems later in life?

Grammar Structures and Practice

A. Changes in Modal Auxiliaries with Reported Speech

Different modals may or may not have to change in reported speech.

4.15 Changes in Modal Auxiliaries with Reported Speech			
Structures	**Explanations**	**Quotations with Modal Auxiliaries**	**Reported Speech**
Can, may, must* (referring to need), and *will	In reported speech, the modal auxiliaries *can*, *may*, *must* (referring to need), and *will* also shift to past forms.	"Ann **can help** Chris." "John **may help** too." "We all **must help** Chris." "Mario **will** also **help**."	Susan said that Ann **could help** Chris. She added John **might help,** too. She repeated that we all **had to help** Chris. She mentioned Mario **would** also **help**.
***Must* (expressing probability)**	When *must* expresses probability, it does not change.	"Chris **must be** tired."	She said that Chris **must be** tired.
***Could, might, ought to, should, would,* and all perfect modals**	*Could, might, ought to, should, would,* and all perfect modals do not change.	Adriana **could help** later. Jenny **could have helped** yesterday.	She mentioned that Adriana **could help** later. She added that Jenny **could have helped** yesterday.

1 Practice Here are tips for a healthy lifestyle. Imagine that your doctor has told you to do these things. Change each sentence to reported speech. Begin your new sentences with *The doctor said that...*, *The doctor told me that...*, *The doctor mentioned that ...*, *The doctor added that ...*, or *The doctor stated that ...*.

Examples   You must get more exercise.
   The doctor said that I must get more exercise.
   You can go to the gym every day.
   The doctor added that I could go to the gym every day.

1. Everyone should get regular exercise.

2. Regular exercise may help to prevent heart disease.

3. We can join a health club.

4. Students could use the gym at school.

5. You should join an exercise class.

6. You could swim at the pool.

7. I may take a yoga class.

8. I might join a basketball team.

9. We could play soccer.

10. You should improve your diet.

11. You should include vegetables and fruits at every meal and for snacks.

12. We must limit French fries, snack chips, and other fried vegetable products.

13. You can choose whole grain rice, bread, pasta, and cereals.

14. We should limit the amount of red meat we eat.

15. Everyone can choose foods that help maintain a healthy weight.

B. Commands, Modal Auxiliaries, and Reported Speech

In reported speech, commands can be changed to clauses with *should* or a form of *have to.*

- Depending on the time frames of the conversation, *have to, has,* or *had to* can be used.
- Commands can also be changed to infinitive phrases. The infinitive expresses the same meaning as *should/have to* + simple form. Chapter 7 has more information on infinitives.
- The verbs *advise, beg, command, direct, encourage, order, urge,* and *warn* follow the same pattern as *tell* in infinitive phrases. The indirect object must be used.

4.16 Commands, Model Auxiliaries, and Reported Speech

Quotations with Commands	Reported Speech with *Should*	Infinitive Phrases
She said, "**Come** home early."	She said that we **should come** home early.	She said **to come** home early.
She told us, "**Come** home early."	She told us that we **should come** home early.	She told us **to come** home early. She advised (urged) us **to come** home early.
Quotations with Commands	Reported Speech with *Have to*	Infinitive Phrases
She said, "**Come** home early."	She said that we **have to come** home early. (close to the present)	She said **to come** home early.
She told us, "**Come** home early."	She told us that we **had to come** home early. (in the past)	She told us **to come** home early. She advised (urged) us **to come** home early.

2 Practice Imagine that you're taking a yoga class. Change the commands first to reported speech with *should* or *had to*. Then change the clauses to infinitive phrases. Remember to add modal auxiliaries and nouns or pronouns when necessary.

Example The instructor said, "Stand up."
The instructor said that we should stand up.
The instructor said to stand up.

1. The instructor ordered, "Be quiet and breathe deeply."
2. The instructor told us, "Stand very straight."
3. The instructor said, "Do not sit down yet."
4. The teacher said, "Stretch your arms and your legs."
5. The teacher said, "Bend and touch your hands to the floor."
6. The teacher told us, "Twist from side to side."
7. The teacher encouraged us, "Loosen up."
8. The teacher advised, "Continue breathing deeply."
9. The instructor told us, "Lie down on your mat."
10. The teacher said, "Close your eyes."
11. The teacher added, "Don't open your eyes till I tell you to."
12. The instructor encouraged us, "Relax."

▲ Yoga is a combination of exercise and meditation. The purpose of yoga is to create strength, awareness, and harmony in both mind and body.

C. Reduction of Requests for Action and for Permission

Certain requests for action or permission can also be reduced to infinitive phrases.

- Requests with *Will you...*, *Can you...*, *Would you...*, and *Could you...* can be reduced to infinitive phrases. The indirect object *must* be used with the infinitive phrase.
- Requests with *May I...*, *Could I...*, and *Can I...* can also be reduced to infinitive phrases, but *no* indirect object is used.

4.17 Reduction of Requests for Action and for Permission

Quotations with Requests for Action	Reported Speech with Modal Auxiliaries	Infinitive Phrases
She asked (us), "**Will** you **come** home early?" She asked, "**Could** you **help** me?"	She asked (us) if we **would come** early. She asked (us) whether we **could help** her.	She asked us **to come** early. She asked us **to help** her.

Quotations with Requests for Permission	Reported Speech with Modal Auxiliaries	Infinitive Phrases
She asked (me), "**Could I speak** to John?"	She asked (me) if she **could speak** to John.	She asked **to speak** to John.

---

3 Practice Change the quotations to reported speech using noun clauses. Then reduce the noun clauses to infinitive phrases. Remember to add nouns or pronouns when necessary.

Example She asked, "Could I help you?"
She asked if she could help me.
She asked to help me.

1. She asked, "Could you tell me the time?"

2. He asked, "May I use your phone?"

3. They asked their lawyer, "Would you please read this?"

4. The little boy asked his mother, "Can I go to Martin's house?"

5. The students asked their teacher, "Will you please postpone the next test?"

6. The policewoman asked, "May I see your driver's license?"

7. I asked, "Could you give me some change?"

8. Omar asked Joel, "Will you help me with my homework?"

9. Bedi asked Ahmed, "Would you lend me some money till the weekend?"

10. Emiko asked Seiji, "Could I borrow your dictionary?"

11. The mother asked her son, "Will you pick up your toys, please?"

12. The tourists asked, "Could you give us directions to the museum?"

D. Reduction of Embedded Questions

Yes/no questions with modal auxiliaries can be reduced to infinitive phrases. *Whether (or not)* is always used with an infinitive form.

- Information questions (with *how, what, when,* and *where*) may also be reduced.
- With both types of questions, the speaker and the subject of the question *must* be the same person(s).
- Indirect objects are not necessary with either type of reduced question.

4.18 Reduction of Embedded Questions		
Quotations with Yes/No Questions	**Reported Speech with Noun Clauses**	**Reduction to Infinitive Phrases**
We asked (her), "**Should** we **leave** now?" We asked (her), "**Should** we **come** at six or at seven?"	We asked (her) if we **should leave** then. We asked (her) whether we **should come** at six or at seven.	We asked (her) whether (or not) **to leave** then. We asked (her) whether **to return** at six or at seven.
Quotations with Information Questions	**Reported Speech with Noun Clauses**	**Reduction to Infinitive Phrases**
We asked (her), "How **can** we **get** to your house?" We asked (her), "Where **should** we **park**?"	We asked (her) how we **could get** to her house. We asked (her) where we **should park**.	We asked (her) how **to get** to her house. We asked (her) where **to park**.

4 **Practice** Change the quotations to reported speech using noun clauses. Then reduce the noun clauses to infinitive phrases.

Example He asked, "Where can I park nearby?"
He asked where he could park nearby.
He asked where to park nearby.

1. The man asked, "Where should I park?"

2. He asked, "Could you give me change for a dollar?"

3. The woman asked, "Why did I get a parking ticket?"

4. She wondered, "What can I do about this ticket?"

5. The bus driver asked, "Would you like some help?"

6. The passenger wondered, "Where should I get off the bus?"

7. The parents asked, "Should we buy that house?"

8. I wondered, "Should I call the doctor?"

9. The tourists asked the officer, "How can we get to the library from here?"

10. We asked, "When should we leave for the play?"

11. Pablo asked, "Which pages should I study for the test?"

12. Nadia wondered, "How long will the test take?"

Using What You've Learned

5 **Reading a Chart** In pairs, read through the following suggestions from the American Cancer Society (ACS) on healthy living in your day-to-day life. Check the meaning of any words or phrases you don't know. Then, add other ideas to the recommendations from the ACS. Try to add at least 10 new suggestions. You can use information from other parts of this chapter, such as the charts on pages 137 and 169.

Now, on your own, create two personal lists. On the first list, include statements of things that you already do. On the second list, put at least five statements of things that you can, may, might, should, or will do to become more active. A month from now, you can report to the class on how well your new lifestyle is going!

Helpful Ways to Be More Active

- Use stairs rather than an elevator.
- If you can, walk or bike to your destination.
- Exercise at lunch with your workmates, family, or friends.
- Take a 10-minute exercise break at lunch or at work to stretch or take a quick walk.
- Walk to visit friends or co-workers instead of sending an email.
- Go dancing with your spouse, friends, or classmates.
- Plan active vacations rather than only driving trips.
- Wear a pedometer every day and watch your daily steps increase.
- Go to the gym or fitness center at your school or work.
- Do stretching exercises throughout the day.
- Join a sports team.
- Use a stationary bicycle while watching TV.
- Take a walk every evening.
- Plan your exercise routine to gradually increase the days per week and minutes per session.

Focus on Testing

Use of Modal Auxiliaries

Model auxiliaries are frequently tested on standardized English proficiency exams. Review these commonly tested structures and check your understanding by completing the sample items below.

Remember that . . .

✔ Modal auxiliaries are followed by the simple form of a verb.
✔ Perfect modal auxiliaries use modal + *have* + past participle.
✔ In reported speech, some modals change while other modals do not.

Part 1 Mark the correct completion for the following sentences.

Example John _____ sick; he didn't go to class yesterday.

    (A) may   (C) must

    (B) may have being   (D) must have been.

1. A person who is physically fit _____ the same weight.

    (A) should able to stay   (C) should being able to stay

    (B) should to be able stay   (D) should be able to stay

2. Syrup of ipecac _____ the best known antidote to most poisons.

    (A) maybe   (C) may be

    (B) may to be   (D) may being

3. If an accident victim is dizzy and cannot move an arm or leg, she _____ a head injury.

    (A) could be have   (C) could be had

    (B) could have   (D) could had had

4. Nestor said they _____ windsurfing because there was no wind.

    (A) must go   (C) couldn't go

    (B) could have gone   (D) may not go

5. When the sea is rough, you _____ take more precautions in the water.

    (A) have to   (C) have

    (B) must to   (D) had to

Part 2 Circle the letter below the underlined word(s) containing an error.

Example An individual <u>may to feel</u> frustrated if she has <u>difficulties</u> in <u>speaking</u>
Ⓐ
                        B   C
the language of the country <u>where she is living</u>.
                D

1. She would <u>much</u> rather <u>to exercise</u> moderately <u>than</u> <u>strenuously</u>.
      A   B   C   D

2. A person <u>may had had</u> a heart attack <u>if he or she</u> has <u>chest pain</u> and <u>breathing</u>
      A   B   C   D
difficulties.

3. Most people <u>who eat</u> a healthy diet should <u>be able get</u> all the calcium
      A   B
<u>they need</u> from their normal <u>food intake</u>.
  C   D

4. Jim <u>may feel</u> a little nervous because this <u>might have be</u> the first
   A   B
<u>snowboarding competition</u> that he <u>will enter</u> this year.
    C   D

5. Mary told <u>us</u> that she <u>will like</u> to hear from you if you <u>have</u> the time <u>to write</u>
    A   B   C   D
her.

Self-Assessment Log

Each of the following statements describes the grammar you learned in this chapter. Read the statements; then check the box that describes how well you understand each structure.

	Needs Improvement	Good	Great
I can use modal auxiliaries and other structures to express ability and expectations.	❑	❑	❑
I can use modal auxiliaries and other structures to make requests, ask for permission, and express preferences.	❑	❑	❑
I can use modal auxiliaries and other structures to discuss needs and advice.	❑	❑	❑
I can use modal auxiliaries to express possibilities and probabilities.	❑	❑	❑
I can use modal auxiliaries in reported speech.	❑	❑	❑
I can take a test about modal auxiliaries and related structures.	❑	❑	❑

High Tech, Low Tech

In This Chapter

The Passive Voice

Part 1 The Passive Voice with Simple Tenses

Part 2 The Passive Voice with Perfect Tenses

Part 3 The Passive Voice with Continuous Tenses

Part 4 The Passive Voice with Modal Auxiliaries

Part 5 Review of Chapters 1–5

> **"** The science of today is the technology of tomorrow. **"**
>
> —Edward Teller
> U.S. nuclear physicist
> (1908–2003)

Connecting to the Topic

1 What is the word "tech" a shortened form of?

2 What is meant by "High Tech, Low Tech?" Can you give some examples of each?

3 What is your favorite new technology?

In this chapter, you will study the forms and uses of verbs in the passive voice. You will notice that the time frame of a passive verb may be the same as that of an active verb, but the focus of the passive sentence is quite different. As you study the chapter, pay careful attention to the focus of the passive constructions.

Reading Read the following passage. It introduces the chapter theme, "High Tech, Low Tech," and raises some of the topics and issues you will cover in the chapter.

Old and New Technology

Old inventions are not necessarily eliminated by new ones. After all, people did not stop riding bicycles after the car was invented. Thus, older inventions may be replaced, but they seldom disappear because new roles are created for them. Some of the best examples of this are from the field of long-distance communication.

Until the 19th century, communication had been limited by distance and time. Then came a series of amazing inventions that extended the range of human communication. Each of these inventions was expected to replace existing technology. For example, when the telephone was invented in 1876, it was feared that letters would become obsolete. When television was introduced in the 1940s, many people predicted the "death" of radio. And as television became more popular, people worried that it would lead to the "death" of books and reading. But it is clear that these predictions were wrong. The older technologies—letters, books, and the radio—have not disappeared. Instead, their roles have been changed by the appearance of new technology. Television, together with the automobile, has provided a new role for the radio. Both television and the radio have created new roles for the newspaper. And all of these have affected the book.

The technology of the 21st century is progressing rapidly. With the availability and affordability of the personal computer, more and more households are wired to the World Wide Web on the Internet. This puts the individual in contact with people and information that can be located anywhere in the world. As a result, communication today is both more global and more personal than ever before.

At the same time, the inventions of one and two centuries before still play important roles in the daily life of millions of people all over the world. The telephone and the television, in their new forms, such as the cell phone and PDAs, are still with us. And, oh yes, that most ancient technology, the book, is still with us, too.

Discussing Ideas Discuss the questions.

Can you think of examples of new inventions that have made old inventions obsolete? Can you think of products or systems that may become obsolete due to new inventions? For example, will email completely replace regular mail?

Part 1 The Passive Voice with Simple Tenses

Setting the Context

Previewing the Passage Discuss the questions.

What do you know about early forms of long-distance communication? How did people communicate with each other from far away?

Reading Read the passage.

The Telephone: Past, Present, and Future

During most of human history, even the most important news was difficult to deliver. Then, in the 1800s, the telephone was invented. At first people were suspicious of the new technology, but today millions of phone calls are made daily by people all over the world. Some offices already have "videophones," telephones connected to video screens that allow callers to see one another as they speak. In the future, videophones will be installed in every home and office, just as ordinary telephones are today.

5

Discussing Ideas Discuss the questions.

What would your life be like today without telephones? What will your life be like in a world of "videophones"?

▲ A meeting using a videophone

Grammar Structures and Practice

A. Introduction to the Passive Voice

Most transitive verbs (verbs that take an object) can be used in both the active voice and the passive voice.

- A form of the verb *be* is always used in passive sentences. It is singular or plural to agree with the subject, and it also tells the tense of the passive construction.
- The time frame of a passive verb may be the same as that of an active verb, but the focus of the sentence is different.

5.1 Introduction to the Passive Voice

	Examples	Focus of the sentence
Active	DIRECT SUBJECT VERB OBJECT Alexander Graham Bell **invented** the telephone.	Alexander Graham Bell
Passive	AGENT The telephone **was invented** by Alexander Graham Bell.	the telephone
Active	DIRECT SUBJECT VERB OBJECT Millions of people **use** the Internet every day.	millions of people
Passive	AGENT The Internet **is used** by millions of people every day.	the Internet

1 **Practice** Which of the following sentences are in the active voice and which are in the passive voice? Label each. Then label the subject (S), verb (V), object (O), and / or agent (A) in each sentence. Put one line under the subjects and two lines under the verbs. Finally, tell the primary focus of each sentence.

Example _Passive_ The first fax machine <u>was manufactured</u> by Muirhead, Ltd., of England. *Focus: the first fax machine*

Active Muirhead, Ltd., of England <u>manufactured</u> the first fax machine. *Focus: Muirhead, Ltd.*

1. _____ The telephone was invented by Alexander Graham Bell in 1876.

2. _____ The phonograph was invented by Thomas Edison in 1877.

3. _____ Warner Brothers introduced movies with sound in 1927.

4. _____ Bank credit cards were first introduced by Bank of America in 1958.

5. _____ Intel Corporation created the first microprocessor for computers in 1971.

6. _____ Martin Cooper invented the first cell phone in 1973.

7. _____ The Walkman was developed by Sony Corporation in 1979.

8. _____ Microsoft released Windows 1.0 in 1985.

9. _____ Apple produced the first version of Powerbook in 1989.

10. _____ Computer companies released the first PDAs for sale in 1993.

11. _____ In the 1990s the BlackBerry was developed.

12. _____ The first iPod was released by Apple in 2001.

B. The Passive Voice with Simple Tenses

- The passive voice of verbs in simple tenses is formed in this way: *(will) be (am, is, are, was, were)* + past participle (+ *by* + agent).
- Adverbs of frequency usually come after the first auxiliary verb.
- The verb *be* is singular or plural, depending on the passive voice subject.
- The passive forms have the same general meanings and time frames as verbs in the active voice.

5.2 The Passive Voice with Simple Tenses		Examples	Focus
Simple Past	Active	A computer company **installed** a new computer network in our office.	a computer company
	Passive	A new computer network **was installed** in our office (by a computer company).	a new computer network
Simple Present	Active	Computer companies **install** new computer networks every day.	computer companies
	Passive	New computer networks **are installed** (by computer companies) every day.	new computer networks
Simple Future	Active	A computer company **will install** a new computer network next week.	a computer company
	Passive	A new computer network **will be installed** (by a computer company) next week.	a new computer network

2 Practice Underline the uses of the passive voice in the passage "The Telephone: Past, Present, and Future" on page 183. Give the tense of each.

3 Practice Complete the following by using the past, present, or future tense of the verbs in parentheses. Use the passive voice. Remember that singular subjects take singular verbs and plural subjects take plural verbs.

Example Until the latter part of the 20th century, most day-to-day information _____*was stored*_____ in a card filing system.

1. The first generation of computers _____ (invent) in the early 1940s.

2. Today the computer _____ (take) for granted by much of the world.

3. Between 1980 and 2000, millions of personal computers _____ (sell) to consumers.

4. Computers _____ (use) by over 500 million people throughout the world.

5. Today, almost the entire world _____ (connect) by the Internet.

6. In many offices, computers _____ (connect) to each other in a network.

7. Messages _____ (received) via email.

8. Written documents _____ (transmit) by computer and then printed out on printers.

9. In the future, even faster computers _____ (invent).

10. Soon the telephone and personal computer _____ (replace) by a handheld communication device.

▲ Computers are widely available on most college campuses.

C. The Passive Voice in Sentences with Indirect Objects

Passive voice sentences may be made from sentences with both a direct and indirect object.

- In active voice sentences with both a direct and an indirect object, either object may become the subject of the corresponding passive sentence.
- Sentence focus is on the passive voice subject.

5.3 The Passive Voice in Sentences with Indirect Objects		
Structures	**Active**	**Passive**
Direct Object	The United States gave **the patent** for the telephone to Bell.	**The patent** for the telephone was given to Bell by the United States.
Indirect Object	The United States gave **Bell** the patent for the telephone.	**Bell** was given the patent for the telephone by the United States.

 4 Practice Sit in groups of three students. Student A should read the active voice sentences that follow. Students B and C should change them to the passive voice. Follow the example.

Example   A: The school secretary gave Sam an important message.
B: Sam was given an important message by the school secretary.
C: An important message was given to Sam by the school secretary.

1. The phone company sent me information about new types of phone service.

2. Mrs. Jones will give the results of the test to the students within the next week.

3. The salesman showed Mr. Sanchez some computer software.

4. Every year, a rich businesswoman gives our town $100,000 to spend on the schools.

5. The judges awarded Joseph first prize in the essay contest.

6. My father lent me that beautiful sports car.

7. Young-hoon gave Ali a cell phone.

8. Martin will buy Camila a PDA.

9. The school gave each student a new computer.

10. My children sent me an iPod for my birthday.

5 Practice The following sentences are in the active voice. Some of the sentences have objects, but others, with linking verbs, do not. Decide which sentences can be changed to the passive voice. Label the subject (S), verb (V), and object (O) in each sentence. Then change the sentence to the passive voice. In sentences with a direct and an indirect object, give both possibilities.

Example
                      S   *V*
Philipp Reis was a German inventor. *cannot be changed*

               S   *V*   *O*
Reis designed an early telephone around 1861.

An early telephone was designed by Reis around 1861.

1. According to most history books, Alexander Graham Bell invented the telephone.

2. The true story is more dramatic, however.

3. In 1876, two inventors completed patent applications on the same day.

4. One was a schoolteacher named Alexander Graham Bell.

5. The other was a professional inventor named Elisha Gray.

6. Gray and Bell did not work together.

7. The two inventors developed very similar telephones.

8. Gray finished first.

9. However, the U.S. Patent Office received Bell's application two hours before Gray's.

10. Thus, the Patent Office gave the official patent to Alexander Graham Bell.

11. Elisha Gray took Bell to court.

12. Gray sued Bell for the rights to the talking machine.

13. Bell won in court.

14. The Patent Office awarded the patent to Bell.

15. To this day, the whole world gives credit to Bell for inventing the telephone.

6 Practice Marc, Sharon, and Annette McLean are planning a surprise party for their parents' anniversary Friday evening. Today is Thursday. The list on page 189 shows which tasks the children completed before today. (These tasks are indicated by a ✔.) Other tasks will be done as indicated. Use the information in the list to write 10 additional passive sentences in the past and future tenses.

Examples *The invitations were ordered by Marc two months ago.*
The turkey will be cooked by Annette on Friday afternoon.

Marc	Sharon	Annette
✓ order invitations—2 months ago	✓ pick up invitations from printer—1 month ago	✓ address and mail invitations—3 weeks ago
buy flowers—Friday afternoon	✓ bake the cake—Wednesday night	cook the turkey—Friday afternoon
set the table—Friday afternoon	✓ buy champagne—Tuesday	buy decorations—last week
clean the house—Friday morning	clean the house—Friday morning	put up the decorations—Friday afternoon

D. *By* + Agent

By + noun (or pronoun) can be used in passive sentences to tell who or what performed the action of the verb.

- Most passive sentences in English do not contain phrases with *by*, however.
- Use *by* + agent only if the phrase gives the following information:

5.4 *By* + Agent

Information Types	Explanations	Examples
Information Necessary to the Meaning of the Sentence	*By* + agent must be used if the sentence is meaningless without it.	The majority of overseas phone calls are transmitted **by satellite**.
A Name or Idea that Is Important in the Context	Proper names are often included because they give specific information. Other nouns and pronouns are often omitted.	The telephone was invented by **Alexander Graham Bell**. Telephones are made ~~by people~~ in factories.
New or Unusual Information	*By* + agent is generally included if the phrase introduces new or unusual information. After the agent is understood, the phrase is usually omitted to avoid repetition.	Today most overseas calls are transmitted **by satellite**. The calls are beamed ~~by satellite~~ from one country to another.

7 **Practice** In a "team" or "group" effort, the final result or product is more important than the effort of each individual. In speaking and in writing, passive sentences are often used to focus on the product or result. Passive sentences without *by* + agent give even more emphasis to *what* was done, not *who* did it. Look at your sentences from Activity 6 again. Rewrite each sentence, but this time, omit *by* + agent. Compare each set of sentences, and notice the difference in emphasis.

Example order invitations—two months ago

The invitations were ordered by Marc two months ago.
The invitations were ordered two months ago.
(The second sentence puts more emphasis on the action.)

8 Practice Read the following passive voice sentences below and underline the phrase with *by* in each sentence. Then decide whether each *by* + agent is necessary to the meaning of the sentence. Tell which phrases you would omit and why.

Examples Before companies like Federal Express, airmail letters and packages were transported by <u>commercial airlines</u>.
Do not omit the phrase because it tells who transported airmail letters and packages.

In those days, letters and packages were often lost <u>by people</u>.
The phrase can be omitted. It is obvious that mail was lost by people.

1. Federal Express, the first overnight package delivery company, was started by Frederick Smith in 1973.

2. Similar companies were created by people in the years that followed.

3. Before Federal Express was created by Smith, packages were always shipped by air freight companies on regular commercial airlines.

4. In those days, fast delivery of packages was never guaranteed by anybody.

5. Commercial airline flights were often delayed by bad weather or equipment problems.

6. Packages were sometimes lost by the airlines.

7. Sometimes packages were delivered by the air freight companies weeks after the mailing date.

8. At Federal Express, overnight delivery is guaranteed by the company.

9. Federal Express planes and trucks are used by the company in order to guarantee service.

10. Currently, over three million packages are delivered worldwide by FedEx each day.

E. Verbs Commonly Used in the Passive Voice

The following verbs are frequently used in the passive voice.
- A variety of prepositions can follow them.
- *By* is also used depending on the context.

5.5 Verbs Commonly Used in the Passive Voice

Verbs		Examples
be based on	be involved in (with)	The movie **was based on** the novel.
be connected to	be located in (at, on)	Wash your hands! You **are covered with** dirt!
be covered with	be made of (from)	He **was known for** his honesty.
be filled with (by)	be made up of	He **was known as** a very honest person.
be formed of (from, by)	be related to	The class **is made up of** students from many places.
be known for (as)	be used for (as, with)	She **is related to** the president.
be known to + *verb*	be used to + *verb* + *-ing*	

Note: See Chapter 7 for information on verbs of emotion in passive constructions *(He's interested in sports. I'm bored with that book.).*

---

9 **Practice** Complete the following sentences by adding appropriate forms of the verbs in parentheses. Use past, present, or future tenses. Then add appropriate prepositions in the spaces provided. Include adverbs when indicated.

Example Today, magazines and newspapers _____*are filled*_____ (fill) _____*with*_____ stories about the Internet.

1. Electronic mail, which _____ (know / commonly)

   _____ email, is the fastest growing means of communication

   in the world.

2. Today, millions of people from all seven continents _____

   (connect) _____ each other through the Internet.

3. Today's Internet _____ (base) _____ a

   network built for researchers in the United States during the 1970s.

4. The original network of the 1970s _____ (use)

   _____ communicating about research projects at different

   universities.

5. At that time, most of the research projects _____ (relate)

   _____ the defense industry.

6. Today, the Internet _____ (make / actually)

   _____ hundreds of regional computer networks.

7. Today, networks _____ (locate) _____

   countries all over the world.

8. Each year the number of companies that _____ (involve)

   _____ Internet sales has increased.

F. Anticipatory *It* and the Passive Voice

The passive voice is often used with *it* to avoid mentioning the agent or source.

- *By* + agent is rarely used with these constructions.
- *It* is often used with the passive form of verbs such as *believe, confirm, deny, estimate, fear, hope, mention, report, say,* and *think.*

5.6 Anticipatory *It* with the Passive Voice

Verbs Commonly Used with *It*		Explanations	Examples	
believe confirm deny estimate fear	hope mention report say think	Past expressions like *it was believed* often indicate that these ideas have changed. *That* is added when a direct quote is changed to reported speech. In reported speech, verbs often shift to past tenses.	**Active** **Passive**	**People said**, "The earth is flat." **It was said**, "The earth is flat." **It was said** that the earth **was** flat. **It was believed** that the earth **was** flat.

10 **Practice** As we learn more about our world, many of our beliefs change. Expressions such as *it was believed, felt, thought,* or *said that . . .* are used to indicate past beliefs that have changed. In these cases, *would* and *was/were going to* express "the future in the past."

Rephrase the following quotations to include these expressions:

It was believed that . . .	It was feared that . . .
It was said that . . .	It was thought that . . .
It was felt that . . .	It was hoped that . . .

Note: Remember to use past forms in the *that* clause.

Examples   "The telephone is going to change people's lives."
It was feared that the telephone was going to change people's lives.

"People won't write letters anymore."
It was believed that people wouldn't write letters anymore.

1. "People will forget how to read."

2. "Parents will not be able to supervise their children's conversations."

3. "Telephones are going to eliminate the postal service."

4. "Paper companies will go out of business."

5. "People are going to gossip more."

6. "People are not going to have any privacy."

7. "People won't send telegrams anymore."

8. "Letters will become obsolete."

Cultural Note

The Spread of New Technology
The radio had existed almost 40 years before it began being used regularly by 50 million people. The TV had existed over 12 years before it reached 50 million viewers. After 16 years in existence, the personal computer was being used by 50 million people. In contrast, within only four years of the Internet's being opened to the public, 50 million people were connected.

11 Practice Read the following passage for meaning. Then complete the passage with either active or passive forms (simple present or past tenses) of the verbs in parentheses. The first two are done as examples.

The Impact of the Telephone

Many new inventions __are used__ every day, but the telephone __became__
                (use)   (become)
an everyday item faster than almost any other invention in history. In May 1877,

six telephones _____ in commercial use. In November 1877,
                1 (be)

there _____ 3000, and by 1881, 133,000. Today, people every-
          2 (be)

where _____ by the telephone, although most of us
         3 (affect)

_____ it without really thinking about it. In the beginning, how-
    4 (use)
ever, many people _____ the telephone. It
                        5 (fear)
_____ by some that the telephone _____ evil,
    6 (believe)   7 (be)
and laws _____ by a few to prohibit telephones in bedrooms in
            8 (suggest)
order to prevent secret conversations. (Telephones would allow private romantic conversations, and this would corrupt people, especially young girls!) But,
these ideas and fears _____ as the demand for telephones
                            9 (overcome)
grew.

At first in the United States, young boys _____ to operate
                                                10 (employ)
the telephone switchboards, but because of their bad language and tricks many
of them _____ their jobs. Soon, in September 1878, Emma M.
            11 (lose)
Nutt _____ as the first woman telephone operator. In France,
        12 (hire)
women _____ from the beginning. This was in part because all
            13 (employ)
boys and young men _____ to serve in the army. More impor-
                        14 (require)
tant, the female voice _____ much clearer over early telephone
                            15 (sound)
lines. In the late 1800s, the telephone, together with the typewriter,
_____ thousands of women to work in offices. New fashions
    16 (bring)
_____ to suit the needs of female workers, and "appropriate"
    17 (create)
clothing for work _____. The shirtwaist dress and the blouse
                        18 (introduce / soon)
_____ for women "going to business." The telephone, obvi-
    19 (design)
ously, _____ begin the social revolution that
            20 (help)
_____ today. Today, the telephone _____ so
    21 (continue)   22 (be)
much a part of our lives that we _____ it unless it
                                        23 (not notice)
_____ out of order. In fact, with hundreds of millions of
    24 (be)
telephones worldwide, no other invention _____ so much.
                                                25 (use)

12 Creating a Classroom Quiz Have you ever played quiz games like $10,000 Pyramid or Trivial Pursuit? These are question-and-answer games based on categories of information. To play a classroom version, first choose five or six categories: music, art, inventions, buildings, discoveries, and so forth. Then separate into two teams, and write at least five questions for each category. For example, "Who invented the sewing machine?" or "Name the composer(s) of 'Hey Jude.'" After you have completed your questions, give them to your teacher. Your teacher will ask each team the questions. The team chooses a category, and a different member must answer each time. You may play until you reach a certain score or until all the questions have been asked.

Part 2 The Passive Voice with Perfect Tenses

Setting the Context

Previewing the Passage Discuss the questions.

What are *gadgets*? Can you give any synonyms—words that have the same meaning?

Reading Read the passage.

Gadgets, Gadgets, and More Gadgets!

Since the last half of the twentieth century, our way of life has been revolutionized by gadgets of all types: television sets and DVDs, microwave ovens and garage door openers, cell phones and laptop computers, just to name a few. However, a century ago, most of these common household items had not even been dreamed of! 5

Discussing Ideas Discuss the questions.

Can you name other common gadgets that did not exist 15 or 20 years ago? What new gadgets do you think will be created soon? Are you familiar with any of the expressions in the cartoon below?

Credit: COMMITTED. Reprinted by permission of United Feature Syndicate, Inc. All rights reserved.

Grammar Structures and Practice

A. The Passive Voice with Perfect Tenses

- The passive voice of verbs in perfect tenses is formed in this way: *have (has, have, had)* + *been* + past participle (+ *by* + agent).
- Adverbs of frequently usually come after the auxiliary *have*.

5.7	The Passive Voice with Perfect Tenses		
Perfect Tenses	**Structures**	**Examples**	**Focus**
Present Perfect	**Active**	New technology **has revolutionized** the communications industry.	new technology
	Passive	The communications industry **has been revolutionized** by new technology.	the communications industry
Past Perfect	**Active**	Before the 1950s, researchers **had not yet developed** high-quality audio and video equipment.	researchers
	Passive	Before the 1950s, high-quality audio and video equipment **had not yet been developed**.	high-quality audio and video equipment

1 **Practice** The following list shows "old" inventions and the newer inventions that have replaced or improved upon them. Form sentences using the present perfect tense, passive voice. If possible, add information to make the sentences interesting.

Example typewriters / word processors

In many offices and homes, typewriters have been replaced by word processors.

1. shoelaces and zippers / Velcro
2. records and turntables / CDs and CD players
3. brooms / vacuum cleaners
4. electric fans / central air conditioners
5. conventional ovens / microwave ovens
6. telephone operators / pagers and voice-mail systems
7. eyeglasses / contact lenses
8. orchestras / music synthesizers
9. home-movie cameras / video cameras
10. letters / email

 2 **Practice** Imagine that you work in a recording studio and you are going to video-tape a TV commercial. In pairs, go over your final checklist before you begin recording. Ask questions using the present perfect tense of the passive voice. Give short answers using the past participle, as in the example.

Example call the actors   A: Have the actors been called?
                                B: Called!

1. test the microphones
2. check the lights
3. clean the camera lenses
4. focus the camera
5. test the loudspeakers
6. adjust the sound
7. load the film
8. close the doors

3 **Practice** Underline the object in each sentence. Then change the sentences from the active to the passive voice. Omit the agent unless it is important to the meaning of the sentence.

Example In just 40 years, companies have introduced an <u>amazing selection of audio and video equipment</u>: color television, transistor radios, cassette players, video recorders, compact discs, and DVDs.
In just 40 years, an amazing selection of audio and video equipment has been introduced: color television, transistor radios, cassette players, video recorders, compact discs, and DVDs.

1. In the past 40 years, researchers have revolutionized audio and video technology.

2. By the mid-1950s, Ampex Corporation had introduced the first modern video recorder.

3. The television industry has used the Ampex system since that time.

4. By the late 1950s, companies had introduced the first stereo record.

5. Since 1960, researchers have developed high-quality sound systems.

6. By the late 1980s, scientists had developed compact discs and lightweight camcorders.

7. In recent years, MCA, RCA, and several European companies have designed and produced videodisc systems.

8. Apple Computer has created a computer program that will program your VCR for you if you don't know how!

9. In many places, DVDs have replaced videotapes for film rentals.

10. Recently, TV options—big screen, flat screen, plasma screen, and high definition—have increased consumer choice.

4 **Practice** Use simple or perfect forms of the verbs in parentheses to complete the following passage. Choose between active and passive forms. The first one is done as an example.

Those Amazing Machines! (Also Known as Microelectronic* Devices)

In recent years, we _____*have grown*_____ very dependent on machines of all
                                  (grow)

kinds—in business, in industry, and in our own homes. Nowadays the average

person _____ every day by hundreds of devices that
              1 (surround)

_____ microelectronic technology. This technology, for
         2 (use)

*Microelectronics has to do with electric currents in small components such as transistors and microchips. Microelectronic devices are found everywhere today.

example, _____ in microwave ovens and digital clocks. In just
          3 (employ)
half a century, microelectronic technology _____ it possible to
                                            4 (make)
produce practical devices for everyday life. High-speed cameras with automatic
focusing _____. Compact disc players _____.
          5 (create)   6 (develop)
Remote control devices _____ for televisions and video
                        7 (produce)
recorders and for telephone answering machines. Fifty years ago, none of these
devices _____ because microelectronic technology
         8 (exist)
_____. All microelectronic devices _____ with
9 (not invented / yet)   10 (construct)
similar types of components, which are smaller, cheaper, and more reliable than
components of the past. This explains why some devices, such as VCRs,
answering machines, and especially home computers, _____
                                                     11 (cost)
much less now than they did when they first _____ on the
                                             12 (appear)
market. It also explains why the average home today _____
                                                      13 (contain)
more than 40 machines and electronic devices!

Using What You've Learned

5 **Discussing What Gadgets You Own** Make a list of all the gadgets that are
mentioned in this section. Put a check mark next to each device that you own or have
owned and count the number of check marks. Then talk with your classmates to see
which student has the largest number of these gadgets. Next, make a list of gadgets
that you have in your home but that were not mentioned in these activities. Again, compare with your classmates to see who has the largest number of gadgets.

6 **Writing About a Useful Gadget** Choose *one* gadget that you absolutely
could not live without and write a paragraph about it. Include the following:

When was the item invented?

By whom was it invented?

How is it made?

How is it used today?

How was it used in the past or what was used instead of it?

How has this item been modified or changed in recent years?

Part 3 | The Passive Voice with Continuous Tenses

Setting the Context

Previewing the Passage Discuss the questions.

When were the first cars developed? Since then, what other major breakthroughs in transportation have occurred?

▲ Hybrid cars may be the transportation of the future.

Reading Read the passsage.

The Future of Transportation

Amazing changes are taking place in methods of transportation that we use every day. It was only about 100 years ago that gasoline-powered cars were being developed. Today, hybrid cars which use gasoline and electric power are being sold by automakers such as Toyota and Honda. High-speed rail is being implemented in many countries of the world. The world is shrinking as trans-   5
portation is becoming faster and faster.

Discussing Ideas Discuss the questions.

Name all the types of transportation that you have used in your lifetime. Can you give the normal speed for each of these today? Does your list include any high-speed transportation? Which? How fast could you travel on this?

Grammar Structures and Practice

A. The Passive Voice with Continuous Tenses

- The passive voice of verbs in the present and past continuous tenses is formed in this way: *be (am, is, are, was, were)* + *being* + past participle (+ *by* + agent).
- Adverbs of frequency generally come after the first auxiliary verb.

5.8 The Passive Voice with Continuous Tenses

Continuous Tenses	Structures	Examples	Focus
Present Continuous	Active	Many cities **are using** computers to help regulate traffic.	many cities
	Passive	Computers **are being used** in many cities to help regulate traffic.	computers
Past Continuous	Active	Ten years ago, cities **were using** traffic officers to regulate traffic.	cities
	Passive	Ten years ago, traffic **was being regulated** by traffic officers.	traffic

Note: The future continuous tense (*will be* + verb + *ing*) and the present and past perfect continuous tense (*have, has, or had been* + verb + *ing*) are not used in the passive voice.

 1 Practice Working in pairs, take turns asking questions and forming answers using the present continuous tense, passive voice. Make up some other examples.

Example A: Why are you wearing your black suit?
B: (brown suit / cleaned) My brown suit is being cleaned.

A	B
1. Why is the traffic so slow today?	Main Street / repaired
2. Why don't you practice piano today?	piano / tuned
3. Why is your office closed?	new computer system / installed
4. Why can't we go into the cafeteria?	floor / washed
5. Why are they staying in a hotel?	their house / painted
6. What is happening to that bus?	it / towed away
7. Where is your new suit?	it / altered
8. Why are you taking the bus to school today?	my car / repaired
9. Why are you writing your essay longhand?	my printer / fixed
10. Why are you walking to school today?	my bike / tuned up

2 Practice With the same partner or a new partner, repeat Activity 1. This time, change the questions and answers to past time.

Example   A: Why was the traffic so slow today?
B: Main Street was being repaired.

3 Practice In pairs, change the following sentences from the present continuous, active voice to the past continuous, passive voice. Do this activity in speaking and in writing.

Example   Today computers are typing letters. (secretaries)
Fifty years ago, letters were being typed by secretaries.

1. Today computers and pilots are navigating planes. (only human pilots)
2. Today private package delivery services are delivering packages. (only the U.S. Postal Service)
3. Today computers are controlling traffic signals. (traffic officers)
4. Today computers are running automobile assembly lines. (assembly line foremen)
5. Today computers are controlling switches in train tracks. (human switch operators)
6. Today Japan is making most of the world's motorcycles. (the United States)
7. Today several countries are operating high-speed trains. (only Japan)
8. Today many countries are exporting cars. (only a few countries)
9. Today many people are recording their appointments in PDAs. (in daily planners)
10. Today lots of students are composing their essays on word processors. (no students)

4 Practice The following sentences give some information about the history of the automobile. Change the sentences to the passive voice. Omit *by* + agent if it is not necessary to the meaning of the sentence.

Example   In 1890, people were already driving gasoline-powered cars in France.
In 1890, gasoline-powered cars were already being driven in France.

1. By 1929, American automakers were producing approximately five million cars a year.
2. In 1950, the United States was manufacturing two-thirds of the world's motor vehicles.
3. By 1960, manufacturers were introducing compact cars because of competition from Europe.

4. By the 1970s, competition from Japan was threatening the U.S. auto industry.

5. By 1980, the United States was producing only one-fifth of the world's cars.

6. Today foreign manufacturers are actually making many so-called American cars.

7. These days, automakers are developing hybrid cars.

8. Several big automakers are building and testing electric cars.

9. They are testing alternative fuels such as methanol.

10. People are also building new mass-transport systems.

5 **Practice** Complete the following passage with either active or passive forms (simple, perfect, or continuous tenses) of the verbs in parentheses. Include adverbs when indicated. In some cases there may be more than one correct answer.

Developments in Transportation

Amazing developments _are currently taking_ place in transportation
                          (take / currently)
technology. Some technological changes _____ and others
                                        1 (implement / already)
_____. In the 21st century, the major forms of transportation
2 (implement / soon)
that _____ in the 20th century—cars, trains, and planes—will
     3 (use)
still be popular, but they _____ in significant ways. An impor-
                           4 (modify)
tant example of work that _____ now to improve our methods
                           5 (do)
of transportation is with electric and hybrid cars.

Why are electric and hybrid cars getting so much attention? Fuel efficiency

and air pollution are the two big reasons. Air pollution is a serious problem in

many large cities, and most of this pollution _____ by exhaust
                                               6 (cause)
from automobiles. In California, a law _____ stating that by
                                        7 (pass)
1998, 2 percent of the cars sold there had to be electric. This percentage had to

go up to 5 percent by 2001 and 10 percent by 2003. Consequently, automakers

worldwide _____ hard to create a cheap, efficient, and attrac-
          8 (work)
tive electric car. Small electric hybrid cars _____ by Japanese
                                              9 (introduce / already)
automakers Honda and Toyota. Other hybrid vehicles _____ by
                                                    10 (develop / currently)
U.S. and European manufacturers. Fuel efficiency is also a serious considera-

tion. Distances of 50 miles per gallon of gas _____ with today's

11 (achieve / now)

hybrid cars, and the fuel ratings may be even better in the near future.

Using What You've Learned

6 **Reporting the News** The time is the year 2025. The place is an airport in New York, where, in about one hour, the new "hyperspace" plane will be taking off on its first regularly scheduled flight to Tokyo. Imagine that you are a radio news reporter at the scene on this history-making day. Your assignment is to describe to your listeners the activities that are taking place during these last moments before takeoff. Try to provide as many details as possible concerning the activities of the following:

the passengers   the ground crew
the plane   the luggage and cargo
the flight crew

Make notes for your description. Use the present continuous tense, active or passive voice.

Then role-play your report for the class.

7 **Writing About Change** Write a paragraph about changes that are occurring in your work or field of study. Try to include information on research that is currently being done, new technology that is being introduced, and other changes that are being implemented.

Use your paragraph as the basis for a small group discussion. You may want to separate according to general areas of interest—for example, those who are interested in business, those who are involved in the sciences, and so on. You might include drawings, diagrams, or other visual aids to help in explaining.

Setting the Context

Previewing the Passage Discuss the questions.

What do you know about the first computers? When were they built? What were
they used for?

▲ ENIAC (Electronic Numerical Integrator and Computer), the first large-scale
computer, had almost 18,000 vacuum tubes and required more than 1,800
square feet (167 square meters) of floor space.

Reading Read the passage.

Computers in Our Lives

It was only in the middle of the 20th century that the first computer, Mark I,
was developed for military use. Since then computers have come to play a vital
role in almost every aspect of our lives. Today, phone calls can be directed by
computers; cars can be assembled by computerized robots; messages, files,
photographs, and music can be sent over the Internet; children may be taught   5
with the help of computers; and much more. Computers can even be used to
arrange people's romantic relationships!

Discussing Ideas Discuss the questions.

What other current uses of computers can you think of? What possible future uses of computers can you suggest?

Grammar Structures and Practice

A. The Passive Voice with Modal Auxiliaries

The passive voice of modal auxiliaries is formed in this way: *modal (can, could, may, might, must, ought to, shall, should, will, would)* + *be* + past participle (+ *by* + agent). Adverbs of frequency generally come after the modal auxiliary.

5.9	The Passive Voice with Modal Auxiliaries	
Structures	**Examples**	**Focus**
Active	Today we **can use** personal computers to write letters.	we
Passive	Today computers **can be used** to write personal letters.	computers
Active	Writers **may use** computers to help them do research.	writers
Passive	Computers **may be used** by writers to help them do research.	computers
Active	A doctor **might use** a computer to get the latest information about a drug.	a doctor
Passive	A computer **might be used** by a doctor to get the latest information about a drug.	a computer

1 **Practice** In the following sentences, change the verbs from the active voice to the passive voice whenever possible. Omit the agent unless it is important to the meaning of the sentence.

Example Nowadays we may find robots in hundreds of different industries.
Nowadays robots may be found in hundreds of different industries.

1. We can define a robot as an "intelligent" machine.

2. Robots can copy the functioning of a human being in one way or another.

3. One early robot, "Planobot," was simply a mechanical arm that people could tilt or rotate.

4. Nowadays, people can design robots to do many jobs that would be dangerous or boring for humans.

5. For example, robots might replace human workers in dangerous areas such as nuclear power plants or coal mines.

6. In hospitals, people can program "nursing" robots to lift patients, wash them, and put them back in bed.

7. In the future, we might use robots for such complex tasks as making beds and preparing a steak dinner.

8. Though some robots are able to "say" a limited number of words, people cannot yet program robots to think like people.

9. In the future, however, people will use artificial intelligence to create robots that are more humanlike.

10. Wouldn't it be wonderful if people could design computers to perform all kinds of unpleasant tasks such as homework?

▲ Robots can be used for welding.

2 **Practice** Complete the following with the active or passive forms of the modals and verbs in parentheses. The first one is done as an example.

HERO

How would you like to have your own personal robot "servant"? Although not quite as advanced as the robots portrayed in Hollywood movies, some household robots are now available. One of them, named HERO, _can be programmed_ to perform a number of useful tasks around the house.
(can / program)

HERO _____ lights on and off. He _____ pack-
1 (can / turn)   2 (also / can / carry)
ages. Amazingly, he _____ to teach languages! Personal robots
3 (can / even / use)
of the future will be more sophisticated. They _____ as com-
4 (will design)
plete entertainment centers, with the ability to sing, dance, even tell jokes!

Moreover, all the electronic equipment in the house—television, radio, phone,

computer, and so on—_____ by these robots. Imagine: Some-
5 (will / regulate)
day, our dinners _____, our dishes _____ our
6 (may / cook)   7 (may / wash)

laundry _____, and our cars _____—all by our
8 (may / fold)   9 (may / repair)

own personal robots! For the time being, however, all of those chores

_____ by humans.
10 (must / still / perform)

3 **Practice** The following passage is written entirely in the active voice. It contains sentences that could be improved by using the passive voice. Rewrite the selection, using sentences in the passive voice when appropriate. Omit the agent if it is not necessary to the meaning of the sentence.

Computerized Robots

Never temperamental, always on time, always efficient, Epistle reads the mail each morning, chooses the most important letters, and marks the most important parts long before the boss arrives. Epistle is not an ordinary secretary. Epistle is a robot.

IBM developed Epistle a number of years ago. Today people are designing   5
computerized robots that are even more sophisticated than Epistle to think and reason like the human brain. These machines will use artificial intelligence to perform their functions.

Artificial intelligence has already begun to affect the lives of millions. People are building both robots and computers that can do amazingly humanlike   10
work. For example, in many U.S. hospitals, computers can diagnose diseases with at least 85 percent accuracy. In England, scientists have developed a "bionic nose" that can distinguish subtle differences in smell. They can use the nose in the food and wine industries to check freshness and quality.

Until recently, we could program robots to perform only routine tasks. In   15
the near future, computers utilizing artificial intelligence may give robots full mobility, vision, hearing, speech, and the "sense" to make logical decisions.

4 **Review** Complete the following passage by using either the active or passive voice of the verbs in parentheses. Use any of the tenses and modals covered in this chapter. The first one is done as an example.

The History of Computers

In 1944, the first general-purpose computer, Mark I, _____ *was put* _____
(put)

into operation. It was very slow and very large. In fact, all the early computers

were extremely large, and several floors of a building _____ to
1 (need)

house them.

By the end of the 1950s, computers _____ to use transistors. Transistors _____ computers smaller, less expensive, more powerful, and more reliable. Today these _____ as second-generation computers.

Third-generation computers, which _____ in the 1960s, _____ chips to store the memory of the computer. These computers were still very large, however. But by the 1970s, when the silicon chip _____, computers _____ truly small and affordable. Computers with these silicon chips _____ fourth-generation computers. Fifth-generation technology is still in development, yet promises refined voice recognition, parallel processing and, at this point, who knows what else.

5 **Review.** Complete the following passage by using either the active or passive voice of the verbs and modals in parentheses. Use any of the tenses and modals covered in this chapter. The first one is done as an example.

Development in Telecommunications

During most of human history, communication _____was limited_____ by
(limit)
time and distance. In the past 200 years, however, revolutionary changes in communication _____. In the 19th century, the telegraph and
1 (occur)
telephone _____. Radio, television, and computers
2 (invent)
_____ in the early and 20th century. Since then, these inven-
3 (develop)
tions _____ the way people live and work.
4 (change / completely)

Today all these communications devices _____ together.
5 (can / link)
This new wave of technology _____ "telecommunications"—
6 (call)
the use of television, radio, telephones, and computers to communicate across distance and time. In the next few years, telephones, computers, and video screens _____, allowing offices to have "videoconference" in
7 (may / connect)
which participants can see and talk to each other and in which computer files

_____. Soon, people with home computers, laptops, and
        8 (could / share)
portable computers _____ to electronic mail services and
                        9 (will / connect)
libraries around the world so that they _____ information
                                        10 (can / communicate and access)
from home, on airplanes, or just about anywhere. Today personal computers
_____ in millions of homes worldwide, and home computer
        11 (can / find)
ownership _____ to grow. Because of technology, people living
                12 (should / continue)
in one part of the world now _____ almost instantly about
                                13 (may / inform)
events occurring thousands of miles away.

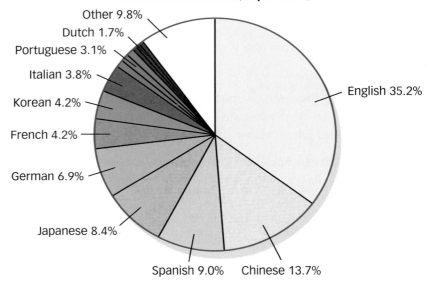

Online Language Populations
Total: 801.4 Million (Sept. 2004)

Other 9.8%
Dutch 1.7%
Portuguese 3.1%
Italian 3.8%
Korean 4.2%
French 4.2%
German 6.9%
Japanese 8.4%
Spanish 9.0%
Chinese 13.7%
English 35.2%

Source: _Online Language Populations_ from www.globalreach.biz

6 **Review** Reread the opening passage "Old and New Technology" on page 182.
Then do the following:

1. Underline the subject and verb of the first sentence. Is the verb in the active or
   passive voice? Can you rephrase the sentence to begin with _new inventions_?

2. Underline the subjects and verbs in the second sentence. Unlike the first
   sentence, the second sentence does not have a phrase with _by_. Can you add
   one? Why do you think the phrase with _by_ was not used?

3. Underline all the other passive voice verbs in the passage. Tell whether they refer to past, present, or future time. Then tell the agent for each. If the agent is not included in the passive construction, tell who or what you think the agent is.

Using What You've Learned

 7 Doing Research The Internet began as an experimental four-computer network established by the U.S. Department of Defense so that researchers could communicate with each other. By 1971, this network linked over two dozen sites, including Harvard and MIT. By 1974, there were over 200 sites.

Learn more about the history of the Internet, and prepare a presentation or a composition. Here are some questions to research:

1. Which universities were involved in developing the Internet?
2. When was the first browser created? Where? By whom?
3. How was hypertext developed?
4. How are Web searches conducted?

 8 Discussing Changes Think of the tremendous changes that computers have brought in recent years. For example, look at the tasks that follow. All of these can now be done electronically. In the past, however, they had to be done manually.

In pairs or small groups, discuss the changes in these tasks and add others that you can think of. Use the passive voice wherever possible.

Example *Until the last 30 years or so, letters could only be handwritten or typed. And they could only be sent by regular mail or by someone who was traveling to a certain place. Today they can be mailed or sent by express mail and delivered overnight to almost any part of the globe. They can be faxed, or sent electronically almost instantly.*

banking
compose music
design cars
diagnose illnesses
draw three-dimensional objects
figure taxes
investing in stocks
keep household records (balance checkbooks, pay bills, and so on)

mix paint
obtain information from libraries
purchase tickets (for airlines, concerts, sports events, and so on)
sort mail
teach children
write and send letters

9 **Writing About Change** Choose one of the topics on page 211. Prepare a brief report for your classmates. Write one paragraph about how the process was done in the past, and one paragraph about how it is done today. If possible, include changes that may occur in the near future too. Use the passive voice whenever possible in your report.

Part 5 Review of Chapters 1–5

Setting the Context

 Previewing the Passage Discuss the questions.

Some languages add new words or change meanings of words frequently. Is that true of your native language? What are some new words, or words with new meanings?

Reading Read the passage.

Techtainment?

English is a language that adds new meaning to old words all the time. In the past 10 to 15 years, an incredible variety of new meanings have been invented because of changes in technology. Just think of the meaning of the word "mouse." Which of these do you think of first?

Completely new words have also been developed. Words like infotainment 5 and edutainment have come into English in recent years. These words are used to describe TV programs and movies that communicate information or educate through entertainment. Now it appears that another new word is being invented: "techtainment." Techtainment is the next step in the spread of technology in our lives. It's where communications, electronics, entertainment, and technology come together. Some examples? Computers with CD and DVD burners, iPods and MP3 players, PDAs, and cell phones with digital cameras are everywhere today—with many more new inventions soon to come.

10

Discussing Ideas Discuss the questions.

Can you give other examples of "techtainment" today? What can you imagine will be developed in the future?

Grammar Practice

1 **Review** Identify the part of speech of each italicized word.

        preposition   *noun*   *noun*   *noun*
            adjective   *conjunction*

Example *Since prehistoric* times, *humans* have tried to combine *art and motion.*

▲ Walt Disney

1. Animation is *an* area where art *and* technology come together.

2. Video games and animated movies are two *very popular* examples.

3. *Walt Disney* is *the* name *that* people *most frequently* associate *with* animation.

4. Walt Disney *was born in* 1901, and in 1920, *he* started working in animation *at* the Kansas City Slide Company.

5. Disney's *friend* Ubbe Iwerks worked *with him.*

6. Walt Disney moved *to Los Angeles, where he* opened a *new* studio in *his* uncle's *garage.*

7. In 1928, Disney *created* Mickey Mouse *while* he *was riding on* a train *to* California.

8. In 1932, Walt Disney *won* his *first* Academy Award for "Flowers and Trees," *and* in 1933, he won his *second* Academy Award for "The Three Little Pigs."

9. *When* Walt Disney died in 1966, he had *already* won 31 Academy Awards.

10. Walt Disney *still holds* the *world record for* the *most individual Oscars.*

11. In 1995, the *first computer-animated movie,* "Toy Story," *was released.*

12. "Toy Story" was the first *movie to be* created *completely digitally.*

2 **Review** Label the subject(s) and verb(s) in the following sentences. Tell whether the sentences are simple, compound, or complex. If the sentence is compound or complex, circle the connecting word.

Example Anime is an art form *that* is very popular today. *complex sentence*

1. Anime is a form of art and animation that is used on TV and in movies.

2. Anime originally came from Japan.

3. In the early 1900s, both Japanese and American filmmakers were experimenting with animation.

4. The first highly popular anime animations did not appear in Japan until Japanese TV began broadcasting Osamu Tezuka's series *Astro Boy* in 1963.

5. What do you know about the series *Astro Boy?*

6. Tell me more about the series *Astro Boy.*

7. I don't know anything about that series.

8. *Astro Boy* was the first series to use anime style artwork with a plot and characters.

9. By the late 1980s, many high-budget anime films were being produced, but most were commercial failures.

10. Although many anime films were commercial failures in Japan, they became very popular overseas.

11. The movie *Spirited Away* shared the first prize at the 2002 Berlin Film Festival and received the Academy Award for Best Animated Feature in 2003.

12. Have you seen the movie *Spirited Away,* which won an Academy Award?

13. I haven't seen *Spirited Away,* so I can't tell you about it.

14. Can you tell me which your favorite film was?

15. I'd like to know who your favorite anime character is.

3 **Error Analysis** All of the following sentences have errors. Find and correct the errors by adding, omitting, or changing words.

but

Example High-tech electronics are glamorous, low-tech "toys" are still lots of fun.

1. Easy to have fun with low-tech toys and games.

2. Just think about how entertaining is a piece of wood.

3. What a person can do with a piece of wood?

4. Here is some examples of ways to have fun with pieces of wood.

5. Baseball is usually play with a wooden bat.

6. In the old days, baseball players could not be hit the ball as far as they can today.

7. We were used to play baseball a lot when we were children.

8. Skiing involves strapping long pieces of wood to you feet.

9. In the old days, skis were wood, but today most skis are made by fiberglass or other materials.

10. In the past, tennis and other rackets was made of wood, too.

11. Do you like to play tennis with me tomorrow?

12. Can you tell me when is the tennis tournament this afternoon?

13. You must to live by the ocean to go surfing, but you can windsurf on rivers and lakes too.

14. Susan has gone windsurfing yesterday.

15. I would like to know where is a good place to rent windsurfing equipment.

4 **Review** First read the following passage for meaning. Then complete the passage by choosing the correct verb form in parentheses.

▲ Windsurfing at sunset

Ride the Wind

Some of today's most exciting sports involve boards, but veteran boarders say windsurfing is the best! Windsurfing, also called windboarding, (must / must to) be the hottest, coolest, smoothest, and fastest way that you (can / could) sail across the water. "It (is / was) really thrilling," (says / say) one windsurfer. "When I (catch / caught) the wind, I (fly / have flown) across the water. I (want / wanted) to keep going. I never (have wanted / want) to stop. I often (became / become) so excited that I (don't / didn't) pay attention to how far away I (am / was) from the shore." To windsurf, you (don't / didn't) need to live close to the ocean. You (can / might) windsurf on a lake or even on a pond. If you (decide / decided) to try windsurfing, remember one thing: you (are / were) sure to fall into the water lots of times. You (can / could) plan on getting very wet your first day. However, even if you (do / did) fall a lot on your first day, you (can / are able to) expect to do better the next time. To windsurf, you (need / needed) to know how to keep your balance and change your position on the board. You (might / might have) learn in as little as three to six hours. You (will / would) begin to feel your body move with the board. People who (windsurf / windsurfed) agree that if you (know / knew) how to ride a bike,

you (can / could) learn to windsurf. Try to pick a hot day for your first day or
rent a wetsuit because you (will / would) definitely get wet.

5 **Review** The following story is about the origin of one of America's most famous games, Monopoly. Choose the correct verb form in parentheses to complete the story.

▲ Checkers is a popular board game with all ages.

Monopoly

One type of "board" that has entertained millions of people is the "board game." Board games such as checkers and chess have been popular for centuries, but the world's most popular game came into being in the 20th century. What is the world's most popular board game? Monopoly. For those who (cannot / might not) know, Monopoly is a game that (manufactures / is manufactured by) Parker Brothers. In the game, each player (buy / buys) and (sell / sells) real estate.

The story of the creating of the game is quite something. It (invented / was invented by) Charles Darrow in 1933. At that time, Darrow (is / was) an unemployed engineer. He (has lost / had lost) his job at the beginning of the Depression, a period of great economic hardship in the United

States that (began / begun) at the end of the 1920s. Darrow (is / was) out of
work for three years. He (did / was doing) a lot of different things to make
money, like walking dogs and fixing electric irons. He also (kept / keeped)
himself busy by trying to invent things. First, Darrow (tried / was trying) to
create score pads for card games, and then he (made / had made) jigsaw
puzzles. Unfortunately, no one (interested / was interested) in Darrow's inventions. Finally, Darrow (began / was beginning) dreaming about the time before
the Depression. Before the Depression, he and his wife
(had taken often / had often taken) vacations at the beach. He
(remembered / was remembering) one special vacation. It (is / was) their visit to
Atlantic City, New Jersey. Darrow (drew / was drawn) maps of the streets of
Atlantic City and (then created / created then) a game using the maps. Soon his
new game (finished / was finished).

Darrow and his wife (spended / spent) every evening playing the new
game. In the game, they (buy / would buy) and (sell / sold) real estate. They
(would play / play) the game with large amounts of money. Of course, the
money (isn't / wasn't) real, but it (maked / made) the Darrows feel rich!

Soon friends and neighbors (begin / began) to stop by to play the game.
They (ask / asked) Darrow if he (made / would make) sets for them. Pretty
soon, Darrow (cannot / could not) make enough sets by hand, so he
(goes / went) to Parker Brothers with his game. At first, Parker Brothers
(rejected / were rejected) Monopoly. However, Darrow (wasn't / didn't)
discouraged. Finally, Parker Brothers (make / made) Darrow an offer, and the
rest (is / was) history. Today's most popular game worldwide, Monopoly
(produce / is produced) in more than 25 languages.

Using What You've Learned

6 **Doing Research** Research a field or pastime that particularly interests you. Learn about changes in technology related to that field. Your research might be on biotechnology and changes in medicine, or it could be on art and digital painting. Gather information and pictures, if possible, and prepare a presentation for your classmates. If possible, do your research on the Web and create a digital presentation for your class.

Review of Problem Areas: Chapters 1 to 5

A variety of problem areas is included in this test. Check your understanding by completing the sample items below.

Part 1 Mark the correct completion for the following.

Example John ———————— never complaining about his work.

     (A) be known for   (C) is known for

     (B) is know for   (D) was know for

1. Nowadays the majority of overseas telephone calls ———————— by satellite.

     (A) transmit   (C) are transmitted

     (B) transmitting   (D) are transmitting

2. Would they mind ———————— late?

     (A) if I coming   (C) if I came

     (B) to come   (D) to coming

3. Before turning on the switch, make sure the machine

————————————.

     (A) plugs in   (C) has plugged in

     (B) is plugged in   (D) be plugged in

4. Whenever you access information from the Internet, it must ———————————— carefully; not all information comes from reliable sources.

     (A) evaluate   (C) have been evaluated

     (B) be evaluated   (D) been evaluated

5. Dust devils spin like tornados but ———————— more than two or three hundred feet in the air.

     (A) rarely reaches   (C) reach rarely

     (B) reaches rarely   (D) rarely reach

6. Vitamins C and E ———————— help to deter cataracts from developing.

     (A) may   (C) must be

     (B) may be   (D) must

7. Using a different order of words can _____ of a sentence.

- Ⓐ change often the meaning
- Ⓑ change the meaning often
- Ⓒ to change often the meaning
- Ⓓ often change the meaning

8. Sherrie _____ stay home because there are no waves to surf here today.

- Ⓐ said we should have
- Ⓑ said to
- Ⓒ told we should
- Ⓓ told us we should have

9. When the sea is rough, you _____ take more precautions in the water.

- Ⓐ have to
- Ⓑ must to
- Ⓒ have
- Ⓓ had to

10. Before Carole met her husband, she _____ she would be single all her life.

- Ⓐ has thought
- Ⓑ would think
- Ⓒ thinks
- Ⓓ had thought

Part 2 Circle the letter below the underlined word(s) containing an error.

Example   Difficulties with <u>culture</u> shock <u>are</u> often <u>relate</u> to an individual's

                A   B   Ⓒ

     ability to speak the language of the country <u>where she is living</u>.

                                            D

1. The top floor of the parking structure <u>collapsed</u> during the earthquake and

                                       A

  <u>could</u> not <u>used</u> for the <u>next six months</u>.

   B   C   D

2. A plane is currently <u>been</u> designed <u>that</u> will <u>allow for</u> travel between New

                      A   B   C

  York and Tokyo in approximately <u>two-and-a-half</u> hours.

                                D

3. A child <u>has</u> <u>been missing</u> for three days, but today, she was <u>find unharmed</u>

          A   B   C

  and <u>safe</u>.

     D

4. Experts <u>predict</u> that by 2020, the population of southern California
   <u>A</u>

   <u>will have growing</u> from <u>16 million to 22 million people</u>, <u>thus creating</u>
   B   C   D

   increasingly greater demands on transportation systems.

5. <u>Physically fit</u> people <u>should</u> be able <u>stay</u> the <u>same weight</u> over a period of
   A   B   C   D

   several years.

6. <u>Before</u> the Second World War <u>had ended</u>, the number of people in the United
   A   B

   States <u>working</u> in agriculture <u>had dropped</u> substantially.
          C   D

7. Doctors <u>has discovered</u> that <u>chronic pain</u> <u>can have</u> a <u>strong</u> psychological
            A   B   C   D

   component.

8. Coal and oil were formed <u>when</u> plants <u>become</u> buried in <u>marshes</u> or swamps
                             A   B   C

   and then <u>decayed</u>.
            D

9. Wendy <u>couldn't have call</u> when she <u>said</u> she did because I was at home
          A   B

   <u>working</u> and I <u>would've heard</u> the phone ring.
   C   D

10. I <u>had been</u> asleep <u>when</u> the robbers <u>broke into</u> the house and <u>take</u> all the
      A   B   C   D

    jewelry.

Self-Assessment Log

Each of the following statements describes the grammar you learned in this chapter. Read the statements; then check the box that describes how well you understand each structure.

	Needs Improvement	Good	Great
I can use a variety of tenses in the passive voice.	❑	❑	❑
I can use singular verbs with singular nouns and plural verbs with plural nouns.	❑	❑	❑
I can use appropriate prepositions after passive voice verbs.	❑	❑	❑
I can omit the *by* + agent phrases after passive voice verbs when appropriate.	❑	❑	❑
I can take a test reviewing problem areas with sentences, verbs, modals, and the passive voice.	❑	❑	❑

Money Matters

In This Chapter

Nouns and Noun Modifiers

Part 1 Count versus Noncount Nouns
Part 2 Indefinite Adjectives and Pronouns
Part 3 The Definite Article
Part 4 Units of Measurement
Part 5 Agreement

❝To understand someone, find out how he spends his money. **❞**

—Mason Cooley
U.S. writer and professor
(1927–2002)

Connecting to the Topic

1 Think of all the ways that money affects you every day. Think about saving money, spending money, making money, and losing money. Can you give a recent example of each?

2 How do you spend your money? Name your top spending categories (food, clothing, transportation, and so on).

3 Do you save money? What are you saving for?

In this chapter, you will study many uses of nouns and noun clauses, pronouns, articles, and adjectives. This will help you with singular and plural forms as well as the various words and expressions used with nouns.

Reading Read the following passage. It introduces the chapter theme, "Money Matters," and raises some of the topics and issues you will cover in the chapter.

The Global Economy

Of all the sciences, only two are subjects that have a direct and noticeable effect on our lives every day. One is meteorology, the study of weather. Heat, cold, sun, and rain affect us in many ways—in the kind of clothing we wear, for example, and the types of activities we do outdoors. Economics is the other science that affects the daily life of all of us. Each time we spend money, or it is   5
spent on us, we are contributing to the economic life of our country, and in fact, of the world.

Most people have a basic understanding of the weather, but how many people feel comfortable with the subject of economics? Often, economics seems to be a mysterious subject. Newspapers and television use terminology that can   10
sound like a foreign language. They speak of *the gross national product*, *the balance of payments*, *the cost of living*, *interest*, *productivity*, *stocks and bonds*, and so forth.

In some ways, economics is like an enormous jigsaw puzzle. Each piece is basic, but the pieces interconnect, one to another, in a large picture. To look at   15
the whole picture, you must begin piece by piece. Knowledge of the individual pieces and their interconnection will help you understand the global picture.

Discussing Ideas Discuss the questions.

According to the passage, which sciences affect us every day? Why? Can you give some examples of economic activities in your daily life? What are other economic terms you have heard? Can you explain them?

Part 1   Count versus Noncount Nouns

 Previewing the Passage Discuss the questions.

What does *wealth* mean? Can you give some examples of wealth?

Reading Read the passage.

What Is Wealth to You?

- To some people, wealth may mean ownership of businesses, houses, cars, stereos, and jewels.
- To others, wealth may mean control of resources, such as oil, gold, silver, or natural gas.
- To the philosophical, wealth may be intangible. It can be found in honesty, love, courage, and trust.
- To much of the world, however, wealth is having enough food: bread, rice, fish, meat, and fruit.

5

 Discussing Ideas Discuss the questions.

How would you describe a *wealthy* person?

Grammar Structures and Practice

A. Introduction to Count and Noncount Nouns

A noun can name a person, a place, an object, an activity, an idea or emotion, or a quantity.

- A noun may be concrete (physical or tangible) or abstract (nonphysical or intangible).
- Both abstract and concrete nouns can be classified into two types: count nouns and noncount nouns.

6.1 Count Nouns

Explanations	Structures	Examples
Count nouns are nouns that can be counted (*apples, oranges*, and so on).	**Singular**	I have a **friend**. My **friend** owns a **car**.
They have both singular and plural forms. Most count nouns are concrete, but some can be abstract.	**Plural**	**Friends** are very important. New **cars** are expensive.

6.2 Noncount Nouns

Explanations	Structures	Examples
Noncount nouns are usually mass concrete nouns (*food, water,* and so on) or abstract nouns (*wealth, happiness,* and so on) that we don't count.	**Mass Concrete Nouns**	**Air** and **water** are necessary for life. We need to buy **coffee, rice,** and **sugar**.
Noncount nouns are singular, even though some end in -s (*economics, mathematics, news, physics*).	**Abstract Nouns**	**Honesty** is the best policy. We need more **information**. We're concerned about your **health**. Have you studied **economics** or **physics**?

1 **Practice** Quickly reread "What Is Wealth to You?" on page 227 and then do the following:

1. Underline all the nouns and make sure that you understand their meanings.

2. Group the nouns in the chart on page 229.

3. Make a list of any nouns that are confusing to you and discuss these as a class. For example, are there nouns that can go in more than one category?

Count Nouns		Noncount Nouns	
Singular	**Plural**	**Concrete (Tangible)**	**Abstract (Intangible)**
	people		

B. Groups of Count and Noncount Nouns

Certain patterns exist with count and noncount nouns.

- Noncount nouns often refer to categories or groups. Count nouns are often specific items in these groups.
- Some nouns or groups of nouns are almost always noncount, such as food items and weather terms.
- Other nouns may be count or noncount, depending on the meaning.

6.3 Groups of Count and Noncount Nouns

Noncount	Count	Nouncount	Count
advice	hints ideas suggestions	information, news	articles magazines newspapers
equipment	machines supplies tools	money	cents dollars quarters
friendship, love	feelings friends relatives	nature	animals forests mountains oceans
furniture	chairs lamps tables	time	days hours minutes
homework	assignments essays pages	traffic, transportation	buses cars trains

Note: Here are some common noncount food items: *bread, butter, coffee, fruit, meat, milk, rice, sugar, tea.*
Here are some common noncount weather items: *air, rain, snow, water, weather, wind.*

6.4 Nouns That Can Be Both Count and Noncount

Structures	Examples	Meanings
Noncount Count	I studied **business** in college. We have **a business** in Florida.	*business* = an idea or activity *a business* = a store or firm
Noncount Count	We had **chicken** for dinner. My uncle has **a chicken**.	*chicken* = a type of food *a chicken* = a bird
Noncount Count	I have **time** to go there now. I have gone there many **times**.	*time* = an unspecified period of minutes, hours, and so on. *times* = occasions
Noncount Count	That window needs new **glass**. Would you like **a glass** of water? I need new **glasses**.	*glass* = a transparent material *a glass* = a container to drink from *glasses* = a device to help people see better
Noncount Count	**Statistics** is an important area in the study of economics. What are the current population **statistics** for your country?	*Statistics* = area of study *Statistics* = measurements of variations

2 **Practice** In each pair of sentences, the same noun acts as a count and a noncount noun. Identify count (C) and noncount (N) nouns.

Example _____N_____ We're having fish for dinner tonight.

_____C_____ My uncle caught three fish this morning.

1. _____ What time is it?

_____ We had a wonderful time on Saturday.

2. _____ Is a tomato a fruit or a vegetable?

_____ Fruit is good for you.

3. _____ My friend eats salad every day.

_____ Would you like a salad?

4. _____ My brother is majoring in business.

_____ We hope to start a small flower business.

5. _____ Do you like fish?

_____ My aunt caught four fish last night.

6. _____ Lucy bought some new wine glasses.

_____ Glass can be recycled fairly easily.

7. _____ We're having turkey on Thanksgiving.

   _____ He's never seen a live turkey.

8. _____ Jane bought some Colombian coffee.

   _____ Could we have two coffees, please?

9. _____ Work is a central part of many people's lives.

   _____ We bought several works of art at the auction.

10. _____ Living abroad can be a wonderful experience.

    _____ How much work experience do you have?

 3 **Practice** Working in pairs, separate these nouns into groups. Make a chart like the following one to help you. *Note:* Many of the following terms appear throughout the chapter; check their meanings if you do not know them.

✔ advice	employment	market	salary
✔ automobile	gasoline	money	supply
✔ belief	gold	news	time
✔ business	honesty	oil	traffic
capitalism	inflation	price	wealth
company	interest	product	weather
consumer	investment	productivity	work
economics	machine	profit	
employee	machinery	resource	

Count Nouns		Noncount Nouns*	Meaning of Nouns That Are Both Count and Noncount
Singular	**Plural**		
automobile	automobiles	advice (abstract)	business-C = store or company
belief	beliefs		
business	businesses	business (abstract)	business-N = activity or idea

*You might try to separate your list of noncount nouns into abstract and mass nouns.

C. Indefinite Articles: *A* and *An*

A and *an* are the indefinite articles. An indefinite article is used before a singular count noun. The indefinite article may mean *one*, or it may mean an unspecified person or thing.

6.5	Indefinite Articles : *A* and *An*	
Structures	**Explanations**	**Examples**
a	*A* is used before a singular count noun that begins with a consonant sound.	I bought **a** banana. I bought **a** house. **A** European man lives next door.
an	*An* is used before a singular count noun that begins with a vowel sound.	I wasted **an** egg. I wasted **an** hour.

Note: A or *an* is never used with a noun that functions as a noncount noun.

---

4 **Rapid Oral Practice** The following nouns are all singular. Some are count and some are noncount. Form complete sentences by starting with *We have* or *We don't have*. Use *a* or *an* with count nouns and nothing with noncount nouns.

Examples imported car
We have an imported car.

delicious food in . . .
We have delicious food in Italy.

1. computer
2. heavy traffic in . . .
3. problem with traffic in . . .
4. income tax in . . .
5. high (low) unemployment in . . .
6. high gas prices in . . .
7. information for you
8. time for. . .
9. news for you
10. hot (cold) weather during . . .
11. suggestion for you
12. advice for you
13. low inflation in. . .
14. high (low) inflation rate in . . .
15. a lot of air (water) pollution in . . .

D. Unspecified or Unidentified Count and Noncount Nouns

Both count and noncount nouns may be used to refer to unspecified or unidentified people, things, and so forth.
- A singular count noun is preceded by *a* or *an*.
- Plural count nouns and noncount nouns are used without articles.

6.6 Unspecified or Unidentified Count and Noncount Nouns

Structures	Explanations	Examples	Meanings
Singular Count Nouns	Either an article or an adjective *must* be used with a singular count noun.	**A house** can be expensive.	*a house* = one house or any house in general
Plural Count Nouns	Articles are not used with unspecified or unidentified plural count nouns.	**Houses** are getting more expensive.	*houses* = all houses in general
Noncount Nouns	Articles are not used with unspecified noncount nouns. Noncount nouns always take singular verbs.	**Love** is wonderful. **Time** is **money**. **Health** is better than **wealth**.	

5 **Practice** What does wealth mean to you? What do you value and why? From the following list, choose three or four items that are important to you. Put them in order (first, second, and so on). Make count nouns plural and use *are*.

Example I think . . . is / are (very) important because . . .

First, I think good health is important because without health, we have nothing. Second, I think . . .

accurate information	good health	love
clean air	good neighbors	money in the bank
courage	good public education	peace in the world
elegant clothes	health insurance	reliable transportation
expensive car	homework	respect
free time	honesty	safe housing
good advice from family and friends	jewelry	
	large family	

6 **Practice** Our societies suffer from many negative issues. From the list on the next page, choose three or four issues that you think are very bad for the physical and mental health of a society. Put them in order, beginning with the worst. Make count nouns plural and use *are*.

Example I think . . . is / are (very) bad because . . .

First, I think little respect for laws is bad because without laws, people do anything they want. Second, I think . . .

air pollution	drug abuse	little respect for laws
alcohol abuse	drug trafficking	poor education
censorship of the news	high interest rates	poor health care
computer crime	high unemployment	poor system of justice
corruption	lack of good, low-cost	violent crime
crowded schools	housing	water pollution

7 **Error Analysis** Many of the following sentences have errors in their use of singular and plural nouns. Find and correct the errors.

glasses

Example Do you know where my ⟨glass⟩ are? I can't see without them.

1. How many time have you been to New York?

2. We need more informations about that.

3. Do you have any advice for me?

4. The office manager recently purchased some new equipments.

5. We have a lot of homeworks to do for Monday.

6. There are several new student here from Taiwan.

7. I brought ten dollar with me.

8. He has some very nice furniture in his new apartment.

9. I have three assignment for tomorrow.

10. Traffic is very heavy today.

11. Economics are very interesting.

12. Are there a lot of air pollution in your home town?

8 **Practice** The following statements include noncount nouns and singular and plural count nouns. Complete each statement by using *a* or *an*, or use *X* to indicate that no article is necessary.

Examples I've always been interested in _____*X*_____ economics.

I've never taken _____*an*_____ economics class.

1. _____ economics is concerned with two basic groups: _____ consumers and _____ suppliers.

2. _____ economists study the interrelationship between the two groups.

3. For example, _____ economist might study the way _____ supplier creates _____ market for _____ new product.

4. _____ economics also deals with the interrelationship between _____ larger groups, including _____ regions and _____ countries.

5. As we all know, _____ change in the economy of _____ country such as Japan can affect _____ people all over the world.

6. Economists study how events in _____ region can affect _____ markets and _____ prices in other regions.

7. For example, _____ weather in California can affect the price of _____ fruit in Massachusetts.

8. Today, _____ important issue involves _____ "new economy" companies and _____ "old economy" companies.

9. _____ "old economy" company is one that makes _____ traditional goods, like _____ cars or _____ furniture or _____ steel, or handles _____ services, like _____ health care, _____ banking, or _____ legal issues.

10. _____ "new economy" company may be _____ Internet-based goods or service company with no store or office, or it may produce _____ computer hardware or software.

9 Practice The following definitions of economic terms include both count and noncount nouns. Complete the definitions by using *a* or *an*, or use *X* to indicate that no article is necessary.

Example The *balance of* _____*X*_____ *payments* is the difference between the amount of _____*X*_____ money that leaves _____*a*_____ country and the amount that comes in through _____*X*_____ imports, _____*X*_____ exports, _____*X*_____ investments, and so on.

1. _____ *black market* is the illegal sale of _____ products.

2. *Capital* is _____ money or _____ assets such as _____ gold or _____ buildings that can be used to make _____ investments.

3. _____ *depression* is _____ very severe drop in economic activity. _____ high unemployment and _____ low production usually occur during _____ depression.

4. _____ *recession* is _____ less severe decrease in economic activity.

5. The *gross national product* (GNP) is the total value of _____ goods and _____ services produced in _____ country during _____ specific period of _____ time (usually a year).

6. _____ *Goods* are _____ physical things, such as _____ cars and _____ televisions.

7. _____ *Services* are _____ actions or _____ activities, such as _____ financial planning or _____ medical care.

8. The *money supply* is the total amount of _____ money in circulation.

9. _____ *Inflation* is _____ increase in _____ prices.

10. _____ *productivity* is the total national output of _____ goods and _____ services divided by the number of _____ workers.

10 Practice The following sentences make generalizations about large companies. Change the nouns or noun phrases in italics from plural to singular or from singular to plural. Add or omit *a* or *an* and make other changes in verbs and pronouns. (Note that in this activity, *multinational* and *multinational corporation* have the same meaning.)

Example *Multinational corporations* are *companies* that operate in more than one country.

A multinational corporation is a company that operates in more than one country.

1. *Multinationals*, such as IBM and Pepsi, may operate in over 100 countries.

2. Because of their size, *multinational corporations* can often make *products* at *lower costs* than *local industries* can.

3. *Multinationals* can also make *countries* dependent on *them*.

4. *A multinational corporation* may import *a raw material* from *a foreign country*.

5. *A multinational* may make *a product* in one country and export it to another country.

6. Today *a country* may require *a company* to build *an assembly plant* in *an area* where *a product* will be sold.

7. Building *a factory* in *a foreign country* can still benefit *a multinational*.

8. It eliminates *a major expense* in transportation.

Using What You've Learned

11 **Making Generalizations** A *generalization* is a general statement that expresses an idea or an opinion about people, things, ideas, and so on. It often gives a general rule or conclusion based on limited or insufficient information. For example, consider these statements. Are they always true?

1. French people drink wine.

2. Japanese people always have dark hair.

3. American men are tall.

4. Latin Americans are fantastic dancers.

Note that these generalizations use nouns without articles. This is one of the most common ways to make generalizations. As a class or in small groups, think of some of other generalizations.

12 **Categorizing** Form teams of two or more students each. Take turns giving noncount noun categories for each of the following groups of count nouns. The team with the highest number of correct answers wins. Your teacher or a classmate can be the judge of correct answers. A classmate can also be the timekeeper. Set a 10- or 15-second limit for answering. Then try to add new items of your own.

Example movies and plays
　　　　entertainment

1. taxis and subways

2. dimes and nickels

3. beds and dressers

4. newspapers and magazines

5. compositions and reading assignments

6. snowstorms and thunderstorms

7. minutes and seconds

8. paintings and sculptures

9. records, tapes, and CDs

10. earrings and necklaces

Part 2 | Indefinite Adjectives and Pronouns

Setting the Context

 Previewing the Passage Discuss the questions.

Is economics a mystery to you? What do you know about economics?

Reading Read one man's explanation of economics in very simple terms.

Economics in My Life

For many people, economics is a mystery, but I deal with it every day. Economics is just a complicated way of explaining why I make only a little money and why another guy makes a lot of money.

 Discussing Ideas Discuss and write a very simple definition of economics.

Grammar Structures and Practice

A. Indefinite Adjectives and Pronouns with Both Count and Noncount Nouns

Indefinite adjectives are used before nouns, and indefinite pronouns can be used in place of nouns.

- Indefinite adjectives such as *some, many,* and *little* are used with nouns instead of giving specific amounts.
- Indefinite pronouns such as *some, someone, any,* and *anyone* replace nouns.
- Certain expressions work with both count and noncount nouns: *any, some, a lot (of), lots (of), plenty (of), no,* and *none*.

6.7 Indefinite Adjectives and Pronouns with Count and Noncount Nouns

Structures	Indefinite Adjectives	Indefinite Pronouns
Count Nouns	Do you have **any** dollar bills? Jack has **some** dollar bills. Harry has **a lot of** dollar bills. I have **no** dollar bills.	I don't have **any**. Jack has **some**. Harry has **a lot**. I have **none**.
Noncount Nouns	Do you have **any** money? Jack has **some** money. Harry has **a lot of** money. I have **no** money.	Do you have **any**? Jack has **some**. Harry has **a lot**. I have **none**.

Note: In formal English, *none* is always followed by a singular verb: *None of the people has arrived.* (formal)
None of the people have arrived. (informal)

---

 1 **Rapid Oral Practice** In pairs, ask and answer questions using these cues and words such as *some, any,* and *a lot (of)*.

Examples homework tonight
A: Do you have any homework tonight?
B: Yes, I have some homework.

money
A: Do you have some money?
B: No, I don't have any.

1. cash
2. checks
3. credit cards
4. interesting news (about . . .)
5. information about good dentists (doctors, therapists, and so on)
6. assignments tonight
7. free time today
8. advice (about . . .)
9. change
10. coins
11. papers to write
12. one-dollar bills

B. (A) *Few* and (Not) *Many* with Count Nouns versus (A) *Little* and (Not) *Much* with Noncount Nouns

Indefinite adjectives are used before nouns, and indefinite pronouns can be used in place of nouns. Some are used only with count nouns, and some are used only with noncount nouns.

6.8	(A) *Few* and (Not) *Many* with Count Nouns	
Explanations	**Examples**	**Meanings**
Few, a few, many, and *not many* are used with count nouns. *Many* can be used in affirmative statements, but it's more common in questions with *how* and in negative statements.	How **many** (dollars) do you have? I have **a few** (dollars). I **don't** have **many** dollar bills. I have **few** dollar bills.	I have some dollars, but not a lot. I have only a small number of dollars, probably not enough. I probably don't have enough.

6.9	(A) *Little* and (Not) *Much* with Noncount Nouns	
Explanations	**Examples**	**Meanings**
A little, little, much, and *not much* are used with noncount nouns. *Much* can be used in affirmative statements, but it is more common in questions with *how* and in negative statements.	How **much** (money) do you have? I have **a little** (money). I **don't have much** money. I have **little** money.	I have some money, but not a lot. I have only a small amount of money, probably not enough. I probably don't have enough.

Note: Other expressions such as *numerous, several, a number of,* and *a couple (of)* can be used with plural count nouns. Expressions such as *a good deal of, a great deal of,* and *a large (small) amount of* can be used with noncount nouns.

---

2 **Practice** *Few* and *little* mean "not many (much)," but *a few* and *a little* mean "some." Indicate the differences in meaning in the following sentences by writing + ("some") or - ("not many or not much").

Example _____**+**_____ There are a few good restaurants in town.

_____**–**_____ There are few good restaurants in town.

1. _____ We have little homework for the weekend.

2. _____ We have a little homework for the weekend.

3. _____ I have a little advice for you.

4. _____ I have a few ideas for you.

5. _____ He has little information on that.

6. _____ There is little traffic today.

7. _____ Do you have a little time?

8. _____ We have a few pages to read for tomorrow.

9. _____ She has a few friends here.

10. _____ She has few friends here.

11. _____ I've got a little money with me.

12. _____ I've got a few dollars with me.

 3 **Rapid Oral Practice** With a partner, take turns making statements and responses modeling the examples that follow. Make count nouns plural and use _a little, little, not much, a few, few,_ or _not many_.

Examples   money with me
   A: I have a little money with me. How about you?
   B: I don't have much money this week.

   dollar with me
   A: I have a few dollars with me. How about you?
   B: I have a few dollars too.

1. free time today

2. furniture in my house (apartment)

3. friend from . . .

4. problem with . . .

5. extra energy

6. homework tonight

7. news from home

8. assignment this week

9. change

10. food at home

11. one-dollar bill

12. plan for the weekend

C. Modifiers with *A Lot Of, A Little, A Few, Little,* and *Few*

A lot of, a little, a few, little, and *few* occur frequently in conversation. They are often used with other modifiers. The most common are *quite, just, only, very,* and *too.*

6.10	Modifiers with *A Lot Of, A Little, A Few, Little,* and *Few*		
	Count Nouns	**Noncount Nouns**	**Meaning**
Quite with *A Lot (Of)* and *A Few*	She has **quite a few** assignments.	She has **quite a lot of** homework.	a large number or amount
Just and *Only* with *A Few* and *A Little*	She has **just a few** assignments.	She has **just a little** homework.	a moderate number or amount
	She has **only a few** assignments.	She has **only a little** homework.	a small number or amount
Very and *Too* with *Few* and *Little*	She has **very few** assignments.	She has **very little** homework.	a very small number or amount
	She has **too few** assignments.	She has **too little** homework.	not enough

Note: Too can also be used with *many* and *much* to mean "more than enough." Compare the following:

That teacher gives *too many* assignments.

That teacher gives *too much* homewrok.

---

4 **Practice** Choose the correct form of the word(s) in parentheses.

Example Changes are occurring in the economies of (many / much) countries around the world.

1. Since the end of the 1980s, tremendous changes have occurred in (many / much) parts of the world.

2. (Few / Little) countries have escaped the major political changes that began in the 1980s.

3. When countries change their political systems, (many / much) other changes also occur.

4. Major economic changes have occurred in more than (a few / a little) countries in the world.

5. With economic changes have come (many / much) social problems.

6. Countries that used to have (very few / very little) difficulty with unemployment and crime are now dealing with serious problems.

7. In controlled economies, often there wasn't (many / much) unemployment or (many / much) crime.

8. In free market economies, there can be (quite a few / quite a little) social problems that hadn't existed before.

5 Practice In pairs, ask and answer questions about your hometown or home country. Use the examples and the following cues, changing any count nouns to plural.

Give your own opinions and offer any additional information you know about the subject. If your country has experienced major changes in recent years, talk about both the past and the present.

Questions: Is there much (any) . . . ?
　　　　　 Are there many (any) . . . ?
Answers:　 There is quite a lot (some, just a little, and so on) . . .
　　　　　 There are quite a few (only a few, too few, and so on) . . .

Examples　oil
　　　　　 A: Is there much oil in your country?
　　　　　 B: Unfortunately, there isn't much oil in my country.
　　　　　 taxi
　　　　　 A: Are there many taxis in Buenos Aires?
　　　　　 B: There are quite a few—maybe thousands!

1. tax	**7.** farm
2. poverty	**8.** factory
3. crime	**9.** unemployment
4. discrimination	**10.** beautiful scenery
5. air and water pollution	**11.** English language schools
6. high-tech industries	**12.** corruption

D. *One, Another, The Other, Others, The Others*

These pronouns and adjectives are often used to list more than one item. The choice depends on how many items are in the group and whether the speaker is referring to the entire group.

6.11	*One, Another, The Other, Others, The Others*			
	Adjective	**Pronoun**	**Meaning**	**Examples**
Singular	one problem	one	one	We have **two problems**. One is lack of money. **The other** is lack of time.
	another problem	another	an additional problem	
	the other problem	the other	the second of two or the last of a group	We have **several problems. One** is lack of money. **Others** are lack of time and transportation.
Plural	some problems	some	some	We have **four problems. One** is lack of money. **Another** is lack of time. **The others** are lack of transportation and equipment.
	other problems	others	additional problems	
	the other problems	the others	the last of a group	

6 Practice Complete the following sentences by using a form of *other (another, other, others, the other, the others)*.

Example We have two problems. One is time, and _____*the other*_____ is money.

1. There are five major areas of business. One is accounting, and _____*another*_____ is data processing. _____ are finance, management, and marketing.

2. Accounting is sometimes divided into two branches. One is public accounting and _____ is private accounting.

3. Marketing experts are responsible for promoting and selling a product. This involves many things, beginning with product design and development. _____ aspects of marketing include packaging, pricing, and advertising.

4. Financial experts can be divided into three major groups. Financial analysts form one group. _____ groups are bankers and stockbrokers.

5. Although they may make different products, most factories are organized in a similar way. Two areas of factory organization are purchasing and inventory control. _____ areas include control of production and of distribution.

7 Practice Complete the following sentences by using *one* or a form of *other (another, other, others, the other, the others)*.

Example We opened three bank accounts last year. _____*One*_____ was a checking account. _____*Another*_____ was a regular savings account. _____*The other*_____ was a college savings fund.

1. For investments, people often deposit their money in a financial institution. Several types of financial institutions exist in the United States. The most common are commercial banks. _____*Other*_____ common types are credit unions and savings and loans.

2. Commercial banks generally handle business customers. They offer many services such as checking and savings accounts. _____ services include short-and long-term loans and certificates of deposit.

3. Credit unions and savings and loans also offer certificates of deposit (CDs). CDs usually offer higher interest rates than regular savings accounts, and they usually have at least two requirements. _____ is to deposit a minimum amount of money ($500, $2,500, and so on). _____ is to agree to leave your money on deposit for a minimum amount of time (six months, two years, and so on).

4. _____ common form of investing is putting money in the stock market. There are two common ways of participating in the stock market. _____ is to buy individual stocks. _____ is to by shares in a mutual fund, which is a pool of money from many people to buy shares in many different companies.

5. Several major stock markets exist in the United States, including two very famous markets. _____ is the New York Stock Exchange and _____ is the NASDAQ. In addition to these two markets, _____ in the United States and abroad include currency markets, commodities markets, and futures markets.

8 **Review** Choose the form of the word(s) in parentheses that is correct in formal, written English.

The Organization of a Business

In ((all)/ any) economic systems today, most businesses plan their organization carefully. (Another /(One)) common organizational system is the division of labor. Division of labor means all of the workers (is / are) specialized. Each worker has (his or her / their) own particular duties to per¹ form. Each duty (is / are) one part of the whole operation. A good example of² the division of labor is an assembly line in an automobile factory. (One / Other)³ worker may install a door while (another / others) is installing the hood.⁴ (The other / The others) add lights, windshield wipers, and so on. Normally, the⁵ workers don't move. Everyone (stay / stays) in one place, and a conveyor belt⁶ moves the product to (him or her / them).⁷

The division of labor permits mass production, but it does have⁸

(any / some) disadvantages. For one thing, (few / little) people know or
      9   10
understand all (aspect / aspects) of an operation. In addition, mass production
                          11
may be efficient, but (many / much) workers complain that they get (few / little)
                                12   13
job satisfaction from working on one small duty, day after day. To them, there is

(many / much) more satisfaction in doing a job from start to finish.
        14

9 **Error Analysis.** Many of the following sentences have errors in indefinite
pronouns and adjectives. Find and correct the mistakes. Use formal, written English.

Example   Motor City is a town with many automobile factories. *Correct*

                         many
            How ~~much~~ factories are there in Motor City?

1. I've worked at Mass Production Motors for a few years.

2. We have a lot problems in this factory.

3. The workers are paid very few money.

4. We don't get no job satisfaction here.

5. There are too much unhappy workers in this factory.

6. Only a little people are happy with their jobs.

7. Last year there weren't much strikes, but this year we're going to have plenty
   of.

8. So far we haven't had much success in changing things.

9. The management has tried to make some changes, but it's had very little
   success.

10. Many of workers are against the changes.

11. Everyone has his own opinion about the situation.

12. One person thinks things are getting better, but other person thinks they're
    getting worse.

Using What You've Learned

10 Discussing a Cartoon The cartoon below was first published on April 14, one day before Americans must file their income tax returns. People try hard to find ways of reducing the amount of taxes they must pay. These ways of reducing taxes are called *loopholes*.

Read the cartoon. Then work in pairs and rewrite the dialogue. Make complete questions for the first two frames. For the second two frames, try to put the ideas in your own words. Then compare your new dialogue with those of your classmates.

cathy®
by Cathy Guisewite

Part 3 | The Definite Article

Setting the Context

▲ Miners use a large drill deep in a coal mine.

 Previewing the Passage Discuss the question.

What are natural resources? Give some examples of natural resources.

Reading Read the passage.

World Resources: Where Are They?

Some of the world's most important resources are coal, iron ore, petroleum, copper, gold, silver, and diamonds. Many deposits are concentrated in small areas, such as the petroleum deposits off the coast of Venezuela and in the deserts around the Persian Gulf.

Discussing Ideas Discuss the question.

Think of an area of the world that you know well. What are this area's most important natural resources?

Grammar Structures and Practice

A. Introduction to the Definite Article

The definite article *the* can be used with both count and noncount nouns when the noun is specifically identified or its identity is already clearly understood. Many times, the particular context determines if *the* should be used or not, but in certain cases, such as with place names and locations, specific rules exist about when to use and not to use *the*.

6.12 *The* with Count Nouns

Structures	Explanations	Examples
Nonspecific (Without *the*)	*The* is not used with nonspecific nouns. *A* or *an* is used with a singular noun, and no articles are used with plural nouns.	**Singular** Today a company may earn over $1 billion annually. **Plural** Today **companies** may earn over $1 billion annually.
Specific (With *the*)	*The* is used before a singular or plural count noun when that noun is specifically identified or its identity is already understood.	Today, **the companies** that earn over $1 billion annually are primarily oil companies.
Unique Nouns	*The* is used with names of people, places, and so on that are considered to be one of a kind. These include *the earth, the world, the moon, the sun, the universe, the president*, and *the pope*. Exception: *on earth*	Many of the largest companies in **the world** are oil companies. Oil companies control most of **the earth's** known oil reserves.
Repeated Nouns	After a noun has been mentioned once, *the* is used with later references to that noun.	He works for **an oil company. The company** has sent him to work in many different countries. He enjoys working for **the company**, but he is tired of traveling.
Identifying Phrases	Phrases that come immediately after a noun often identify it, so *the* is used. *The* + noun + *of* is a frequent combination.	**The majority of companies** with billion dollar incomes are oil companies.
Identifying Clauses	Like phrases, clauses may identify or specify *which* person, place, or thing.	Today, **the companies that earn over $1 billion** are primarily oil companies.
Superlatives and Ordinal Numbers	*The* is normally used with superlatives (*the most, the least*) and ordinal numbers (*the first*).	The company with **the highest income** is an oil company.

---

1 Practice The following sentences include both specific and nonspecific count nouns. Complete them by using *the,* or use *X* to indicate that no article is necessary.

Example _____X_____ natural resources are important to all countries.

1. _____ most important resources in England are tin and iron ore.

2. _____ raw materials are used to make _____ products.

3. _____ raw materials that are used to make _____ cars include iron ore, rubber, and petroleum.

4. _____ petroleum deposits are located in many parts of the world.

5. _____ petroleum deposits in the Amazon will be difficult to extract.

6. _____ mines can be _____ very dangerous places to work.

7. _____ mines near Bogotá, Colombia, produce large quantities of salt.

8. _____ coal mines in West Virginia have caused many deaths.

B. *The* with Noncount Nouns

Articles are not generally used with noncount nouns. However, noncount nouns, like count nouns, may be preceded by *the* when the noun is *specifically identified*.

6.13	*The* with Noncount Nouns	
	Explanations	**Examples**
Nonspecific (Without *the*)	No articles are used with unspecific nouns.	**Gold** is a precious metal.
Specific (With *the*)	*The* is used with a noncount noun when the noun is identified by a phrase or clause.	**The gold in jewelry** is mixed with other metals.
		The gold that is used in jewelry is mixed with other metals.
	The is usually used with superlatives.	South Africa produces **the most gold** in the world.

2 **Practice** The following sentences include both specific and nonspecific noncount nouns. Complete them by using *the*, or use *X* to indicate that no article is necessary.

Example _____X_____ silver is valuable.

1. Most of _____ silver in the United States is used to make photographic and X-ray film.

2. _____ iron ore is used to make _____ steel.

3. _____ iron ore from eastern Canada is high in quality.

4. Japan produces some of _____ best steel in the world today.

5. _____ oil from Saudi Arabia is lighter in weight than _____ oil from Venezuela.

6. _____ oil is the most important single factor in the world's economy.

7. _____ gold is perhaps _____ most highly treasured metal.

8. Since 1910, one-third of _____ gold in the world has been mined in South Africa.

C. *The* with Proper Nouns

The has specific uses with proper nouns, especially with geographical locations. Because proper nouns identify specific places, *the* is often used. There are few exceptions to the rules. Study the information in Appendix 3 and use it for reference.

3 **Rapid Oral Practice** Use *the* or *X* with the following phrases. Do this exercise orally and then in writing.

Examples _____*the*_____ Hawaiian Islands

_____*X*_____ Hawaii

1. _____ Great Lakes

2. _____ Lake Superior

3. _____ America

4. _____ United States

5. _____ Golden Gate Bridge

6. _____ equator

7. _____ Saudi Arabia

8. _____ 2004

9. _____ 1990s

10. _____ Philippine Islands

11. _____ Japanese (people)

12. _____ Rocky Mountains

13. _____ earth

14. _____ Canada

15. _____ president

16. _____ President Kennedy

17. _____ University of Ohio

18. _____ Harvard University

19. _____ 18th of March

20. _____ British Museum

4 **Practice** Complete the following sentences by using *the*, or use *X* to indicate that no article is necessary.

Example Spectacular sapphires come from _____*X*_____ Madagascar,

_____*the*_____ world's fourth largest island.

1. The world's major source of diamonds is _____ southern Africa.

_____ Star of _____ Africa, the world's largest cut diamond, was found there. Today _____ Star of _____ Africa is one of _____ British crown jewels kept in _____ Tower of _____ London.

2. The world's finest emeralds are mined in _____ Andes Mountains _____ in Colombia, _____ South America. The most important mine is located near _____ town of _____ Muzo on _____ Minero River.

3. The world's largest rock crystal, 1,000 pounds, was found in _____ Burma. A piece of this rock crystal is displayed at _____ National Museum in _____ Washington, D.C.

4. The largest known pearl was found in _____ Philippine Islands in _____ 1930s. It weighed 14 pounds, 1 ounce. The largest known black pearl was found near _____ Fiji in _____ 1984.

5. _____ world's largest gold mine is in _____ South Africa. _____ South Africa supplies 60 percent to 70 percent of _____ gold in _____ world. _____ largest uranium field in _____ world is also located in _____ South Africa.

5 **Practice** Make complete sentences from the following cues. Add *of, from,* and *in* and be sure to include *the* when necessary.

Example large gold deposits / exist / Andes Mountains / South America
Large gold deposits exist in the Andes Mountains in South America.

 1. oil / be a valuable resource
 2. oil / Saudi Arabia / be lightweight and high in quality
 3. copper / South America / be easy to mine
 4. copper / be important for the communications industry
 5. silver / United States / be primarily found / Rocky Mountains
 6. silver / be used to make photographic film
 7. forty percent / silver / United States / be used for photography
 8. diamonds / be / precious gems
 9. large diamond mines / exist / Ural Mountains / Russia
10. twenty-five percent / diamonds / world / be found / West Africa

6 **Practice** Complete the passage by using *the* or *X* (to indicate that no article is necessary). The first one is done as an example.

Mineral Resources

_____ X _____ minerals are abundant in _____ 1
nature. _____ 2 earth is made up of _____ 3
minerals, and even _____ 4 most valuable minerals are found in
_____ 5 common rocks everywhere. Nevertheless, many of
_____ 6 minerals near _____ 7 earth's surface
exist _____ 8 in small amounts. As a result, they cannot be mined
economically. Only _____ 9 big deposits can be mined at a
reasonable cost. _____ 10 biggest deposits of _____ 11
minerals are distributed unequally around _____ 12 world. Some
minerals, like _____ 13 iron in _____ 14 Mesabi
Mountains in _____ 15 Michigan, are almost gone. Others, like
_____ 16 copper, cobalt, and _____ 17 petroleum,
are located under _____ 18 Atlantic and _____ 19
Pacific Oceans and _____ 20 Persian Gulf.

We have already taken many of _____ 21 mineral deposits that
were easy to mine. Today _____ 22 companies have to look harder
and deeper to find _____ 23 minerals, and _____ 24
cost of _____ 25 minerals reflects this. Unless
_____ 26 exploration and _____ 27 technology keep
up with our use of _____ 28 resources, _____ 29
cost of _____ 30 minerals will increase dramatically.

7 Practice Complete the following by adding *the* or *X* (to indicate that no article is necessary).

Where Minerals Are Located

Some of _____ the _____ earth's most valuable resources are found
in only a few countries. For example, _____ 1 South Africa and
countries in _____ 2 former Soviet Union produce one-third to

one-half of many vital resources. They are _____ world's
                                                    3
largest producers of _____ manganese, _____
                              4   5
chrome, _____ platinum, and _____ gold.
                  6   7
_____ Australia is another country that contains major re-
        8
sources. It has large deposits of _____ oil,
                                              9
_____ gas, _____ iron ore, and
          10   11
_____ coal. In fact, _____ Japan gets almost
        12   13
one-half of its iron ore (which is used to make _____ steel) and
                                                            14
_____ large quantities of _____ coal from
          15   16
_____ Australia. _____ Canada, too, has
          17   18
_____ large mineral deposits. _____ oil and
          19   20
_____ natural gas deposits in _____ Canada
          21   22
are some of _____ biggest in the world.
                      23

8 Practice Reread the opening passage "The Global Economy" on page 226. Then
do the following:

1. Look at the last paragraph of the passage, and underline the nouns. Which are
   singular and which are plural? Which are count nouns and which are
   noncount?

2. Look at the word(s) that come before each noun. Which nouns are preceded
   by articles (*a, an,* or *the*)? Which are preceded by adjectives? Which nouns
   stand alone?

3. Look at the second and third sentences in the last paragraph. Can you explain
   why *a* is used with *picture* in the second sentence, but *the* is used in the third
   sentence?

4. Look at the phrase *the study of weather* in the first paragraph. The pattern
   the + noun + *of* + noun is common in English. Underline all other examples of
   this pattern in the passage.

5. Does *economics* take a singular or a plural verb? Can you think of other
   examples of singular nouns that end in *-s*?

9 **Researching a Natural Resource** Are you interested in knowing more about gold? petroleum? diamonds? a certain kind of wood—mahogany, teak, ebony? a certain kind of rock—marble, slate, granite? As a group, pair, or individual project, choose one resource that you would like to learn more about and briefly research it at a library or on the Internet. Gather information on where this resource is found today, how it is extracted, and how it is used. Use your research as the basis for a short composition. Finally, share your information with the rest of the class in a three- to five-minute presentation.

Part 4 Units of Measurement

Setting the Context

Previewing the Passage Discuss the question.

Can you think of some factors that influence what types of foods people eat in different parts of the world?

Reading Read the following passage and identify three factors that influence food choices.

Diet and the Demand for Food

The demand for different food products depends on three factors: the number of people in the area, their standard of living, and their cultural attitudes. The first two factors are obvious. The third, cultural attitudes, often depends on diet habits and religion. Take attitudes toward diet in the United States, for example. Changes, preferences, and prices have had an interesting effect on consumption in the U.S. In 1940, Americans consumed 19.4 pounds of butter and margarine per person, and most of it was butter. Now they eat less than 13 pounds, most of it margarine. 5

Before World War II, people in the U.S. averaged 155 pounds of wheat flour a year; now they average about 135. Americans are also eating much less fruit, but they're eating many more vegetables. They are eating more chicken and turkey, too. 10

Discussing Ideas Discuss the questions.

According to the passage, how are eating habits changing in the U.S.? Have your eating habits changed in the last 10 years? How?

▲ In the U.S. in the 1950's, a typical meal included bread.

Grammar Structures and Practice

A. Units of Measurement

Units of measurement are commonly used in this pattern: number or percent + unit + of + name of item. Note that *of* is not used with *dozen* or *half dozen*, however.

6.14	Units of Measurement
Units of Measurement	**Items**
bar	hand soap, candy
bottle	liquids such as juice, soda, and water
box	solids such as cereal and crackers
bunch	items that grow together, such as bananas, celery, or grapes; and items that are tied together, such as flowers. In informal English, a *bunch* is often used to mean "a lot."
can	liquids and solids such as soda and vegetables
carton	eggs, milk, ice cream, and other dairy products
dozen, half dozen	eggs, cookies, rolls, and other items bought in quantities of six or twelve
gallon, quart, pint	most liquids and ice cream
head	lettuce, cabbage, cauliflower
jar	jam, mayonnaise, and other items that are spread with a knife
loaf	bread
piece, slice	most solids, such as bread, cake, cheese, and meat
pound, ounce	cheese, butter, fruit, meat, poultry, and other solids
roll	paper towels, toilet paper
six- (twelve-) pack	soda
tube	toothpaste, creams, and ointment

1 Practice Complete the following grocery lists by adding appropriate units of measurement. Be sure to use *of* when necessary. The first one is done as an example.

2 _pounds of_ ground beef

1 _____ butter

1 _____ milk

6 _____ bottled water

1 _____ lettuce

3 _____ cereal

2 _____ paper towels

1 _____ jam

1 _____ eggs

12 _____ soda

1 _____ grapes

2 _____ crackers

1 _____ mayonnaise

1 _____ toothpaste

2 _____ juice

1 _____ wine

1 _____ ice cream

3 _____ bread

1 _____ celery

2 _____ cheese

2 Practice Using the chart of equivalents below, convert the amounts from metric to British units. You may give approximate (rounded-off) equivalents.

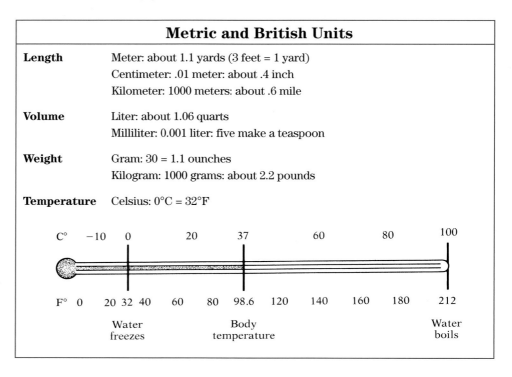

Metric and British Units	
Length	Meter: about 1.1 yards (3 feet = 1 yard) Centimeter: .01 meter: about .4 inch Kilometer: 1000 meters: about .6 mile
Volume	Liter: about 1.06 quarts Milliliter: 0.001 liter: five make a teaspoon
Weight	Gram: 30 = 1.1 ounches Kilogram: 1000 grams: about 2.2 pounds
Temperature	Celsius: 0°C = 32°F

C°   −10   0   20   37   60   80   100

F° 0   20 32 40   60   80 98.6 120   140   160   180   212

Water   Body   Water
freezes   temperature   boils

Example 4 liters of milk

Four liters of milk are approximately equal to one gallon of milk.

1. 1 liter of milk

2. 3 meters of fabric

3. 32 liters of gas

4. 10 centimeters of tape

5. 3 kilograms of cheese

6. a meter of rope

7. 10 milliliters of sugar

8. 20 degrees Celsius

3 Practice Use the list of equivalents above again. This time convert the following amounts from British to metric units. You may give approximate (rounded-off) equivalents.

Example 4 gallons of gas

Four gallons of gas is approximately equal to 16 liters of gas.

1. 2 pounds of cheese

2. 1 quart of milk

3. 5 pounds of chicken

4. 2 yards of fabric

5. 1 teaspoon of salt

6. 10 feet of rope

7. 3 inches of string

8. 3 teaspoons of sugar

4 **Review** Complete the next passage by using *a, an,* or *the,* or by using *X* to indicate that no article is necessary. Explain any cases where you feel more than one choice may be appropriate.

The Green Revolution

In 1910 _____X_____ farmers represented 33 percent of _____the_____ U.S. workforce, and it took more than _____(1)_____ hour of _____(2)_____ work to produce _____(3)_____ bushel of _____(4)_____ corn. By 1980 two minutes of _____(5)_____ work produced _____(6)_____ same amount, and _____(7)_____ farm employment had fallen to about three percent. In 1950 _____(8)_____ very good dairy cow could produce 1,200 gallons of _____(9)_____ milk per year. By 1990 _____(10)_____ dairy cows were averaging over 2,500 gallons _____(11)_____ year, and some prize cows had even reached 6,000 gallons. During _____(12)_____ 1990s, _____(13)_____ milk production increased by about 20 percent. These are only two examples of _____(14)_____ dramatic changes that have occurred in _____(15)_____ agriculture. Through _____(16)_____ advances in _____(17)_____ science and _____(18)_____ technology, _____(19)_____ modern agriculture has become one of _____(20)_____ world's greatest success stories. Today, _____(21)_____ global agriculture produces 17 percent more calories per _____(22)_____ person than it did 30 years ago, despite _____(23)_____ 70 percent population increase.

5 **Review** Complete the following passage by using *a, an, the,* or *X* (to indicate that no article is necessary). Explain any cases where you feel more than one choice may be appropriate.

Changing Eating Habits

___The___ eating habits of ___X___ people around _____ 1 _____ world are changing. In general, as _____ 2 _____ country becomes richer, its people consume more meat. This causes _____ 3 _____ increase in _____ 4 _____ demand for meat, and as _____ 5 _____ result, _____ 6 _____ meat production begins to increase.

_____ 7 _____ meat production is not always _____ 8 _____ good use of _____ 9 _____ land, however. _____ 10 _____ meat production normally uses more resources in _____ 11 _____ land, _____ 12 _____ water, and _____ 13 _____ work. When _____ 14 _____ farmland is poor, raising _____ 15 _____ cows is efficient, but when _____ 16 _____ farmland is rich, raising _____ 17 _____ crops gives much more food. _____ 18 _____ wheat, _____ 19 _____ rice, or _____ 20 _____ other crops grown for _____ 21 _____ direct human consumption produce much more human food per acre. _____ 22 _____ reason for this is that _____ 23 _____ cow uses up to 90 percent of _____ 24 _____ energy from grain to convert it to meat. Today, about _____ 25 _____ third of _____ 26 _____ world's grain production is fed to _____ 27 _____ livestock (cows, pigs, and so on). This amount of grain is enough to supply _____ 28 _____ human energy needs of _____ 29 _____ China and _____ 30 _____ India.

Using What You've Learned

6 **Taking an Inventory** What food do you have at home? What personal care or cleaning products do you have? Choose two different cupboards or closets in your home. One should have food or cooking items. The other should have cleaning or personal care items. Make a list of the contents of each. Bring your lists to class and share your information with your classmates.

7 **Comparing Prices** How well do you know grocery prices? Check your budgeting ability. First, make a list of at least 10 items that you need to buy. Your list should include food and household items. Use specific units of measurement in your list, and write down what you believe each item costs. Then work with a partner. Do not let your partner see your estimated prices. Your partner should write down estimates for your list, while you write down estimates for your partner's list. Finally, go to a grocery store and check the prices. Report back to the class on how accurate you were. You can use the following chart to help you.

Item	My Cost Estimate	Partner's Cost Estimate	Actual Store Price
1.			
2.			
3.			
4.			
5.			
6.			
7.			
8.			
9.			
10.			

Setting the Context

Previewing the Passage Discuss the questions.

What does the word *security* mean? What does security mean to you?

Reading Read the passage.

Security

Although some jobs may seem secure, in today's world no one is certain of keeping the same job for his or her entire lifetime. Change is occurring constantly. Today's jobs may not exist tomorrow; likewise, today's companies may not, either. While everyone everywhere is interested in security, the fact is that nothing ever stays exactly the same. All things and situations change—people, jobs, careers, technology, the economy, politics, and the weather. As the Greek philosopher Heraclitus said many centuries ago, "There is nothing permanent except change." 5

Discussing Ideas Discuss the question.

At this particular stage in your life, what does financial security mean for you?

Grammar Structures and Practice

A. Subject / Verb Agreement

In formal English, subjects and verbs must agree in number (singular or plural).
- A singular verb is used with a subject that is a singular count noun or a noncount noun. Certain nouns are singular, even though they end in *-s (economics, news)*.
- Plural verbs are used with subjects that are plural count nouns.
- In general, words or phrases that come between the subject and verb do not affect the use of singular or plural verbs.

6.15 Subject / Verb Agreement

	Explanations	Count Nouns	Noncount Nouns
Singular Subject and Verb	A singular verb is used with a subject that is a singular count noun or a noncount noun. Certain nouns are singular, even though they end in *-s (economics, news).* See below.	**A friend is** a person who cares about you. **Our aunt**, along with several friends, **is coming** for dinner.	**Friendship is** very important to me. Good **news** about friends **is** wonderful to hear.
Plural Subject and Verb	Plural verbs are used with subjects that are plural count nouns.	**Friends are** people who care about you. **Our aunt and uncle are coming** for dinner. **Our sons**, as well as their friend Paul, **are coming** for dinner.	

1 **Practice** In these sentences, choose the correct form (singular or plural) of the verb in parentheses.

Example John and Susan (is / are) taking economics this semester.

1. John's classmates (is / are) important to him.

2. Classmates (is / are) people who attend classes with you.

3. John, along with several classmates, (is / are) arriving shortly.

4. John, as well as his classmates, (is / are) arriving soon.

5. Economics (is / are) John's favorite class.

6. His assignments for economics (is / are) very difficult.

7. (Is / Are) there any news about the final exam for that class?

8. John and his classmates (is / are) worried about the exam.

B. Subject / Verb Agreement with Collective and Other Nouns

Some nouns are always plural, and other nouns can be either singular or plural.

- Some count nouns are called "collective" because they refer to a group as *one* unit. Collective nouns can be singular or plural, but in American English, they are generally singular.
- Other nouns that refer to one item, especially names of tools, are always plural.
- For all nouns used as subjects, words or phrases that come between the subject and verb do not usually affect the use of singular or plural verbs.

6.16 Subject / Verb Agreement with Collective and Other Nouns

Structures	Explanations	Nouns		Examples
Common Collective Nouns (generally singular)	Some count nouns are called "collective" because they refer to a group as *one* unit. Collective nouns can be singular or plural, but in American English, they are generally singular.	army assembly audience class committee congregation congress couple crew	faculty family government group public senate series staff team	**The assembly is** meeting at 10:00. **The audience was** eager for the show to begin. **The committee was** well-organized. **The government is** responsible for that. **The public is** upset about the issue. **The staff was** in agreement.
Nouns with No Singular Form (always plural)	Other nouns that refer to one item, especially names of tools, are always plural.	binoculars clothes glasses pajamas pants pliers police	premises scissors shears shorts slacks tongs tweezers	**Those binoculars were** expensive. **Your pants are** in the laundry. **Those pliers were** expensive. **The scissors are** in that drawer. **Your blue slacks are** dirty. Where **are the tweezers**?
Nouns with No Plural Form (always singular)		economics news physics		**Economics** is an interesting subject. The **news** is on at 6:00 P.M.

2 **Practice** In these sentences, choose the correct form (singular or plural) of the verb in parentheses.

Example News from home ((is) / are) very important to me.

1. Finance (is / are) one of five major area studies in business.

2. The class (is / are) preparing a report on international finance.

3. Economics (is / are) a difficult subject for many people.

4. Economists often (helps / help) shape government policies.

5. The economic theories of John Maynard Keynes (has / have) shaped the policies of many governments.

6. Supply-side economics (was / were) the name given to the policies of President Ronald Reagan.

7. The government (has / have) changed economic policies several times.

8. The advice from the accountants (was / were) very valuable.

9. Congress (has / have) voted not to raise taxes.

10. The staff (has / have) written a full report on the issue.

11. The police (is / are) on the way here.

12. These premises (is / are) off limits to unauthorized individuals.

13. The general public (is / are) not allowed to enter this area.

14. The information we were given about the machines (was / were) useful.

15. The new equipment (has / have) worked very well.

16. The news (was / were) very good.

17. That series of articles (was / were) highly informative.

18. Do you know where my glasses (is / are)? I want to read this.

19. Do you know where the binoculars (is / are)? I can't see the game.

20. The team (is / are) coming on the field now.

C. Agreement with Nouns, Pronouns, Adjectives, and Verbs

These pronouns and adjectives—*any-, every-, no-, some-, each, all,* and *none*—affect whether verbs or other pronouns are singular or plural.

6.17 Agreement with Nouns, Pronouns, Adjectives, and Verbs

Structures	Explanations	Examples
anyone　no one anybody　nobody anything　nothing everyone　someone everybody　somebody everything　something	In formal English, indefinite pronouns such as *anyone* and *anybody* are singular. They are used with singular verbs. Singular pronouns and adjectives are used to refer to them. In informal English, plural pronouns are often used.	*Formal* **Everyone has his or her** own problems from time to time. **Everyone has his** own problems at times. *Informal* **Everyone has their** own problems at times.
each	*Each* and *each* + noun is always singular.	**Each person was** counted. **Each was** counted.
all	*All* uses a plural verb when it modifies or refers to a count noun. *All* uses a singular verb when it modifies or refers to a noncount noun.	*Count Nouns* **All assignments are** due on Friday. **All are** due on Friday. *Noncount Nouns* **All homework is** due on Friday. **All is** due on Friday.
none	*None* generally uses a singular verb in formal English, but a plural verb is sometimes considered correct.	*Formal* **None was** missing. *Informal* **None were** missing.

3 Practice Choose the form of the word(s) in parentheses that is correct in formal, written English.

Example No one (want /(wants)) to be in a bad economic situation.

1. Everyone (hope / hopes) to get and keep a good job.
2. With today's changing economy, anyone with a good job (is / are) very fortunate.
3. Everyone (worry / worries) about losing (her / their) money.
4. None (want / wants) to lose (his / their) money.
5. All of the people (was / were) concerned about the safety of (his or her / their) savings.
6. Each of them (was / were) very concerned about the situation.
7. Anyone who (don't / doesn't) currently have a job (is / are) welcome to apply.
8. Every company (has / have) (its / their) own employment policies.
9. Some companies allow everyone to give (his or her / their) ideas.
10. In some companies, all workers (is / are) able to contribute (his or her / their) ideas.
11. Nobody (is / are) surprised when people complain.
12. Anybody can bring (his or her / their) complaints to meetings.
13. None of the workers (was / were) at the meeting last night.
14. No one (was / were) available to give (his / their) opinion.
15. Nothing (was / were) resolved.

4 Practice Reread the sentences in Activity 3 starting on page 266. Identify and rewrite any sentences that have an informal, conversational alternative.

Example 3. Everyone (worry / worries) about losing (her / their) money.
Everyone worries about losing their money. —Informal

5 Review Complete the following passage by using *a, an, the,* or *X* (to indicate that no article is necessary). Explain any cases where you feel more than one choice may be appropriate.

Food Insecurity and World Hunger

Today, no one should go hungry. Everyone's food supply should be secure. _____*The*_____ world produces enough food to feed _____*the*_____ entire global population, yet _____*X*_____ hunger plagues _____ 1 _____ earth. According to _____ 2 _____ World Bank, over 800 million people are malnourished—so poorly fed that they are unable to lead _____ 3 _____ normal, active lives. Approximately one in seven people goes hungry. One in three children is underweight. Why does _____ 4 _____ hunger exist? These are some of _____ 5 _____ reasons according to the United Nations World Food Programme:

Nature

_____ 6 _____ Natural disasters such as _____ 7 _____ floods, _____ 8 _____ tropical storms, and _____ 9 _____ drought are increasing, with horrific consequences for food security in poor, developing countries. _____ 10 _____ Drought is now _____ 11 _____ single most common cause of food shortages.

War

Since 1992, _____ 12 _____ number of short and long-term food crises caused by _____ 13 _____ humans has more than doubled—from 15 percent to more than 35 percent. In _____ 14 _____ war, _____ 15 _____ food sometimes becomes _____ 16 _____ weapon. _____ 17 _____ Food and _____ 18 _____ livestock is taken or destroyed. _____ 19 _____ Fields and _____ 20 _____ water wells are often mined or contaminated.

Poverty

In many places, _____ 21 _____ poor farmers often cannot afford to buy _____ 22 _____ seeds that would grow _____ 23 _____ food for their families. They lack _____ 24 _____ money to pay for _____ 25 _____ tools that they need. They don't have _____ 26 _____ land or _____ 27 _____ water or _____ 28 _____ education to lay _____ 29 _____ foundation for

_____ secure future. In short, _____ poor are
           30   31
hungry and their hunger traps them in _____ poverty.
                                              32

6 **Review** Complete the following passage by using the appropriate form (active or passive) of the verb in parentheses. Add adverbs and negatives when indicated, and pay close attention to use of singular and plural forms.

Working Toward Positive Change

Change _____*is*_____ a reality in everyone's life. Everyone in the
                (be)
world _____*is faced*_____ with change every single day. If change
              (face)
_____ to occur, what can we do to try to make change positive?
   1 (have)
What positive changes can one person make?

   Heifer Project International _____ an excellent example of
                                        2 (be)
the work of one person toward positive change. Heifer _____ in
                                                            3 (begin)
the 1930s through the vision and practical work of Dan West. During the Spanish Civil War, West _____ to Spain to help as a relief worker.
                          4 (travel)
While he _____ there, he _____ the tremendous
              5 (work)   6 (feel)
challenge of feeding hungry people. He _____ that he
                                              7 (believe)
_____ to find a process to help guarantee a supply of food. But
   8 (have)
how? As fast as he _____ milk to the hungry children, they
                          9 (give)
_____ the milk and it _____. The cost of import-
   10 (drink)   11 (go)
ing more milk _____ too expensive for a country recovering
                    12 (be)
from war.

   Then one day an idea _____ to West: "These children
                              13 (come)
_____ a cup; they _____ a cow." Why not bring
   14 (not need)   15 (need)
cows to Spain and produce the milk there? West _____ to give
                                                      16 (want)
each cow to a family. The offspring of that cow _____ to be
                                                      17 (have)
given to another family. The second family _____ to give a calf
                                                  18 (have)
to yet another family. And so on! His idea _____ "Little steps
                                                 19 (be)

climb big mountains."

West _____ home and _____ *Heifers for*
        20 (return)   21 (form)

Relief. His organization _____ to ending hunger permanently
           22 (dedicate)

by providing families with livestock and training. In 1944, the first shipment of

17 heifers _____ from York, Pennsylvania, to Puerto Rico.
       23 (send)

These heifers _____ to families whose children
         24 (go)

_____ milk.
  25 (taste / never)

Why _____ Dan West _____ heifers? Heifers
     26 (do)   27 (choose)

_____ young cows that _____ birth yet. They
   28 (be)   29 (not give)

_____ perfect not only for supplying a continued source of milk,
   30 (be)

but also for supplying a continued source of support. How

_____ the Heifer program _____? Each family re-
   31 (have)   32 (work)

ceiving a heifer _____ to "pass on the gift." In other words, each
      33 (agree)

family _____ the female offspring to another family. Because of
    34 (donate)

this "chain," the gift of food _____.
      35 (end / never)

This simple idea of giving families a source of food rather than short-term

relief _____ for almost 60 years. As a result, millions of families
   36 (continue)

in 115 countries today _____ better health, more income, and
      37 (experience)

the joy of helping others.

▲ A young Kenyan woman with the Heifer Project International cow
received by her family.

Using What You've Learned

7 **Discussing Proverbs** Proverbs are wise sayings that have endured over time. Some proverbs deal with how we manage money—are we wise or foolish with our resources? In groups, read the proverbs and compare them to proverbs in your first languages. Can you explain the meaning of each?

1. A penny saved is a penny earned.

2. The best things in life are free.

3. An ounce of prevention is worth a pound of cure.

4. A fool and his money are soon parted.

5. A bird in the hand is worth two in the bush.

6. You can have too much of a good thing.

7. Beauty is potent but money is omnipotent.

8. Money is a good servant but a bad master.

Use of Articles and Singular and Plural Forms

Singular and plural forms of nouns and verbs are frequently tested on standardized English proficiency exams. Review these commonly tested structures and check your understanding by completing the following sample items.

Remember that . . .

✔ A singular subject uses a singular verb. Plural subjects use plural verbs. Generally, words that come between the subject and verb do not affect the use of singular or plural forms.

✔ A noncount noun always takes a singular verb.

✔ A singular count noun must be preceded by an article or adjective. Plural count nouns do not have to be preceded by an article or adjective.

✔ A collective noun (*committee, staff,* and so on) generally takes a singular verb.

✔ Many indefinite pronouns and adjectives are singular.

Part 1 Mark the correct completion for the following:

Example   John ——————— happy with his classes.

    (A) seem   (C) seeming

    (B) is seem   (D) **seems**

1. Physics ——————— the study of matter, energy, force, and motion.

    (A) is being   (C) is

    (B) are   (D) have been

2. The economic theorist who has perhaps most influenced government policy making in the last 60 years ——————— John Maynard Keynes.

    (A) is   (C) have been

    (B) are   (D) has being

3. ——————— is often a problem for students studying far from their homes.

    (A) Homesickness   (C) The homesickness

    (B) A homesickness   (D) Another homesickness

4. ——————— stock exchanges in the United States are the New York and the NASDAQ exchanges.

    (A) Largest   (C) The largest two

    (B) The largest   (D) Largest two

5. The students have two tests: one test on Monday and
_____ on Tuesday.

    Ⓐ other   Ⓒ the others

    Ⓑ others   Ⓓ the other

Part 2 Circle the letter below the underlined word(s) containing an error.

Example   Anyone can <u>feel frustrated</u> if <u>they have</u> <u>difficulties</u> in speaking
                                    A   Ⓑ   C

        <u>a foreign</u> language.
         D

1. The committee <u>has</u> been discussing the issue of how <u>each</u> member should
                A   B

<u>officially</u> register <u>their</u> opinion on a particular issue.
  C   D

2. In recent years, unemployment <u>have</u> grown <u>considerably</u> among <u>certain</u>
                               A   B   C

segments of the population, especially <u>those</u> in urban areas.
                                  D

3. In 1900, <u>typical</u> chocolate candy bar weighed two ounces, but today it weighs
           A

seven ounces, <u>a</u> 350 percent increase in <u>the</u> average size of <u>candy bars</u>.
          B   C   D

4. Almost everyone who <u>lives</u> on earth is in one way or <u>another</u> affected by <u>the</u>
                    A   B   C   D

global economics.

5. The committee <u>has</u> already made <u>their</u> selection from <u>the</u> various candidates
   A   B   C   D

for that job.

Self-Assessment Log

Each of the following statements describes the grammar you learned in this chapter. Read the statements; then check the box that describes how well you understand each structure.

	Needs Improvement	Good	Great
I can use *a* and *an* appropriately.	❑	❑	❑
I can use *the* appropriately.	❑	❑	❑
I can use a variety of indefinite pronouns and adjectives appropriately.	❑	❑	❑
I can use units of measurement appropriately.	❑	❑	❑
I can use singular and plural verbs and pronouns appropriately.	❑	❑	❑
I can take a test about articles, pronouns, and singular and plural forms.	❑	❑	❑

Remarkable Individuals

In This Chapter

Gerunds, Infinitives, and Related Structures

Part 1 Introduction to Gerunds

Part 2 Introduction to Infinitives

Part 3 Verbs Followed by Gerunds; Verbs Followed by Infinitives

Part 4 Verbs Followed by Either Gerunds or Infinitives

Part 5 Special Uses of Other Verb Forms

" People become really quite remarkable when they start thinking that they can do things. When they believe in themselves, they have the first secret of success. **"**

—Norman Vincent Peale
U.S. clergyman and motivational speaker (1898–1993)

Connecting to the Topic

1. What does it mean to be remarkable?
2. Are remarkable people always successful people?
3. Does true success always involve achieving something remarkable?

Introduction

In this chapter, you will read about both famous and not-so-famous people who have done remarkable things. You will study the use of gerunds and infinitives, including how they can function as nouns, which verbs they often follow, and how the use of one or the other can change the meaning of a sentence. You will also look at a few uses of other verb forms: simple, present participle, and past participle forms.

Reading Read the following passage. It introduces the chapter theme, "Remarkable Individuals," and raises some of the topics and issues you will cover in the chapter.

Remarkable People

- A teenager who was brain damaged at birth learns to ride a bicycle and begins to compete in long-distance races.
- A former U.S. president devotes the rest of his life to promoting peace, to helping resolve conflicts, and to building homes for the needy around the world. 5
- A young woman who wants to make a difference in environmental issues and in education spends a year counting penguins and teaching school to children in a lonely outpost at the bottom of the world.
- A group of scientists brings help and hope to desperately poor farmers by developing high-quality corn that is able to grow well in difficult terrain. 10
- A professional golfer uses his fortune to support organizations in helping children to excel and to reach their dreams.

Some of these people are rich and famous, and some are not. Some are young, and some are old. What do they have in common? All of them are remarkable.

What makes a person remarkable? The word *remarkable* means "notably 15 unusual" or "worthy of notice." A remarkable person, then, is someone who is unusual, who is worthy of our noticing. Of course, being "unusual" or "worthy of notice" does not necessarily mean being famous or well known. Many famous people are not remarkable, and many people who are truly remarkable are not famous. 20

These people are remarkable because all them set difficult goals and then worked hard to achieve them. Perhaps that is the measure of remarkable individuals: people with the courage, strength, and perseverance to work—and keep on working—toward something that they believe in. As Booker T. Washington once said, "Success is to be measured not so much by the position that one has reached 25 in life as by the obstacles which he has overcome while trying to succeed."

We can learn a great deal from people we consider to be remarkable. We can be inspired by their work and their way of being because they enable us to see what is possible in one life.

Discussing Ideas Disuss the questions.

Who are some remarkable people that you know or that you have read about? Why do you think they are remarkable?

Part 1 Introduction to Gerunds

Setting the Context

Previewing the Passage Discuss the questions.

What does having a second job mean to you? Who do you know that has a second job?

Reading Read the following passage about Jimmy Carter, a former president of the United States.

A Second Job

For some people, retiring after years of hard work is a lifetime goal. However, former U.S. President Jimmy Carter did not retire after serving four years as the president of the United States. Instead of staying home and relaxing, Carter created a "second job" for himself as an ambassador for world peace. He went from being president to being a humanitarian.[1] As a humanitarian, Carter   5
spent his time helping people and countries in need. Sometimes this meant intervening between two countries in conflict. Other times it involved working with opposing sides in the same country. And often it meant devoting time to the poor. For example, he did a tremendous amount of work with Habitat for Humanity, a volunteer agency involved in building homes for the poor. In all,   10
Carter's work has been remarkable. Even more remarkable is that Carter chose to do humanitarian work, even though he could easily have stayed at home as a "retiree."

------

[1] *humanitarian* someone who works for the good of all humankind

▲ Former U.S. President Jimmy Carter building homes for the poor

 Discussing Ideas Disuss the questions.

Do you know of any other leaders who have done work like Carter who have done a "second job" after their time in office? Do you know of other individuals who have gone back to work after retirement?

Grammar Structures and Practice

A. Introduction to Gerunds

Gerunds have the same form as present participles: simple form + *-ing*. See Appendix 2 for spelling rules for the *-ing* ending.

7.1 Functions of Gerunds

Explanation	Structures	Examples
Although gerunds look like verb forms, they function as nouns and can be used at many points in a sentence.	**Noun Object of a Verb**	I enjoy **books**.
	Gerund Object of a Verb	I enjoy **reading**.
	Gerund Subject	**Reading** is my favorite pastime.
	Gerund Complement	My favorite pastime is **reading**.
	Gerund Object of a Preposition	By **reading** a lot, I learn about the world.

Like verbs, gerunds have affirmative and negative forms and active and passive forms.

7.2 Forms of Gerunds

Structures	Explanations	Active	Passive
Affirmative	Active gerunds are the *-ing* form of a verb. Passive gerunds are formed by using *being* + past participle.	**Governing** a country is difficult.	**Being governed** by a good leader is what most citizens want.
Negative	*Not* comes before the gerund. Possessive nouns or pronouns may also be used before gerunds.	**Not dedicating himself to peace** is unthinkable for a man like Jimmy Carter.	**Not being dedicated** to peace is unthinkable for a man like Jimmy Carter.
***By* Phrase with Passive**	As with most passive sentences, the *by* phrase is commonly omitted.	Everyone was delighted by the **committee's inviting** Jimmy Carter.	Everyone was delighted by **Jimmy Carter's being invited** (by the committee).

Gerunds can also have subjects and objects. In formal English, a possessive is used before a gerund. In informal English, nouns or object pronouns are often used.

7.3 Use of Possessives and Pronouns with Gerunds

	Explanations	Active	Passive
Formal	In formal English, a possessive is used before a gerund.	Everyone was moved by **Carter's committing himself** to the poor. Everyone was delighted by **the committee's inviting** Jimmy Carter. Everyone was delighted by **its inviting** Jimmy Carter.	Everyone was moved by **his being committed** to the poor. Everyone was delighted by **Jimmy Carter's being invited**. Everyone was delighted by **his being invited**.
Informal	In informal English, nouns or object pronouns are often used.	Everyone was delighted by **the committee inviting** Jimmy Carter. Everyone was delighted by **it (them) inviting** Jimmy Carter.	Everyone was delighted by **Jimmy Carter being invited**. Everyone was delighted by **him being invited**.

1 Practice Reread the selection "A Second Job" on page 277. Underline all uses of gerunds. Tell how they are used (as a subject, after a verb, and so on).

2 Practice Complete the second sentence in each pair with either an active or passive gerund. Use the example as a model.

Example Our children like being read books. We like
reading books to our children.

1. We enjoy reading stories to our children. Our children enjoy
   _____.

2. Our children enjoy being sung to. We enjoy _____.

3. Our children like being given gifts. We like _____.

4. We like inviting friends to our house. Our friends like _____.

5. Our children enjoy being played with. We enjoy _____.

6. Our children like being helped. We like _____.

7. We enjoy including our friends. Our friends enjoy _____.

8. We like telling stories to each other. Each of us likes _____.

9. We enjoy applauding a good speaker. A good speaker enjoys
   _____.

10. We enjoy calling our family on holidays. Our family enjoys
    _____.

11. We like sending our family cards and letters. Our family likes
    _____.

12. People enjoy being praised for doing a good job. We enjoy
    _____.

3 Practice Doing a good job at something usually involves enjoying what you are doing. What do you enjoy doing? Here are ideas from a "work aptitude inventory." These inventories help young people make choices about jobs and careers. Which activities do you enjoy? Which don't you enjoy? Make at least 10 sentences with active gerunds after the verb *enjoy* or *like*. Use these ideas and add some of your own.

Example *I enjoy building things like furniture and model ships and planes.*

- build things
- care for animals or plants
- cook and bake
- design or draw things
- fix machines
- help people with medical problems
- plan and organize
- read alone
- read to children
- solve problems
- teach people how to do things
- travel
- use a computer
- work with numbers
- work with people

4 Practice Complete the following sentences with active or passive gerunds formed from the verbs in parentheses. Include negatives when indicated.

Example ___*Reading about*___ (read about) Jimmy Carter is inspirational.

1. For Carter, _____ (help) the poor is important work for humankind.

2. _____ (serve) others has been a full-time job for Carter.

3. By _____ (not give up) and by _____ (continue) to fight against poverty, he has given hope to millions of people.

4. Anyone who visited President Carter could not help _____ (inspire) by his dedication.

5. Carter has spent a great deal of time _____ (work) with Habitat for Humanity.

6. Habitat for Humanity International (HFHI) is a nonprofit organization. That is, the organization is not involved in _____ (make) money.

7. HFHI was founded in 1976 by Millard and Linda Fuller because they were interested in _____ (build) housing that poor people could afford.

8. Since 1976, HFHI has been successful at _____ (build) more than 200,000 houses around the world.

9. Through HFHI, thousands of volunteers have done remarkable jobs at _____ (construct) safe, low-cost housing in a very short time.

10. It is famous for _____ (give) people a new start. Through the help of HFHI, more than 1 million people in more than 3,000 communities now have safe, decent, affordable shelter.

B. Gerunds Following Prepositions

Because gerunds act like nouns, they can also follow prepositions.

7.4 Gerunds Following Prepositions		
Explanations	**Structures**	**Examples**
Gerunds are used to replace nouns as the objects of prepositions. Infinitives (*to* + verb) may *not* be used.	**Noun Object of a Preposition**	Thanks **for the invitation**. Thanks **for the performance**.
	Gerund Object of a Preposition	Thanks **for inviting us**. Thanks **for performing for us**.

Common Expressions with Prepositions That Are Often Followed by Gerunds			
be accused of be afraid of be dissatisfied with be famous for be in favor of be fed up with be good at	be interested in be involved in be satisfied with be sick of be tired of	approve of blame someone for can't (cannot) help complain about disapprove of excuse someone for get through instead of	plan on (praise) someone for put off talk about (talk over) think about try hard at work hard at worry about How about . . .?

There are many common expressions with prepositions that are often followed by gerunds. Some of these use the preposition *to*.

7.5 Common Expressions with *To* That Are Often Followed by Gerunds

Explanation	Expressions		Structures	Examples

In these idiomatic expressions, *to* is a preposition, and the gerund form follows it if a verb form is used.
 	
Do not confuse the preposition *to* with the *to* used in infinitives (*to* + verb).
	be accustomed to
	be committed to
	be devoted to
	be opposed to
	be subjected to
	be used to
		devote time
		  (money, effort) to
		donate time
		  (money) to
		in addition to
		look forward to
		object to
		plead guilty to
		plead innocent to
			Noun Object of *to*
			
			Gerund Object of *to*
				I am looking forward to **the party**.
				
				I am looking forward to **seeing** you. (*Not* I am looking forward to see you.)

5 **Practice** Complete the following by using the appropriate preposition and including the gerund form of the verbs in parentheses.

at	for	in	of	to

Example Jimmy Carter and his wife Rosalynn are famous _____*for*_____

_____*doing*_____ (do) humanitarian work.

1. Throughout their lives, the Carters have been committed

_____ _____ (work) for social justice.

2. In addition _____ _____ (promote) peace and human rights, the Carters developed the Jimmy Carter Work Project (JCWP).

3. The JCWP is involved _____ _____ (help) Habitat for Humanity to construct affordable housing.

4. Each year, Mr. and Mrs. Carter look forward _____

_____ (donate) a week of their time to the JCWP.

5. The Carters never get tired _____ _____

(build) homes and _____ _____ (raise) awareness of the need for affordable housing.

6. The Work Project is interested _____ _____ (do) projects in different locations each year.

7. It's good _____ _____ (attract) volunteers from around the world.

8. In 2001, the JCWP attract 9,000 volunteers who devoted time _____ _____ (work) on construction projects in South Korea.

9. In 2002, the Work Project was devoted _____

_____ (construct) 1,000 homes in 18 African countries.

10. Grateful people everywhere have thanked the Carters _____

_____ (help) to provide them with safe, affordable housing.

Cultural Note

Volunteerism in the U.S.

Americans of all ages volunteer their time (and give their money) to a great variety of causes. "Causes" can range from remodeling or building homes, donating blood, and teaching children to planting trees, reading to the elderly, and picking up litter along a highway. Large numbers of Americans volunteer. In 2005, for example, over 65 million people volunteered their time to work for a particular cause. That equals over 28 percent of the U.S. population, a percentage that has remained fairly constant for several years.

Using What You've Learned

6 **Describing Skills** Late in life, former President Jimmy Carter found that he was good at building houses! How about you? Are you good at something? Cooking? Dancing? A sport or a craft? How did you learn this? Use this activity to tell your classmates about how you learned and how they can learn. Use the following cues and add gerunds and any other necessary information. You may want to use the verbs *do, watch, listen (to), try, study,* and *buy.*

- I'm (some people, many people are) interested in . . .
- Some people learn best by . . .
- Other people learn from . . .
- Here are my recommendations for . . .
- You should start by . . .
- Before . . . , you should . . .
- While . . . , you should. . .
- Instead of . . . , you should . . .
- After. . . , you . . .

Example *Today, many people are interested in creating websites. Some people learn about website design by taking classes or going workshops. I started by watching a friend create her own website . . . .*

7 **Discussing Plans** What do you feel like doing this afternoon? Tonight? Take turns making suggestions with *how about* + gerund. Make a chain around the class. One student can begin: turn to your neighbor and make a suggestion. Your neighbor will respond and then turn to his or her neighbor with a suggestion. Continue until the whole class has had a turn.

Example   A: How about going to a movie tonight?
             B: Sorry, but I have a lot of homework.
             B: How about ordering a pizza for dinner?
             C: That sounds great!

Setting the Context

 Previewing the Passage Discuss the questions.

Do you know how to ride a bicycle? Have you ever participated in a bicycle race?
Can you imagine racing a bicycle without using your legs?

Reading Read the following passage.

A Remarkable Bicyclist and a Remarkable Human Being

Justin Johnson is a remarkable human being. He was born with numerous
handicaps, but none of these has stopped Justin. Unable to walk without help,
Justin began to ride a hand-powered bicycle several years ago. At first, it was
very difficult for him to go more than a short distance. Soon Justin's trainer Jeff
Frame suggested a three-wheel pedal bicycle since Justin had some use of his   5
legs. Justin worked hard to master the pedal bike and then decided to try to
compete in bicycle races. In 2004, he entered *El Tour de Tucson*, an Arizona
bicycle race. It was almost impossible for him to finish the race, but finally, after
dark, Justin made it across the finish line—with a police escort! It had taken
him 5 hours 19 minutes to complete the course. In 2005, when Justin raced   10
again, he was able to finish the 38-mile race in 4 hours 51 minutes. His training
and hard work had made it possible to cut 30 minutes off his previous record.

Justin's experience with bike racing has encouraged him to shoot for other
goals. Although he has limited vision and hand movements, he's now studying in
a Tucson college and hopes to graduate. Justin also plans to write a book about   15
his life. He wants to share his experiences so that others can find the strength to
succeed against difficult odds.

▲ Justin Johnson and his three-wheel pedal bicycle

Discussing Ideas Discuss the questions.

Do you know anyone like Justin? Do you know someone who has managed to fulfill a dream despite a handicap?

Grammar Structures and Practice

A. Introduction to Infinitives

The infinitive is *to* + simple form.

7.6	Functions of Infinitives	
Explanations	**Structures**	**Examples**
Like the gerund, the infinitive is a verb form that can replace a noun, but it may *not* be the object of a preposition. Infinitives of purpose can be used with or without the expression *in order*.	**Noun Phrase Object of a Verb**	I would like **a new bicycle**.
	Infinitive Object of a Verb	I would like **to buy a new bicycle**.
	Infinitive Subject	**To choose** the right one takes a little time.
	Infinitive Complement	It is fun **to look at** all the models at a bicycle store.
	Infinitive of Purpose	**To buy** a really good bicycle costs a lot of money. He'll save for a year **(in order) to buy** that bicycle.

Like verbs, infinitives have affirmative and negative forms and active and passive forms. Infinitives can also have subjects and objects.

7.7 Forms of Infinitives

Structures	Explanations	Active	Passive
Affirmative	Active infinitives are *to* + the simple form of a verb. Passive infinitives are formed by using *to be*+ the past participle.	We have **to tell** John about the sale on bicycles.	John has **to be told** about the sale on bicycles.
Negative	To make a negative, *not* comes before the infinitive.	Mary said **not to tell** him.	There is a reason for him **not to be told**.
With *for*	*For* + a noun or pronoun may also be used as the subject to an infinitive. "Anticipatory *it*" is often used in this pattern: *it* + *be* (+ *for* + noun or pronoun) + adjective + infinitive.	**For John to know** about this is important. It's important **for John to know** about this. It's important **for him to know** about this.	**For John to be told** is important. It's important **for John to be told**. It's important for **him to be told**.

1 **Practice** Reread the selection "A Remarkable Bicyclist and a Remarkable Human Being" on page 285. Underline all uses of infinitives. Tell how they are used (as a subject, after a verb, and so on).

2 **Practice** Although he has severe handicaps, Justin Johnson is a normal 22-year-old in most respects. Use the following cues to tell about things Justin likes to do, loves to do, and doesn't like to do.

Example *Justin likes to listen to music.*

Likes to Do	Loves to Do	Doesn't Like to Do
go shopping	learn about cars	clean up his room
listen to music	play basketball	wash dishes
send emails	watch football games	write essays

3 Practice Make complete sentences from the following. Begin your sentences with *It's important*. Use the example as a model.

Example   exercise all his muscles
It's important for Justin to exercise all his muscles.

1. get daily exercise
2. do physical therapy
3. spend time with friends
4. practice biking
5. be patient
6. study hard
7. balance priorities
8. work toward new goals

4 Practice Gerunds are used more often than infinitives as subjects of sentences. However, infinitives are frequently used with anticipatory *it* as a subject. Change the following sentences to begin with *it*. Describe some common challenges that face people with handicaps or medical problems.

Example   For a person who is blind, going up and down stairs can be difficult.
It can be difficult for a person who is blind to go up and down stairs.

1. For people who are blind, walking on a bumpy sidewalk is often difficult.
2. For a person who is blind, going shopping can be hard.
3. For a person who is hearing impaired, participating in conversations can be a challenge.
4. For people who are hearing impaired, learning another language is often very difficult.
5. For people with severe arthritis, opening a bottle or a jar can be almost impossible.
6. For a person with arthritis, tying a shoelace may not be easy.
7. For someone with allergies, eating in a restaurant is not always simple.
8. For people with allergies, spending time outdoors can be very difficult.
9. For anyone with a handicap, doing sports can be a big challenge.
10. For Justin Johnson, competing in bicycle races is a great thrill.

B. Infinitives Following Adjectives, Nouns, and Adverbs

Infinitives are frequently used after certain expressions with nouns and adjectives.

7.8 Adjectives and/or Nouns + Infinitives

Structures	Explanations	Examples
Infinitives of Purpose	Infinitives are used to express purpose or goals. *In order* is not necessary for this meaning; it may be omitted. A common expression with infinitives of purpose is *it* + *take* + time or effort + infinitive.	**In order to finish** the race, Justin had to train for many months. **To finish** the race, Justin had to train a lot. It took Justin over five hours **to finish** the race.
Noun + Infinitive	Similarly, infinitives can be used after nouns to show what should or can be done with the nouns. A common expression is *there* + *be* + noun + infinitive.	I have **a pass to use** for the grandstand. She needs **a pass to get in**. Do you have **an extra pass to give me**? There are free passes **to be had**.
Adjective + Infinitive	Infinitives often follow adjectives of emotion or feelings (*happy, sad, eager*).	I was very **happy to meet** Justin Johnson. I was **eager to watch** the race.
Ordinal Numbers + Infinitive	Infinitives often follow ordinals (*the first, the second*, and so on) or adjectives such as *the last* and *the only*.	Justin was **the first to ride** a special bicycle in the Tour de Tucson. Justin probably won't be **the last to do** so.
***It + be* Adjective + Infinitive**	Many adjective / infinitive combinations follow this pattern: *it* + *be* + adjective + infinitive. *Of* + an object often follows adjectives such as *nice, good*, and *polite*.	It was **fun to meet** Justin. It was **great to talk** with him. It was **nice of Justin to spend** time with us.

7.9 Adverbs + Infinitives

Structures	Explanations	Examples
too	The adverb *too* is often followed by an adjective or adverb and an infinitive: *to* + phrase + infinitive. This expression often implies a negative result.	That hill was **too steep to ride** up. I had to walk my bicycle. It was **too difficult to climb** on a bike.
not enough	Infinitives frequently follow *not enough*: *not* + adjective or adverb + *enough* + infinitive *not* + *enough* + noun + infinitive These expressions also imply a negative result.	She was **not old enough to enter** the race. I was**n't strong enough to finish** the race. I did**n't** have **enough energy to finish** the race. We did**n't** have **enough time to train** well for the race.
enough	*Enough*, in affirmative statements, can also be followed by an infinitive. These expressions imply a positive result.	Justin was **strong enough to finish** the race. Justin was **a strong enough bicyclist to finish** the race.
what, when, where, which, and *how*	Phrases with *what, when, where, which,* and *how* are reduced forms of noun clauses: *I would like to know where I can get a good bicycle.* = *I would like to know where to get a good bicycle.*	I would like to know **where to buy** a good bicycle. I would like to know **how to choose** a good bike. I would like to know **which brand to choose**.

5 Pracitce Add infinitive phrases to complete the following.

Example I'm interested in learning how *to ride a mountain bike.*

1. I'm looking for a good mountain bike. Can you tell me where . . . ?
2. Have you considered talking with members of the local bicycle club? It would be a good idea . . .
3. Many beginners have a hard time because their muscles get sore. It's hard . . .
4. It usually takes a few weeks or months . . .
5. Where can I get a mountain bike? Do you know of a good place . . . ?
6. I don't want to look for a bike by myself. Do you have time . . . ?
7. I don't know anything about good places for mountain biking. Can you tell me where . . . ?
8. You can always rent a bike if you don't have enough money . . .
9. Can you tell me where I can rent bicycles? I don't know where . . .
10. Thanks for your time. It was really nice of you . . .

▲ Today's mountain bikes can cost several thousand dollars.

6 Practice Complete the following passage by using active or passive infinitive forms of the verbs in parentheses. Be sure to include negative or noun objects when indicated.

Bicycling

Bicycles were invented in the early 19th century as "toys" for the rich, the only people who could afford _____to buy_____ the early models. Later,
_(buy)

bikes became more affordable, but few people would dare _____
1 (ride)

one. In order _____ _____ a bike, you have
2 (learn)   3 (ride)

_____ _____ a lot! By 1899, however, one out
4 (prepare)   5 (fall)

of every six Americans had bought a bike and started _____.
6 (ride)

The bicycle boom was on! People everywhere began _____ for
7 (ride)

pleasure, and many began _____. Even the *New York Times*
8 (race)

hired _____ races and encouraged _____ bicy-
9 (reporters / cover)   10 (local groups / sponsor)

cle events. But then the automobile was invented, and its popularity threatened

_____ the bicycle entirely.
11 (eliminate)

Of course, the bicycle was not eliminated by the car. People everywhere

have continued _____ their bicycles for pleasure. Likewise,
12 (ride)

many people bicycle in order _____ in good shape, especially
13 (stay)

as doctors have been advising _____ their lifestyles and encouraging _____ more exercise. At the same time, various energy crises have caused _____ their cars at home and _____ their bicycles _____ to work. During one energy crisis alone, bicycle sales skyrocketed from fewer than 7 million in 1970 to over 15 million in 1973. This trend has continued, and today in Washington, D.C., 70,000 alone, for example, over seventy thousand bicyclists commute to their jobs daily.

So, bicycles aren't likely _____. In fact, their popularity is expected _____ as millions of people worldwide rely on bikes for transportation and recreation.

(Blanks labeled: 14 (people / reconsider), 15 (they / get), 16 (many people / leave), 17 (use), 18 (commute), 19 (disappear), 20 (increase))

C. Verbs Followed by Either Gerunds or Infinitives

Many verbs may be followed by either gerunds or infinitives. The basic meaning of the sentence does not change.

7.10	**Verbs Followed by Either Gerunds or Infinitives**	
Verbs	**Structures**	**Examples**
begin like* can (not) afford love* can't bear neglect can't stand prefer continue start hate	**Verb + Gerund** **Verb + Infinitive** **Verb + Gerund** **Verb + Infinitive**	It **began raining**. It **began to rain**. I **like swimming**. I **like to swim**.

* Note that *would like* and *would love* are followed by infinitives.

D. Parallel Structure with Gerunds and Infinitives

Parallelism involves using the same grammatical forms in a series of words in a sentence.

7.11	**Parallel Structure with Gerunds and Infinitives**	
Explanations	**Correct Usage**	**Incorrect Usage***
When two or more infinitives appear in a series, it is not necessary to repeat *to*.	He loves **to eat, to drink,** and **to be** merry. He loves **to eat, drink,** and **be** merry.	✗He loves to eat, drink, and to be merry.
In any series, it is important to use parallel structure. Do *not* mix infinitives and gerunds, if possible.	He loves **to eat, to drink,** and **to be** merry. He loves **eating, drinking,** and **being** merry.	✗He loves to eat, drinking, and to be merry. ✗He loves to eat, drinking, and being merry. ✗He loves eating, to drink, and to be merry.

* Note that each of these is incorrect.

7 **Error Analysis** Many of the following sentences have errors in use of parallel structures. Find and correct the errors.

Examples   Jack loves to bicycle and playing tennis.
  Incorrect:
    Jack loves to bicycle and (to) play tennis.
    OR
    Jack loves bicycling and playing tennis.

  Jack likes to ski and surf.
  Correct as is.

1. When bicycles were first invented, most people were too poor to buy or maintaining a bicycle.

2. In the early days, owning and to maintain a bicycle was expensive.

3. By the late 1800s, bicycles were cheaper and people everywhere began buying and riding them.

4. People everywhere began to ride for pleasure, and some began racing.

5. After the invention of the automobile, bicycle riding decreased and driving increased.

6. Bicycle riding became very popular in the U.S. again in the 1970s because to ride a bicycle was a way of saving gasoline.

7. Many people couldn't afford to pay for gasoline, so they began to ride their bicycles to work.

8. During that time, some of today's great cyclists started riding bicycles and doing short races as children.

9. Cyclists like Lance Armstrong began to ride and compete as young children and continued to race as adults.

10. People everywhere love watching Lance Armstrong and hear his amazing story.

8 **Practice** Complete the following passage by adding the gerund or infinitive form of the verbs in parentheses. Add subjects when indicated.

Lance Armstrong: An Inspiration to All

Lance Armstrong is a remarkable person. The multiple winner of the Tour de France is an outstanding athlete and excellent bicycle racer. He is also a cancer survivor.

Lance Armstrong has always worked hard at _____*doing*_____ every-
                                                    (do)
thing well. He's worked hard at _____ every day of the week in
                                        1 (train)
order _____ fit enough _____ "the big race."
           2 (be)   3 (win)
He's worked even harder at _____ the cancer that had spread
                                  4 (fight)
through his body.

It was in 1996 that Armstrong was named the top cyclist in the world. It was also in 1996, just four months before his 25th birthday, that Armstrong was diagnosed with advanced stages of cancer. Chances for his recovery were 50-50.

Armstrong began _____ chemotherapy treatments—the
                         5 (have)
strongest, most aggressive available. This therapy was almost too much
_____, though. Even though Armstrong was a young athlete in
   6 (his body / take)
excellent condition, the therapy was so potent that it completely weakened
him. He couldn't continue _____ as he had trained before. It
                                   7 (train)
was very difficult _____ even basic, day-to-day activities.
                       8 (Armstrong / do)
Miraculously, the chemotherapy finally began _____, and
                                                        9 (work)
Armstrong started _____ about _____ once
                        10 (think)   11 (race)
again. In May of 1998, Lance Armstrong celebrated his return to cycling with a

victory at the Tour de France. He then won the Tour again each year from 1999 to 2005. He's the first person ever _____ the Tour seven con-
12 (win)
secutive times.

Armstrong has won an even greater race, the race against cancer. And he has survived with a remarkable spirit. He says, "It's ironic, I used to ride my bike to make a living. Now I just want to live so that I can ride."

▲ Lance Armstrong, breaking records and making history by winning the 2005 Tour de France

Using What You've Learned

9 **Talking About Bicyclists and Bicycle Racing** Are you a fan of bicycle racing? What do you know about the Tour de France, the Vuelta a España, or the Gira d'Italia? What do you know about the top cyclists today? Choose one topic to research using the Internet or the library. Prepare a short composition to share with your classmates. Try to use the following verbs and expressions in your composition.

be good at	begin	like
be famous for	can (not) afford	love
be interested in	can (not) stand	prefer
be involved in	continue	start
be satisfied with	hate	

10 **Describing a Person** In pairs or small groups, use the following phrases in a discussion about someone you admire. After you have finished, choose one member of your group to give a brief summary of your discussion for the entire class.

. . . is interested in . . .   For. . . , it's fun . . .

. . . is excited about . . .   It's enjoyable . . .

. . . is turned off by . . .   For. . . , it's boring . . .

. . . is good at . . .   It's great . . .

Part 3	Verbs Followed by Gerunds; Verbs Followed by Infinitives

Setting the Context

 Previewing the Passage Discuss the question.

Imagine living in the harshest climate on earth. What qualities would a person need not only to survive but also to be well-adjusted in a very difficult setting?

Reading Read the following passage.

Living in Antarctica

Antarctica is a frozen continent where the temperature seldom manages to reach 25°F (- 4°C). It tends to hover around -20°F (-30°C), and it can plunge to -100°F (-80°C) or less. The winds can reach 200 miles per hour (320 km). The sun shines most of the day during the very short summer, but the winter is month after month of dusk and darkness.   5

You might like to pay a short visit to Antarctica to see its frozen beauty from the warmth of your cruise ship, but would you like to live there? Approximately 1000 people live in Antarctica year-round, and two of those remarkable people are Adriana Romero and Victor Figueroa, from Argentina.

Victor Figueroa has spent many years in Antarctica, and one year, he was   10 joined by his wife Adriana. Victor was commander of the scientific station at Esperanza (Hope). Adriana was hired to help run the Antarctica radio station, and she also volunteered to teach in the Esperanza school, to help with the Adelie penguin counts, and to translate for foreign visitors.

For them, living in Antarctica was exciting, but both also admit being bored   15 and even being frightened at times. Through all, they persisted with high spirits and courage, both making major contributions to our knowledge of this forbidding continent.

▲ Adriana Romero, radio broadcaster and teacher, bicycling near Argentina's Esperanza Station in Antarctica.

Discussing Ideas Disuss the questions.

Have you (or someone close to you) ever had any experiences similar to those of Adriana Romero and Victor Figueroa—living for an extended time in a very difficult environment? Can you describe the experience?

Grammar Structures and Practice

A. Verbs and Verb Phrases Commonly Followed by Gerunds

Some verbs may be followed by gerunds, some by infinitives, and some by either. This is a short list of verbs commonly followed by gerunds. More are covered later in the chapter.

7.12 Verbs and Verb Phrases Commonly Followed by Gerunds				
Verb + Gerund				**Examples**
admit	decide	involve	risk	**I appreciated** your **telling** us your story.
anticipate	delay	keep (on)	suggest	
appear	dislike	know (how)	tolerate	**I can't help wondering** why you did that.
appreciate	enjoy	learn (how)	understand	
avoid	escape	mind		**Can** you **imagine living** there for a year?
be	finish	miss	be worth	
be able	forgive	postpone	have trouble	You should **spend** some **time reading**
be supposed	have	practice	spend time	about Antarctica.
consider	hope	recommend		
dare	imagine	regret		We can't **tolerate having** problems.

B. Verbs Commonly Followed by Infinitives

Some verbs may be followed by gerunds, some by infinitives, and some by either. This is a short list of verbs commonly followed by infinitives. More are covered later in the chapter.

7.13 Verbs and Verb Phrases Commonly Followed by Infinitives				
Verb + Infinitive				**Examples**
afford	fail	manage	volunteer	Can you **afford to go** there?
agree	forget	offer	wait	I've **decided to travel** there.
appear	happen	plan	wish	She **happened to mention** that.
be	have	prepare	would like	I **hesitate to spend** so much money.
be able	hesitate	pretend	would love	We **offered to make** some plans.
be supposed	hope	refuse		You **seem to be** tired.
care	intend	seem		I'll **wait to make** my decision.
decide	know (how)	tend		I **would like to** learn how to do that.
deserve	learn (how)	threaten		

---

1 **Practice** Complete the following, using gerund or infinitive forms of the verbs in parentheses. Be sure to include negatives and make other changes when indicated.

Example We can't afford . . . (take that trip)

We can't afford to take that trip.

1. They agreed . . . (not tell anyone)

2. We appreciated . . . (he / tell us that)

3. He had avoided . . . (tell us)

4. She deserved . . . (tell) (*passive*)

5. I can't forgive . . . (they / not tell us)

6. He happened . . . (mention / the subject)

7. We regretted . . . (not tell) (*passive*)

8. He waited . . . (tell / officially) (*passive*)

2 **Practice** Going to Antarctica was a major move for Adriana Romero, and living there was seldom easy. Following is information about her experiences and daily life. Rephrase each sentence using the cues below. Pay attention to the use of infinitives and gerunds.

Examples Would you like to live in a remote place for a year?
Can you imagine *living in a remote place for a year?*

Adriana Romero was able to spend an entire year in Antarctica.
Adriana Romero managed *to spend an entire year in Antarctica.*

1. Adriana decided to move with her husband to Antarctica.

   Adriana agreed . . .

2. She was interested in living in Antarctica for a year.

   She wished . . .

3. When Adriana was in Antarctica, she managed to do some exercise almost every day.

   When Adriana was in Antarctica, she spent time . . .

4. At first, she didn't want to exercise outside.

   At first, she hesitated . . .

5. Later, she really enjoyed getting on her bicycle and riding on the ice.

   Later, she really appreciated . . .

6. Adriana missed not being able to swim.

   She regretted not . . .

7. She offered to teach at Argentina's School No. 38 on the base.

   She volunteered . . .

8. While there, Adriana was able to speak English and French through her radio broadcasts at Station LRA 36.

   While there, Adriana practiced . . .

9. She was also always ready to speak with visiting scientists and tourists.

   She was always prepared . . .

10. Adriana disliked not having a lot of fresh fruit to eat.

    Adriana missed . . .

11. She couldn't help feeling afraid sometimes.

    She admitted . . .

12. Adriana hopes to return to Antarctica someday.

    Adriana intends . . .

C. Verbs That May Be Followed by a Noun or Pronoun Object Before an Infinitive

Some verbs may optionally be followed by a noun or promoun object before an infinitive.

7.14	Verbs That May Be Followed by a Noun or Pronoun Object Before an Infinitive	
Explanations	Verb + (Noun or Pronoun) + Infinitive	Examples
Infinitives may follow these verbs directly, or a noun or pronoun object may come between the verb and the infinitive. The meaning of the sentence changes with the use of a noun. Note that *for* is not used before the noun or pronoun.	ask beg dare expect need promise want would (may, might) like use	She **asked to play** soccer with us. She **asked her friend to play** soccer. She **wanted to play**. She **wanted her friend to play**.

D. Verbs That Must Be Followed by a Noun or Pronoun Object Before an Infinitive

Some verbs *must* be followed by a noun or pronoun object before an infinitive.

7.15	Verbs That Must Be Followed by a Noun or Pronoun Object Before an Infinitive			
Explanations	Verb + (Noun or Pronoun) + Infinitive			Examples
A noun or pronoun object *must* follow these verbs if an infinitive is used. The object comes between the verb and the infinitive. Note that *for* is not used before the noun or pronoun.	advise* allow* cause* convince enable* encourage* force	get hire invite order permit* persuade	remind require teach* tell urge warn	The doctor **encouraged him to get** more exercise. She **persuaded him to start** a regular exercise program. She **told him to begin** today.

*These verbs are followed by gerunds if no noun or pronoun object is used after the main verb.

3 Practice Complete the following sentences by using *for* or *X* (to indicate that nothing is needed).

Example We asked _____ X _____ Victor to go camping with us.
It was difficult _____ for _____ him to decide.

1. We had expected _____ him to say yes immediately.

2. He promised _____ us to ask for vacation time.

3. It wasn't easy _____ him to get time off from work.

4. We told _____ him to keep trying.

5. We finally convinced _____ Victor to come.

6. Then, he invited _____ his friends to come.

7. In order _____ all of them to come, we had to find more tents.

8. Our neighbor wanted _____ us to use his tent.

4 Practice Complete the following sentences in your own words. Use *me* in each sentence. Be sure to add *for* when necessary.

Examples My parents have asked *me to try hard in school.*
It is difficult *for me to understand spoken English.*

1. I need to learn more English, and my parents have encouraged . . .

2. My parents have told . . .

3. They have warned . . .

4. They won't permit . . .

5. I have a test soon, and it's important . . .

6. It's necessary . . .

7. My teacher wants . . .

8. My teacher expects . . .

9. It isn't easy . . .

10. In order . . .

11. My teacher has advised . . .

12. Soon it will be easier . . .

5 Practice Complete the following, using gerund or infinitive forms of the verbs in parentheses. Be sure to include subjects when indicated.

Watching Birds and Counting Penguins

▲ A chinstrap penguin

Some pastimes can be done almost anywhere—observing birds, for example. Bird _____*watching*_____ is a pastime, even a competitive sport, for mil-
(watch)
lions of people around the world. And for Adriana Romero and many scientists in Antarctica, it is an important job. The work of many of the scientists there is _____ track of the penguins. They spend a lot of time
1 (keep)
_____ and _____ penguins, especially the
2 (observe)   3 (count)
Adelie penguins. Observing and counting penguins is a way for
_____ possible changes in the environment. It allows
4 (scientists / notice)
_____ changes in the ecosystem of Antarctica and even warns
5 (scientists / detect)
_____ weather disturbances. Over the long term, penguin
6 (they / expect)
births and migration seem _____ important indicators of global
7 (be)
weather changes. Warmer temperatures cause penguins _____
8 (stay)
longer in Antarctica and _____ more babies. Colder tempera-
9 (have)
tures bring shorter stays and earlier migrations. Because polar weather changes indicate changes worldwide, scientists from many countries are urging

_____ more programs like the penguin observation programs
10 (governments / fund)
in Antarctica.

6 Practice Adriana's husband, Victor Figueroa, was commander of Esperanza Station and later was the leader of Argentina's 1999–2000 expedition to the South Pole. Learn about his trek by completing the following sentences with appropriate gerund or infinitive or forms of the verbs in parentheses.

Example The entire team was excited about _____*hiking*_____ (hike) to the South Pole.

1. All of us were used to _____ (spend) long hours outdoors in the frigid weather.

2. All of us were accustomed _____ (hike) long distances with heavy loads.

3. Because of our _____ (train), each one of us knew how

    _____ (survive) under terrible conditions.

4. All of us looked forward to _____ (trek) to the Pole. Of course, we all felt nervous, too.

5. It was thrilling for _____ (me / lead) the 1999–2000 expedition.

6. Of course, I was worried about _____ (have) accidents or injuries.

7. I anticipated _____ (encounter) some very bad weather.

8. In fact, we delayed _____ (start) our expedition because of an accident and some bad weather.

9. And, we weren't able _____ (arrive) at the Pole in time for The start of the millennium on January 1 because of bad snow storms.

10. All of us risked _____ (lose) our lives on this trek, but none of us regret _____ (make) the trip.

11. Amazing sights such as the *aurora* or the beautiful star-filled nights never failed _____ (boost) our courage.

12. And, none of us will ever forget _____ (stand) at the bottom of the world, the South Pole!

7 Practice Complete the following, using gerund or infinitive forms (active or passive) of the verbs in parentheses. Be sure to include negatives, possessives, or subjects when indicated.

Amateur Astronomy

Would you like _____ to know _____ more about the stars but don't know
(know)

where _____? Well, even though there appear
1 (begin)

_____ millions of stars, only about 6,000 are visible. The visible
2 (be)

stars are the brightest but not necessarily the closest. Many of these seem

_____ together. These groupings are called constellations, and
3 (group)

many have unusual names, such as Taurus the Bull and Orion the Hunter. You

can learn _____ many of them by _____ what
4 (recognize)   5 (remember)

they represent.

The best time for _____ the stars is during cold, clear
6 (you / study)

nights. It is easier _____ many of the fainter stars then because
7 (see)

the atmosphere lets more light reach the earth. Don't be discouraged by

_____ a telescope. You can always see important stars, like
8 (not / have)

Polaris (the North Star) or the Southern Cross. Early navigators knew how

_____ direction by _____ Polaris because it is
9 (tell)   10 (find)

almost directly over the North Pole. In order _____ a steady
11 (keep)

direction east or west, you have _____ sure Polaris is in the
12 (make)

same position each night. Explorers have used this method of

_____ for over three thousand years. If you are interested in
13 (navigate)

_____ more, consider _____ in a course or
14 (learn)   15 (enroll)

_____ a local group of astronomers. And, of course, before
16 (join)

_____ in a telescope or any expensive equipment, ask your lo-
17 (invest)

cal science museum or school department for advice.

8 Practice Imagine that your class will live on a base in Antarctica for one year. You are the commander. Life will be very difficult, so you will need to have clear rules. Make a list of rules for your subordinates (your classmates). Complete the following sentences. Then share your lists of commands.

Example I advise *you to take this mission seriously.*

1. I encourage . . .
2. I expect . . .
3. You must (not) finish . . .
4. It's (not) important . . .
5. It's (not) necessary . . .
6. I promise . . .
7. I will require . . .
8. I will (not) allow . . .
9. I will (not) force . . .
10. I will (not) forgive . . .
11. I will (not) permit . . .
12. I will (not) tolerate . . .
13. You will risk . . . if you . . .
14. I urge. . .
15. I would like . . .

Using What You've Learned

9 Describing Travels and Vacations Think about a special trip that you've taken or a special thing that you've observed. It doesn't have to be as exotic as an *Adelie* penguin or the southern *aurora*, much less a trek to the South Pole. It only needs to be special to you. Take 15 minutes and write about this place or thing. Then go back and try to rephrase some of your sentences to use gerunds or infinitives.

10 Describing a Special Place or Thing Living in Antarctica is not easy, and sometimes for Adriana Romero it was lonely and frightening. She found ways to keep herself encouraged and optimistic. One source of inspiration for her was a giant petrel, a sea bird that flew near Esperanza Station often.

Read her description of this petrel and its impact on her. Then think of something from nature that has had an impact on you, has inspired you, or has helped give you courage or peace or persistence. It could be a place, a bird or animal, or a thing, for example.

Finally, spend 15–20 minutes writing about it and its inspirational impact on you. Try to use infinitives and gerunds in your writing. If you wish, share your piece with the class.

My Magnificent Bird

Driven by gusts of freezing wind of the Antarctic Peninsula, the Giant Petrel kept soaring higher and higher. This magnificent bird coasted across Hope Bay from one extreme to the other in just a few minutes. Then it disappeared behind the huge glacier in front of me.

I could follow his flight from my house at Esperanza Station. I saw him gliding effortlessly, and I heard him cawing his message to me often during the year I lived and worked in the "uttermost confines of the world," as people who'd been in Antarctica for a while used to say. The giant petrel was a winged presence that constantly reminded me "to reach for the skies." He invited me to dream and to imagine great adventures. His presence encouraged me to explore the frigid spaces around me. As he gave me hope and courage, he persuaded me to become completely wrapped up in my fascination with the cruel, glacial beauty of this frozen continent.

—Adriana Romero, Esperanza Station, Antarctica

Setting the Context

▲ Athlete jumping hurdles.

 Previewing the Passage Discuss the questions.

Are you a sports fan? What are your favorite sports to watch? To participate in?
Have you ever participated in competitive sports?

Reading Read the following passage.

Olympic Athletes

Not every athlete who competes in the Olympics is successful. Not every
athlete who competes in the Olympics becomes rich and famous. But, every
single Olympic athlete is remarkable.

What does it take to become an Olympic athlete? Reaching the Olympics
means doing years and years of training. And that means training virtually every   5
day. Potential Olympians can't stop training for a few months in order to take a
vacation or take some classes. Even if they feel like they can't bear to go to the
gym or dive into the pool even one more time, they have to continue to work at
their sport.

Their years of training, discipline, and perseverance make all of these young   10
athletes remarkable. Whether they win or lose is almost irrelevant. Their
tremendous effort is perhaps the most important measure of success.

Discussing Ideas Disuss the questions.

Do you prefer the Summer or the Winter Olympic Games? What is your favorite Olympic sport?

Grammar Structures and Practice

A. Verbs Followed by Gerunds or Infinitives

Some verbs are followed by gerunds or inifinitives depending on the use of a noun or pronoun object.

7.16	Verbs Followed by Gerunds or Infinitives, Depending on the Use of Noun or Pronoun Object		
Verbs	**Structures**	**Explanations**	**Examples**
advise allow be worth cause encourage permit teach	**Verb + Gerund** **Verb + Noun or Pronoun + Infinitive**	These verbs are followed by gerunds if **no** noun or pronoun object is used. If a noun or pronoun object is used, it **must** be followed by an infinitive.	We **don't permit smoking** here. They **permitted him to smoke** in the other room.

1 **Practice** What sports or other activities do you enjoy? Which do you dislike? Complete the following sentences in your own words. Use at least one infinitive or gerund in each.

Example I like ___to bicycle a lot___.

OR: I like ___bicycling a lot___.

1. I like _____.

2. I love _____.

3. I would like _____.

4. I don't like _____.

5. I can't stand _____.

6. I prefer _____.

7. Last year (month, summer, and so on), I began _____.

8. I still haven't started _____.

9. My teachers always encourage me _____.

10. My parents usually allowed me _____.

11. My parents never permitted _____.

12. I'd advise _____.

2 **Practice** Two great female athletes of the 20th century were Olga Korbut, from the former Soviet Union, and Nadia Comaneci, from Romania. Learn more about them by completing this passage, using gerund or infinitive forms of the verb in parentheses. Note any instance where either an infinitive or a gerund is possible.

Gymnastic Superstars

Olga Korbut and Nadia Comaneci are two remarkable athletes who changed the world of gymnastics forever. Both began _practicing / to practice_ (practice) and _____ in the sport at a very early age, and both continued
1 (compete)
_____ excellent athletic and artistic skills. Olga Korbut was
2 (develop)
born in 1956 in what is now Belarus. At age 11, she started _____ gymnastics at a government school and within a few
3 (study)
years became one of the best Soviet gymnasts. Her persistence paid off, but it wasn't easy. She tells many stories of her early years of _____.
4 (train)
For example, the first time she stood on the high beam, she fell off and was close to tears. She wanted _____ then and there.
5 (quit)

Her coach told _____ and start over. He encouraged
6 (she / get up)
_____ more relaxed. He asked _____
7 (she / be)   8 (she / imagine)
_____ in a beautiful meadow, not on a thin beam. Olga hated
9 (walk)
_____ these things, and she almost refused _____.
10 (hear)   11 (continue)
She was frightened, and as she said, "I was too young _____
12 (know)
that this was the greatest wisdom that a coach can have. After a fall, a tiny molecule of fear is born, somewhere deep in the soul. If time is lost—even an hour or two—that molecule will grow into an enormous beast. This beast will push you off the apparatus every time you climb on to it, and one day, you will simply be too scared _____ it at all." Olga learned
13 (approach)

_____ her fears, kept on _____, and soon be-
14 (overcome)   15 (practice)

came a star.

Nadia Comaneci was born in Romania in 1961 and began
_____ serious gymnastics after she'd been "discovered" at age
16 (do)

6 by the national coach. The coach taught _____ many amazing
17 (she /do)

exercises, and she herself created others. Even as a very young athlete, Nadia

was rarely afraid of anything—of _____ difficult or dangerous
18 (try)

moves or of _____ in front of millions of people. Perhaps the
19 (perform)

truly difficult thing for her was press conferences. Journalists seemed

_____ her age, and they would ask _____ to
20 (forget)   21 (she / respond)

every kind of question imaginable! Once a journalist asked her about her great-

est wish, and she answered, "I want _____ home." Another
22 (go)

journalist questioned her about her plans for _____, and she re-
23 (retire)

sponded, "I'm only 14."

Both Olga Korbut and Nadia Comaneci achieved greatness in gymnastics.

They created new and beautiful moves, they received incredibly high scores

from judges, and they won numerous medals, Olympic and others. Their infec-

tious smiles and great performances captured the hearts of people around the

world and caused _____ gymnastics. Above all, perhaps,
24 (millions of young girl / take up)

the talent and persistence of these two athletes encouraged people

everywhere _____ hard, _____ persistent, and
25 (work)   26 (be)

_____ their dreams.
27 (follow)

3 **Practice** One of America's great female athletes was the tennis player Billie Jean
King. Learn more about her by completing these sentences. Use gerund or infinitive
forms of the verbs in parentheses. Note any instance where either an infinitive or a
gerund is possible.

Example Billie Jean King always liked _____ _to do / doing_ _____ (do) sports.

1. From a very early age, Billie Jean King loved _____ (play)
   tennis.

2. She continued _____ (practice) and _____ (play) as an amateur even though she was seldom invited _____ (participate) in important tennis competitions because she didn't have "the right connections."

3. People often neglected _____ (inform) her about key amateur competitions.

4. Billie Jean King also began _____ (notice) how little female tennis stars were paid and how much male stars could earn.

5. She couldn't stand _____ (see) good female athletes treated poorly, so she decided _____ (do) something about the problem.

6. She started _____ (discuss) the issue with other female tennis players and asked if they would like _____ (to join) together in contract negotiations.

7. Billie Jean King's breakthroughs into the "male" world of sports encouraged _____ (many young females / get) involved.

8. Her efforts allowed _____ (young women everywhere / dream) of _____ (be) successful in professional sports.

B. Verbs That Change Meaning Depending on the Use of Infinitives or Gerunds

These verbs may be followed by either infinitives or gerunds, but the choice between infinitives and gerunds affects the meaning of the sentence. In general, the infinitive refers to the future and often involves a purpose, whereas a gerund refers to the past. The clearest example of this is with the verb *remember*.

7.17 Verbs That Change Meaning Depending on the Use of Infinitives or Gerunds

Structures	Examples	Meanings
Mean + Infinitive *Mean* + Gerund	I **meant to visit** Brazil. A trip to Brazil **meant spending** much more money.	I planned to visit Brazil, but I couldn't. A trip to Brazil involved spending much more money.
Remember + Infinitive *Remember* + Gerund	I always **remember to buy** the paper I **remember buying** the paper.	I never forget to buy the paper. I remember that I bought the paper.
Stop, Quit + Infinitive *Stop, Quit* + Gerund	He **stopped (quit) to smoke.** He **stopped (quit) smoking.**	He stopped his work in order to smoke a cigarette. He does not smoke any more.
Try + Infinitive *Try* + Gerund	The room was hot, so we **tried to open** the window. The room was hot, so we tried the fan, but it didn't work. Then we **tried opening** the window.	We were not able to open the window. Opening the window was another possibility.

---

4 **Practice** Complete the following by using the infinitive or the gerund forms of the verbs in parentheses.

Example Did you remember _____*to buy*_____ tickets for the game?

1. After the volleyball game, we all stopped _____ (have) a cup of coffee, but Joanie didn't join us. She said that she'd stopped _____ (drink) coffee because the caffeine bothered her.

2. Everyone at work was surprised when John quit _____ (work) _____ (take) a long vacation in South America. He said that we should quit _____ (work) so hard and take off for faraway places too!

3. A: I tried _____ (open) the front door, but it seems _____ (be) stuck.

   B: Have you tried _____ (use) the key? It's locked, you know.

4. A: Did you remember _____ (buy) some golf balls?

   B: Of course, I didn't remember _____ (buy) any. I didn't know you needed some.

A: You knew, but you forgot _____ (get) some. I distinctly remember _____ (tell) you _____ (buy) some this morning.

B: Oh no . . . you meant _____ (tell) me, but *you* forgot. I didn't forget!

5 **Practice** Complete the following by using the infinitive or the gerund forms of the verbs in parentheses. Note any cases whether either form could be used and explain why you chose the form you did.

▲ Golf phenomenon Tiger Woods

Example Tiger Woods never stops _____*doing*_____ (do) great things, both on and off the golf course.
Both "doing" and "to do" are grammatically correct, but "doing" has the right meaning.

1. Tiger Woods has used his fame and fortune from golf to help _____ (foster) self-esteem in young children.

2. The Tiger Woods Foundation "encourages _____ (youth / dream) big dreams."

3. It tries "_____ (engage) communities in _____ (help) youngsters pursue their goals."

4. The Foundation looks for ways _____ (teach) children "_____ (care) about and _____ (share) with others."

5. His work involves _____ (team) up with other organizations interested in _____ (help) kids.

6. Tiger Woods tries hard _____ (foster) in young children the same qualities he himself values the most.

7. That means _____ (help) "_____ (foster) tenacity, integrity, courage, self-esteem and drive for excellence."

8. He wants _____ (kids / keep on) _____ (improve) themselves. He says, "Never quit _____ (try) hard! Never stop _____ (work) toward your dream."

9. Tiger Woods speaks from experience because he remembers _____ (do) all those long hours of practice and exercise.

10. He always kept on and on even though many times he wanted _____ (quit) _____ (work) so hard.

11. He urges _____ (kids / do) the same—keep on _____ (strive) forward.

12. Above all, Tiger hopes _____ (show) young children everywhere "the power they possess to improve their own circumstances."

6 **Review** Complete the following sentences by using either the infinitive or gerund form (active or passive) of the verbs in parentheses. Include negatives and subjects where indicated. Use parallel structures when possible.

Example _____*Mastering*_____ (master) golf may be frustrating, but it can also be rewarding.

1. It will take time and patience for _____ (you / learn) the game of golf well.

2. _____ (learn) the uses of each club is the first step.

3. In order _____ (learn) faster, it is best for _____ (you / watch) other players.

4. It is also helpful _____ (teach) by a good player.

5. Good players will advise _____ (you / spend time) _____ (walk) around the golf course in order _____ (get) (know) its contours.

6. _____ (plan) a sequence of moves, rather than just one at a time, is one secret to good strategy.

7. _____ (not pay) attention to your opponent's moves can be disastrous.

8. _____ (watch) by spectators distracts some golfers.

9. Some spectators need _____ (tell) _____ (be) quiet.

10. _____ (win) the game is important, but _____ (play) well, _____ (develop) strategies, and _____ (not get) nervous are just as important.

Using What You've Learned

7 **Talking About Outdoor Activities** In pairs or in small groups, use as many of the following verbs as possible to talk about and explain your favorite outdoor activity or game. It may be an organized sport, or it may be an activity such as camping or hiking. As you talk, be sure to explain any rules involved.

allow	hate	remember
begin	like	start
can't stand	love	stop
continue	permit	try
dislike	prefer	

Example In golf, you begin by looking over the course, by choosing your first club (usually a driver), and by teeing up. Then . . .

8 **Complaining** Are you frustrated about something? How about getting it out of your system? In groups or as a class, vent your frustrations by making complaints with _can't bear, can't stand,_ and _hate_ + gerund or infinitive or with _be fed up with, be sick of, be tired of,_ and _be sick and tired of_ + gerund. Make sure that everyone has the chance to make at least one complaint. Some of you may have more!

Example I can't stand to do any more homework!

9 **Telling Stories** In small groups, make up a story together. One member of your group will begin, and the rest will add to it to create an entire story. Each student must talk continuously for at least 30 seconds. Use as many verbs as possible. (To make this activity more difficult, you may use the rule that no verb can be repeated!) Try to use an infinitive or gerund with each. You may use your own opening to begin the story, or you may use one of the following lines:

1. "It was a dark and stormy night." (from _Paul Clifford_)

2. "Romeo, Romeo, wherefore art thou Romeo?" (from _Romeo and Juliet_)

3. "As Gregor Samsa awoke one morning from uneasy dreams, he found himself transformed in his bed into a gigantic insect." (from _The Metamorphosis_)

4. "Once upon a time there lived . . ."

5. "This is the tale of a meeting of two lonesome, skinny, fairly old men on a planet which was dying fast.. . ." (from *Breakfast of Champions*)

Part 5 | Special Uses of Other Verb Forms

Setting the Context

Previewing the Passage Discuss the question.

Barbara McClintock was a very successful American scientist who did research in the field of genetics beginning in the 1920s. What characteristics do you think a woman of that time needed to have in order to succeed in such a field?

▲ Barbara McClintock

Reading Read the following passage.

Barbara McClintock: A Pioneer in Genetic Research

As a young child, Barbara McClintock was always interested in science and the natural world around her. She would look carefully at the plants growing in the yard and could notice even small variations among the same types of plants.

By the time she entered Cornell University just after World War I, she was fully committed to botany. Plants of all kinds were interesting to her, vegetables

5

were definitely inspiring to her, but she was absolutely fascinated by corn (maize). Needless to say, Barbara McClintock was unusual.

Her incredible interest in plants was not the only unusual thing about her. Being a woman in science was also unusual, though in her day, botany was somewhat "acceptable" for women to study. However, being a woman made it very difficult for her to become a researcher. Many universities "let" women study or teach but did not "let" them do research. So despite her tremendous talents and ground-breaking[1] work, Barbara McClintock never obtained a permanent position as a researcher at any university. 10

Barbara McClintock's long and productive career greatly helped expand our knowledge of plant genetics. And her work most certainly helped open the path for other women to work in the field of genetics. 15

[1]*ground-breaking* innovative, first-of-its-kind

 Discussing Ideas Disuss the question.

Since Barbara McClintock began her career in the 1920s, the world of scientific work has changed a great deal for women. Can you give examples of other areas of science where women are very active in research or development today?

Grammar Structures and Practice

A. Causative Verbs and Related Structures: *Help, Let, Make, Have, Get,* and *Need*

Help, let, and *make* are followed by the simple form of a second verb. They are not generally followed by passive constructions. These verbs are often followed by the active or passive form of a second verb.

7.18	*Help, Let,* and *Make*	
Verbs	**Explanations**	**Examples**
Help	*Help* may take the simple form or the infinitive of another verb as an object.	I **helped** (him) **carry** the packages. I **helped** (him) **to carry** the packages.
Let	*Let* is followed by a noun or a pronoun and the simple form of another verb. It *does not* take an infinitive.	I **let** him **borrow** my car. I **let** them **help** me.
Make	*Make* is followed by a noun or pronoun and the simple form of another verb. *Make* + noun or pronoun + adjective is also frequently used.	I **made** him **wash** my car. I **made** them **help** me. The news **made** me **unhappy**. The bad weather **made** us **late**.

Constructions with *have* are often used when you pay for a service: You *have* someone *do* something, or you *have* something *done* by someone.

7.19	*Have*		
Explanations	**Active**	**Passive**	
With *have*, the active form is *have* + noun or object pronoun + simple form. The passive form is *have* + noun or object pronoun + part participle.	I **had** him **wash** my car. I **had** the barber **cut** my hair.	I **had** my car **washed** (by him). I **had** my hair **cut** (by the barber).	

Get and *need* are two more causative verbs. The passive form of *get* is similar in meaning to the passive form of *have*. *Get* is frequently used in conversational English.

7.20	*Get* and *Need*		
Explanations	**Active**	**Passive**	
With *get* and *need*, the active form is *get / need* + noun or object pronoun + infinitive. The passive form is *get / need* + noun or object pronoun + past participle.	I **got** him **to wash** my car. I **needed** him **to wash** my car.	I **got** my car **washed** (by him). I **needed** my car **washed** (by him).	

1 **Practice** Barbara McClintock succeeded despite many obstacles in her path. Use the following cues to form complete sentences with *make*.

Example being a female researcher / try twice as hard
Being a female researcher made her try twice as hard.

1. being a woman / others suspicious of her work
2. one colleague's support / her feel confident
3. her research / think differently about genetic transfer
4. what she found out about jumping genes in corn / believe that genes could move
5. the first reaction of the scientific community / feel rejected
6. eventually her careful and innovative research / earn the respect of the world
7. her discovery of transposable elements in genetic structure / win the Nobel Prize
8. this final recognition / her friends happy for her

2 Practice Answer the following questions. Use *let* in your answer.

1. Do you let other people tell you how to think?
2. In general, do you let others decide things for you?
3. Do you sometimes let yourself do less than your best?
4. Do you ever let yourself daydream about doing one great thing?
5. Did your parents let you follow your dreams?
6. What situations let you do your best?
7. Do you know anyone who doesn't let society tell him / her how to lead his / her life?
8. Have you ever let someone know he / she has done something great for you?

3 Practice Many people have lots of responsibilities at home and at work. Sometimes we need to get things done, to take care of these responsibilities, before we can do our best work. Follow the cues to form complete sentences with *have, need,* or *get.*

Example children / pick up from school
I'll need the children picked up from school.

1. shopping / do
2. dinner / prepare for tonight
3. my appointments / cancel
4. someone / walk the dog
5. someone / clean up the house
6. my assistant / screen my calls
7. someone / bring my car in for servicing
8. my neighbor/pick up my mail

4 Practice Imagine you are a scientific researcher, and you are beginning a great project, something that you have really been wanting to do. Imagine what preparations you would need before getting into your work. Complete each sentence with appropriate verb forms (infinitive, past participle, simple form). You can choose from the following verbs or add your own.

cancel	find	interrupt	plan	take
deliver	form	organize	postpone	write
feel	help	photocopy	reserve	

Example I'll have my daily schedule _____*cancelled by*_____ my secretary.

1. I'll have important meetings _____ until we have finished the work.

2. I'll have my assistant _____ a quiet conference room for us to work.

3. I'll get my ideas _____ down on paper before we begin.

4. I'll get the plans _____ by Monday.

5. I'll have a team of co-workers _____ to help me on the project.

6. I'll get work groups _____ for different parts of the project.

7. I'll need leaders _____ responsibility for each work group.

8. I won't let people _____ us while we're working.

9. I'll get my friends _____ me relax after working sessions.

10. I'll have all our lunches _____ to the conference room so we can work through lunch.

11. We'll make everyone _____ proud of us.

12. We'll have a big party _____ when we finish the work.

B. Verbs of Perception

The verbs *see, look (at), watch, observe, listen (to), hear, smell, taste, perceive,* and *feel* are verbs of perception.

- These verbs can be followed by a second verb.
- The second verb can be in the simple or the present participle form.

7.21	Verbs of Perception		
Explanation	**Forms**	**Examples**	**Meanings**
Often, there is little difference in meaning between the two forms but the *-ing* form usually stresses an action in progress.	**Present Participle**	We **heard** the bell **ringing**.	Action in progress
	Simple Form	We **heard** the bell **ring**.	Action completed
	Present Participle	We **saw** the building **burning** down.	Action in progress
	Simple Form	We **saw** the building **burn** down.	Action completed

5 **Practice** Imagine that you have just had a tour of a botanist's laboratory. Use the information in parentheses to complete the following sentences describing what you saw, felt, and so forth.

Example While we were in the lab, we saw (a lab assistant / examine plant cells under a microscope.)

While we were in the lab, we saw a lab assistant examining plant cells under a microscope.
OR: . . . we saw a lab assistant examine plant cells under a microscope.

1. We watched (a scientist / perform an experiment).

2. We heard (a parrot / speak). It was Polly, the lab mascot.

3. We felt (the humid air / wet our faces).

4. We looked at (the many species of corn / grow in the greenhouse).

5. We observed (the scientists / concentrate on their work).

6. We felt (the air temperature / grow warmer as we entered the greenhouse).

7. We smelled (roses / give off their fragrance).

8. We listened to (Polly / say hello and good-bye a thousand times).

C. Present and Past Participles Used as Adjectives

The participle forms of many verbs may also be used as adjectives after linking verbs such as *be, become, feel,* and *get.* In particular, verbs that express emotions are often used in this way.

7.22	Present and Past Participles Used as Adjectives	
Structures	**Explanations**	**Examples**
Verbs	Verbs that express emotions include: amaze disappoint interest surprise annoy excite intrigue thrill astonish fascinate please tire bore frighten relax worry confuse inspire satisfy	That book doesn't **bore** me. The study of botany **fascinates** me. The descriptions of plants **intrigue** me. Lab work **doesn't tire** me.
Present Participle	The present participle expresses the effect of the subject on someone or something.	The ideas in that book were very **interesting** to me. Lab work isn't **tiring** for me.
Past Participle	The past participle tells the reaction of the subject to someone or something. Note the variety of prepositions used with the past participle.	I was very **interested in** the ideas in that botany book. I am getting more **excited about** botany every day. I never feel **bored with** that book.

6 **Practice** Think about a plant, a tree, a rock, a crystal, an animal, or a flower that you've learned about recently or have seen recently in nature. Describe how you felt at that time by answering the following questions.

Example How did you become interested in learning about this?
I became interested in learning about butterflies because I saw a beautiful butterfly last month.

1. What did you become interested in?

2. How did you become interested in learning about it?

3. Is its appearance interesting?

4. Were you surprised by anything you found out about it?

5. Was there anything confusing about it?

6. Was it satisfying to learn about it?

7. Were you excited about it?

8. Tell three fascinating things about it.

7 Practice Complete the following by using either the present or the past participle of the verbs in parentheses.

Example Walking alone in the forest is _____*frightening*_____ (frighten) to many people.

1. For many people, walking in the woods is _____ (relax).

2. However, some people are _____ (frighten) about spending time in the woods.

3. They're _____ (worry) about encountering wild animals.

4. Humans are more _____ (frighten) to most animals than most animals are to humans.

5. Some people get _____ (worry) about eating wild foods, like wild mushrooms.

6. Yet people everywhere are _____ (interest) in trying new foods.

7. Looking for new varieties of mushrooms is _____ (excite) to many people.

8. They are _____ (thrill) at the thought of finding food in the wild.

9. It is _____ (amaze) to think that we could survive on wild plants and other foods if we had to.

10. City folk are _____ (surprise / often) by what country people eat from nature.

8 Review Complete the following passage with gerund or infinitive forms of the verbs in parentheses. Include negatives and objects where indicated.

How Corn Can Change Lives

Life in rural China can be very, very hard. An example is the province of Guizhou. There, typical farms are less than one hectare (two acres) and are often perched on almost inaccessible mountainsides. Until recently, annual incomes were less than $50 per person. For up to three months a year, families had almost no food because of weather conditions and crop cycles.

In 1994, life began _____*to change / changing*_____ for many farmers in Guizhou,
(change)
and today it promises _____ even better. In 1994, technicians
1 (get)
from the Guizhou Academy of Agricultural Sciences offered

_____ farmers in the area and encouraged _____
2 (help)   3 (they / plant)

"quality protein maize." They recommended _____ this high-
                                          4 (plant)

quality corn because it is a hybrid that grows well in difficult areas. In fact, its

yields are about 10 percent higher than normal yields, and it has a high content

of certain amino acids that are vital for children's growth. The corn is also used

_____ animals, especially pigs. By _____
5 (feed)   6 (raise)

larger, healthier pigs, farmers have been able _____ major
                                               7 (make)

changes in their lives. By _____ 30 pigs during three years'
                          8 (sell)

time, one farmer was able _____ a new house, _____
                          9 (build)   10 (educate)

his children, and _____ new equipment for _____
                  11 (get)   12 (irrigate)

and _____.
    13 (compost)

The Guizhou Academy of Agricultural Sciences has been responsible for

_____ and _____ with the farmers on
14 (educate)   15 (work)

_____ this hybrid corn. _____ the corn itself
16 (introduce)   17 (develop)

involved _____ traditional Chinese corn with international vari-
         18 (cross)

eties. First, the technicians had _____ the new seeds, and after
                                 19 (several farmers / try)

others saw this special corn _____ and _____
                             20 (grow)   21 (produce)

well, many wanted _____ in the project. The university techni-
                  22 (join)

cians didn't even need _____ _____ it because
                       23 (persuade)   24 (other farmers / try)

the good results were obvious. The university technicians themselves were very

_____ about the project and willing to work in difficult condi-
25 (excite)

tions. They were _____ _____ the tremendous
                 26 (thrill)   27 (see)

results. Today, it is in rural corners like these in China that you can see agricul-

tural research _____ a major impact on people's lives. You can
               28 (have)

look at corn stalks _____ with ears of corn, and you can watch
                    29 (burst)

healthy children _____ and _____. Above all,
                 30 (play)   31 (work)

you can hear these subsistence farmers[1] _____ their stories. As
                                          32 (tell)

_____
[1]*subsistence farmer*s farmers able to produce only the minimum necessary for survival

a 78 year-old woman who had obviously gone through many, many hard times said, "We have always worked hard, but this barely kept us alive until [the researchers and the high protein corn] arrived. Thank you for helping us. Now my family is happy, I have a good house, good clothes, and I can travel to the local town."

▲ A healthy cob of corn with the husk peeled back

9 Review Reread the opening passage "Remarkable People" on page 276. Underline and label all gerunds, infinitives, present and past participles, and simple forms of verbs.

Using What You've Learned

10 Making a To-Do List What is on your to-do list? What are some repairs or services that you need to take care of? What are some that you have had done lately? Go around the room in a chain, giving statements with *get, have,* or *need.*

Examples

To Do	Done
I have to get my glasses repaired.	*I had my teeth checked last week.*

11 Talking About Likes and Dislikes When your life is busy, it's hard to find time to get everything done that you need to do. It can also be very pleasant to have things done for you. First, make a list of things you enjoy having done for you. Try to give at least five. Then, make a list of things you don't like having done for you. After you have made your lists, work in pairs or small groups. Compare your lists, explaining why you do or do not enjoy each.

Examples

Like	Don't Like
I like getting my laundry done.	*I don't like having my teeth cleaned.*

12 Describing a Place Think of a place with lots of unusual sights and sounds. It may be a place that you've visited recently, or it may be a place that you remember from the past. In small groups, take turns telling about the place. Use verbs of perception to describe things that you saw, smelled, heard, and so forth. As an alternative, write a short composition about your place and then share it with your classmates.

Examples

There's a beautiful place in the mountains where we used to camp. From the camp, we could see the mountains rising sharply above us. We would sit and watch deer and moose eating in the meadow below us.

Last week I went to Disneyland, and it was incredibly crowded. In every direction, I saw thousands of people walking, standing, eating, laughing, arguing, getting sunburned and tired. I heard hundreds of people screaming as they rode on the different rides.

13 **Describing an Event or Location** Think about a trip you've taken; a sport you've played; or a restaurant, store, or museum you've visited during the past few weeks. Give several original sentences using either present or past participles. Choose from the following verbs or add your own.

Positive Feelings		Negative Feelings	
amaze	interest	annoy	disappoint
amuse	intrigue	bewilder	shock
excite	relax	bore	tire
fascinate	surprise	confuse	worry

14 **Imagining an Exotic Place** Traveling to faraway places is one of the most fascinating ways to spend your leisure time. Imagine yourself in the Middle East, in the Amazon, or in Paris. Imagine where you have been and how you arrived at this destination. Imagine what you will do next. As you imagine, describe everything that you see, hear, smell, feel, perceive. Are you excited? Are you nervous? What are the most interesting things around you?

Use of Gerunds, Infinitives, and Other Verb Forms

Gerunds, infinitives, and other verb forms are frequently tested on standardized English proficiency exams. Review these commonly tested structures and check your understanding by completing the sample items below.

Remember that . . .

✓ Different verbs are followed by different forms. Make sure the appropriate form is used.

✓ Gerunds, not infinitives, are used after propositions.

✓ In lists containing verb forms, make sure that the same form is used whenever possible. Don't mix forms (for example, gerunds and infinitives) unless it is unavoidable. Try to use parallel structures.

Part 1 Mark the correct completion for the following.

Example   John apppears ———————— happy with his work.

    Ⓐ to be   Ⓑ be

    Ⓒ been   Ⓓ being

1. The pitching of the waves on the open sea caused the small vessel ————————.

    Ⓐ capsize   Ⓑ capsizing

    Ⓒ to capsize   Ⓓ have capsized

2. It is always helpful ———————— a map while hiking in wilderness areas.

    Ⓐ to carry   Ⓑ to carrying

    Ⓒ carrying   Ⓓ carry

3. Of the various activities she does, Mary likes swimming and ———————— the best.

    Ⓐ to ride a horse   Ⓑ to horseback ride

    Ⓒ horses   Ⓓ horseback riding

4. ———————— a mistake is not to bring on the end of the world.

    Ⓐ To made   Ⓑ Making

    Ⓒ To make   Ⓓ Having made

5. Remarkable people are able ———————— in order to achieve a goal.

    Ⓐ persevere   Ⓑ to persevere

    Ⓒ persevering   Ⓓ persevered

Part 2 Circle the letter below the underlined word(s) containing an error.

Example   An individual <u>may</u> feel frustrated and <u>confusing</u> if <u>she</u> doesn't know
               (Ⓐ)   B   C
          the language of the country <u>where she is living</u>.
                                         D

1. The Park Service always advises visitors <u>using</u> extra caution when <u>hiking</u> or
                                    A   B
   camping in areas <u>where</u> bears <u>have been sighted</u>.
                   C   D

2. <u>The popularity</u> of bicycles <u>increased greatly</u> during the 1970s, as more
      A   B
   people began to ride them for pleasure and <u>using</u> them <u>to commute</u> to work.
                                      C   D

3. Polaris, <u>the North Star</u>, has helped <u>guiding</u> seafarers <u>ever since</u> ancient times
              A   B   C
   when <u>sophisticated</u> navigational tools did not exist.
             D

4. <u>Do you</u> really <u>want</u> <u>learn</u> <u>to play</u> a musical instrument?
    A   B   C   D

5. It's <u>fascinated</u> <u>to learn</u> about all the <u>amazing</u> projects former Jimmy Carter did
       A   B   C
   after <u>leaving</u> the U.S. presidency.
          D

Self-Assessment Log

Each of the following statements describes the grammar you learned in this chapter. Read the statements; then check the box that describes how well you understand each structure.

	Needs Improvement	Good	Great
I can use gerunds after prepositions and certain verbs.	❑	❑	❑
I can use infinitives after adjectives, adverbs, nouns, and certain verbs.	❑	❑	❑
I can use appropriate verb forms after causative verbs.	❑	❑	❑
I can use appropriate verb forms after verbs of perception.	❑	❑	❑
I can use appropriate present and past participle forms with verbs of emotion.	❑	❑	❑
I can use a variety of structures and vocabulary to talk and write about remarkable individuals and their accomplishments.	❑	❑	❑
I can take a test about gerunds, infinitives, simple verb forms, present and past participles, and parallel structure.	❑	❑	❑

Creativity

In This Chapter

Compound and Complex Sentences; Clauses of Time and Condition

Part 1 Compound Sentences

Part 2 Adverb Clauses of Time and Condition: Unspecified or Present Time

Part 3 Adverb Clauses of Time and Condition: Past Time with the Simple Past and Past Perfect Tenses

Part 4 Adverb Clauses of Time and Condition: Past Time with the Simple Past and Past Continuous Tenses

Part 5 Adverb Clauses of Time and Condition: Future Time

❝To raise new questions, new possibilities, to regard old problems from a new angle requires creative imagination and marks real advances ...❞

—Albert Einstein
German-born Swiss-U.S. physicist
(1879–1955)

Connecting to the Topic

1. What does it mean to look at something from a new angle, a new direction?

2. Can you think of some examples of people who looked at an old problem from a new direction?

3. Can you give an example of when you have used your creativity to solve a problem?

Introduction

In this chapter, you will review the variety of sentence types in English, and you will study both compound and complex sentences. This chapter focuses on complex sentences with adverb clauses of time and condition. Chapters 9 and 10 cover other types of complex sentences. As you study this chapter, pay close attention to the time frames expressed by the different constructions.

Reading Read the following passage. It introduces the chapter theme, "Creativity," and raises some of the topics and issues you will cover in the chapter.

The Creative Urge

If an inventor builds an astounding machine or an artist produces a stunningly original work, we call this creative genius. Yet, creativity is not only in the realm of artists and scientists: it is an attribute we all have within us. The creative urge is the most profoundly human—and mysterious—of all our attributes. Without fully understanding how or why, each of us is creative. 5

Since earliest times, humans have produced marvelous creations. Learning to use fire and to make tools were incredibly creative achievements. Above all, early humans produced our most extraordinary creation: language.

After our ancestors had learned to communicate with each other, a long series of amazing developments began. Creativity flourished among such peoples as the ancient Egyptians, Minoans, Greeks, Mayans, and the Benin of Africa. Long before the modern age of machines, our ancestors had already developed sophisticated techniques and systems in mathematics, astronomy, engineering, art, architecture, and literature. 10

Of course, creativity varies in time and place. While the Egyptians were developing mathematics and building libraries, other societies were still learning to use fire. By the time Europeans began to use money, the Chinese had already been trading with paper currency for hundreds of years. Nevertheless, every new achievement represents human creativity. If one attribute characterizes humans, it is our creative urge to improve, to find new ways of doing things. 15 20

Discussing Ideas Discuss the question.

Who are some creative people you know about? They may be living now or they may be from another time.

Part 1 Compound Sentences

Setting the Context

Previewing the Passage Discuss the question.

Creativity is difficult to define. It means different things to different people. What is your definition of creativity?

Reading Read the passage.

What Is Creativity?

To *create* means "to bring into being, to cause to exist." According to this dictionary definition, ordinary people are creative every day. We are creative whenever we look at or think about something in a new way.

Discussing Ideas Discuss the questions.

Can you identify the activities in the photos on page 333? Can you add a few more examples of day-to-day activities that involve creativity?

Grammar Structures and Practice

A. Review of Sentence Types

Sentences may be simple, compound, complex, or a combination of compound and complex.

8.1 Review of Sentence Types		
Structures	**Explanations**	**Examples**
Simple Sentences	Simple sentences have one subject-verb combination.	Creativity is part of everyday life.
Compound Sentences	Compound sentences are two simple sentences connected by a comma and *and, but, for, nor, or, so,* or *yet.* A compound sentence may also be formed by joining two sentences with a semicolon. Transition words or phrases are often used with compound sentences.	Many artists are highly creative, **but** ordinary people can be just as creative. Some people are creative from childhood; **however,** others show their genius later in life.
Complex Sentences	Complex sentences consist of two or more clauses: a main clause that is complete by itself and one or more dependent clauses introduced by a connecting word such as *although, because, if, that, when,* or *who.*	**Although** some people are creative from childhood, others show their genius later in life.
Compound-Complex Sentences	Compound-complex sentences sentences can have several clauses. There is always one main clause, but other clauses can be joined by a variety of connecting words.	Some people are creative from childhood, **but** others show their genius **when** they are much older.

Punctuation Guidelines

Structures	Explanations	Examples
Coordinate Clauses	A comma is normally used before conjunctions that join two independent clauses. *Note:* The comma is optional in short sentences.	_____ and _____ .
Transitions	Most transitions are used at the beginning of a sentence or after a semicolon. They are normally followed by a comma. In some cases, transitions may be used in the middle or at the end of a sentence.	In addition, _____ . _____ ; in addition, _____ .
Subordinate Phrases and Clauses	Adverb phrases and clauses may begin or end complex sentences. A comma is normally used after introductory phrases and clauses.	_____ while _____ . While _____ , _____ .

---

1 **Review** Label subject(s) and verb(s) in the following sentences. Then indicate what type of sentence each is (simple, compound, or complex). If the sentence is compound or complex, circle the connecting word.

              S   V   S   V   V

Example We are creative (whenever) we look at or think about something in a new way. *complex sentence*

1. First of all, creativity involves an awareness of our surroundings.

2. It is the ability to notice things that others might miss.

3. A second part of creativity is an ability to see relationships among things.

4. Creativity is involved when we remake or reorganize the old in new ways.

5. We might find a more efficient way to study, or we could rearrange our furniture in a better way.

6. Third, creativity means having the courage and drive to make use of our new ideas.

7. To think up a new concept is one thing; to put the idea to work is another.

8. These three aspects of creativity are involved in all the great works of genius; however, they are also involved in many of our day-to-day activities.

9. As human beings, we respond to and are curious about new things.

10. This is part of our natural thought process.

2 Review Indicate the type of each sentence below (simple, compound, or complex). If the sentence is compound or complex, circle the connecting word. Underline the *dependent* clauses in the complex sentences.

Examples   In order to (create), there must be a dynamic force. *simple sentence*
What force is more potent than <u>love is</u>? —*Igor Stravinsky*
complex sentence

1. The creative person is both more primitive and more cultivated, more destructive, a lot madder, and a lot saner than the average person is. —*Frank Barron*

2. Creative minds always have been knows to survive any kind of bad training. —*Anna Freud*

3. All men are creative, but few are artists. —*Paul Goodman*

4. Human salvation lies in the hands of the creatively maladjusted. —*Martin Luther King, Jr.*

5. In creating, the only hard thing's to begin; a grass blade's no easier to make than an oak. —*James Russell Lowell*

6. One must still have chaos in oneself to be able to give birth to a dancing star. —*Friedrich Nietzsche*

7. He who does not know how to create should not know. —*Antonio Porchia*

8. A creative artist works on his next composition because he was not satisfied with his previous one. —*Dmitri Shostakovich*

9. The urge for destruction is also a creative urge. —*Michael Bakunin*

10. Two roads diverged in a wood, and I—I took the one less traveled by, And that has made all the difference. —*Robert Frost*

B. Coordinating Conjunctions

Coordinating conjunctions are used to join two independent clauses into one compound sentence.

- The coordinating conjunctions are *and, but, for, or, so, yet,* and *nor*.
- A comma is normally used between the two clauses. In short sentences, however, the comma can be omitted.

8.2 Coordinating Conjunctions: *And, But, For, Or, So, Yet*

	Explanation		Examples
and	*And* expresses addition.		**and** he is quite funny.
but	*But* expresses contrast.		**but** he sometimes loses his temper.
for	*For* expresses reason.	Martin is easy-going,	**for** he enjoys just about everything.
or	*Or* expresses choice.		**or** at least he seems that way.
so	*So* expresses result.		**so** many people like him.
yet	*Yet* expresses contrast.		**yet** he gets nervous about tests.

8.3 Coordinating Conjunction: *Nor*

Explanation	Simple Sentences	Compound Sentences
Nor is used to join two negative clauses.	The box is not very big. It is not very heavy.	The box is not very big, **nor** is it very heavy.
When *nor* begins the second clause, the auxiliary verb or the verb *be* is placed before the subject. A negative is not used in the second clause.	Ann doesn't like cold weather. She doesn't enjoy snow. Ben hasn't done his homework. He hasn't cleaned the house.	Ann doesn't like cold weather, **nor** does she enjoy snow. Ben hasn't done his homework, **nor** has he cleaned the house.

Note: And, but, or, and *yet* are often used to join words or phrases also.

---

3 **Practice** Form compound sentences using the coordinating conjunctions indicated for each set. Add commas. You may have to change nouns (to pronouns), word order, or sentence order. For sentences with more than one possibility, form two sentences and try to explain any difference in meaning or emphasis.

Example   (nor) Some people do not use all their senses very often.
They do not have a very great awareness of their surroundings.
Some people do not use all their senses very often, nor do they have a very great awareness of their surroundings.

1. (but / yet) Some people use all five senses often. Most of us rely heavily on our sight.

2. (nor) Many people do not pay attention to sounds. Many people do not take time to listen.

3. (for / so) Musicians pay attention to all types of sounds. Musicians want to find interesting new combinations.

4. (and / yet) A musician can find music in exotic sounds. A musician may also hear music in ordinary noises.

5. (or / and) A car horn may produce a new rhythm. A bird may sing a new sequence of notes.

6. (but / yet) Another person may not hear these combinations. A music lover will find these combinations.

7. (but) Smell is important in chocolate tasting. Taste is perhaps more important.

8. (or) A chocolate taster must have a good sense of taste. A chocolate taster won't last long on the job.

9. (and) A chocolate taster must be able to recognize the smell of a high-quality chocolate. A chocolate taster must be able to recognize the flavor of a high-quality chocolate.

10. (but) Chocolate tasters and musicians may use their sight while working. Sounds and tastes are very important in their work.

C. Transitions

Transitions are words or phrases that link two related ideas. The list in the chart contains some of the most common transitions.

8.4	Transitions		
Function	**Transitions**	**Explanations**	**Examples**
Provide Examples	*for instance* *for example*	*For instance* is also used to give examples. Like *for example*, it is common in conversational English.	Anyone can be creative. **For example,** a cook who tries a new recipe is creative.
Express Emphasis	*in fact*	*In fact* emphasizes important or little-known information.	Each of us is creative and, **in fact,** we are creative more often than we realize.
Give Additional Information	*in addition*	*In addition* has the same meaning as "also."	Creativity involves looking at things in a new way; **in addition,** it means trying new things.
Show Contrast	*however*	*However* has the same meaning as "but."	Everyone can be creative; **however,** many people are afraid to try.
	on the other hand	*On the other hand* refers to the opposite side of an issue. *In contrast* is also common.	Some people never try new ideas; **on the other hand,** there are many people who constantly try new things.
Provide a Reason or Result	*therefore*	*Therefore* means "as a result" or "so."	Creativity is a mysterious process; **therefore,** it is difficult to define.
Show Sequence (by Time or Order)	*first, second, now, then, next, earlier, later, after that, finally, etc.*	Sequence transitions are not normally used with a semicolon. Commas are sometimes used after these transitions.	Creativity involves several steps. **First,** it is being aware of something. **Next,** it involves seeing a relationship with something else. **Then,** it means using the new ideas.

4 Practice Describe the process of taking a digital photograph by putting the following steps in order. Use sequence transitions (*first, second,* and so on) as you reorder the sentences. More than one sequence is possible.

Example *First, turn on the camera.*

1. Focus the lens on your subject.
2. Shut off the camera.
3. Review the photo in your viewfinder.
4. Keep the photo if you like it, or delete it if you don't.
5. Take the photo.
6. Hold the camera steady.
7. Look through the viewfinder and compose your photo.
8. Check the battery.
9. Turn on the camera.
10. Make sure your memory card is in the camera.

▲ With a digital camera, you can instantly see the picture you have taken.

5 Practice Two of the 20th century's most creative musicians have been the jazz greats Louis Armstrong and Miles Davis. Both played the trumpet, but in other aspects, they were two very different individuals. Read the following information about them. Then write sentences with *in contrast* and *on the other hand*.

▲ Louis Armstrong

▲ Miles Davis

Example Louis Armstrong always tried to please his audiences and his fans.

Miles Davis did not seem to care about popularity.

Louis Armstrong always tried to please his audiences and his fans; in contrast, Miles Davis did not seem to care about popularity.

1. Louis Armstrong came from a relatively poor family in New Orleans.

   Miles Davis was born into a prosperous middle-class family in East St. Louis.

2. Louis Armstrong was friendly and fun-loving.

   Miles Davis was often called mysterious, rebellious, and even shy.

3. Armstrong was a film star and comedian as well as a musician.

   Davis concentrated only on jazz.

4. Armstrong maintained a consistent style throughout his career.

   Miles Davis changed his musical style numerous times.

5. There is a simplicity and clarity to most of Louis Armstrong's music.

   The music of Miles Davis is often abstract and complex.

6. Louis Armstrong was noted for his singing style as well as his playing style.

   Miles Davis did not sing at all.

7. Armstrong's speaking voice was warm and sunny with a pleasant New Orleans twang.

   Davis's voice was thin and scratchy, almost as if it hurt him to speak.

8. Louis Armstrong generally wore suits on stage.	Miles Davis was well-known for his unusual and trendy clothes.
9. Armstrong's sound was bold and moody.	Davis's sound was mellow[1] and brassy.[2]
10. Louis Armstrong was part of the "mainstream" of American music.	Miles Davis was always on the "cutting edge" of music.

---

[1]*mellow* soft and rich sounding
[2]*brassy* noisy and metallic sounding

6 **Practice** This passage is about the artist Georgia O'Keeffe and her husband, Alfred Stieglitz. First, read the passage to understand the ideas. Then, complete it by adding transitions: *however, in addition, in fact, therefore.* Use each at least once. You will also need to add punctuation.

Note: In general, a writer would not use this many transitions in one short passage. Other connecting words such as *although, because, but,* and so on would also be used to give more variety.

▲ Georgia O'Keeffe and Alfred Stieglitz

Georgia O'Keeffe and Alfred Stieglitz

Georgia O'Keeffe was perhaps the most famous female artist of the 20th century. She was born and raised on a large farm in Wisconsin; _____*therefore*_____, she felt more at home in wide open spaces than she did in cities _____1_____. O'Keeffe moved to New York City in the 1920s because of the large artist community there.

It was difficult for a woman to be an artist at that time _____2_____ she had to work very hard to support herself. She sold paintings _____ she worked as a teacher in order to make a living. In her early years, O'Keeffe received little recognition for her work, and her life in New York was difficult. _____ after her marriage to the famous photographer Alfred Stieglitz, she became very well known.

Stieglitz and O'Keeffe were a brilliantly creative couple. _____ together, they produced more creative works than perhaps any other 20th-century couple.

7 **Practice** Combine the following sentences, using *for example, however, in addition, in fact, on the other hand,* or *therefore.* Use each transition at least once. Add appropriate punctuation and make other necessary changes. For example, change nouns to pronouns when appropriate.

Example   Being creative involves making the best use of your senses. Being creative means looking at the same object from many different perspectives.
Being creative involves making the best use of your senses; for example, it means looking at the same object from many different perspectives.

1. A good photographer looks at the object itself. A good photographer considers the distance, angle, texture, and light.

2. Light is one of the most important aspects of a good photo. The same scene can be either unusual or boring, depending on the light.

3. Creative photographers experiment with light. They may take the same photo at many different times of day.

4. Mornings and evenings give warm light, rich colors, and long shadows. Noon gives harsh, bright light to a photo.

5. Morning and evening light is richer. Most outdoor photographers work between sunrise and 10:00 A.M. and between 4:00 P.M. and sunset.

6. Bright sunlight makes colors seem pale. Good photos can be produced even on very sunny days by using a "sunlight" filter.

7. Today, most people take color snapshots. Art photographs are still mostly done in black and white.

8. Good photographers share a bond with their subjects. Good photographers know how to "bring out the best" in their photos.

8 **Teaching Others** Do you have a pastime or hobby that you enjoy? It might be taking photos, drawing, playing an instrument, or making crafts. Think about how you do this activity. Then work in pairs or small groups and take turns describing some of the steps involved in the activity. Try to include sequence transitions in your description.

9 **Making Comparisons** Reread your comparisons of Louis Armstrong and Miles Davis in Activity 5, page 340. Then think of two other individuals who do the same activity but who have very different styles or personalities. The two may be musicians, artists, sports figures, actors or actresses, or politicians, for example. Write a paragraph comparing the two individuals, using transitions when possible. Then work in pairs or small groups and tell each other about these people.

Part 2 — Adverb Clauses of Time and Condition: Unspecified or Present Time

Setting the Context

Previewing the Passage Discuss the questions.

In your opinion, are "thinking" and "doing" equally important? What happens when you have one without the other?

Reading Read the quotation.

Creativity and Innovation

"If creativity is thinking up new things, innovation is doing them. Ideas are useless unless they are used, and the proof of their value is in their implementation.

There is no shortage of creativity or creative people. . . . If there is a shortage, it is a shortage of innovators."

—Theodore Levitt, Harvard University

5

Discussing Ideas Discuss the questions.

Do you agree with Levitt? Are ideas useless unless they are implemented, that is, used or put into action? Is there a shortage of innovators in our world?

Grammar Structures and Practice

A. Clauses of Time: Present Time or Unspecified Time

Time clauses can relate ideas or actions that occur at the same time or in a sequence.

- Time clauses in the present can relate habitual, repeated activities.
- They can also relate events occurring in the present.
- These clauses may begin or end sentences.

8.5 Habitual Activities

Structures	Explanations	Examples
when *whenever*	*When* joins two actions that happen at the same time or in sequence. In many cases, *when* means "at any time" and is he equivalent of *whenever*. The simple present is generally used in both clauses.	**When** Tim Astor gets a new idea for a novel, he writes it down immediately. He begins a new book **whenever** he gets an inspiration.
after *before* *until*	*After*, *before*, and *until* join actions that occur in sequence. Either the simple present or the present perfect may be used in the dependent clause. The present perfect emphasizes the completion of the action.	He edits his material **after** he finishes the entire first draft. He never starts a new project **before** he has completed the current one. He works on a project **until** he is fully satisfied with it.
as *while*	*As* and *while* may join two actions that happen at about the same time. The present continuous can be used in the dependent clause to emphasize continuity. The verb in the main clause shows whether the action is habitual or happening at the moment of speaking.	**As** he is writing, he often listens to classical music. He often listens to music **while** he is writing.

8.6 Present Activities

Structures	Explanations	Examples
as *while*	*As* and *while* can join two actions that are happening at the present. In this case, both clauses are in the present continuous.	Tonight he is listening to Beethoven's Fifth Symphony **as** he is writing. He is humming **while** he is writing.

8.7 Past and Present Activities

Structures	Explanations	Example
since	*Since* joins a previous action or situation to an action or situation in progress. The main clause is in the present perfect (continuous).	He has been writing **since** he woke up at six this morning.

1 **Practice** Complete the following with present forms of the verbs in parentheses. The first one is done as an example.

A Method to Our Madness

For most of us, when we _____think_____ of the work of creative
(think)

artists and scientists, we _____ a mysterious world of geniuses.
1 (imagine)

When an inventor _____ an amazing new machine, when a mu-
2 (develop)

sician _____ a beautiful piece of music, or when a scientist
3 (create)

_____ a major discovery, we _____ in awe. We
4 (make)   5 (feel)

_____ that these geniuses _____ very different
6 (assume)   7 (be)

from us. Yet, geniuses or not, we all _____ a similar creative
8 (use)

process whenever we _____ at something in a new way or
9 (look)

_____ new solutions to a problem. It _____ a
10 (try)   11 (be)

process of first looking at a situation carefully and then making and following a

plan of action.

2 **Practice** Think about the process of writing a composition or essay. Make a step-by-step plan of action for writing by forming complete sentences from the following clauses.

Example Whenever you write something, . . .

Whenever you write something, it's a good idea to work in a
quiet place without distractions.
Whenever you write something, you need to be able to
concentrate on your ideas.

1. Before you begin to write a composition, . . .

2. While you are thinking about the topic, . . .

3. After you have gathered your ideas, . . .

4. When you need more information on a topic, . . .

5. . . . as you are writing.

6. After you have finished writing, . . .

7. . . . until you are satisfied with your composition.

8. . . . before you hand in your composition.

3 **Practice** Describe the following processes by making statements with time clauses. Explain (a) what you should do before you begin . . . , (b) what you should do while you are . . . , and (c) what you should do after you have finished. Add modal auxiliaries such as *can* or *should* and combine steps when necessary.

Example *Before you begin painting a watercolor, you should choose a good piece of watercolor paper. After you have sketched your drawing lightly, wet the paper with water . . .*

1. Painting a watercolor
   - Choose a good piece of watercolor paper.
   - Sketch your drawing lightly.
   - Wet the paper with water.
   - Use watery paint for large areas.
   - Catch any drips.
   - Use a drier brush for details.
   - Let your painting dry completely.
   - Mount your picture.

2. Sculpting clay
   - Put a mat down to protect the table.
   - Work the clay with your hands.
   - Add water to soften the clay.
   - Shape individual parts of the sculpture.
   - Attach each part by pinching it on.
   - Smooth the sculpture with water.
   - Use tools to draw any details.
   - Carefully put the sculpture on a piece of paper.
   - Let the sculpture dry at least 24 hours.

3. Designing a web page
   - Spend some time looking at other web pages.
   - Think of a URL that is not already taken.
   - Make some sketches of how you want the web page to look.
   - Choose a background pattern and color for the first page.
   - Decide on the font styles and sizes that you wish to use.
   - Create a logo for your web page.
   - Enter your information.
   - Add hypertext to link parts of your document and to link to other websites.

B. Clauses of Condition: Present Time or Unspecified Time

In sentences with clauses of condition, the main clause shows the effect, or result, of the dependent clause. *If* and *unless* are used in these clauses.

8.8 Clauses of Condition: Present Time or Unspecified Time		
Structures	**Explanations**	**Examples**
if	The main clause is the effect or result of the dependent clause. These sentences refer to habitual activities or activities that are true in general.	**If** Tim writes a lot during the week, he usually has time to relax on the weekend. Tim usually has time to relax on the weekend **if** he writes a lot during the week.
unless	*Unless* is used similarly to *if . . . not* in many sentences. However, *unless* is more emphatic.	Tim rarely writes on the weekend **unless** he has a deadline. **Unless** he has a deadline, Tim doesn't work on the weekend.

4 Practice According to Paul Heist in *The Creative College Student*, the following are some of the chief characteristics of creative students and creative people in general:

Creative people are flexible, independent, innovative, spontaneous, and open to a wide range of experiences. They develop their own styles and their own sense of beauty.

The following deals with some of these characteristics. Form complete sentences from each pair by matching a main clause with a dependent clause. Be sure to pay attention to the difference in meaning of *if* and *unless*.

Example If you develop your own style, _____ *b* _____

Unless you develop your own style, _____ *a* _____

a. you end up imitating other people.

b. you don't have to imitate other people.

1. If a person is independent, _____

   Unless a person is independent, _____

   a. he or she usually relies on others for support or encouragement.

   b. he or she doesn't have to depend on others for support or encouragement.

2. If you are flexible, _____

   Unless you are flexible, _____

   a. you can adapt more easily to new situations.

   b. it may be difficult for you to adapt to new situations.

3. If people are open to new ideas, _____

Unless people are open to new ideas, _____

    a. they can take better advantage of unusual opportunities.

    b. they may miss many unusual opportunities.

4. If you are innovative, _____

Unless you are innovative, _____

    a. it may be difficult for you to find solutions for many problems.

    b. you can usually find solutions for most problems.

5. If you have your own sense of style, _____

Unless you have your own sense of style, _____

    a. you will merely copy what is in fashion.

    b. you will create a unique image for yourself.

6. If you have your own sense of beauty, _____

Unless you have your own sense of beauty, _____

    a. you can find beauty in your work and in your life.

    b. you won't really know how to judge a work of art.

5 **Practice** Complete the following sentences in your own words.

Example I feel most creative when *I am relaxed.*

    1. It is easiest for me to write (sing, draw, and so on) if . . .

    2. Most of my best ideas come after . . .

    3. It is hard for me to concentrate unless . . .

    4. I have done my best work since . . .

    5. I really enjoy listening to music while . . .

    6. I am fascinated whenever . . .

    7. It is not easy for me to start a project before . . .

    8. I am often afraid to . . . until . . .

    9. I feel satisfied after . . .

   10. I never give up on my idea unless . . .

6 Practice What type of student are you? What type of person are you? Answer the following questions in complete sentences.

Example When do you do two things at once?
> *If I have a lot of laundry to fold or clothes to iron, I usually watch TV at the same time.*

1. When do you do two things at once?
2. Do you watch TV while you are doing your homework?
3. What else do you do while you are doing your homework?
4. Can you concentrate if people around you are talking or doing other things?
5. Are you nervous before you take a test?
6. Do you celebrate after you have turned in a big assignment?
7. Do you always take notes (listen carefully) when you are in class?
8. Do you get depressed if you get less than an A?
9. Do you usually compare grades with classmates after a test?
10. Do you make it a point to introduce yourself to your instructor when you start a new class?

Using What You've Learned

7 Describing a Creative Person Whom do you consider to be creative? Do you have a friend or relative who is good at making or fixing things, at painting, at cooking or baking, at playing or writing music? Give a brief presentation on a creative person you know. Use the following questions to help you prepare.

1. How is this person creative?
2. When is he or she the most creative? What seems to inspire him or her?
3. Has this person always been creative?
4. What interesting things has he or she done or produced?
5. What is this person doing now? Is he or she still involved in creative activities?

8 Describing a Work of Art What do you consider to be a very creative work? Have you seen a piece of original art, a photograph, a play, a musical performance that you really liked? Write a paragraph describing this work. Use the following questions to help you prepare.

1. What is the medium (type) of this work? (plastic arts, photography, performing arts, other?)

2. What makes this work creative?

3. How does it make you feel?

4. What do other people think of this work? Do they agree with you?

5. Do you know who created this work? Has this person or have these people created something else that you also like?

▲ *Whistler in the Dark* (self-portrait)

Part 3

Adverb Clauses of Time and Condition: Past Time with the Simple Past and Past Perfect Tenses

Setting the Context

 Previewing the Passage Discuss the question.

A Renaissance person is someone who is knowledgeable and accomplished in a wide variety of fields. The following passage is about such a person, Leonardo da Vinci (1452–1519). What do you know about his accomplishments?

Reading Read the passage.

Leonardo da Vinci

Most people recognize Leonardo da Vinci as the painter of the *Mona Lisa* and *The Last Supper*. Yet Leonardo was a master of design, engineering, science, and invention, as well as a master of art.

After Leonardo had painted his most famous works, he began to spend

more time on his other dreams. As a military engineer, Leonardo had drawn 5
plans for primitive tanks and airplanes long before they were ever dreamed possible. He is also credited with having designed the first parachute and having
constructed the first elevator.

In the sciences, Leonardo was equally amazing. He had discovered complex
principles of physics nearly a century before Galileo did his own work. In 10
anatomy, Leonardo studied muscle and bone structure to improve his painting,
and even after he had tired of painting, he continued to study the workings of
the heart. He had even speculated on the circulation of blood a century before
William Harvey proved it. Leonardo da Vinci was so far ahead of his time that
not until this century did his genius become truly evident. 15

▲ The *Mona Lisa*

 Discussing Ideas Discuss the questions.

This passage tells about only some of da Vinci's works. Can you tell about any other
of da Vinci's projects? Can you name other individuals who have been ahead of
their time?

Grammar Structures and Practice

A. Adverb Clauses of Time: Past Time with the Simple Past and Past Perfect Tenses

Clauses of time can relate events that occurred at different times in the past.

8.9	Clauses of Time: Past Time with the Simple Past and Past Perfect Tenses		
Structures	**Explanations**		**Examples**
before *by the time (that)* *until* *when*	The past perfect is used to refer to an event or situation that came before another event or time in the past. With *before, by the time that, until,* and *when,* the past perfect is used in the main clause.		Leonardo da Vinci **had painted** the *Mona Lisa* **before he worked** on many of his ideas for inventions.
after *as soon as* *once*	In complex sentences with *after, as soon as,* and *once,* the past perfect (continuous) is used in the dependent (not the main) clause.		**After** Leonardo da Vinci **had painted** his major artworks, he **spent** more time on his inventions.

1 Practice Reread "Leonardo da Vinci" on page 350. How many sentences can you find with adverb clauses of time? For each such sentence, find the connecting word. Then explain which action came earlier and which action came later.

B. Adverbs with Time Clauses

Adverbs of frequency and other expressions are often used with the past perfect tense.

8.10	Adverbs with Time Clauses	
Structures	**Explanations**	**Examples**
already *barely* *hardly* *just* *no sooner* *scarcely*	Adverbs such as *already, hardly, just,* and *scarcely,* are often used with the past perfect tense. They generally come between *had* and the past participle. *Yet* usually comes at the end of a negative sentence.	Leonardo da Vinci **had already worked** as a civil engineer, military engineer, and architect **by the time** he **began** his major paintings.

C. *After, Before, By,* and *Until* as Prepositions

After, before, by, and *until* can also be used as prepositions in phrases of time.

- Sentences with *before, by,* and *until* may use the past perfect tense.
- Sentences with *after* would generally use the simple past tense. Compare these:

8.11	*After, Before, By,* and *Until* as Prepositions	
Structures	**Examples**
Subordinating Conjunction	**Before** he began his major paintings, da Vinci had already worked as an engineer and architect. **After** da Vinci had painted many of his major artworks, he spent more time on his inventions.
Preposition	**Before** 1495, da Vinci had already worked as an engineer and architect. **After** 1500, da Vinci spent more time on his inventions.

2 Practice Everyone develops special talents during his or her lifetime, but few are able to equal the extraordinary feats of the following individuals. Complete the following passages by using simple past or past perfect forms (active or passive) of the verbs in parentheses. Note any case where you feel both tenses are appropriate. The first two are done as examples.

1. Ibn Sina

Ibn Sina _____*was*_____ a Persian who _____*wrote*_____ *The*
        (be)   (write)

Canon of Medicine. This medical encyclopedia _____ very
        1 (be)

advanced; as a result, scholars _____ it for five centuries.
        2 (use)

Before his death in 1037, Ibn Sina _____ an additional 150
        3 (complete)

books on such varied subjects as philosophy, mathematics, theology, and as-

tronomy. Like many learned men, he _____ early. By the age of
        4 (begin)

10, he _____ the Koran. By the age of 18, he _____
        5 (memorize)   6 (work)

as a physician for a sultan.

2. King Sejong

King Sejong _____ Korea from 1418 to 1450. He
        1 (rule)

_____ a scholar as well as one of the greatest and most virtu-
        2 (be)

ous of Korean kings. Peace for Korea _____ one of his finest
        3 (be)

accomplishments. Once he _____ the barbarians on Korea's
                              4 (defeat)
northern border, Korea _____ a long period of peace. Within
                          5 (enjoy)
his government, Sejong _____ men of talent, no matter what
                          6 (promote)
their social status. He _____, "The prosperity of the state
                          7 (say)
depends upon the character of the government." He also _____
                                                          8 (invent)
hang'ul, the Korean alphabet, which _____ literacy to the
                                        9 (bring)
common people. By the time Sejong _____, he
                                      10 (die)
_____ culture blossom and _____ learning
    11 (see)   12 (watch)
truly flourish in his beloved Korea.

3. Sor Juana Inés De La Cruz

   Sor Juana, the great Mexican poet, was born in Mexico City around 1651.
She _____ to read before she _____ three
       1 (start / already)   2 (be)
years old. By her seventh birthday, she _____ to enter the
                                           3 (try)
university. Because girls _____ in the university, Sor Juana
                            4 (not allow)
eventually _____ the convent. During her life, she
              5 (join)
_____ extraordinary prose and poetry. Before she
    6 (write)
_____ in 1695, she _____ a library of over
    7 (die)   8 (collect)
4,000 books.

4. Johann Wolfgang von Goethe

   Goethe _____ from 1749 to 1832. He _____
             1 (live)   2 (be)
a scientist as well as the greatest of German poets. By age 16, he
_____ religious poems, a novel, and a prose epic. While
    3 (write / already)
continuing to write, he _____ both law and medicine. After he
                           4 (study)
_____ to live in Weimar, Goethe _____
    5 (be invited)   6 (become)
minister of state. Because of his position, he _____ himself in
                                                  7 (educate)
agriculture, horticulture, and mining. He then _____ to master
                                                  8 (proceed)
anatomy, biology, optics, and mineralogy.

5. John Stuart Mill

Perhaps John Stuart Mill _____ more at age 13 than most
1 (master / already)
people learn in their entire lives. He _____ reading Greek at age
2 (begin)
three and Latin at seven. By age 12, he _____ all the master-
3 (read)
pieces in both languages. He then _____ to logic and political
4 (turn)
economy; by age 18, he _____ articles on these topics for the
5 (write)
Westminister Review.

6. Margaret Mead

By the time Margaret Mead _____ 26, she
1 (be)
_____ curator of the American Museum of Natural History.
2 (name / already)
Before she _____ age 30, she _____ two major
3 (reach)   4 (publish)
books on people of Oceania. Before her death in 1978, she _____
5 (write)
hundreds of articles and books on topics ranging from anthropology to nuclear

warfare and disarmament.

3 **Practice** The following sentences give you information about Michelangelo
Buonarroti (1475–1564) and some of his accomplishments. The sentences are listed in
chronological order (order by time of occurrence). Use the cues in parentheses to
combine each pair. Change nouns and verb tenses, omit words, and add punctuation
when necessary.

Example   Artists used methods of fresco[1] painting for many centuries. The
Italians perfected the technique. (before)
*Artists had used methods of fresco painting for many centuries
before the Italians perfected the technique.*

1. Both Michelangelo and Leonardo da Vinci worked with fresco. Michelangelo
and Leonardo were commissioned for a painting in Florence. (before)

2. Michelangelo began his work on the Council Room in Florence. Michelangelo
was called to Rome by Pope Julius II. (soon after)

_____

[1]*fresco* the art of painting on a moist plaster surface

3. Michelangelo left for Rome. The two artists never worked together again. (once)

4. Michelangelo arrived in Rome. The pope commanded Michelangelo to fresco the Sistine Chapel. (as soon as)

5. Michelangelo didn't finish the ceiling. The pope impatiently opened the Sistine Chapel in 1509. (when)

6. Michelangelo, without help, covered 5,800 square feet with fresco painting. Michelangelo finished the Sistine Chapel ceiling. (by the time that)

▲ A detail from the Sistine Chapel ceiling painted by Michelangelo Buonarroti

4 **Practice** First read the following passage for meaning. Then complete it by using appropriate connecting words and transitions. Choose from *after, and, at the same time, but, by, by the time that, for example, in addition, in fact, once, whenever*. Try to use each at least one time.

The Italian Renaissance

Many cultures have produced great thinkers and great artists,

_____*but*_____ the collection of brilliant minds that lived in Italy in the

1400s and 1500s may never be repeated. It was a very special time for the world.

_____ the end of the 13th century, Florence and other Italian
             1

cities had reached very high standards of living. The aristocracy used its wealth

to promote the arts and the sciences. _____ Leonardo da Vinci
                                                          2

was born in 1452, even the growing middle class of craftspeople and merchants

had already begun to participate in and benefit from the "explosion of learning and creativity" evident in Florence, Lucca, and other Italian cities. Knowledge was highly valued; _____, learning was important even for the common people—not just the rich.

The creative and reflective atmosphere of that time led to great achievements across many fields. New ideas about mathematical and geometric proportions led to changes in music, architecture, and of course, art. _____ other thinkers had worked out ideas about depth and perspective, masters such as Botticelli, da Vinci, and Michelangelo began applying these theories in their paintings and sculptures. _____, architecture changed dramatically. _____ various mathematical and structural theories had been developed, taller and wider buildings became possible. _____, great new domed cathedrals like Santa Maria del Fiore in Florence were built, _____ old gothic styles were abandoned.

The sciences also blossomed. Geniuses like Leonardo da Vinci and Galileo Galilei worked across many disciplines. _____, Galileo worked with mechanics, astronomy, temperature, and magnetism. He invented the microscope, _____ he also built a telescope powerful enough to make the discovery of the satellites of the planet Jupiter. _____, he experimented with ideas of motion such as the pendulum and gravitation. _____, it is said that he used the tilt of the Tower of Pisa to do his experiments on the acceleration of falling bodies.

Renaissance Italy produced tremendous achievements that still impact us today. _____ we admire great works of art, listen to lyrical music, appreciate beautiful buildings, or look through a lens at the starry night sky, we must thank Italians of the Renaissance for their many creative contributions to our world.

▲ Santa Maria del Fiore in Florence, Italy   ▲ The Leaning Tower of Pisa in Pisa, Italy

Using What You've Learned

5 **Talking About da Vinci** Leonardo da Vinci was "far ahead of his time." He had drawn plans for a number of inventions that were not developed until centuries later. Some of these plans included an airplane, an elevator, a helicopter, lock gates for canals, a submarine, and a tank.

In small groups, discuss one or more of these inventions. Try to imagine what da Vinci had been thinking, doing, or feeling before he created his plans and how he arrived at them. You might want to use the following questions to help you. After you have finished, choose one member to give a brief summary for the class.

1. What do you think led da Vinci to these ideas? What problems had he been trying to solve?

2. Can you think of any reasons why he didn't develop the actual invention? (He *did* design and build a type of gate for canal locks.) Were all the necessary materials available at that time?

3. When were these inventions actually developed?

4. How have they changed since then?

5. How have they affected our lives?

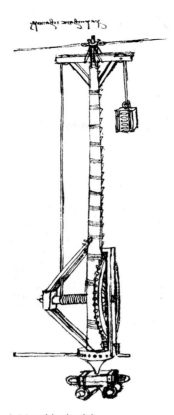

▲ Movable derrick

▲ Tank

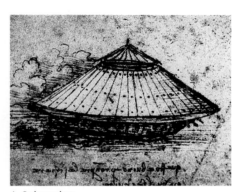

▲ Submarine

6 **Describing Someone You Admire** Is there someone whom you particularly admire for his or her knowledge or accomplishments? He or she may be a musician, a scholar, a sports figure, a politician, a friend, or a family member. What did this person do? How did he or she accomplish this?

Write a paragraph describing this person's accomplishments. Organize your composition in chronological order, and be sure to pay close attention to your use of verb tenses. Later, work in small groups and share your descriptions with your classmates.

Setting the Context

▲ Albert Einstein

 Previewing the Passage Discuss the questions.

Who was Albert Einstein? What do you know about his work?

Reading Read the paragraph.

Creativity and Genius in Science

One of history's greatest revolutionary thinkers has been Albert Einstein, yet virtually no one foresaw his creativity. When he was a child, his parents feared that he was mentally handicapped. For example, while he was learning to talk, he had great difficulties. When he entered school, he was considered "average" at best. Later, after he had finally graduated from a technical school, he was not able to find a job teaching science. Yet Einstein went on to become one of the world's greatest scientists, and today his name is synonymous with genius.

5

Discussing Ideas Discuss the questions.

In many ways, Einstein was what we call a *late bloomer*, someone who develops his or her potential later than other people do. Do you know of other people who began great accomplishments later in life? What about the opposite? Do you know of people who were *precocious*, who produced a great deal early in life, and then perhaps stopped?

Grammar Structures and Practice

A: Clauses of Time and Condition: Past Time with the Simple Past and Past Continuous Tenses

Clauses of time can relate events that occurred at the same time in the past.

8.12	Clauses of Time and Condition: Past Time with the Simple Past and Past Continuous	
Structures	**Explanations**	**Examples**
when	The simple past tense is used with *when* to show a direct connection in the time of occurrence of two events.	**When** Einstein **had** extra time during the day, he **wrote** down his ideas.
if *unless*	*If* and *unless* express a cause and effect relationship between two events. The main clause is the effect, or result, of the dependent clause. Use the simple past.	**If** he **had** enough time, he **wrote** out long mathematical equations. **Unless** he **had** no time, he **would** usually **write** down notes each day.
as *while*	*As* and *while* connect to events that were in progress at the same time. The past continuous is used with *as* and *while*. Both clauses may use the past continuous to emphasize that both activities were in progress at the same time.	**As** Einstein **was doing** his work, he **was** also **thinking**. **While** Einstein **was working** in the patent office, he **had** plenty of time to think.

1 **Practice** Complete the following passage by using simple past or past continuous forms of the verbs in parentheses. Include adverbs where indicated. The first one is done as an example.

Albert Einstein

When Einstein _____*was*_____ a child, he _____ no
                    (be)   1 (show)
early evidence of genius. While he _____ to talk, he
                                        2 (learn)
_____ tremendous difficulties, and his parents
    3 (have)

_____ about his being mentally handicapped. In high school, he
        4 (worry / even)

_____ an average student. When he _____
        5 (be)   6 (graduate / finally)

from a technical institute in Zurich, Switzerland, he _____ able
                                                              7 (not be)

to find a teaching appointment in science. He _____ up work-
                                                    8 (end)

ing in a patent office in Bern, Switzerland.

Einstein _____ that type of job, but as he _____
              9 (not want)   10 (work)

in the office, he _____ able to spend time thinking. Several
                        11 (be)

years later he _____ five papers in one year, 1905. These papers
                    12 (publish)

_____ an explanation of his special theory of relativity, which
        13 (include)

_____ a worldwide scientific revolution.
        14 (begin)

2 **Practice** Many of science's greatest findings or events have come as a result of
good luck combined with hard work. Complete these passages by using simple past or
past continuous forms of the verbs in parentheses. The first verb is done as an example.

1. During the late 1800s, Louis Pasteur _was experimenting_ with bacteria.
                                              (experiment)

   When Pasteur _____ chickens old bacteria by accident,
                      1 (give)

   they _____ sick, but they _____. When he
          2 (become)   3 (not die)

   _____ the injections several times, the chickens
        4 (repeat)

   _____ a resistance to infection. This discovery
        5 (develop)

   _____ his work on immunization.
        6 (begin)

2. While von Mering and Minkowski _____ the pancreas
                                          1 (study)

   (which helps to metabolize sugar), they _____ the organ
                                                  2 (remove)

   from several dogs. Later, a laboratory assistant _____
                                                          3 (notice)

   something unusual. Flies _____ around the cages of these
                                  4 (swarm)

   dogs, but they _____ near the cages of other dogs. When
                        5 (not go)

   the two researchers _____ the dogs without pancreases,
                              6 (test)

   they _____ that the dogs _____ the
          7 (discover)   8 (have)

362   Chapter 8 ■ ■ ■

symptoms of diabetes. This incident _____ medical
                                        9 (give)
science the first information connecting the pancreas to the cause of
diabetes.

3. In 1929, the English bacteriologist Alexander Fleming _____
                                                            1 (experiment)
with a bacteria culture when it _____ contaminated by a
                                    2 (become)
mold. When the mold _____ the bacteria, the bacteria
                          3 (touch)
_____. Fleming _____ this mold and
        4 (die)   5 (save)
_____ it grow in a liquid. While this mold _____,
        6 (let)   7 (grow)
it _____ a substance that _____ able to
        8 (produce)   9 (be)
kill a number of bacteria. Moreover, the substance _____
                                                          10 (harm / not)
animals. This substance later _____ known as penicillin.
                                    11 (become)

3 Practice Complete the following sentences about Marie Curie by using simple
past, past continuous, or past perfect forms (active or passive) of the verbs in
parentheses.

1. Born in Poland in 1867, Marie Sklodowska _was not allowed_ to attend
                                                (not allow)
   school there beyond the high school level.

2. After an older brother and sister _____ for university
                                          (leave)
   education in Paris, Marie _____ to send them money and to
                                  (work)
   save for her own education.

3. While she _____, Marie _____ herself from
                  (work)   (teach)
   family books.

4. As soon as she _____ enough money, she _____
                        (save)   (go / also)
   to Paris.

5. While Marie _____ at the Sorbonne, she _____
                    (study)   (live)
   as economically as possible and _____ all her time studying.
                                          (spend)

6. When she _____, Marie Sklodowska _____
   (graduate)   (be)
   at the top of her class.

7. In 1894, she _____ to Pierre Curie, who
   (introduce)
   _____ somewhat famous for his work in physics.
   (become / already)

8. After Marie _____ Pierre Curie, she _____
   (marry)   (begin)
   to apply his earlier discoveries to the measurement of radioactivity.

9. Scarcely six years after Marie _____ in Paris, she
   (arrive)
   _____ major discoveries about radioactivity; Pierre
   (make)
   _____ the potential and _____ his own
   (see)   (drop)
   research to join her.

10. In December 1898, the Curies _____ other experiments with
    (conduct)
    uranium ore when they _____ a new radioactive substance:
    (detect)
    radium.

11. In 1903, Marie Curie _____ her dissertation on radioactivity,
    (write)
    and for it, she and Pierre _____ that year's Nobel Prize with
    (give)
    Antoine Becquerel.

12. After Pierre Curie's death in 1906, Marie _____ her study of
    (continue)
    radioactive elements, and in 1911 she _____ the Nobel Prize
    (award)
    in chemistry.

4 Practice The following sentences tell about the life of Albert Einstein. The sentences are in chronological order (order by time of occurrence). Combine each group of sentences by using coordinating or subordinating conjunctions or transitions. You can choose from the following connecting words or you can use others: *after, and, as soon as, as a result, before, for example, in addition, when, while, until*. Change words, phrases, verb tenses, and punctuation when necessary.

Example   In 1900, Albert Einstein graduated from the Polytechnic Academy in Zurich. Later that year, Albert Einstein became a Swiss citizen. Later that year, Albert Einstein took a job in a Swiss patent office.

In 1900, after Albert Einstein had graduated from the Polytechnic Academy in Zurich, he became a Swiss citizen and took a job in a Swiss patent office.

1. Albert Einstein worked in the patent office for three years. Then, Albert Einstein married Mileva Marié.

2. Albert Einstein worked in the patent office for several years. During that time, he developed many of his theories.

3. Albert Einstein worked at the patent office. He financed some of his research by writing patents for better refrigerators.

4. Einstein did not produce any notable scientific work. Then he published five papers in 1905.

5. Einstein published his papers in 1905. Before then, he had been completely unknown in the scientific community.

6. These papers were published. Einstein immediately became famous in the scientific community. These papers contained many revolutionary ideas. They outlined the "special theory of relativity," the "equivalence of mass and energy $(E = mc^2)$," and the "photon theory of light."

7. During the next six years, Einstein continued to develop his theory of relativity. During that time, Einstein continued to study the relationship between mass and energy. During that time, Einstein tried to incorporate gravity into his theory.

8. Einstein taught in Prague for a brief time. Then the Einstein family returned to Switzerland. Einstein was offered a position at the Polytechnic Academy in Zurich.

9. Einstein accepted a position at the Prussian Academy of Sciences. The Einstein family moved to Berlin.

10. Einstein's wife and sons were vacationing in Europe. World War I broke out.

5 Practice The following is a continuation of the chronology of Albert Einstein's life. Use the information to write a short paragraph about him. Combine ideas by using coordinating conjunctions, subordinating conjunctions, and transitions. Change words, phrases, verb tenses, and punctuation when necessary.

1914

Einstein accepted a position at the Prussian Academy of Sciences.

The Einstein family moved to Berlin.

Einstein's wife and sons vacationed in Switzerland.

World War I began.

His family was unable to return to Germany.

This forced separation eventually led to divorce.

1916

Einstein published his paper on the general theory of relativity.

This theory was revolutionary.

It contradicted Newton's ideas on gravity.

It predicted irregularities in the motion and light from Mercury.

During this time, Einstein devoted much of his time to pacifism.

Einstein began to write and distribute antiwar literature.

1919

The Royal Society of London verified Einstein's predictions about Mercury.

Einstein quickly became famous.

Einstein married Elsa, the daughter of a cousin of his father.

Einstein stayed in Berlin.

Einstein continued to work for pacifism.

1921

Einstein was awarded the Nobel Prize in physics.

Using What You've Learned

6 Researching a Historical Figure Use information from this section, along with other information you can gather from the Internet or the library, to write a short paragraph about one of the following:

• Marie Curie and the discovery of radium

• Alexander Fleming and the discovery of penicillin

• Louis Pasteur and immunization, pasteurization, or other processes

• Galileo and observation of our universe

• Chinese astronomer Chang Heng and the seismograph

Part 5 — Adverb Clauses of Time and Condition: Future Time

Setting the Context

Previewing the Passage Discuss the questions.

How do you go about making decisions? Do you decide quickly? Or do you look carefully at alternatives? Have you ever seen or used a "decision tree" like the one on the following page?

Reading Read the passage.

Decision Making

Making a good decision is one of the most creative things we do. In many ways, creativity is the ability to see all the alternatives. It can be an analytical process. When you need to make an important decision, using a decision tree can be a great help, especially if the decision is a complicated one.

Imagine that you are in charge of identifying a supplier of silk fabric for your clothing company. Look at the a decision tree on page 368 to help you make your decision.

5

Supplier A: higher grade silk, cost is $0.50 more per meter, delivery is cheaper than supplier B, supplier A wants to dye silk, won't ship otherwise

Supplier B: slightly lower grade silk, cost is cheaper than supplier A, delivery costs about $0.25 more per meter of silk fabric, supplier B will ship raw fabric, not dyed

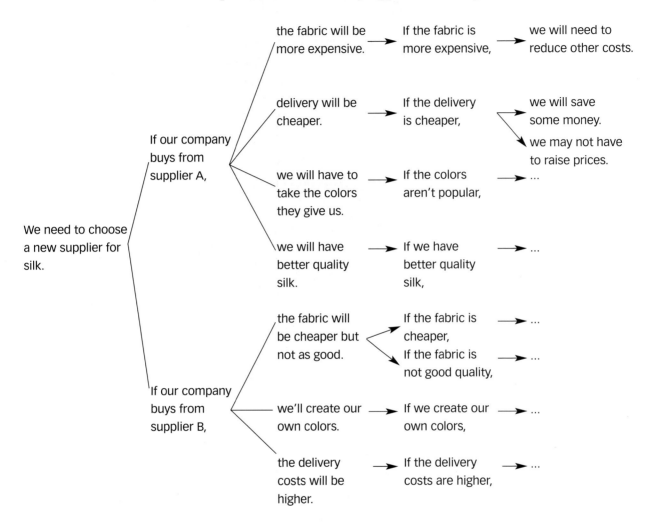

▲ Hong Kong is a fabric buyer's paradise!

 Discussing Ideas Discuss the questions.

What were the possible results for each situation on the decision tree? What was your final decision? What effect does this decision have on the company?

Grammar Structures and Practice

A. Clauses of Time: Future Time

Clauses of time can relate events that will occur at different times in the future.

8.13	Clauses of Time: Future Time	
Structures	**Explanations**	**Examples**
after *as soon as* *before* *once* *until* *when*	With these words, the verb in the dependent clause is in the simple present or the present perfect tense. The present perfect emphasizes the completion of the action. The verb in the main clause is in a future tense. Modal auxiliaries such as *can* and *should* are often used in either clause.	**After I finish**, I will take a long vacation! I'm going to call you **as soon as I finish**. I won't call you **before I have finished**. **Once I've finished**, I'll call you. I should work **until I have finished**. **When I finish**, I'll give you a call.
as *while*	With *as* and *while*, the present continuous is often used in dependent clauses to emphasize an action in progress.	I'll have to concentrate a lot **as I'm working**. **While I'm working**, I won't think about my vacation.

1 Practice Imagine that you have a business that offers a service such as insurance, travel, or computer consulting. In your own words, complete the following about "your business."

Example After the sales meeting is over, *we'll make some decisions.*

1. After I finish this report, . . .
2. When we have finished our business plan, . . .
3. Tonight, I'm going to finish my work before . . .
4. While I'm reviewing our balance sheet tonight, . . .
5. As soon as I get to the office, . . .
6. I'll call them once . . .
7. As we're redoing our office, . . .
8. I will keep on trying to contact the buyer until . . .
9. When I reach the buyer, . . .
10. If I close the sale . . .

2 Practice Imagine that you're going to start your own online business. What are you going to do before you start the business? While you are thinking about the product you will sell? After you have decided on a product? Write a paragraph by forming complete sentences from the cues. Add specific information about your own "business" for numbers 9 and 10.

Example Think of a product to sell online.

Before I start this business online, I am going to think about what my product will be. While I am thinking about the product, I'll do market research on . . .

1. Research the competition.
2. Decide what advantage selling online can give.
3. Fnd a supplier.
4. Set up a distribution system.
5. Design a website.
6. Create packaging.
7. Market my product on the Internet.
8. Hire an accountant to handle my record keeping.
9. Add more information about "your" business.
10. Add another piece of information about "your" business.

3 Practice Complete these sentences, giving more ideas about your "company."

Example If the product sells, *we'll expand our company.*

   1. If we make a profit, . . .

   2. If the product is successful, . . .

   3. If we add a new product, . . .

   4. If we don't sell a lot of the product, . . .

   5. If my friends want to invest in my company, . . .

   6. If my financial backers are willing to lend me more money, . . .

   7. If we sell a lot of products online, . . .

   8. If we get more orders than we expected in the first year, . . .

   9. If we start selling internationally, . . .

 10. If our company goes public,[1] . . .

---

[1]*goes public* offers shares of company stock for the public to buy

B. Clauses of Condition: Future Time

Factual conditional sentences that refer to the future generally express predictions or intentions. The main clause shows the effect or result of the *if* clause.

8.14	Clauses of Condition: Future Time	
Structures	**Explanations**	**Examples**
if	The verb in the dependent clause is in a present tense. The verb in the main clause is *be going to* or a modal auxiliary: *will, may, might, should,* and so on.	**If I finish** my work, **I will** (*may, might,* and so on) go to the party. **I am not going** to go (*can't go, shouldn't go,* and so on) **if I haven't finished** my work.
unless	*Unless* is similar in meaning to *if . . . not* in many sentences, but *unless* is more emphatic.	**Unless I finish** my work, **I am not going** to go (*can't go, shouldn't go,* and so on) to the party.

---

4 Practice Complete the following in your own words.

Example If the weather is nice this weekend, *we'll take a trip.*

   1. If I have enough money, . . .

   2. If it rains tomorrow, . . .

   3. If I finish my homework early, . . .

   4. If I don't finish my homework, . . .

5. If my friends invite me to visit, . . .

6. If my parents don't call soon, . . .

7. If I win a scholarship, . . .

8. If I get a perfect score on the TOEFL test, . . .

9. If I get accepted to graduate school, . . .

10. If I have the chance to study abroad, . . .

5 **Practice** Imagine that you are trying to decide about a place to live. Use the following decision tree, similar to the one on page 368, to help you decide what to do. Use the correct forms of the verbs in parentheses and add more information. Then make your decision and explain why you made that decision.

I can spend up to $500 a month for my expenses (housing, meals, transportation).
Apartment A: with Americans; $280 a month; near school
Apartment B: with people from my own country; $200 a month; far from school

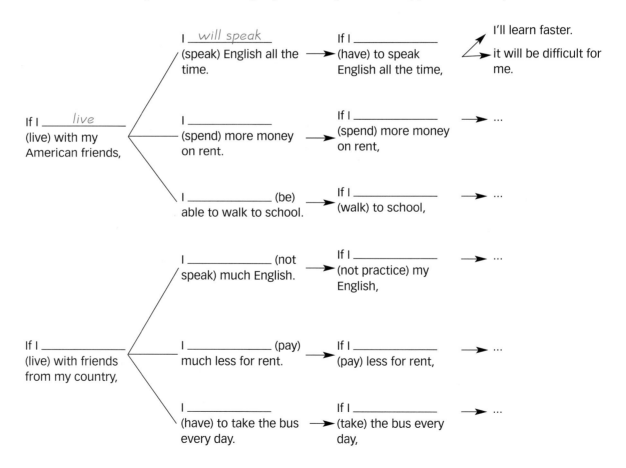

6 **Practice** Combine the following pairs to form new sentences with *unless*.

Example I should speak English more often. If I don't, I'll never become fluent.
Unless I speak English more often, I'll never become fluent.

1. I should find a cheaper place to live. If I don't, I'll run out of money soon.

2. We should save more money. If we don't, we'll never be able to take a long vacation.

3. You should send your application for school soon. If you don't, you may not be accepted this year.

4. I should write my parents soon. If I don't, they'll start to get worried about me.

5. You should start your research project soon. If you don't, you may not be able to finish in time.

6. They should prepare more for the test. If they don't, they may not pass.

7. Deb should see the doctor soon. If she doesn't, her condition may get worse.

8. Jack should take a long vacation. If he doesn't, he might have a nervous breakdown.

9. I shouldn't have to take any more English classes. If I don't pass this one, I will.

10. Mary should see a counselor about studying abroad. If she doesn't, she might not choose the right school.

7 **Practice** The following guidelines for excellence in business are from *In Search of Excellence* by Thomas J. Peters and Robert H. Waterman. According to Peters and Waterman, these are the eight attributes of "excellent, innovative companies." After reading the list, think about the causes and effects of these attributes. Then think about the consequences for a company that does not have them. Form sentences using *if, unless, before, after,* and *when* to express your ideas. You may have several opinions for each.

Excellent, Innovative Companies

Example take action
They make theories and analyses, but most important, they try new ideas.
If a company is innovative, it will try new ideas.
When a company takes action, it will be able to see results, rather than guess the results.
If a company doesn't try something new, another company will probably try it first.
Unless a company tries new ideas, it won't make any progress.

1. are close to the customer
They get their ideas from the people they serve; they listen carefully to their customers.

2. encourage independence and ingenuity
   They don't hold people back. They encourage employees to be creative and to take risks. They support experimentation.

3. work for productivity through people
   They treat everyone in the company as an important source of ideas. They never encourage a "we / they" management / worker situation.

4. keep "quality" as the basic philosophy of the organization
   Quality is the most important thing, not status, organization, resources, or technology.

5. stick to their own business
   They don't get involved in things that are outside of their area of expertise. They don't acquire jobs or businesses they don't know how to run.

6. keep their organization simple and their staff to a minimum
   Their structures and systems are simple; they avoid having too many managers.

7. are both centralized and decentralized
   Control is loose because workers at all levels have authority and responsibility; on the other hand, control is tight because top management decides the basic direction of the company.

C. Sentence Problems: Fragments, Comma Splices, and Run-ons

Fragments, comma splices, and run-on sentences are some of the most common errors in writing. These errors involve incomplete ideas or incorrect punctuation.

8.15 Sentence Problems: Fragments, Comma Splices, and Run-Ons		
Structures	**Explanations**	**Examples of Errors***
Fragment	Fragments are incomplete sentences. They are missing a subject or a verb.	✗ Thinking up new ideas.
Comma Splice	A comma splice is two sentences combined with a comma but without a connecting word.	✗ Thinking up new ideas can be difficult, it is important.
Run-On	A run-on sentence is two sentences combined without proper punctuation. A period, a semi-colon, or a connecting word must be added.	✗ Thinking up new ideas can be difficult it is important.

* Note that each of these is incorrect.

8 **Error Analysis** Some of the following sentences are well written. Others are incomplete or are punctuated incorrectly. For each sentence, indicate complete (C), incomplete (I), or punctuation error (PE). Then, rewrite the incorrect sentences correctly.

Example   _____I_____ If a scientist makes an outstanding discovery.
A scientist may make an outstanding discovery.
OR
If a scientist makes an outstanding discovery, we call this creativity or genius.

1. _____ When an artist produces a masterpiece.

_____

2. _____ People are creative not only in art or science, they are also creative in their daily lives.

_____

3. _____ Ordinary people are creative every day.

_____

4. _____ Creativity involves awareness it means noticing the world around us.

_____

5. _____ To think up a new concept.

_____

6. _____ It is the courage and drive to make use of new ideas.

_____

7. _____ Creativity combining old ideas in new ways.

_____

8. _____ According to an old saying, there is nothing new under the sun.

_____

9. _____ Is not always easy to look at the same ideas in a different way.

_____

10. _____ Being open to new ideas is sometimes difficult, however, every one of us has the ability to do it.

_____

9 Error Analysis The following passage contains errors in punctuation: sentence fragments, comma splices, and run-on sentences. First, read the passage once to understand the ideas. Then correct the passage by changing or adding punctuation when necessary.

Creativity

One form of creativity is the sudden flash of insight. When an idea pops into your head. This is what Arthur Koestler called the Eureka process. *Eureka* comes from the story of the ancient Greek scientist Archimedes. Archimedes supposedly leapt naked from his tub. Shouting "Eureka!" *Eureka* means "I have found it." He had suddenly figured out why some things float.

Not all creative discoveries come like a flash of light, however. In fact, Thomas Edison, the inventor of the lightbulb, tried hundreds of metal combinations in his laboratory. Before he found the right one to conduct electricity. Edison was able to create something new and valuable because of his energy and tenacity. He gave his own definition of genius it is 1 percent inspiration and 99 percent perspiration.

Despite their differences, Edison and Archimedes had much in common, they followed the same process. First, both recognized a problem. And were aware of previous steps to solve it. Both consciously or unconsciously worked toward a solution. Finally, both arrived at a solution, this was the creative idea.

Using What You've Learned

10 Comparing Superstitions Consider the world of myths and superstitions. In small groups, share some traditional beliefs and/or superstitions. Use these ideas and add some of your own. Then, share your information with the whole class.

	if you break a mirror?
	if you step on a crack in the sidewalk?
What will happen . . .	if you walk under a ladder?
	if a black cat crosses your path?

11 Using a Decision Tree Reread "Decision Making" on page 367. In pairs or small groups, discuss the possible options and complete the decision tree. Finally, try to decide which supplier your company should choose.

12 Creating an Invention Rube Goldberg was a creative American cartoonist. He "created" some of the world's most amazing "inventions." The invention in the accompanying cartoon is designed to attract a waiter's attention. Read the text and then follow the drawing to get the step-by-step process.

Then design your own invention and explain it for the class.

Example *My invention is a musical air conditioner with a remote control. When I want to relax, I want both the right temperature and the right music. Now let me show you how it works. If you push this button,...*

13 **Designing an Ideal School** Think about the various descriptions of creativity, innovation, and excellence in this chapter. Try to put these ideas to use as you consider the problems of teaching and learning a language. Imagine that you and your classmates have been asked to design a program for a language school. Work in small groups. Discuss your ideas on the best ways to learn languages. Then make a list of recommendations for planning a language program. Consider the following questions, and add ideas of your own.

1. How many students should there be per class? How many different teachers should students have?

2. How many hours a day should students have classes? When should the classes be offered?

3. What kinds of classes should be offered?

4. Should there be a language lab? Should use of the lab be optional or mandatory?

5. How should you plan if you want to offer economical and effective classes? Remember that both money and time may be problems for the students. Some may be working. Some may have families. Many will not be able to afford expensive classes.

14 **Writing Short Essay Tests** Short essay tests are frequently used in both the sciences and the humanities. Your scores are usually determined by the content. However, an answer with few grammatical errors will most likely receive a better score than one with many errors. So, as you write, also pay attention to the grammar you studied in this chapter. Practice your skills at writing short answers to these questions regarding content in this chapter. Try to spend no more than 10 minutes per answer.

Hint: You can often begin your answer by making the question into a statement.

1. Who is the only woman to have been awarded two Nobel Prizes? In short essay form, give a brief history of her life. Be sure to include information on the Nobel Prizes she received.

2. Create a decision tree for one of these situations. Make your decision regarding the situation. Then write a brief essay explaining your choice.

    Situation 1: Toshio has been awarded two scholarships: one full scholarship to a smaller state university and one a partial scholarship to a well-known and expensive East Coast college. His parents cannot afford to pay for his tuition.

    Situation 2: Anna has two job offers: one at a small firm in her hometown and the other in a large firm in a large city about five hours from her home. The job offers are similar in terms of money and benefits. In her hometown, she can live with her parents and use public transportation. In the city, she will need to have a car and an apartment.

3. Briefly describe the steps involved in taking a good photograph.

Use of Connecting Words

Connecting words are frequently tested on standardized English proficiency exams. Review these commonly tested structures and check your understanding by completing the sample items that follow.

Remember that . . .

✓ Subordinating conjunctions must be followed by a subject / verb combination.
✓ Prepositions are followed by nouns or noun forms.
✓ Transitions use semicolons when joining two sentences.

Part 1 Mark the correct completion for the following.

Example _____ John is satisfied with his work, he will submit the project.

    (A) When   (B) Therefore

    (C) During   (D) In fact

1. _____ Georgia O'Keeffe was living in New York, she worked as a teacher to support herself.

    (A) If   (B) Unless

    (C) While   (D) After

2. _____ you have problems with motion sickness, you can take over-the-counter antihistamines before traveling.

    (A) If   (B) On the other hand

    (C) Unless   (D) After

3. In Europe, most Internet users pay per message; _____, Internet users in the United States usually pay flat rates.

    (A) in contrast   (B) while

    (C) therefore   (D) once

4. We have an important test on Monday, _____ I haven't started studying yet.

    (A) however   (B) but however

    (C) but   (D) so

5. _____ the age of 10, the Persian scholar Ibn Sina had memorized the Koran.

    (A) During   (B) By the time that

    (C) When   (D) By

Part 2 Circle the letter below the underlined word(s) containing an error.

Example An individual often <u>feels frustrated</u> <u>unless</u> she has difficulties <u>speaking</u>
                                    A   Ⓑ   C
       the language of the country <u>where she is living</u>.
                                                    D

1. Louis Armstrong was one of <u>the</u> 20th <u>century's</u> greatest jazz musicians;
                                A   B

   <u>in contrast</u>, he starred in movies and <u>did</u> comedy shows.
        C   D

2. <u>While</u> April <u>of</u> 1999, Europeans sent <u>more than</u> a billion messages on their
      A   B   C
   <u>mobile</u> phones.
      D

3. <u>During</u> Pope Julius II opened <u>the</u> Sistine Chapel in 1509, Michelangelo
      A   B
   Buonarroti had <u>not yet</u> finished his <u>fresco painting</u> of the ceiling.
                      C   D

4. <u>Before</u> her death in 1978, Margaret Mead <u>was written</u> hundreds of articles
      A   B
   and books on numerous subjects <u>including</u> anthropology, museum <u>curating</u>,
                                      C   D
   and nuclear disarmament.

5. Hong Kong <u>is often</u> <u>called</u> the fabric capital of the world; <u>as a result most</u>
                A   B   C
   textile manufacturers send representatives there <u>to buy</u> fabric.
                                                      D

Self-Assessment Log

Each of the following statements describes the grammar you learned in this chapter. Read the statements; then, check the box that describes how well you understand each structure.

	Needs Improvement	Good	Great
I can use coordinating conjunctions in compound sentences.	❏	❏	❏
I can use a variety of transitions.	❏	❏	❏
I can use clauses of past, present, and future time.	❏	❏	❏
I can use clauses of condition.	❏	❏	❏
I can use appropriate punctuation.	❏	❏	❏
I can use a variety of connecting words and sentence types to talk and write about creativity.	❏	❏	❏
I can take a test about compound and complex sentences.	❏	❏	❏

Human Behavior

In This Chapter

Adjective Clauses

Part 1 Review of Modifiers and Introduction to Adjective Clauses

Part 2 Clauses with *That, When,* and *Where*: Replacement of Subjects, Objects, and Adverbials of Time or Place

Part 3 Restrictive and Nonrestrictive Clauses; Clauses with *Who, Which,* and *Whose*: Replacement of Subjects and Possessives

Part 4 Clauses with *Whom* and *Which*: Replacement of Objects

Part 5 Clause-to-Phrase Reduction; Agreement with Adjective Phrases and Clauses

“Religion is a candle inside a multicolored lantern. Everyone looks through a particular color, but the candle is always there. ”

—Mohammed Neguib
First president of Egypt
(1901–1984)

Connecting to the Topic

1. Do you practice a formal religion?

2. Can you name the major religions of the world?

3. Which religion are you the most knowledgeable about? The least knowledgeable?

In this chapter, you will review basic word order of modifiers, and you will study adjective clauses. As you study the chapter, pay close attention to the role of punctuation with these clauses.

Reading Read the following passage. It introduces the chapter theme, "Human Behavior," and raises some of the topics and issues you will cover in the chapter.

Religion and Human Behavior

Does life have meaning? What gives it meaning? Why do we act the way we do? What is the best way to live? How can we be happy? How can we find peace? How can we find fulfillment in our lives? These are questions that people have struggled with throughout human history. Philosophers, psychologists, sociologists, and physicists all have tried to give us answers. We also look for answers   5
within ourselves. We try to cultivate the spiritual side of our lives. For many people in the world, spiritual questions are answered by organized religion.

Hundreds of spiritual traditions exist in the world, yet they all try to answer the same questions. They teach basic ideas that help humans understand their nature and their behavior. They describe oppositions between the spirit and the   10
body, good and evil, earthly and divine. Often these opposites cause conflict in people. Each spiritual tradition gives people a method that they can follow to walk the path of goodness. Each spiritual tradition moves toward a goal. Often that goal involves moving from earth to the divine and from the body to the spirit. This goal has a name like heaven, nirvana, or salvation. All cultures in the   15
world have spiritual traditions and usually some form of organized religion. The spiritual side of existence, whether organized into a religion or not, has a strong effect on the daily lives of people around the world.

Discussing Ideas Discuss the questions.

Think about religion in your culture. Is there one major religion? Or are there several? Is religion an important influence in your culture? To what extent does it affect or control the way people think and behave?

Part 1 Review of Modifiers and Introduction to Adjective Clauses

Setting the Context

 Previewing the Passage Discuss the questions.

This chapter talks about five of the major world religions. It begins with Hinduism, the oldest of the five. What do you know about Hinduism? Is it practiced in your area or country? What religious buildings are shown in the photos below? (Turn to page 419 to check your answers.)

Read the passage.

Hinduism

The religious tradition that we call *Hinduism* is the product of 5,000 years of development. *Hindu* is the Persian word for *Indian*. Hindus themselves, however, call their religious tradition the eternal teaching or law *(sanatana dharma)*. Hinduism has no founder and no prophet.[1] It has no specific church structure, nor does it have a set system of beliefs defined by one authority. The emphasis is on a way of living rather than on a way of thought. Radhakrishnan, a former president of India, once remarked: "Hinduism is more culture than a creed."

5

---

[1]*prophet* a person who claims to speak for God

Discussing Ideas Discuss the questions.

Where did the name *Hindu* come from? Who founded Hinduism? Does Hinduism have a strictly organized system of beliefs? Do you think Hinduism is somewhat different from other religions in these regards? Do you know of any Hindu customs or Hindu beliefs?

Grammar Structures and Practice

A. Review of Modifiers

Remember that English has fairly strict rules for the word order of modifiers in a sentence. To review the order of modifiers, see Chapter 1, pages 31–33.

1 Practice Look at the italicized modifiers in the following sentences and indicate which word(s) each modifies. Try to identify the modifiers (adjective, adverb, article, and so on).

article   *preposition*   *preposition*
                 noun   *noun*

Example *The* majority *of Hindus* believe *in karma.*

   1. *An important* concept *of Hinduism* is karma, *which means "action" or "work."*

2. Because *most* Hindus believe *in reincarnation*, karma *also* means the consequences *of actions from one life to the next.*

3. To *some* social scientists, karma is *heredity*, or genetic inheritance, and dharma is *free will*, the ability to make choices.

4. Reincarnation means *an* individual has lived *many* lives and will live many more until the *final* liberation.

5. Because of karma and reincarnation, respect *for life, customs, and laws* is very important to Hindus.

6. *Some* Hindus believe that being a vegetarian is *the best way* to show respect *for life.*

2 **Practice** Quickly reread the passage "Hinduism" on page 386. Then do the following:

1. Read the first sentence of the passage. Name the subject, verb, and complement in the main clause. Name the subject, verb, and connecting word in the independent clause.

2. In the same sentence, name the parts of speech of the following:

religious; Hinduism; the; of; development

B. Introduction to Adjective Clauses

An adjective clause is a dependent (relative) clause that modifies a noun or pronoun.

- An adjective clause usually comes immediately after the word(s) it modifies. In some cases, a pronoun or prepositional phrase may come between the noun or pronoun and the clause.
- English has several different types of adjective clause constructions. You will study each one in detail in later sections.

9.1 Adjective Clauses

Types of Clauses	Examples
Subject Clauses: *that, which,* and *who*	Hinduism is a religion **that** did not have one founder.
Object Clauses: *that, which,* and *who(m)*	The man **whom** I met yesterday is a Hindu. The man **to whom** I was introduced is a Hindu.
Possessive Clauses: *whose*	Hinduism is a religion **whose** beliefs form a major part of Hindu culture.
Time and Place Clauses: *when* and *where*	India is a country in Asia **where** a majority of the population is Hindu.

3 Practice Each of the following sentences has an adjective clause. Underline the dependent clauses and circle the word(s) they modify.

Example The Ganges is a (river) <u>that flows through northern India</u>.

1. It is a river <u>whose water is sacred to Hindus</u>.

2. Hindus from all over the world travel to the Ganges, <u>which is the symbol of life without end</u>.

3. Every day, the Ganges is filled with hundreds of thousands of people <u>who come to drink or bathe in the sacred water</u>.

4. Millions of people come for the great Kumbh Mela Festival, <u>which is held once every 12 years</u>.

5. This festival takes place at Allahbad, <u>where the Ganges and the Jumna rivers join</u>.

6. The Kumbh Mela Festival is a special time <u>when all Hindus hope to bathe in the sacred waters of the Ganges</u>.

7. A very important festival is the Kumbh Mela Festival, <u>during which millions of people drink or bathe in the sacred river</u>.

8. Varanasi, <u>which is another city on the Ganges</u>, is the most sacred for Hindus.

9. Varanasi is the city <u>that Hindus believe to be the most sacred</u>.

10. All Hindus hope to die at Varanasi, <u>where the sacred water gives eternal life</u>.

11. A hope <u>that all Hindus have</u> is to die at Varanasi.

12. The sacred ashes of those <u>who have died at Varanasi</u> are thrown on the river, and their lives will continue forever.

▲ The Ganges River

4 **Practice** Work with a partner. Reread the sentences in Activity 3. Decide by what type of adjective clause the noun or pronoun is modified: a subject clause, an object clause, a possessive clause, or a time and place clause. Use the chart on page 387 as a guide.

Example The Ganges is a river <u>that flows through northern India.</u> *subject clause*

5 **Practice** Reread the sentences in Activity 3 one more time. On a separate piece of paper, try to rewrite each sentence as a simple sentence, but try to include all the important information, information which might be expressed in the adjective clause.

Example It is a river whose water is sacred to Hindus.
  The water of the Ganges River is sacred to Hindus.

Using What You've Learned

6 **Describing Holidays** The word *holiday* originally was "holy day," and it had a strictly religious meaning. Today, we use *holiday* to mean any vacation day. Just as religions celebrate special holidays, so do cities, states, countries, and cultures.

Get into four groups. Each group will take a season (spring, summer, winter, or fall). In your group, make a list of holidays you know that are celebrated during that season. Include a brief description of how and where they are celebrated. After you have finished, share your information with the rest of the class. Later, you will be asked to give a brief presentation about one holiday.

Part 2   Clauses with *That, When,* and *Where*: Replacement of Subjects, Objects, and Adverbials of Time or Place

Setting the Context

Previewing the Passage Discuss the questions.

Hinduism and Buddhism are closely related in many ways. Siddhartha Gautama was a Hindu who sought knowledge throughout his life, and his teachings developed into Buddhism. Why do you think Buddhism became a separate religion? Has this happened in other religions?

Reading Read the passage.

Buddhism

Buddhism developed from the teachings of Siddhartha Gautama (the Buddha or "enlightened one"). However, it is not a religion that honors one person, human or divine. Buddha is neither a god nor a god-sent mediator. He is not a "redeemer" who can save others. In Buddhism, teaching *(dharma)* and knowledge are more important than the person, Buddha. This knowledge is a special religious knowledge that people attain through transcending human limitations. It is knowledge that goes far beyond the limits of thought. It leads to the ultimate goal, where the personality is transformed. The path to this transformation is a method of forming "right" habits.

Today, Buddhists refer to Buddha as the great example, but every person has to seek his or her own enlightenment. Selflessness and the seeking of peace on earth are the ways to enlightenment.

▲ The Great Buddha of Kamakura, Japan

 Discussing Ideas Discuss the question.

According to the passage, every person has to seek his or her own enlightenment. What does *enlightenment* mean to you?

Grammar Structures and Practice

A. Clauses with *That*: Replacement of Subjects

That may be used to form adjective clauses replacing subjects.

9.2 Clauses with *That*: Replacement of Subjects

Connecting Words	Explanations	Sentence Types	Examples
That	When two sentences share an identical noun or noun phrase, you can use *that* to replace the noun or noun phrase in the second sentence. *That* is used for ideas and things.	**Simple Sentences**	Buddhism is a **religion. This religion** teaches a way of life.
		Complex Sentence	Buddhism is a religion **that** teaches a way of life.
That **(instead of *who*)**	*Who* is generally preferred to refer to people. In informal spoken English, *that* is sometimes used.	**Simple Sentences**	Siddhartha was a **person. This person** tried to overcome suffering.
		Complex Sentence	Siddhartha was a person **that (who)** tried to overcome suffering.

Note: Commas are *not* used with adjective clauses beginning with *that*.

---

1 Practice Combine the following sentences to form adjective clauses with *that*. Make any necessary changes in the sentences.

Example We visited a Buddhist temple. The temple was in Tokyo.
We visited a Buddhist temple that was in Tokyo.

1. I bought a book. The book was about Buddhism.

2. Buddhism is a religion. It has over 350 million followers.

3. Buddhism has many beliefs. These beliefs help people to deal with their problems.

4. I have a problem. It has been bothering me for a while.

5. I talked about it with a friend. The friend had a similar problem.

6. My friend had some ideas for me. These ideas were very helpful.

7. I visited a Buddhist temple. The temple was made of wood.

8. Buddhists often sit in meditation. Meditation quiets the mind and body.

2 Practice Combine the following sentences to form adjective clauses with *that*. Make any necessary changes in the sentences.

Example "Buddha" is a word from Sanskrit. This word from Sanskrit means "the enlightened one."
"Buddha" is a word from Sanskrit that means "the enlightened one."

1. Through meditation, Buddha learned laws of life. Laws of life include the "Four Noble Truths" of Buddhism.

2. The first law is about suffering. The suffering comes from our past actions, or "karma."

3. The second law talks about desires. The desires are for the wrong things.

4. The third law says changing our lives will solve the problems. The problems come from desires.

5. The fourth law describes a way of living. The way of living is Buddha's path to inner peace.

6. According to Buddha, these "Four Noble Truths" are the laws. These laws will lead us to enlightenment.

7. Funerals in East Asia are often marked by Buddhist services. These services are a little different in each country of that region.

8. Buddhists believe in the unity of all living things. Living things are part of this world.

3 **Practice** Summarize the information given in Activity 2 by completing the following in your own words:

Buddha taught a way of thinking and acting that . . .

B. Clauses with *That, When,* or *Where*: Replacement of Objects of Verbs and Adverbials of Time or Place

That may be used to form adjective clauses replacing objects of verbs.

9.3	Clauses with *That*: Replacement of Objects of Verbs		
Connecting Word	**Explanations**	**Sentence Type**	**Examples**
That	To form an adjective clause, the relative pronoun *that* can replace the object of the verb in a simple sentence.	**Simple Sentences**	The **ideas** helped relieve suffering. Siddhartha taught **these ideas**.
	That normally refers to things or ideas, and in informal English, it may be used to refer to people.	**Complex Sentence**	The ideas **that** Siddhartha taught helped relieve suffering.
Omitted *That*	*That* is sometimes omitted in informal English; this is possible only when *that* replaces an object (not the subject).	**Complex Sentence**	The ideas Siddhartha taught helped relieve suffering.

When and *where* can be used as relative pronouns that replace adverbials of time or place.

9.4 Clauses with *When* or *Where*: Replacement of Adverbials of Time of Place

Connecting Word	Explanations	Sentence Type	Examples
When	*When* is used to replace adverbials of time.	**Simple Sentences** **Complex Sentence**	Siddhartha lived at a **time**. People suffered tremendously **then**. Siddhartha lived at a time **when** people suffered tremendously.
Where	*Where* is used to replace adverbials of place.	**Simple Sentences** **Complex Sentence**	Nepal is a **country**. Buddhism and Hinduism are practiced **there**. Nepal is a country **where** Buddhism and Hinduism are practiced.

Note: Do not confuse adjective clauses with *when* or *where* (which follow the noun(s) they modify) with adverb clauses (which may begin or end sentences).

---

4 **Practice** Combine the following sentences by using *that, when,* or *where*. Eliminate words whenever necessary.

Example Nirvana is a state of being. People can reach nirvana through learning.
Nirvana is a state of being that people can reach through learning.

1. The word is *nirvana*. Buddhists use this word to describe inner peace.

2. Nirvana is the goal. Every Buddhist hopes to achieve this goal.

3. It is a feeling. People describe the feeling as inner peace.

4. According to an early Buddhist scripture, nirvana is a place. There is no earth, water, fire, and air there.

5. It is a time. An individual achieves the end of suffering then.

6. The way is through meditation. People can reach nirvana this way.

7. Some people know the way. The way follows the practice of Siddhartha.

8. The stillness of the very early morning is a time. Many people feel meditation is best then.

Cultural Note

In the 1960s, many people in the United States became interested in yoga and meditation. Today millions of Americans practice yoga or meditation for health and fitness as well as for spiritual benefits.

▲ Buddhist monk meditating

5 **Practice** Whenever you study a new subject, you need to define and understand key words. Definitions often use adjective clauses. In order to understand Activity 6, which follows, you will need to know the meanings of the following words. Complete their definitions by choosing the appropriate adjective clause.

1. Our lifestyle is the way . . .

2. Our livelihood is the way . . .

3. Discipline is the effort . . .

4. Wisdom is knowledge and understanding . . .

5. Our intentions are actions . . .

6. Our morals are the guidelines . . .

7. Suffering is the sad part of life . . .

8. Right livelihood is the way . . .

a. that we gain through study and experience.

b. that we choose to live, act, and think.

c. that we plan to do.

d. that we earn money.

e. that we use to determine right from wrong.

f. that we use to control our thoughts and actions.

g. that a Buddhist believer must work in the world.

h. that we cannot avoid.

6 **Error Analysis** Many of the following sentences have errors in the formation of adjective clauses. Find the errors and correct them. Indicate sentences that have no errors.

Examples The way to nirvana is a method that Buddhists call the "Eightfold Path."
correct

where
People who follow the Eightfold Path reach a point ~~that~~ extremes and impulses are avoided ~~there~~.

1. The Eightfold Path gives a moral way of living that it includes "right speech, action, and livelihood."
2. It has instructions on discipline that they involve "right effort, mindfulness, and concentration."
3. The Eightfold Path also discusses the wisdom that we develop this wisdom through "right views and intentions."
4. It is not a set of teachings that emphasizes strictness or severity.
5. It teaches a moderate lifestyle where avoids strong feelings.
6. The Eightfold Path leads to Nirvana, a feeling of peace when a person no longer has inner conflicts or suffering.
7. Vegetarianism is a diet choice means you don't eat meat.
8. Vegetarians honor the right that all things have to live.

7 **Practice** Summarize the information given in Activity 6 by completing the following in your own words:

The lifestyle that Buddha . . .

8 **Practice** Have you felt moments of real inner peace? Describe one by completing the following sentences. Add other information if you wish.

1. I've felt the kind of peace that . . .
2. It was at a time (in my life) when . . .
3. I had reached a point (in my life) where . . .
4. It gave me the sensation that . . .
5. For me, inner peace comes at the times when . . .
6. Peace is a feeling that . . .
7. There is a place where . . .
8. To achieve inner peace, you need a personal space where . . .

9 **Practice** Quickly reread the passage "Buddhism" on page 390. Then answer the following:

1. What is the function of the clause *that honors one person* in line 2?
2. What is the function of the clause *that people attain through transcending human limitations* in lines 6 to 7?

Using What You've Learned

10 **Writing Definitions** After you have completed this section, there still may be words that confuse you. Make a short list of new vocabulary that you don't completely understand. Then, in small groups, write your own definitions for them.

After you have written your own definitions, check with other groups, with your teacher, or with your dictionary to see if the definitions are correct. You may also want to define some of the following words:

atheism	festival	ritual
belief	prayer	sin
doctrine	prophet	tradition
faith	religion	worship

Part 3 · Restrictive and Nonrestrictive Clauses; Clauses with *Who, Which,* and *Whose*: Replacement of Subjects and Possessives

Setting the Context

Previewing the Passage Discuss the questions.

The following passage tells about the third major world religion, Judaism. What do you know about Judaism? Are you familiar with any of its customs, traditions, or teachings?

Judaism

Judaism, which dates from the 2nd century B.C., is the oldest of the world's three monotheistic[1] religions. The core of Judaism is the belief in only one God who is the creator and ruler of the whole world.

We can trace the origin of Judaism to the time of Abraham. According to Jewish tradition, Abraham made an agreement with God that he and his family   5 would teach the doctrine of only one God. In return, God promised Abraham the land of Canaan for his descendants.

Judaism is based on two fundamental texts: the Torah (the Old Testament of the Bible) and the Talmud, which is a collection of poetry, anecdotes, laws, traditions, biographies, and prophecies of the ancient Jews. All of Judaism's   10 teachings, laws, and customs are also called the *Torah*, which means "to teach."

---

[1] *monotheistic* believing in one God

Discussing Ideas Discuss the questions.

About one-half of the world's religions are monotheistic (believing in one God), while the others are polytheistic. In your opinion, is this a major difference in beliefs? Is this more important than any similarities among religions?

Grammar Structures and Practice

A. Restrictive versus Nonrestrictive Clauses

Adjective (relative) clauses are either restrictive or nonrestrictive in the information they add. Restrictive clauses are essential to the meaning of the sentence.

9.5 Restrictive versus Nonrestrictive Clauses

Structures	Explanations	Examples
Restrictive Clauses	Restrictive clauses identify the nouns they describe. They explain *which* people, places, things, or ideas are being described. The information in these clauses is *essential* to the meaning of the sentence. *No* commas are used with restrictive clauses. *That* may be used.	I met a professor **who teaches a religious studies course at the college**. I took a religious studies course **that was very informative**. A course **that will be offered next semester** is about the spread of Buddhism.
Nonrestrictive Clauses	Nonrestrictive clauses do *not* define or identify the nouns they describe. They do *not* explain, *which* people (places, and so on). Rather, they give *extra* information because the identity of the noun is already known. Clauses that modify proper names, entire groups, or nouns that are unique (the sun, and so on) are normally nonrestrictive. A comma is used at the beginning and at the end of a nonrestrictive clause. *That* may not be used with nonrestrictive clauses (with commas).	I met Dr. Chang, **who teaches a religious studies course at the college.** I took a course called The Study of Islam, **which was very informative.** The course Buddhism in China, **which will be offered next semester,** is about the spread of Buddhism from India eastward. Dr. Gomez, **who is a colleague of Dr. Chang,** lived in India for many years.

In some cases, the same clause may either identify or give extra information, depending on the situation. Compare the following examples.

9.6 The Same Clause as Restrictive or Nonrestrictive

Structures	Explanations	Examples
Restrictive Clause	This clause tells *which* brother. No commas are used.	My brother **who lives in Iowa** is a teacher. (I have several brothers; the brother in Iowa is a teacher.)
Nonrestrictive Clause	This clause gives extra information. Commas are used.	My brother, **who lives in Iowa,** is a teacher. (I have only one brother, or I'm talking about one brother now. By the way, he lives in Iowa.)

Note: In spoken English, speakers often pause before and after a nonrestrictive clause. This tells you that the information is *extra*. Thus, pauses are likely in the second sentence in the table but not in the first.

---

1 **Practice** As your teacher reads the following sentences aloud, underline the adjective clause in each. Some are nonrestrictive, and some are restrictive. Decide whether the information is *essential* (telling *which* person, thing, and so on) or *extra*. Add commas if the information is extra.

Example People <u>who believe in Judaism</u> are called Jews. *essential information; no commas*

1. Steve Wise who comes from Maryland is Jewish.

2. Steve's brother who lives in Chicago is a rabbi. (Steve has only one brother.)

3. Joan's brother who lives in Chicago is a rabbi. (Joan has several brothers.)

4. Judaism is based on the Talmud and the Torah which is also part of the Christian Bible.

5. The Bible which has two parts is the basis for both Judaism and Christianity.

6. A synagogue is a place where Jews worship and study.

7. The Touro Synagogue which is in Rhode Island is the oldest in the United States.

8. The synagogue which is in Rhode Island is the oldest in the United States.

9. The Talmud which is part of Judaism's holy texts is not part of Christianity's holy texts.

10. The Sabbath which is the weekly holy day for Jews falls on Saturday.

B. Clauses with *Who* or *Which*: Replacement of Subjects

To form an adjective clause, the relative pronoun *who* or *which* can replace the subject of a simple sentence.

9.7 Clauses with *Who* or *Which*: Replacement of Subjects

Connecting Word	Explanations	Sentence Types	Examples
who	*Who* refers to people only. It may be used in both restrictive and nonrestrictive clauses.	Simple Sentences	We spoke with **Dr. Chang**. **Dr. Chang** is an exchange scholar.
		Complex Sentence	We spoke with Dr. Chang, **who** is an exchange scholar.
which	*Which* refers to things or ideas. In nonrestrictive clauses (with commas), *which* (not *that*) must be used.	Simple Sentences	Dr. Chang will lecture on **Judaism**. **Judaism** is his specialty.
		Complex Sentence	Dr. Chang will lecture on Judaism, **which** is his specialty.
which or *that*	In restrictive clauses (without commas), either *which* or *that* may be used, but *that* is preferred.	Simple Sentences	Dr. Chang will lecture on a **topic**. **This topic** is very interesting.
		Complex Sentence	Dr. Chang will lecture on a topic **that (which)** is very interesting.

2 Practice Use *who* or *which* to form an adjective clause from the second sentence in each pair. Combine the sentences, omitting words and adding commas when necessary. Both nonrestrictive and restrictive clauses are included.

Example   Yesterday I met Mr. Preston. Mr. Preston is a world-famous scholar.
Yesterday I met Mr. Preston, who is a world-famous scholar.

1. Mr. Preston will give a talk about archeology. Archeology is the study of past human life and activities.

2. Mr. Preston will speak about various ruins in the Middle East. Mr. Preston has spent many years doing archeology.

3. The Middle East includes countries in Southwest Asia and North Africa. The Middle East is also called the Mideast.

4. The Middle Eastern countries are Egypt, Israel, Jordan, Saudi Arabia, and Yemen. These Middle Eastern countries are on the Red Sea.

5. The Red Sea borders the Sinai. The Sinai is a vast desert of plains, mountains, and white sandy beaches.

6. Mr. Preston used to live in Jerusalem. Jerusalem is a very important center for Judaism, Christianity, and Islam.

7. Mr. Preston told me about several archeologists. These archeologists are doing interesting work in Jerusalem.

8. Mr. Preston conducts archaeological digs. Archaeological digs uncover artifacts from past civilizations.

9. Jerusalem has many important archaeological sites. Jerusalem is an ancient city.

10. The City of David is visited by thousands of tourists each year. The City of David is a very large and ancient ruin in Jerusalem.

3 Practice Use *who* or *which* to form an adjective clause from the second sentence in each pair. Combine the sentences, omitting words and adding commas when necessary.

Example   Many religions have spring festivals like Passover. Passover marks the end of winter.
Many religions have spring festivals like Passover, which marks the end of winter.

1. Passover commemorates the Jews.
   These Jews made the Exodus from Egypt.

2. Rosh Hashanah celebrates the creation of the world.
   Rosh Hashanah is the Jewish New Year in the fall.

3. The Shofar is a trumpet.
   This trumpet is blown at Rosh Hashanah.

4. The 10 days are a time for confessing sins and asking forgiveness.
These 10 days follow Rosh Hashanah.

5. This period ends with Yom Kippur.
Yom Kippur is the "Day of Atonement."

6. On Yom Kippur, the synagogues are filled with people.
These people are praying and asking forgiveness for their sins.

7. At Passover Jews prepare a special meal.
This meal is called a seder.

8. Jews follow ancient traditions.
These ancient traditions have their roots in the Old Testament and the Talmud.

4 **Practice** Summarize the information given in the preceding exercise by completing this sentence in your own words:

Three important Jewish holidays are Passover, which . . . ; Rosh Hashanah, which . . . ; and Yom Kippur, which . . .

5 **Practice** In the following sentences, decide whether you may change *who* or *which* to *that*. Explain why or why not.

Example A rabbi is a person who teaches and leads worship.

> *A rabbi is a person that teaches and leads worship.*
> *You can change "who" to "that" because the clause is restrictive (no commas are necessary).*

1. *Rabbi* is a Hebrew word which means "teacher" or "my master."

2. Only a person who has learned the Torah may be called a rabbi.

3. A rabbi has many duties, which include interpreting Jewish law and giving spiritual guidance.

4. Originally, rabbis were scholars who lived and studied at the synagogues.

5. Rabbis were the people who taught young children the Jewish faith.

6. Rabbi Gordon, who is a friend of ours, teaches several classes each week.

7. Rabbi Gordon's oldest brother, who teaches at a university, is a world-famous scholar.

8. Rabbis often counsel people who find themselves in a spiritual or emotional crisis.

C. Clauses with *Whose*: Replacement of Possessives

The relative pronoun *whose* can be used to form an adjective clause.

9.8	Clauses with *Whose*: Replacement of Possessives		
Connecting Word	**Explanations**	**Sentence Types**	**Examples**
whose	*Whose* replaces a possessive. *Whose* normally refers to people, but it may also refer to places, ideas, or things.	**Simple Sentences**	I never miss a class with **Dr. Chang**. **Dr. Chang's (his)** lectures are always fascinating.
		Complex Sentence	I never miss a class with Dr. Chang, **whose** lectures are always fascinating.
		Simple Sentences	I particularly enjoyed **the last lecture**. **Its** topic was "Judaism and the Legal System."
		Complex Sentence	I particularly enjoyed the last lecture, **whose** topic was "Judaism and the Legal System."

6 **Practice** The following sentences include adjective clauses with *whose*. Rephrase these sentences to form two complete sentences by eliminating *whose* and adding a possessive (or a prepositional phrase).

Example The Jewish tradition of learning comes from the Torah, whose chapters stress the importance of education.

The Jewish tradition of learning comes from the Torah.
The Torah's chapters (the chapters of the Torah) stress the importance of education.

1. The tradition of learning centers around children, whose education begins at an early age.

2. Education begins with the parents, whose duty is to teach the Commandments.

3. The education of the child continues with the rabbi, whose teaching includes both religious and social ideas.

4. Traditionally, all rabbis were scholars whose studies and teachings have shaped modern Judaism.

5. Religious education follows a strict progression whose order and methods have changed little over centuries.

6. Many countries have been influenced by Judaism, whose teachings form the bases of many legal systems.

7. Judaism offers an ancient spiritual message to modern people, whose lives are often filled with doubt.

8. Judaism is a religion whose tenets, or basic beliefs, have remained the same over thousands of years.

7 Practice Use *whose* to form an adjective clause from the second sentence in each pair. Combine the sentences, omitting words and adding commas when necessary.

Examples Last night I talked with a professor. His class meets on Tuesdays and Thursdays at 10:00.
Last night I talked with a professor whose class meets on Tuesdays and Thursdays at 10:00.
Last night I talked with Dr. Lee. His class meets on Tuesdays and Thursdays at 10:00.
Last night I talked with Dr. Lee, whose class meets on Tuesdays and Thursdays at 10:00.

1. We met a professor. His name is Dr. Lee.

2. Dr. Lee teaches a class. Its name is *World Religions*.

3. Dr. Lee teaches *World Religions*. Its focus is on the five major religions and several smaller religions.

4. Last semester we couldn't register for the class. Its class roster was already full.

5. Dr. Lee allowed us to visit the class from time to time. Dr. Lee's kindness is well known.

6. We wanted to learn more about Judaism. Its roots go back thousands of years.

7. The first great monotheistic religion was Judaism. Its teachings honored only one God.

8. Judaism later gave birth to Christianity and Islam. Their traditions also stem from Abraham.

8 Practice Complete the following 10 sentences with *who, which, that, whose,* or *X* (to indicate no relative pronoun is needed). In some cases, more than one relative pronoun may be used. In other cases, the relative pronoun may be omitted. In these cases, give all possibilities, but indicate the preferred form.

Examples The Talmud, _____*which*_____ is a sacred Jewish text, gives detailed rules about daily life. *only one possibility*
The Talmud was developed by ancient rabbis _____*who (that)*_____ wrote stories and parables about daily life. *who is preferred*

1. The Talmud explains rituals _____ many Jews perform daily.

2. Children learn Jewish rituals from their parents and from the rabbi, _____ work includes teaching as well as leading worship.

3. The first rituals _____ Jews perform in the morning are to thank God and to wash their hands.

4. Washing the hands is a ritual _____ symbolizes purity.

5. Cleanliness, _____ is very important in Judaism, is the basis for many Jewish customs.

6. The Talmud gives many rules _____ cover food preparation.

7. Food _____ has been prepared in special ways is called "kosher."

8. Foods like pork, _____ spoils easily, have traditionally been forbidden.

9. This is an example of a religious custom _____ basis was practical. It protected against food poisoning.

10. Jews _____ follow these rules strictly are called "orthodox."

9 **Error Analysis** Many of the following sentences have errors in their use of adjective clauses. Correct the errors. Then look for the sentences in the passages "Hinduism" on page 386, "Buddhism" on page 390, and "Judaism" on page 397 to see if your answers are correct.

Example Judaism which dates from the 2nd century B.C. is the oldest of the world's three great monotheistic religions.
The clause is nonrestrictive and needs commas.
Correction: Judaism, which dates from the 2nd century B.C., is the oldest of the world's three great monotheistic religions.

1. The religious tradition that we call *Hinduism* is the product of 5,000 years of development.

2. Buddhism is not a religion that it honors one person.

3. Knowledge in Buddhism is a special kind of religious knowledge people attain through transcending human limitations.

4. It is knowledge goes far beyond the limits of thought.

5. In Buddhism, knowledge leads to the ultimate goal where the personality is transformed there.

6. The core of Judaism is the belief in only one God who is the creator and ruler of the world.

7. Judaism is based on the Torah and the Talmud, which it is a collection of poetry, anecdotes, and so on.

8. All of Judaism's teachings are also called the *Torah* which means "to teach."

Using What You've Learned

10 Describing a Holiday What is your favorite holiday? Is it a religious, cultural, or national holiday? How is it celebrated? Is there special food, clothing, dancing, or music? Prepare a brief (three- to five-minute) presentation on the holiday of your choice. If possible, bring any special clothing, music, or pictures to show the class as you are describing the holiday.

Example This is a picture of the Passover celebration at my parent's home. My father is the man who . . . He is wearing a yarmulke, which symbolizes . . .

11 Writing Definitions Write definitions for the following words and expressions from American popular culture. You may need to ask people outside your class for help. When you prepare your definitions, use adjective clauses whenever possible. Then try to add one or two other expressions you are familiar with. Finally, work in small groups and share your definitions.

Example What is a yuppie?

A yuppie is a "young urban professional." It is someone who might be single or married, but who probably doesn't have children. It's a person who has a good job and a fair amount of money. . . .

What is a potluck?	What is a skateboard?
What is a fender bender?	What is the tooth fairy?
What is a nerd?	What are "jammies"?
What are jelly beans?	What is leap year?
What is an all-nighter?	What was the Twist?

12 Describing Someone Write at least three sentences describing one of your classmates. Use adjective clauses in your descriptions. Then, read your descriptions to the class, but don't say the person's name. Can the other students guess who you are describing? (Don't make your description too easy!)

Example *I'm thinking of someone who is in this class. She's a woman who has been in this city only a few months. She's someone who wants to study business. I think she will succeed because she's responsible and hardworking.*

Setting the Context

Previewing the Passage Discuss the question.

The teachings of Jesus have had a tremendous impact on our world. What do you
know about his teachings?

Reading Read the passage.

Christianity

Christianity is based on the teachings of Jesus Christ, whom Christians call
the "Son of God." At the same time, Christians commemorate Jesus as an actual
historical figure. He was a man of lowly social standing who was unknown outside of the small part of the Roman Empire where he lived and died.

Jesus was born in Bethlehem, in Judea, in about 4 B.C.E.[1] and was raised in   5
Galilee, where he spent most of his short life. Little is known about Jesus' early
years. Our knowledge of Jesus comes from the last three years of his life, which
he spent preaching a doctrine of brotherly love and repentance. During these
three years of teaching, he and his closest followers traveled throughout Pales-
tine. Wherever Jesus went, he drew large crowds. Before long, he was known as   10
a healer, and people came from far and wide to ask his help.

As Jesus grew popular with the common people, who saw him as their long-
awaited savior, he became a political threat. Within a short time, Jesus was ar-
rested as a political rebel and was crucified.

---

[1]*B.C.E.* before the common era

Discussing Ideas Discuss the questions.

Christianity has many different sects (or divisions). Are you familiar with any of
them? Which?

A. Clauses with *Whom* and *Which*: Replacement of Objects of Verbs

The relative pronouns *who, whom,* and *which* can replace the object of a verb in a simple sentence.

9.9 Clauses with *Whom* or *Which*: Replacement of Objects of Verbs

Connecting Word	Explanations	Sentence Types	Examples
whom	*Whom* is used to refer to people only. Note that *whom* is used in formal speaking and writing; *who* is often substituted in informal English.	**Simple Sentences**	**Dr. Gill** will teach a class on the early Christians. I met **Dr. Gill** last week.
		Complex Sentences	Dr. Gill, **whom** I met last week, will teach a course on the early Christians. (formal) Dr. Gill, **who** I met last week, will teach a course on the early Christians. (informal)
which	*Which* is used to refer to things or ideas. *Which* must be used in nonrestrictive clauses (with commas).	**Simple Sentences**	**History 410** covers early Roman history. Dr. Gill teaches **History 410**.
		Complex Sentence	History 410, **which** Dr. Gill teaches, covers early Roman history.
that	*That* is preferred in restrictive clauses (without commas) that describe things or ideas.	**Simple Sentences**	**The course** meets on Tuesday and Thursday morning. Dr. Gill teaches **the course**.
		Complex Sentence	The course **that** Dr. Gill teaches meets on Tuesday and Thursday morning.

1 **Practice** Underline the adjective clauses in the following sentences. Then decide whether the clauses are restrictive or nonrestrictive. Add commas if the clauses are nonrestrictive.

Example After Christ's death, the followers <u>whom Jesus had chosen</u> met privately.
restrictive, no commas needed

1. Peter was a fisherman whom Jesus had selected to lead his new religion.

2. Peter whom Jesus had chosen as leader kept the followers together.

3. The followers of Jesus were Jews, and they believed in Judaism which they continued to practice.

4. Christianity as a separate religion actually began with Saint Paul whom many scholars consider to have been the main organizer of the new movement.

5. Both Peter and Paul were probably executed around 60 A.D. in Rome which Christians had made the center of the new religion.

6. At that time, only a small sect of "fanatics" believed in Christianity which most people ignored.

7. By 400 C.E., however, Christianity was the official religion of the Roman Empire which the Emperor Trajan had extended throughout the Mediterranean.

8. Today over 2 billion people believe in the group of religions which we call Christianity.

9. The largest denomination of Christianity is Roman Catholicism which has several hundred million followers.

10. In the latter part of the 20th century, many Christians returned to a literal interpretation of the Bible which is the basis of Christian belief.

2 **Practice** Combine the following sentences by using *whom* or *which*. Form an adjective clause from the second sentence in each pair. Change words and add punctuation when necessary.

Example   The word *holiday* actually came from the words *holy* (religious) and *day*. We use the word *holiday* to mean a vacation day.
The word "holiday," which we use to mean a vacation day, actually came from the words "holy" and "day."

1. Holidays such as Christmas have become more like social occasions than religious events. Christianity instituted Christmas.

2. Christmas originally honored only the birth of Jesus Christ. People of many religions now celebrate Christmas.

3. Perhaps the best-known character in the Christmas celebration today is Santa Claus. We see Santa Claus in every store window.

4. The symbol of Santa Claus came into being in 1822 in the poem "The Night Before Christmas." Clement Clark Moore wrote this poem.

5. The Christmas tree is a popular tradition. German farmers began this tradition many, many years ago.

6. The custom of decorating the tree began in the 1800s. Bohemians started this custom.

7. The manger, or nativity, scene is one of the oldest Christmas symbols. St. Francis of Assisi first created a manger in 1223.

▲ Santa Claus

8. The birth of Jesus Christ marks the beginning of the Roman calendar. Much of the world uses the Roman calendar.

9. A Roman abbot and astronomer set Christ's birth as the beginning of the calendar. The Catholic Church commissioned this person.

10. Other calendars include the Islamic, the Chinese, and the Jewish calendars. Many groups or countries follow these calendars.

B. Clauses with *Whom* and *Which*: Replacement of Objects of Prepositions

Relative pronouns may replace the object of a preposition. Several constructions are possible, depending on how formal or informal the statement should be.

9.10 Clauses with *Whom* and *Which* : Replacement of Objects of Prepositions

Explanations	Sentence Type	Examples
In formal English, the preposition begins the adjective clause. In informal English, the preposition usually follows the verb in the adjective clause. If the preposition begins the clause, *whom, which,* or *whose* must be used. In restrictive clauses with the preposition at the end, the relative pronoun may be dropped.	Simple Sentences	**Dr. Church** teaches a course in Roman history. I was introduced to **Dr. Church** yesterday.
	Complex Sentences	Dr. Church, **to whom** I was introduced yesterday, teaches a course in Roman history. *(formal)* Dr. Church, **who(m)** I was introduced to yesterday, teaches a course in Roman history. *(informal)*
	Simple Sentences	**Bascom Hall** is the building. The course is taught in **Bascom Hall**.
	Complex Sentences	Bascom Hall is the building **in which** the course is taught. *(formal)* Bascom Hall is the building **which** the course is taught **in**. *(informal)* Bascom Hall is the building **that** the course is taught **in** (*or* **where** the course is taught). *(informal)* Bascom Hall is the building **the course is taught in**. (*Note:* This construction is possible only with restrictive clauses with the preposition at the end.)

3 Practice Combine the following sentences by using *whom* or *which* with prepositions. Form adjective clauses from the second sentence in each pair. Use the adjective clause to modify the italicized word(s). Change words and add commas when necessary. Give all possibilities, but indicate the preferred form.

Example The Greek word *biblia* simply means "the books." The word *Bible* is derived from *biblia*.
The Greek word "biblia," from which the word "Bible" is derived, simply means "the books."

1. The Bible is a collection of *books*. Both Christians and Jews take their doctrines from these books.

2. These books were written over a period of more than one thousand *years*. During that time, numerous authors contributed their own styles and perspectives.

3. The *Old Testament* is the longer of the Bible's two sections. Judaism is based on the Old Testament.

4. The Old Testament has given us many rules of behavior such as *the Ten Commandments*. Most Western legal codes are founded on the Ten Commandments.

5. The *New Testament* consists of 27 writings completed during the first century C.E. Christianity derives its teachings from the New Testament.

6. Its gospels, revelations, and letters were written by *many authors*. We get a variety of perspectives on the life and teachings of Jesus from these authors.

7. *The message of the gospels* is the central teaching of Christianity. Christians lead their lives according to this teaching.

8. Many politically active Christians base their work on *the New Testament*. The New Testament provides a justification for their actions.

4 Review Complete the following sentences by adding *which, whose, that,* or *X* to indicate that no relative pronoun is needed. Give all possibilities, but indicate the preferred form. Add commas when necessary.

Example Christ is the name ___*X / that / which*___ the Greeks used for the "messiah." *Preferred: "that" or no relative pronoun*

1. The name *Christianity* _____ includes all Christian sects was not used during the lifetime of Jesus.

2. *Jesus* is the Greek name for Joshua _____ means "Jehovah is salvation" in Hebrew.

3. *Christ* comes from a Greek word _____ means "messiah" or "anointed one."

4. *Christ* was a name _____ the people of Antioch, Syria, gave to Jesus.

5. The ending *-ian* _____ comes from Latin was added to Christ.

6. The name *Christian* _____ was soon adopted by the followers of Jesus appeared in later portions of the New Testament.

7. Many words in Christianity come from Greek _____ the Romans used as the common language of their empire.

8. Greek was the language of the great missionary Saint Paul _____ 13 letters (or *epistles*) are an important part of the New Testament.

5 **Review** Combine the following sentences by using *who, which, whose, that,* or *when*. Form adjective clauses from the second sentence in each pair. Omit or change words when necessary and pay close attention to punctuation.

Example Christianity is the largest religious movement in the world. Christianity has over 2 billion followers.

Christianity, which has over 2 billion followers, is the largest religious movement in the world.

1. Christianity consists of three major branches: Roman Catholic, Eastern Orthodox, and Protestant. Christianity has over 2 billion followers.

2. The largest branch is the Roman Catholic church. The Roman Catholic church is headed by the Pope, the bishop of Rome.

3. The origins of Christianity's major branches were two historic movements. The attempts of these movements to make reforms divided the Roman Catholic Church.

4. The second branch, Eastern Orthodox, dates from 1054. The "great schism" occurred between East and West (Greek and Latin Christianity) in 1054.

5. Actually, differences had begun centuries before 1054. These differences centered around authority and control.

6. The third branch developed from a sixteenth-century movement. The movement is called the Reformation.

7. The Protestant Reformation began as a protest against some practices. German Catholics opposed these practices.

8. Protestants had hoped to reform the Catholic Church. Protestants saw abuse of faith, power, and money in the Catholic Church.

9. The Protestant Reformation was led by Martin Luther. The Catholic Church excommunicated Martin Luther.

10. Martin Luther then founded his own religion. This religion became known as Lutheranism.

11. Eventually, other divisions led to the formation of over 250 Protestant sects. The divisions concerned specific beliefs and practices.

12. Lutheranism is the largest branch of Protestantism. The various churches of Protestantism are now loosely united by the World Council of Churches.

6 Practice Summarize the information given in the preceding activity by completing this sentence in your own words:

Christianity has three major branches: Roman Catholic, which . . . . . .

Using What You've Learned

 7 Describing Ceremonies and Customs Most religions and cultures have special ceremonies to mark important stages in life. Birth, adolescence, and death are commemorated in special ways around the world. In pairs or in small groups, discuss one or more of these ceremonies and prepare a brief presentation for the entire class. Make sure to include descriptions of actions, food, special clothing or music, and so forth.

Example   *Baptism, or christening, is the ceremony that Christians use to welcome a child into the world and into the faith. The ceremony often uses a baptismal font, which is a large basin filled with holy water.*

8 Describing Events Think about the high points and low points of your life. Think about the best and worst, the most interesting, and the most frightening. Tell or write several brief stories about them. Following is some vocabulary to give you ideas. Begin your story with *The* (adjective + noun) *that (whom) I have ever . . .*

Examples   *The strangest dream that I have ever had was when I was about seventeen . . .*
OR: The most embarrassing situation that I have ever been in was during eighth grade . . .
OR: The most interesting teacher whom I have ever known was . . .

Adjectives		Nouns	
best	funny	dream	person
bizarre	interesting	experience	situation
embarrassing	strange	friend	teacher
exciting	worst	meal	trip
frightening	nightmare		

Part 5 | Clause to Phrase Reduction; Agreement with Adjective Phrases and Clauses

Setting the Context

Previewing the Passage Discuss the questions.

Islam is the "youngest" of the five major world religions. What do you know about Islam? Who founded it? When?

Reading Read the paragraph.

Islam

Beginning in Mecca about 610 C.E., Islam is the youngest of the great religions. It was founded by Muhammad, a respected and influential citizen of Mecca. Not feeling satisfied with success and security, Muhammad continued to search for answers to the many questions that bothered him. Finally, leaving friends and family, Muhammad sought the desert and its solitude. In the desert, an event occurred which changed his life and affected the history of the world. According to Islamic tradition, on a lonely night, the angel Gabriel appeared to Muhammad. Muhammad returned from the desert to proclaim the words of Allah, revealed to him by the angel. This event began the religion we now call Islam.

5

▲ Muslims pray in the direction of Mecca.

Discussing Ideas Discuss the question.

Most religions have some form of meditation. Many great thinkers have gone to the desert or the mountains in order to be alone, to think, and to search for answers. What is the role of solitude in this search?

Grammar Structures and Practice

A. Appositives

Appositives are nouns or noun phrases that describe nouns.

9.11 Appositives		
Structures	**Explanations**	**Examples**
Clause	Nonrestrictive adjective clauses (clauses that use commas) can be shortened to appositives by eliminating the relative pronoun and the verb *be*.	We recently met Dr. Carlson, **who is a professor of Islamic studies.**
Appositive Phrases	The order of the noun and the appositive can usually be reversed without affecting the meaning of the sentence. Appositives, like nonrestrictive clauses, are normally preceded—and may be followed—by commas.	We recently met Dr. Carlson, **a professor of Islamic studies.** We recently met a professor of Islamic studies, **Dr. Carlson.**

1 **Practice** In the following sentences, change the adjective clauses to appositive phrases.

Example The Koran, which is the sacred book of the Muslims, takes its name from the Arabic word meaning "recite."
The Koran, the sacred book of the Muslims, takes its name from the Arabic word meaning "recite."

1. The Koran is based on revelations to Muhammad, who was the founder of Islam.

2. The whole book, which is the length of the Christian New Testament, is memorized by many Muslims.

3. Those who memorize the Koran earn a special title, which is "Hafiz."

4. The first chapter, which is *Sura 1*, is the most common prayer among Muslims.

5. The followers of Islam, who are more than 1 billion worldwide, say prayers from the Koran five times each day.

6. Muslims pray five times daily in a prescribed manner, which is "Salat" in Arabic and "Namaz" in Persian or Urdu.

2 **Practice** Summarize the information given in the preceding exercise by completing this sentence in your own words:

The Koran, . . .

B. Past Participial Phrases

Adjective clauses with verbs in the passive voice may be shortened to phrases that use the past participle.

9.12	Past Participial Phrases		
Explanation		**Structures**	**Examples**
To form a phrase with a past participle, eliminate the relative pronoun and the verb *be* from an adjective clause.		**Clause**	Dr. Carlson recently taught a course **that was called Islam and the Arts**.
		Phrase	Dr. Carlson recently taught a course **called Islam and the Arts**.

3 **Practice** In the following sentences, change adjective clauses to phrases with past participles.

Example Muslims follow a set of rules and traditions that is called the "Five Pillars of Islam."

Muslims follow a set of rules and traditions called the "Five Pillars of Islam."

1. The *shahada*, which is repeated each day, is the Muslim's statement of faith.

2. The second pillar consists of prayers that are said five times a day while facing toward Mecca.

3. The second pillar, which is called *Salat* in Arabic, involves saying prayers each day in a specific way.

4. The third pillar is a donation of money that is determined by a Muslim's income.

5. The fourth pillar is to fast during the ninth month of the Muslim calendar, which is known as Ramadan.

6. The last pillar of Islam is a pilgrimage to Mecca, which is made at least one time in a person's life if health and finances permit.

C. Present Participial Phrases

Some adjective clauses with verbs in the active voice may be shortened to phrases using present participles.

9.13	Present Participial Phrases		
Explanation		**Structures**	**Examples**
The adjective clause must have *who*, *which*, or *that* in the subject position.		**Clause**	Over 1 billion people, **who represent** every race and continent, believe in Islam
To form a phrase, omit *who*, *which*, or *that* and use the present participle of the verb.		**Phrase**	Islam, **which began** in Arabia, spread quickly throughout the world.
The order of the noun and the phrase can often be reversed.		**Clause**	Islam, **beginning** in Arabia, spread quickly throughout the world.
		Phrase	**Beginning** in Arabia, Islam spread quickly throughout the world.

4 Practice In the following sentences, change the adjective clauses to phrases with present participles.

Example Islam, which spread from Spain to Indonesia, brought new art forms to many parts of the world.

Islam, spreading from Spain to Indonesia, brought new art forms to many parts of the world.
OR: Spreading from Spain to Indonesia, Islam brought new art forms to many parts of the world.

1. Islam contributed to numerous art forms, which included weaving, painting, metalwork, literature, and architecture.

2. Islamic architects, who followed the plan of Muhammad's seventh-century house in Medina, designed magnificent mosques such as the Great Mosque in Córdoba, Spain, and the Royal Mosque in Isfahan, Iran.

3. A Muslim who travels in a foreign country will find the same design in all mosques.

4. Mosques may be large or small, but they have the same design, which consists of an open courtyard and enclosed prayer halls.

5. Artisans who work with ceramic, wood, and metal have created magnificent decorations, such as at the the mosquesin Medina.

6. Pilgrims who come to Medina try to visit both the Mosque of the Prophet and the Quba Mosque.

▲ Interior of mosque dome, Córdoba, Spain

5 **Review** First, underline the appositive or participial phrase in each of the following sentences. Then expand the sentences by changing the phrases to adjective clauses.

Example Modern science owes a tremendous debt to the Islamic Empire, <u>the center of Western learning from the 9th to the 14th centuries</u>.
Modern science owes a tremendous debt to the Islamic Empire, which was the center of Western learning from the 9th to the 13th centuries.

1. Islam has given us the knowledge of Greek science, preserved and developed by the Muslims.

2. Much of Islam's scientific development was done at Baghdad, the capital of the Islamic Empire.

3. Caliph Ma'mum, ruler from 813 to 833, created the "House of Wisdom."

4. The House of Wisdom, containing a library, a translation bureau, and a school, was a sophisticated center of learning.

5. At the House of Wisdom, scholars studied Greek, Persian, and Indian scientific works translated into Arabic.

6. Scientists studying ancient Greek manuscripts developed the foundations for modern medicine.

7. Muslim scientists experimenting with a variety of laboratory techniques developed the foundation for modern chemistry.

8. In mathematics, Muslims gave us three extremely important ideas—the use of numerals, the decimal system, and the concept of zero.

D. Agreement with Adjective Phrases and Clauses

The subject of a sentence determines if the verb should be singular or plural.

9.14	Agreement with Adjective Phrases and Clauses		
Structures	**Explanations**	**Examples**	
		Singular Verb	**Plural Verb**
Adjective Phrases	Adjective phrases and clauses that come between the subject and verb do not affect the agreement. Adjective clauses are singular or plural depending on the noun(s) they modify.	The **Koran**, the sacred book of the Muslims, **comes** from the Arabic word "recite."	**Muslims**, followers of Muhammad, **recite** from the Koran each day.
Adjective Clauses	In adjective clauses with their own subjects (object clauses), however, the subject and verb of the clause should agree.	The **Koran**, which is the sacred book of the Muslims **comes** from the Arabic word "recite." *Sura I*, which a **believer** in Islam **recites** daily, comes from the Koran.	**Muslims**, who **are** followers of Muhammad, **recite** from the Koran each day. *Sura I*, which **Muslims recite** daily, comes from the Koran.

6 **Practice** Choose the correct form of the verbs in parentheses to complete the following sentences.

Example The Koran, which is held sacred by Muslims, (contain /(contains)) 114 chapters or *Sura*.

1. The Koran, the sacred book of the Muslims, (take / takes) its name from the Arabic word meaning "recite."

2. Many scholars who study Christianity (consider / considers) St. Paul to have been the main organizer of Christianity as a separate religion.

3. Peter, who was one of the fishermen, (was / were) chosen by Jesus to be a leader.

4. Traditionally, all rabbis were scholars whose knowledge (has / have) shaped modern Judaism.

5. Rituals that are explained in the Talmud (is / are) performed by many Jews every day.

6. Judaism, which is the parent of both Christianity and Islam, (is / are) the oldest of the world's three great monotheistic religions.

7. Muslims follow a set of rules and traditions that (is / are) called the "Five Pillars of Islam."

8. Mosques may be large or small, but they have the same design, which (consist / consists) of an open courtyard and enclosed prayer halls.

9. The House of Wisdom, containing a library, a translation bureau, and a school, (was / were) a sophisticated center of learning.

10. Santa Claus, whom we see in store windows and television commercials, (is / are) one of the most popular Christmas symbols.

Using What You've Learned

7 Discussing Beliefs George Bernard Shaw said, "There is only one religion, though there are a hundred versions of it." After studying this chapter, do you agree with Shaw's thoughts? If this is true, why have the religions of the world created so many divisions among people? How would the world be different if everyone believed in only one religion? Use information from this chapter and your own ideas and opinions to write a short essay agreeing or disagreeing with Shaw's thoughts.

8 Creating an Unusual Sentence How many adjective clauses can you put in one sentence? While this may be very poor writing style, it certainly is a test of your knowledge of adjective clauses!

First, read the following attempt by one student. How many clauses do you find? (The answer is on page 420.) Then try an original one. *But remember that this is only for practice.* We do not recommend using dozens of adjective clauses in your sentences!

There was an old man who lived in Mexico City, which is the capital of Mexico, which is situated between North and South America, who had a big house that was surrounded by a large garden in which a lot of old trees grew and where sat the old Rolls-Royce, in which the old man had driven through the city until he had an accident in which he hurt his legs and arms, which were 5 then put in casts by a doctor who came from the hospital that had been built by the father of the old man who had the accident, and it is now the best hospital in Mexico, the one in which all the most talented surgeons work, most of whom come from the University of Mexico City, which has a large painting on its front wall that was done by Salvador Dali, who is a Spanish surrealistic painter and 10 who is, unbelievably, related to our old man who had the accident in Mexico City, which is, as mentioned above, the capital city of Mexico.
—Hans Jurgen

The buildings shown on page 385 are: (top left) Buddhist temple in Thailand; (top right) Saint Louis Cathedral, Christian church in New Orleans; (bottom left) Dome of the Rock, Islamic shrine in Jerusalem, Israel; (bottom right) Jewish synagogue, Jerusalem, Israel.

Adjective Clauses and Phrases

Modifiers such as adjective phrases and clauses are frequently tested on standardized English proficiency exams. Review these commonly tested structures and check your understanding by completing the sample items that follow.

Remember that . . .

✔ *That* may not be used in nonrestrictive clauses (with commas).

✔ In formal English, *who* (not *that*) is preferred when describing people.

✔ In formal English, *whom* (not *who*) must be used with object clauses.

✔ When adjective clauses are reduced, the appropriate participle form must be used.

✔ Verbs must agree in number with subjects.

Part 1 Mark the correct completion for the following.

Example   John appears happy with his new boss, _____ is from Spain.

        Ⓐ that   Ⓑ whom

        Ⓒ whose   ⬤Ⓓ who

1. *Hindu* is a word _____ Persians gave to the people of India.

        Ⓐ that   Ⓑ that was

        Ⓒ who   Ⓓ whose

2. The Old Testament, _____ Judaism is based, is the longer of the Bible's two sections.

        Ⓐ which   Ⓑ on which

        Ⓒ on whom   Ⓓ what

3. The gentleman _____ we were introduced is an archaeologist.

        Ⓐ to whom   Ⓑ whom

        Ⓒ who   Ⓓ to who

4. The desert is the place _____ Mohammed meditated to find answers to his question.

        Ⓐ which   Ⓑ that which

        Ⓒ where   Ⓓ when

Answer for Activity 8, page 419: 21 clauses

5. In 1863, the first drawings of "the American Santa Claus" were published in *Harper's Weekly* by a political cartoonist —————————— Thomas Nast.

(A) named   (B) who named

(C) who his name   (D) whose name

Part 2 Circle the letter below the underlined word(s) containing an error.

Example   <u>Overseas</u> travelers <u>often</u> experience culture shock, <u>which are</u> a
           A   B   (C)

combination of <u>confusion</u>, frustration, and depression.
                 D

1. *Nirvana* is the word <u>that</u> Hindus <u>use it</u> <u>to describe</u> <u>a</u> sense of inner peace.
                       A   B   C   D

2. Sociologists are researchers <u>who</u> <u>studies</u> the science of society, <u>along with</u>
                           A   B   C

<u>its</u> social institutions and social relationships.
D

3. Mosques <u>may be</u> large or small, but <u>they</u> have the same design <u>consist of</u> an
              A   B   C

open courtyard and <u>enclosed</u> prayer halls.
                     D

4. Jesus, <u>born</u> a Jew, preached a message of brotherly love <u>that</u> <u>it</u> <u>is</u> now part of
        A   B C D

Christianity.

5. Hinduism is a religion <u>that</u> <u>it</u> was not <u>developed</u> <u>from</u> the teachings of one
                         A B   C   D

founder or prophet.

Self-Assessment Log

Each of the following statements describes the grammar you learned in this chapter. Read the statement; then check the box that describes how well you understand each structure.

	Needs Improvement	Good	Great
I can use a variety of adjective clauses to describe the major world religions.	❑	❑	❑
I can use appropriate punctuation with nonrestrictive and restrictive clauses.	❑	❑	❑
I can use a variety of phrases and appositives.	❑	❑	❑
I can use appropriate punctuation with phrases and appositives.	❑	❑	❑
I can take a test about adjective clauses and phrases.	❑	❑	❑

Crime and Punishment

In This Chapter

Hope, Wish, and Conditional Sentences

Part 1 *Hope* and *Wish*

Part 2 Conditional Sentences: Present or Unspecified Time

Part 3 Perfect Modal Auxiliaries

Part 4 Conditional Sentences: Past and Past-to-Present Time

Part 5 Review of Chapters 6–10

❝Justice is the ligament which holds civilized beings and civilized nations together. **❞**

—Daniel Webster
U.S. politician and orator
(1782–1852)

Connecting to the Topic

1. Justice is rewards or punishments according to the rule of law, and a ligament is the tissue in your body that holds bones together. Why would Daniel Webster call justice a ligament?

2. How could justice hold people or communities together?

3. Would people be "civilized" without justice?

Introduction

In this chapter, you will look at the difference in expressing hopes, wishes, and dreams, in contrast to describing reality. To do so, you will review the modal auxiliaries, and you will study the verbs *hope* and *wish* and various conditional sentences.

Reading Read the following passage. It introduces the chapter theme, "Crime and Punishment," and raises some of the topics and issues you will cover in the chapter. Note that many of the selections in this chapter come from people who have spent time in prisons for a variety of crimes—both violent and nonviolent.

Crime in Our Society

Imagine what you would do if you were in the following situations. If you didn't have enough money to pay your income taxes, would you cheat on them? If you were drunk, would you drive your car? If you were the president of a corporation, would you allow your employees to dump waste into the ocean? Would you ever take something from a store without paying if you didn't have 5 the money for it? Would you become violent if you were angry with your friends or family? These are just some examples of the types of situations in which people may make a decision that can lead to criminal behavior.

Why do people do things that are illegal and can hurt others? Criminologists suggest that the reason we have so much crime is that it is a symptom of other 10 social problems, such as a poor educational system, lack of family values, unemployment, and drug use.

Everybody hopes that crime will decrease, but what can we do to prevent it? Some people wish that we had tougher judges and mandatory sentences for those people who break the law. Others wish that more tax money were spent 15 to fight crime; they wish we had more police on the streets. Still others believe we need to work on changing society. These people hope that social change will lead to a reduction in crime. No matter how we choose to fight crime, everyone wishes we could feel safer in our homes and on the street.

Discussing Ideas Discuss the questions.

In your opinion, what causes crime? If you were working on a crime prevention committee, what would you suggest we do to prevent crime?

▲ Convicted criminals are put in prison behind bars.

Setting the Context

Previewing the Passage Discuss the question.

What does *doing time* mean?

Reading Read the passage.

Doing Time

When I was a child, my ma[1] always talked about taking responsibility for your own actions. Sometimes I don't care anything about what she said, but many days I wish I'd listened to her and I'd thought about what she was trying to teach me. Here I am—doin' time in the joint.[2] I'm caged like an animal because I did some horrible things to some people who were probably nice. Sure, I wish I weren't here. Sure, I wish they'd never caught me.   5

But that ain't[3] all. I wish this life I've got now had never happened. I wish I'd done it differently. I wish I'd believed that someday I'd be responsible for what I'd done. I hope somebody will look at my life and will learn from it. I hope somebody will pay attention to the words of people like my ma.   10

I wish I'd known . . . I wish I'd listened. And I wish I were out on the street.

—Phillip Moton, A Quad, California Men's Colony

---

[1]*ma* Mother, Mama
[2]*the joint* slang for *jail*, the *prison*
[3]*ain't* slang for *am not, isn't,* or *aren't*

Discussing Ideas Discuss the questions.

Do you think that most prisoners have feelings such as Phillip Moton's? Why or why not?

Grammar Structures and Practice

Hope and *Wish*

Hope and *wish* are used to express a speaker's desires or future plans. When showing a contrast with reality, the subjunctive mood is used. The subjunctive mood shows that the ideas are imaginary, improbable, or contrary to fact.

10.1	*Hope* and *Wish*		
	Explanations	**Examples**	
hope	The verb *hope* is generally used to express optimism; the speaker feels that something is possible.	I **hope** (that) he **will visit** us. (It is quite possible that he'll visit us.)	I **hope** (that) they **are going**. (I think that they are going to go.)
wish	The verb *wish* is often used to express impossibility or improbability; the speaker wants reality to be different than it is. To show the contrast to reality, *would*, *could*, or a special verb form—the subjunctive mood—is used after *wish*.	I **wish** (that) he **would visit** us. (It is doubtful that he'll visit.)	I **wish** (that) they **were going**. (I don't think they're going to go.)

Wishes are expressed by using *would, could,* or a subjunctive verb form in the dependent clause.

10.2 The Subjunctive Mood with *Wish*

	Explanations	Examples	Implied Meaning
Wishes About the Future	For future wishes the subjunctive is the same as the simple past tense, in most cases.	I **wish** (that) I **could go** home soon. I **wish** (that) things **would change**.	I can't go home soon. Things probably won't change.
Wishes About the Present	For present wishes, in most cases the subjunctive is the same as the simple past tense. In formal English, *were* is used for all forms of the verb *be*. In informal English, *was* is often used with *I*, *he*, *she*, and *it*, although this is considered incorrect.	I **wish** (that) I **weren't** here. I **wish** (that) I **weren't living** here I **wish** (that) I **didn't have** to be here.	I am here, but I'm not happy about it. I am living here, but I don't like it. I have to be here, but I don't like it.
Wishes About the Past	Past wishes are also expressed by using a subjunctive verb form in the dependent clause. In all cases, this form is the same as the past perfect tense (*had* + past participle).	I **wish** (that) my life **had gone** differently. I **wish** (that) I **had been** good.	I don't like the way my life has gone. I wasn't good then, and I regret it.

1 **Practice** Quickly reread the passage "Doing Time" on page 425. Underline the dependent clauses that follow the verbs *hope* and *wish*. Identify the verb(s) in these clauses and tell the time frame (past, present, or future) for each.

2 **Practice** Underline the verbs in the dependent clauses, and indicate the time frame of each. Then rephrase each sentence to show its meaning.

Examples I wish I <u>were going</u> to see my family soon. *present-to-future*
(*I'm not going to see my family soon, but I would like to.*)
I wish that you <u>were</u> here. *present* (*You're not here, and I miss you.*)
I wish that I <u>hadn't done</u> it. *past* (*I did it, but I regret it now.*)

1. I wish that I'd done a lot of things differently.

2. I wish I'd worked harder at my old job.

3. I wish I'd finished school.

4. I wish that my husband (wife) could find a better job.

5. I wish that I had more free time.

6. I wish that I were sleeping.

7. I wish I were living on a Caribbean island.

8. I wish that my friends lived closer to me.

9. I wish that I hadn't stolen the money.

10. I wish I had a better place to live.

11. I wish that my landlord would lower the rent.

12. I wish I could understand myself better.

3 **Practice** Anyone who is spending time in prison would most likely rather be somewhere else and be doing something else. Rephrase the following sentences to use *wish*.

Example I'd rather be with my friends.
I wish I were with my friends.

1. I'd rather be outside in the fresh air.

2. We'd rather be jogging.

3. I'd rather be home.

4. I'd rather be at the beach.

5. I'd rather be driving.

6. We'd rather be playing soccer.

7. I'd rather be with my children.

8. I'd rather be free.

 4 **Practice** In pairs, take turns making statements and responses.

Example My cousin graduated last year.
A: My cousin graduated last year.
B: Don't you wish that you had graduated last year too?
A: Of course. (or: Not really.)

1. My friend traveled around the world last year.

2. My sister will get married next year.

3. My brother got a scholarship at the university.

4. My father learned to speak German.

5. My mother is a computer whiz.

6. My brother-in-law is trilingual.

7. My nephew is a professional football player.

8. My cousin won the lottery!

5 Practice The following are quotes from people who have been convicted of crimes and who have spent time in prison. Complete them by adding appropriate forms of the verbs in parentheses. Add modal auxiliaries when necessary.

1. You don't want to know about what I've done. I wish I ___had never done___
   (do / never)
   it, that's for sure. Look at me. Do I look like a criminal? No, but I am. I

   wish I _____ in prison, but that's only part of it. I wish I
   (not / be)

   _____.   —Jack B., bank robber
   (be born / never)

2. I did something I believed was right. I still don't know if it was the right

   thing to do. I wish that I _____. I kidnapped someone. I
   (know)

   kidnapped someone important. I wanted to create a revolution because I

   wanted social justice. Here I am behind bars, and the revolution never

   came. I hope someday we _____ justice in our society. I
   (have)

   wish I _____ the answers because what I did hasn't
   (know)

   seemed to help.   —Bill H., kidnapper

3. I carried drugs across the border. For that, I got five years to life here in

   the U.S. I wish I _____ what was going to happen. I
   (know)

   thought I was going to make some money. Now here I am and my wife's

   alone with my kids and they don't even remember their father. I hope that

   someday they _____ me again. I wish I _____
   (love)   (see)

   them. I am so sad and lonely.   —Ramón G., drug smuggler

4. I killed some people, famous people. The family—we killed some people. I

   don't think about it much now. I have asked forgiveness from my God, and

   I hope he _____ me. Many people in the joint, we find
   (forgive)

   religion. I found it here. Today, I can hope that tomorrow I

   _____, tomorrow I _____. I wish I
   (sleep)   (rest)

   _____ to be here, but it has led me to some hope.
   (not have)

   —Tex W., murderer

Using What You've Learned

6 **Making Choices** Each one of us has choices to make, and sometimes we make the wrong ones. Think of three bad choices you have made: in your studies, your career, or your personal life, for example. Looking back, what do you wish that you had done? Write a short paragraph telling what you wish had happened. Later, in a small group discussion, share your composition with your classmates.

7 **Making Wishes** Aladdin found his Genie of the Lamp. Imagine that you've found yours! What three wishes would you wish for? Orally or in writing, tell what you desire and why you'd like to make those particular wishes.

8 **Expressing Preferences** North Americans love to put bumper stickers on their cars. One popular type of bumper sticker begins, "I'd rather be . . . ," meaning "I wish I were . . ." Such bumper stickers usually tell about our hobbies and interests. In pairs or small groups, create your own bumper stickers with *wish*. Try to create at least five slogans beginning with *I wish I were* or *I wish we were*.

Examples *We wish we were sailing.*
We wish we could be studying more grammar.

9 **Expressing Hopes and Wishes** The verbs *hope* and *wish* often represent the attitudes of the optimist and the pessimist. The optimist hopes that everything will work out, while the pessimist *wishes* it would. In small groups, write short dialogues that include people who are optimistic and people who are pessimistic. The dialogue may be serious or it may be comical. Be sure to include a role for everyone in your group. After you have finished, role-play your dialogues for the class. Here are some suggestions for topics:

1. The menu at the dormitory tonight: Imagine that you all live in a dormitory. The food is almost always bad! Some of you would like to send the cook to the moon or at least to a cooking school. Yet a few of you try to be kind in your attitude toward the cook. Some of you optimistically hope for a miracle.

2. The first date with a new boyfriend / girlfriend: Imagine that you are going out with a new person tonight. You will have to meet his or her family, and you hope to make a good impression on everyone. You are worried about not saying and doing the right things. The people in the family are nervous too. You imagine that your evening could be a complete disaster, or perhaps it could be the beginning of a wonderful relationship.

Setting the Context

Previewing the Passage Discuss the questions.

Do you feel safe? What can you do to lower your risk of becoming a victim of crime?

Reading Read the passage.

The Risk of Being a Victim

In a recent survey, 17 percent of the people interviewed said that at least one member of their household had been either a victim or a witness to a crime in the past year. However, if you had been a victim of a crime, it most likely wouldn't have been a violent one. Even though a violent crime is three times more likely to occur now than it was 30 years ago, today 94 percent of all crimes don't involve any threat of violence. Most crimes are not the sensational type that become headlines or top stories on the evening news. 5

So what are your chances of being involved in a crime? If it were 1960 and you were living in the United States, the chances of your experiencing a crime would be low. Today, the odds of experiencing a crime vary. For example, if you lived in an impoverished household, you would be at a greater risk than if you lived in a well-to-do household. If you were an adult, you would be less likely to be victimized than if you were a youth. If you used drugs and committed crimes yourself, you would raise your chances. Interestingly, the odds of being a victim are highest for criminals themselves. 10 15

Discussing Ideas Discuss the questions.

Why do you think youths, criminals, and people living in poverty have the greatest chances of being victims of crimes? What does this tell us about how we can prevent crime?

 Crime and Punishment   **431**

Grammar Structures and Practice

A. *Otherwise*

Otherwise is a transition that contrasts reality with wishes and dreams. It means "if the situation were different" or "under other circumstances."

10.3 *Otherwise*		
Explanations	**Examples**	**Implied Meaning**
The auxiliaries *could, might,* and *would* are often used after *otherwise*. As with other transitions, a semicolon is used when two sentences are joined into one.	I'm scared to walk alone at night; **otherwise**, I would go to the party. I don't have any money. **Otherwise**, I might buy a new car. No one knows where the criminal is hiding. We could arrest him, **otherwise**.*	I am scared to walk home alone at night, so I won't go to the party. I don't have any money, so I can't buy a new car. We don't know where the criminal is hiding. As a result, we cannot arrest him.

*This placement of *otherwise* is informal. It is used in conversation only.

1 **Practice** Complete the following sentences in your own words.

Example I don't have a car; otherwise, I could *take a trip to the mountains.*

1. I don't have much money this month. Otherwise, I might . . .

2. I have a lot of homework tonight; otherwise, we could . . .

3. The reviews of that movie weren't very good; otherwise, . . .

4. I have to work during vacation. Otherwise, . . .

5. I'm out of shape. Otherwise, I . . .

6. I'm afraid of the ocean; otherwise, . . .

7. My roommate is taking a test on Saturday. Otherwise, . . .

8. I don't know how to . . . ; otherwise, . . .

B. Imaginary Conditionals: Present or Unspecified Time

Imaginary conditions express ideas that the speaker or writer thinks are unlikely, untrue, or contrary to fact. They may be wishes or dreams, or they may express advice to others.

10.4 Imaginary Conditionals: Present or Unspecified Time

Explanations	Examples	Implied Meaning
Could, *might*, or *would* is used in the main clause, and a subjunctive form is used in the *if* clause.	If I **had** more money, I **could take** some trips.	I don't have much money, so I am not able to take many trips.
	If I **were** rich, I **would** never **worry**.	I'm not rich, so I worry sometimes.
In most cases, the subjunctive form is the same as the simple past tense, but with the verb *be*, *were* is used for all persons in formal English.	If I **were** you, I **would save** money.	My advice to you is that you should save money.
	If I **was** you, I **would save** money.*	My advice to you is that you should save money.

* This form is incorrect but is frequently used in coversation.

---

2 **Practice** Combine the ideas in the following sentences by forming sentences with *if*. Use the example as a model.

Example I wish this town were stricter about drinking and driving. Then I wouldn't worry so much about driving at night.

If this town were stricter about drinking and driving, I wouldn't worry so much about driving at night.

1. I wish that there weren't so much crime in this neighborhood. Then I wouldn't feel so nervous about living here.

2. I wish the streets were safer here. Then I could walk home at night.

3. I wish that there weren't so many robberies. Then I wouldn't need five locks on my door.

4. I wish there were more police walking through this neighborhood. Then I would feel safer.

5. I wish that I knew more of my neighbors. Then I would feel more comfortable.

6. I wish there weren't so many bike thefts. Then I could park my bike outside.

7. I wish apartments weren't so expensive here. Then I could get a bigger place.

8. I wish that I had a car. Then it would be much easier to get around.

3 **Practice** Crime isn't the only way to get money or things without working long and hard. Imagine that the following situations happened to you through good luck. How would you feel? What would you do? What wouldn't you do? Make at least three statements for each, using *if* clauses.

Example Imagine that you were awarded a one-year scholarship at your school—all expenses paid.

> *If I were awarded a scholarship, I would feel very proud.*
> *If I had a full scholarship, my parents wouldn't have to send me more money.*
> *If I didn't have to pay tuition, I could concentrate more on my work because I wouldn't be worried about money all the time.*

1. Imagine that you were offered a special promotion by the phone company for one month's long distance calls—*free*.

2. Imagine that you were the winner of a sweepstakes at your grocery store—for $500 worth of purchases.

3. Imagine that you won a shopping spree at the mall—for everything you could purchase in three hours.

4. Imagine that you had a winning ticket in the local lottery—for $10,000.

5. Imagine that you won an unlimited mileage air pass from an international airline—for one month of travel to anywhere.

6. Imagine that you hit the jackpot in Las Vegas—for $1 million.

 4 **Practice** We often use *If I were you . . .* instead of *you should . . .* or *you'd better* as a way of giving advice. In pairs, take turns giving advice for the following. If possible, give two pieces of advice for each.

Example A: I often leave my room unlocked.
> B: *If I were you, I wouldn't do that. I would lock the door whenever I left.*

1. I don't feel very safe in my apartment. The windows are very low, and the locks are not very good.

2. I worry about parking my car on the street.

3. I usually leave my backpack (briefcase, purse, and so on) in my office near my desk, but I often forget to lock the door when I go out.

4. I often stay late at the lab. Sometimes I work until 12:30 or 1:00 A.M., and then I walk home by myself.

5. All my important documents, such as my passport, are in a box in my closet, I think. I'm not really sure where I put them.

6. I don't believe in banks, so I keep all my cash in my home.

Using What You've Learned

5 **Discussing Crimes and Possible Punishment** Both crimes and punishments vary from culture to culture. Do you know how these crimes would be punished in your country? In small groups or as a class, share any information you have on your country's justice system. If you don't know what the crime is, look it up.

arson	drug possession	littering	tax evasion
assault	kidnapping	speeding	theft

6 **Giving Possible Solutions to Problems** Is crime a serious problem in your hometown or in the town where you live now? If you had the chance, how would you deal with the problem? In a short composition explain how you would handle it. Begin with *If I were the chief of police in (your city). . . .* Then, in pairs, small groups, or as a class, share your ideas.

7 **Discussing Current Events** Check your local newspaper, watch the television news, or listen to the radio. Make notes about any recent crimes. Come to class prepared to discuss crime in your town or in the nation.

8 **Describing Personality Traits** Are you talkative, shy, impatient, calm? Are you a good listener? Do you have a good memory? Reflect for a moment on your personality. Is there anything about yourself that you'd like to change? What are some characteristics or traits that you wish you had? Are there any you wish you didn't have? Give several original sentences using *If I were . . .* or *If I weren't . . . .*

Example *If I weren't so careless, I would do better on tests.*
If I were more patient, I'd have less stress.

9 **Describing Possibilities** In a speech at Harvard University in 1953, future president of the United States John F. Kennedy said, "If more politicians knew poetry, and more poets knew politics, I am convinced the world would be a better place in which to live."

In your opinion, how might the world be a better place? Share your ideas in a discussion with your classmates or in a brief composition.

Previewing the Passage Discuss the question.

Crimes do not always involve hurting someone or damaging property. What other types of crime are there?

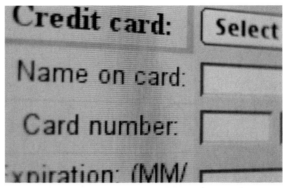

▲ Online purchases usually require credit card information.

Reading Read the passage.

Crimes Without Violence

Wife:	I can't believe this!
Husband:	What happened? What's wrong?
Wife:	Someone must have gotten my credit card number and used it. I've got charges here that I never made!
Husband:	But how could it have happened?
Wife:	I know I haven't been careful about receipts lately. Someone may have gotten my number out of a receipt from a wastebasket in some store. Or maybe it happened because I gave my credit card information for an Internet auction. Do you remember those CDs I bought online? Somebody might have gotten access to my account there. Oh, I should have been more careful.
Husband:	No matter what, these things shouldn't happen. It's wrong. Well, let's call the credit card company and put a stop on the card.

Unfortunately, this scenario is not unusual. Worldwide, nonviolent but equally reproachable criminal acts take place all too frequently. These nonviolent crimes are often called white-collar crimes. They do not hurt us physically, but they can have other terrible effects.

Discussing Ideas Discuss the questions.

Have you ever been a victim of a nonviolent crime, such as the one described in the reading? What happened? What did you do about it?

Grammar Structures and Practice

A. Perfect Modal Auxiliaries

Perfect modal auxiliaries express past activities or situations that were not real or that did not occur. Often, they express our wishes in hindsight.

10.5	**Perfect Modal Auxiliaries**		
Uses	**Structures**	**Explanations**	**Examples**
Unfulfilled Intentions and Preferences	*would*	*Would have* refers to past intentions that were not fulfilled.	I **would have gone**, but it was impossible.
	would rather	*Would rather have* refers to past preferences that were not fulfilled.	I **would rather have gone** with you than stay here.
Unfulfilled Advice	*should*	*Should have* and *ought to have* refer to actions that were advisable but did not take place.	You **should have gone** too.
	ought to	*Ought to have* is less common than *should have*.	He **ought to have stayed** longer.
Past Possibilities	*could* *might* *may*	*Could have, may have,* and *might have* refer to past possibilities. In many cases, the speaker or writer is uncertain whether the action took place. In some contexts, *could have* also refers to past abilities.	I **could have gone** later. He **might have called**. He **may have left** already.
Past Probabilities	*must*	*Must have* refers to past probabilities. The speaker or writer is fairly certain that the action took place.	He **must have left**.

1 **Practice** Quickly reread "Crimes Without Violence" on page 436. Underline all the modal auxiliaries in the passage and give the function and time frame of each.

2 Practice Change the modals to perfect forms in the following sentences. Then listen carefully as your teacher reads both the present and past forms rapidly. Try to distinguish between the two. What clues can you find to help you distinguish the two forms in rapid speech?

Example He may go to jail.
He may have gone to jail.

1. She may get fired.

2. Someone might steal your bike.

3. It must be dangerous to walk on that path.

4. He might cheat on his taxes.

5. John must be worried.

6. John should be more careful.

7. We could have a serious problem.

8. They may use someone else's credit card.

9. Sandy could have an accident.

10. Jim should think more about that.

11. They might rob a bank.

12. Debbie could do very well on the test.

3 Practice We often use responses with modal auxiliaries as a way of empathizing, saying that we understand how someone else feels. In pairs, take turns making statements and responses based on the model. Use *would (not) have* and *too* or *either* in your responses.

Example Someone got my credit card number and used it. I was really shocked.
A: *Someone got my credit card number and used it. I was really shocked.*
B: *I would have been shocked too!*

1. Someone stole my bicycle. I felt just awful.

2. Someone broke into our apartment, and it scared me to death. I wasn't able to sleep for a week.

3. Another student took my ideas for a project. I was infuriated!

4. Someone sent me some threatening emails. I was scared and nervous.

5. Someone stole my purse with my address book in it. I felt terrible.

6. Someone got access to my computer and erased several files. I was furious!

7. Someone picked my pocket on the bus. I got so angry!

8. I had to go to the police station to file a complaint. I felt really nervous.

4 Practice In each of the following statements, a person had a problem but did something wrong to solve it. What could, should, or might the person have done instead? Give at least two alternative actions for each. Use *could have, should have,* or *might have* in your suggestions.

Example Pedro didn't study for his math exam, so during the exam he cheated and copied down the answers from the test of the woman sitting next to him.
He should have studied for his exam.
He could have tried his best on the exam.

1. Jack was failing his history course and needed a high score on his final exam. The class was very large, and the final exam was given in a large hall. He paid someone to take his test for him.

2. Mary had a term paper due for a history class. She would fail the course if she didn't complete it. She did not finish her work, so instead, she bought a term paper from another student.

3. Taka did not want to pay for a book for his class, so he photocopied it chapter by chapter, even though the photocopies cost almost as much as the book.

4. Ravi didn't want to buy lots of CDs, so he downloaded hundreds of songs form the Internet. This was still technically legal, but then Ravi began to sell "pirated" CDs to his friends.

B. Perfect Modal Auxiliaries and Past Advice

In the perfect tense, the modal auxiliaries *should* and *ought to* can be used to express advice that was given but not taken.

10.6 Perfect Modal Auxiliaries and Past Advice

Explanation	Present-to-Future Advice	Past Advice Not Taken
In the present, English has words to express advice, such as *ought to* and *should*. When you want to show that the advice was not taken in the past, use *ought (not) to have* + past participle or *should (not) have* + past participle.	He **ought to go**. He **ought not to say** that. He **should go**. He **should not say** that.	He **ought to have gone**. He **ought not to have said** that. He **should have gone**. He **should not have said** that.

Note: See chart 10.5 on page 437 for more examples of unfulfilled advice (advice not taken).

5 Practice In pairs, take turns making the following statements and responding to them. Use *should (not) have* or *ought (not) to have* in your responses. Then add a few original statements and your partner will respond to them.

Example A: Eun didn't want to wrinkle her blouse, so she didn't wear her seatbelt.

B: She really should have worn her seatbelt.

A: Yes, if she had worn her seatbelt, she might not have been injured in the accident.

B: Right, maybe she would be home and not in the hospital right now.

1. Miki was in a hurry, so she parked her car in a "handicapped" zone.

2. Bill wasn't paying attention and ran a red light. He almost hit another car.

3. Dorothy didn't have any change, so she didn't put any money in the parking meter.

4. Abdul didn't pay any of his parking tickets, and one day his car was impounded.

5. While David was driving, he didn't notice his children were throwing candy wrappers out of the car window.

6. Maria was late for an appointment, so she drove 50 miles per hour through a residential area in order to get to a highway.

6 Practice Rephrase the following sentences to use *otherwise*. Use *may have*, *might have*, *could have*, or *would have* in your new sentences.

Example He was a dangerous criminal, so I was nervous to be near him.
He was a dangerous criminal; otherwise, I wouldn't have been nervous to be near him.

1. There was a lot of crime in that part of town, so I didn't go there very often.

2. The man knew she was a thief, so he didn't hire her.

3. Her boyfriend never paid his parking tickets, so the police towed his car.

4. I worry about Internet fraud; that's why I don't use my credit card to buy things online.

5. There are so many social problems; that's why we have so much crime.

6. The prisons are overcrowded, so we need to build more jails.

Using What You've Learned

7 **Making Excuses** We often use *otherwise* to make excuses when we haven't done something. What haven't you done recently that you should have done? Think of at least six sentences that use *otherwise* and perfect modals. Some ideas are assignments, trips, calls or letters, problems with a friend, cleaning, and fixing things.

Example *I didn't have much free time last weekend; otherwise, I would have written my family.*

8 **Discussing Poetry** The American poet Robert Frost wrote about choices in his poem "The Road Not Taken." Read the poem and discuss the questions. You may want to use your ideas for the basis of a composition.

What do you think Frost is telling us about choices in this poem? What does this poem tell us about his life? What crossroads have you had in your life?

The Road Not Taken

Two roads diverged in a yellow wood,
And sorry I could not travel both
And be one traveler, long as I stood
And looked down one as far as I could
To where it bent in the undergrowth;   5
Then took the other, as just as fair,
And having perhaps the better claim,
Because it was grassy and wanted wear;
Though as for that the passing there
Had worn them really about the same,   10
And both that morning equally lay
In leaves no step had trodden black.
Oh, I kept the first for another day!
Yet knowing how way leads on to way,
I doubted if I should ever come back.   15
I shall be telling this with a sigh
Somewhere ages and ages hence:
Two roads diverged in a wood, and I—
I took the one less traveled by,
And that has made all the difference.   20

—Robert Frost

Setting the Context

Previewing the Passage Discuss the questions.

Do you believe that abuse of the environment is a criminal act? Can you give any specific examples?

Reading Read the paragraph.

Crimes Against Our Environment

OK, it's true. We humans have made a mess of our world. We've committed many criminal acts against our environment. If we'd been a little smarter, if we had done more planning, if we hadn't been so greedy, our world would be a much better place. We wouldn't have created giant cities without efficient trans-portation systems. We wouldn't have polluted our air, land, and water. We wouldn't have let people become so desperate that drugs and crime were their only escape. We would have created healthy, *livable* cities that showed respect for humanity and for the environment. Is it too late? Absolutely not! We got our-selves into this mess; we can certainly get ourselves out.

—Jack Powers, age 40

Discussing Ideas Discuss the question.

Can you give any examples of cases where individuals or companies have been found guilty of environmental crimes?

Grammar Structures and Practice

A. Imaginary Conditionals: Past Time

Conditional sentences with *if* can be used to describe past situations or events that did *not* take place.

10.7 Imaginary Conditionals: Past Time		
Explanations	**Examples**	**Implied Meaning**
For imaginary conditionals in past time, a subjunctive form, which is the same as the past perfect tense, is used in the *if* clause. Perfect modal auxiliaries are used in the main clause.	If I **hadn't needed** the money, I **wouldn't have done** that. We **would have taken** better care of our environment if we **had been** wiser.	I did something because I needed the money. We didn't take good care of our environment because we were not wise.

1 **Practice** Complete the following sentences with the appropriate form of the verbs in parentheses.

Examples If I have time, I _____ will go _____ (go) to the party.

If I had time, I _____ would go _____ (go) to the party.

If I had had time, I _____ would have gone _____ (go) to the party.

1. If she _____ (be) here, I'm sure she will help us.

   If she were here, I'm sure she _____ (help) us.

   If she _____ (be) here, I'm sure she would have helped us.

2. If I _____ (study) harder, I'd get better grades.

   If I _____ (study) harder, I'd have gotten better grades.

   If I _____ (study) harder, I'll get better grades.

3. If he _____ (want) a raise, he would have worked hard.

   He _____ (work) hard if he wants a raise.

   If he wanted a raise, he _____ (work) hard.

4. There will be less air pollution if people _____ (drive) less.

   There _____ (be) less air pollution if people had driven less.

   There would be less air pollution if people _____ (drive) less.

5. If environmental laws had been stricter, the automotive industry _____ (make) vehicles with higher gas mileage.

The automotive industry would make vehicles with higher gas mileage if environmental laws _____ (be) stricter.

The automotive industry will make vehicles with higher gas mileage if environmental laws _____ (be) stricter.

B. Imaginary Conditionals: Past-to-Present Time

Conditional sentences with *if* can be used to describe past actions or situations that have affected the present.

10.8	Imaginary Conditionals: Past-to-Present Time	
Explanation	**Examples**	**Implied Meaning**
For imaginary conditionals of past-to-present time, a subjunctive form (*had* + past participle) is used in the *if* clause. A simple modal auxiliary is used in the main clause.	If we **hadn't bought** the house, we **might** still **be** in an apartment.	We bought a house, so we don't live in an apartment now.
	If we **hadn't bought** the house, we **would** still **have** to pay rent.	We bought a house, so we don't have to pay rent.
	We **would have** much less space if we **hadn't bought** the house.	We have much more space now because we bought a house.

2 Practice Imagine the following possible situations and how they might have affected your life. Complete the following sentences in your own words. Give at least two sentences for each item.

Example If I had been born a millionaire, . . .

If I had been born a millionaire, my money problems today would be completely different! I would have trouble spending it, not making it.

1. If I had never studied English, . . .

2. If I had not come to this school, . . .

3. If I had been born the opposite sex, . . .

4. If I had been born 50 years ago, . . .

5. If I had been elected president of my country 10 years ago, . . .

6. If I had gotten married at age 15, . . .

3 Practice Imagine how our lives might be different today if these events had not occurred. Make notes in the chart on page 445. Try to give at least one negative and one positive effect or result for each event. Then write complete sentences with *if*.

	Negative	Positive
Example: If internal combustion engines hadn't been developed, . . .	If internal combustion engines hadn't been developed, we wouldn't have cars, buses, and taxis. Transportation and travel would be much more difficult.	If they hadn't been developed, however, we also wouldn't have so much air pollution.
1. If petroleum hadn't been discovered, . . .		
2. If cars hadn't been invented, . . .		
3. If no one had invented paper clips, . . .		
4. If zippers hadn't been created, . . .		
5. If computers hadn't been invented, . . .		

4 Practice In recent years, many major improvements have been made in the city of Boston. The following sentences tell about some of the changes that have made Boston a more pleasant place to live. Rewrite them to show what *might, could,* or *would (not)* have occurred if things had been the opposite. Use clauses with *if* and appropriate modal auxiliaries.

Example Bostonians valued their past; as a result, they restored their historic buildings.

If Bostonians had not valued their past, they would not have restored their historic buildings.

1. Bostonians were concerned about historic parts of the city; as a result, they fought very hard to preserve them.

2. Bostonians cared about the beauty of the city; as a result, they preserved many historic areas.

3. The city made major improvements in the old waterfront area; as a result, it is a great attraction today.

4. The old waterfront warehouses in Boston were renovated; as a result, a wide variety of shops and restaurants opened there.

5. The city developed parks and gardens along the harbor; as a result, the waterfront area is very attractive.

6. The city needed new income to pay for some of the improvements; as a result, it tried to attract more tourists.

7. Boston wanted to attract more visitors; as a result, it promoted the development of hotels and tourist facilities.

8. The Boston community was very proud of its history and beauty; as a result, citizens invested in its preservation.

▲ The Boston skyline shows a mix of old and new.

5 **Review** Complete the following passage with the appropriate forms of the verbs in parentheses. Be sure to add modal auxiliaries when necessary. The first one is done as an example.

City Living

My name's Mario. I live in a big city. It's a beautiful city in a lot of ways, but our neighborhood is pretty tough. I wish things _____*were*_____ a lot

(be)
different. For example, I live a long way from school. I wish that I

_____ to get up at 6:00 A.M. to take a bus to school. I wish my

1 (not have)

school _____ right next door. And I wish the whole neighbor-

2 (be)

hood _____ nicer and cleaner. I wish people _____

3 (be)   4 (clean)

up around here—and not just the garbage! I wish there _____

5 (not be)

any drugs on the streets. I wish I _____ out alone at night.

6 (go)

Sometimes I wish that my parents _____ here. I hope things

7 (never move)

_____. I hope I _____ to college and help my

8 (change)   9 (go)

family.

6 **Review** First read the following passage for meaning. Then choose the appropriate form from the words in parentheses to complete the passage.

Los Angeles

At the beginning of the 1900s, Los Angeles ((was)/ were) a sleepy little town, and even as recently as the early 1960s, there (was /(were)) farms and orchards close to our house. Gardens (thrived / had thrived) here, and you could have
₁
(could find / found) an incredible variety of exotic plants and shrubs. Of course,
₂
there (wasn't / weren't) any freeways, and there (used to be / used to being) a
₃   ₄
good transportation system of electric trains. The air (was usually / usually was)
₅
very clear, and as a young child, I (could see / could have seen) the mountains to
₆
the north and east almost every day.

Now, we (get / have got) freeways, traffic, and pollution. What a shame! If
₇
you (had seen / would have seen) Los Angeles 40 years ago, you
₈
(had been /would have been) amazed.
₉

If the city (knew / had known) what (was / was going to) happen. . . . If Los
₁₀   ₁₁
Angeles (kept / had kept) its train system, we (might / should) have avoided
₁₂   ₁₃
some of the traffic problems. If city planners (had only thought / had thought only)
₁₄
more about the future, they could (have put / had put) more money into public
₁₅
transportation. If fewer people (have / had) moved to southern California, the
₁₆
population wouldn't have (grew / grown) so fast. If L.A. (didn't grow / hadn't grown)
₁₇   ₁₈
so fast, we (might not have / might not have had) so many problems today. No
₁₉
one (anticipates / anticipated) all these things; otherwise, we
₂₀
(had been / might have been) a lot more careful. I certainly (hope / wish) that
₂₁   ₂₂
we (had / had had) better foresight and planning. I (hope / wish) that things
₂₃   ₂₄
(will improve / would improve) in the future. Otherwise, we
₂₅
(might have / might have had) even worse problems in the upcoming years.
₂₆

—Debra Love, 54, second-generation native of Los Angeles

Using What You've Learned

7 **Describing Changes** Think about your hometown or the town where you are living now. Have changes taken place in recent years? Have these been good or bad? What if these changes hadn't taken place? What would your area be like? Make at least four statements using conditional sentences with both past and present time.

8 **Hypothesizing** "What if" you had been born at a different time? How would your life be different? "What if" you had been born in a different place? How would your life be different today? Test your knowledge in a game like Trivial Pursuit. Separate into four different groups. In your groups, make up questions about history, geography, languages, social customs, and so on. (Be sure that you know the answers!) The questions should use clauses with *if*.

Example   *If you had lived in London in 1900, who would have been the ruler of your country? (Queen Victoria)*
If you had been in Buenos Aires in 1930, what kind of music might you have listened to? (tangos)

When you have prepared eight to ten questions, get together with another group. Take turns asking the other group members your questions and answering theirs. Keep a count of correct answers, and the group with the highest score wins.

9 **Looking Back** Read the following passage, and think about *second chances*, the opportunities to try again. Then discuss the questions on page 450 in a group.

If I Had My Life to Do Over

I'd make a few more mistakes next time. I'd relax. I would limber up. I would be sillier than I had been this trip. I would take fewer things seriously. I would climb more mountains and swim more rivers. I would eat more ice cream and fewer beans. I would perhaps have more actual troubles, but I'd have fewer imaginary ones.   5

You see, I'm one of those people who live sensibly and sanely hour after hour, day after day. Oh, I've had my moments, and if I had it to do over again, I'd have more of them. In fact, I'd try to have nothing else. Just moments, one after another, instead of living so many years ahead of each day. I've been one of those persons who never goes anywhere without a hot water bottle and a para-   10
chute. If I had it to do again, I would travel lighter.

If I had my life to do over again, I would start barefoot earlier in the spring and stay that way later in the fall. I would go to more dances. I would ride more merry-go-rounds. I would pick more daisies.

—Nadine Stair, 85, Louisville, Kentucky   15

Is this passage about reality or dreams? How do you know? Look at the title of this passage. What verb is used? Does it refer to the past or the present? Most of the passage is written in the conditional with *would*. What is the meaning of *would* in these sentences? Are there things you would do differently if you had the chance? Tell or write about your ideas.

Part 5 Review of Chapters 6–10

Setting the Context

 Previewing the Passage Discuss the questions.

What do you know of President John F. Kennedy? Have you ever heard any of his speeches?

▲ John F. Kennedy, 35th president of the United States, shortly before his assassination

Reading Read the passage.

> Only a few months before his death in 1963, John F. Kennedy talked about our world during a commencement address at American University. Kennedy very eloquently said:
>
> We can help make the world safe for diversity. For, in the final analysis, our most basic common link is that we all inhabit this small planet. We all breathe the same air. We all cherish our children's future. And we are all mortal.

5

Discussing Ideas Discuss the questions.

Describe some of the bonds that you now share with others because of your English studies. What have you learned about other peoples and other cultures? How has this affected you?

Grammar Practice

1 **Review** Complete the following exercise with appropriate active or passive forms of the verbs in parentheses. In some cases, you will need to add modal auxiliaries. Some items may have more than one correct answer. The first one is done as an example.

Life on Earth

Life on earth ___*developed*___ because the conditions _____
         (develop)   1 (be)

suitable for it. If the earth _____ smaller or colder, for example,
                               2 (be)

life _____ different forms. If the conditions _____
     3 (have)   4 (not be)

suitable, no living organisms _____ on earth at all. The simplest
                               5 (develop)

living creatures _____ of a single living unit, the cell. More
                  6 (consist)

complex creatures _____ up of hundreds and even millions of
                7 (make)

cells. However, all living organisms _____ certain characteris-
                          8 (share)

tics. These _____ reproduction, response, growth, and use of
         9 (include)

energy. Plants and animals _____ different only in the way that
                10 (be)

the basic activities of life _____ out by each organism.
             11 (carry)

Of all the creatures alive on earth, humans _____ the great-
                        12 (have)

est impact. The impact of humans _____ because we
                13 (come / often)

_____ able to think. The power to think _____
  14 (be)   15 (give)

us ways both to create and to destroy.

In the past, humans _____ less impact, especially on the
                  16 (have)

environment. Because early humans _____ from place to place,
                    17 (move)

their movement _____ nature a chance to recover. For exam-
         18 (give)

ple, even though humans _____ trees, forests
                19 (cut)

_____ to their former size after the humans
 20 (return / soon)

_____ to a different place. Today, nature _____
  21 (move)   22 (give / seldom)

a chance to recover. Our demands on the earth _____ steadily.
23 (increase)

All human activity _____ to require more and more land and
24 (seem)

more and more resources. Humans _____ this earth with mil-
25 (share)

lions of other animals and plants, yet we _____ without ever
26 (act / often)

thinking about our impact on our world.

2 **Review** First read the passage on the next page for meaning. Then complete it by adding appropriate connecting words: *and, as, but, if, that, when, where, while.*

Our Planet

It's often hard to remember, _____*but*_____ the world _____
1

we live in today is only a fragment in history and in the universe. We may have

different countries and languages, _____ we are all part of this
2

same small fragment of life.

Sometimes it takes an extraordinary event or point of view to remember the

larger picture beyond our world. For astronaut Russell Schweikert, this came in

1969 _____ he was orbiting the earth from space in the Apollo
3

IX Lunar Module. _____ Schweikert looked at the earth, he
4

gained a totally different perspective on life. _____ Schweikert
5

hadn't had the opportunity to orbit the earth, he might never have had this

realization.

Schweikert said, "_____ you go around it [the earth] in an
6

hour and a half, you begin to recognize our identity is with that whole thing.

And that makes a change.

"You look down there, _____ you can't imagine borders
7

and boundaries you cross, again and again and again, _____
8

you don't even see them. There you are—hundreds of people killing each other

because of some imaginary line _____ you're not even aware of
9

because you can't see it. From _____ you see the earth [from a
10

spacecraft], the thing is a whole, _____ 11 it's so beautiful. You wish _____ 12 you could take one person in each hand and say, 'Look at it from this perspective. What's important?'

"You realize on that small spot, that little blue and white thing, is everything _____ 13 means anything to you. All of history and music and poetry and art and birth and love: tears, joy, games. All of it on that little spot _____ 14 you can cover with your thumb."

▲ Earth viewed from space

3 Review What kind of world would you like to live in? Imagine building your own country. How would you organize it? Be creative in answering some or all of the following questions! You may want to use ideas from your composition from Activity 9 in Part 2.

Example *I would love to have my own country. I can imagine living in a beautiful place that has both warm ocean beaches and snow-capped mountains. . . .*

1. Where would you like to locate your country? What type of climate and geography do you want to have? What types of plants and animals? Describe the sights, sounds, and smells of your country.

2. Would you have open borders in your country? Who would you allow to live there? Would you permit citizens to come and go as they pleased?

3. What kinds of architecture would you permit people to have? Would people be allowed to choose the style of their houses? Would you require citizens to follow certain guidelines?

4. Would you prefer to have private education or public education? For primary school? For secondary school? For college or university?

5. Would you plan to have private health care? Or, are you in favor of providing universal public health care? How would you plan to pay for this? Would you ask citizens to pay for part of the cost?

6. Would you require people to serve in an army? Would you have all young people serve? Would you allow people to do alternative service, such as teaching or nursing, instead of serving in an army?

7. What forms of transportation would you allow to exist in your country? Would you permit everyone to have a car? Or, would you limit individual cars?

8. What system of money would you use? Would you have paper money, credit cards, or some other form of currency for buying and selling?

4 **Review** Choose the correct forms of the words in parentheses. An X indicates that no word is necessary.

Living Together on a Small Planet

The environment is (X / the) world (that / who) all living things share. It is
            1   2
what is—air, fire, wind, water, life, and sometimes (the / X) culture. The
                                          3
environment consists of all the things that act and (is / are) acted upon. Living
                                        4
creatures (is / are) born into the environment and (are / were) part of it too. Yet
        5   6
there is (no / none) creature (who / whom) perceives all of what is and what
          7   8
happens. A dog perceives things (that / what) we can't, and we perceive and
                            9
understand (much / many) things beyond (its / it's) world. For a dog, a book
            10   11
isn't much different from a stick, (but / so) for us, one stick is pretty much like
                              12
every other stick. There is no world (that / who) is experienced (by / from) all
                          13   14
living creatures. We all live in the same environment, (so / but) we create many
                                    15
worlds.

We actually know very (little / few) of the world, even of what surrounds us
                          16
every day. It is worth (to take / taking) the time (to think / thinking) of the
                     17   18
variety of ways in (that / which) the environment (could / could be) structured
                    19   20

and (to discover / discovering) how different living things actually structure it.
                    21
We are all collections of atoms, specks in (X / the) universe, just the right size in
                                                          22
our own worlds, giants to fleas, midgets to whales. Our view of the world is only

one of (many / much). It enriches our understanding of ourselves to move away
              23
from familiar worlds and attempt to understand the experience of others. . . .

The respect for life we can (gain / to gain) from these efforts (might / might have)
                                         24   25
in some small way help us work toward preserving the world we share.

—Adapted from Judith and Herbert Kohl, *The View from the Oak*

Using What You've Learned

5 **Talking About Hopes and Dreams** Robert F. Kennedy paraphrased a line from a George Bernard Shaw play when he said, "Some people see things as they are and say why. I dream things that never were and say, why not?"

Give thought to Kennedy's statement, and then think about yourself. At this point in your life, what are some of the dreams that you have for the future? In a discussion or in writing, share some of the possibilities that you imagine and the dreams that you hope for.

6 **Creating Poetry** Poetry is a beautiful form of expression in any language, but it is often difficult to write. In poetry, every word plays an important role, so each must be chosen with care. Interestingly, it is sometimes easier to write poetry in a second or foreign language. A language learner can bring different perspectives and ideas to poetry and thus produce unusual combinations of words and images. Individually, in small groups, or as a class, use the following directions to help you write short poems. You may choose your own topic or select from the suggestions below.

1. Choose the name of another classmate and write a poem about your classmate.

2. Write a poem about English (grammar, composition, and so on).

3. Write about an emotion or idea: love, friendship, homesickness, curiosity.

4. Write about a favorite place.

5. Write about your home area or country.

(continued)

Here are some guidlines for writing a poem. (You need not follow these strictly.)

Line 1: Write a sentence of three to five words about your topic.
Line 2: Take a noun from line 1 and describe it.
Line 3: Add movement to the idea in line 2.
Line 4: Pick a word in line 3 and compare it to something *(X is like . . .)*.
Line 5: Take the idea in line 4 and describe it or add more action.
Line 6: Take the idea in line 5 and compare it to something *(X is . . .)*.
Line 7: Make the idea in line 6 either very big or very small.
Line 8: Describe the idea in line 7.
Lines 9 to 10: Make a final statement (your opinion, and so on).

A SMALLER WORLD

We came from so many places,
Gentle, crowded, warm, noisy, icy places,
Excited travelers, nervous and naïve,
Like newborns entering a new world.
Babbling and blundering our way to English,
Like babies learning to talk.
Mountains of words, ideas, customs to climb,
A struggle for understanding.
Yet our world has become smaller
Because we have known each other.

—Class poem written by students from Mexico, Brazil, Japan,
Colombia, Kuwait, Honduras, Switzerland, and Indonesia

Review of Problem Areas: Chapters 6–10

A variety of problem areas are included in this test. Check your understanding by completing the sample items below.

Part 1 Mark the correct completion for the following.

Example   John wishes that his boss _____ him a long vacation.

    (A) gave   (B) would give

    (C) will give   (D) was giving

1. If she _____ chosen to study in San Francisco, she would have had to find a new house.

    (A) has   (B) would have

    (C) will have   (D) had

2. Professional musicians often rehearse their music mentally in order _____ better.

    (A) performing   (B) being performed

    (C) to perform   (D) to be performed

3. If Los Angeles had not dismantled its system of electric trains, mass transportation there _____ better today.

    (A) might be   (B) might

    (C) might have been   (D) might had been

4. John's roommate wishes that John _____ a set of drums.

    (A) would never have bought   (B) would have never bought

    (C) had never bought   (D) never bought

5. Einstein had some of his most brilliant ideas _____ he was working in a Swiss patent office.

    (A) by the time that   (B) unless

    (C) in addition   (D) while

6. The child appears healthy; _____, it's a good idea for her to have a checkup soon.

    (A) otherwise   (B) therefore

    (C) nevertheless   (D) moreover

7. Most minerals near the earth's surface are located in
_____ amounts.

    (A) a small   (B) small

    (C) the small   (D) the very small

8. The lightbulb, along with over 1,000 other useful items,
_____ by Edison.

    (A) were patented   (B) patented

    (C) patenting   (D) was patented

9. Until barbed wire was invented, _____ land in the Great
Plains had been fenced.

    (A) few of   (B) few of the

    (C) little of   (D) little

10. By 1911, Marie Curie _____ two Nobel Prizes in science.

    (A) had been awarded   (B) had being awarded

    (C) awarded   (D) was being awarding

Part 2 Circle the letter below the underlined word(s) containing an error.

Example It's a good idea for overseas travelers to know something of the
                                 A   B

language of the new country; otherwise, they might have had many
                                      C   (D)

difficulties in adapting.

1. The Great Pyramid in Egypt, that has stood for over four thousand years,
                          A   B

was built without the use of the wheel.
  C   D

2. Companies may have respond more quickly if the United States had imposed
              A   B   C

stricter penalties for pollution much earlier on.
                             D

3. One of the greatest wishes of humans today is that we could have discovered
         A   B   C

a cure for cancer in the next few years.
                    D

4. Keynesian economics has influenced a number of key governmental policies
                    A   B

and policy makers involved with monetary decision making during the last
                          C

five decade.
    D

5. It is hoped that computerized health care would help to reduce the mistakes
      A   B   C

   that are currently being made—causing injuries to about 20 percent of U.S.
                      D

   patients.

6. After Leonardo da Vinci had painted the *Mona Lisa*, he had gone on to pursue
                       A   B

   research in such varied fields as physics, anatomy, and military science.
             C   D

7. The physiological and psychological benefits of exercise has been shown
                    A   B

   through numerous studies done on stress reduction.
                         C   D

8. When Einstein's five papers, including his special theory of relativity,
    A   B

   were published in 1905, a scientific revolution began to unfolding.
      C   D

9. Unless you want to explore much of Lanai, the most secluded of the Hawaiian
     A   B   C   D

   Islands, you will need a four-wheel drive vehicle.

10. The professor who he spoke at the conference was a worldwide specialist in
             A   B   C

    the use of radio frequency identification.
     D

Self-Assessment Log

Each of the following statements describes the grammar you learned in this chapter. Read the statements; then check the box that describes how well you understand each structure.

	Needs Improvement	Good	Great
I can use subjunctive verb forms with conditional sentences to talk and write about crime and punishment.	❏	❏	❏
I can use conditional verb forms with conditional sentences to talk and write about crime and punishment.	❏	❏	❏
I can use *otherwise* appropriately.	❏	❏	❏
I can use appropriate punctuation in writing.	❏	❏	❏
I can take a test reviewing problem areas with nouns and noun modifiers, gerunds and infinitives, compound and complex sentences, adjective clauses, *hope, wish,* and conditional sentences.	❏	❏	❏

Appendix 1

Irregular Verbs

Simple Form	Past	Past Participle	Simple Form	Past	Past Participle
arise	arose	arisen	find	found	found
awake	awoke/awaked	awaked/awoken	flee	fled	fled
be	was/were	been	fly	flew	flown
bear	bore	borne/born	forbid	forbade	forbidden
beat	beat	beat	forget	forgot	forgotten
become	became	become	forsake	forsook	forsaken
begin	began	begun	freeze	froze	frozen
bend	bent	bent	get	got	got/gotten
bet	bet	bet	give	gave	given
bite	bit	bitten	go	went	gone
bleed	bled	bled	grind	ground	ground
blow	blew	blown	grow	grew	grown
break	broke	broken	hang	hung/hanged	hung/hanged
breed	bred	bred	have	had	had
bring	brought	brought	hear	heard	heard
broadcast	broadcast	broadcast	hide	hid	hidden
build	built	built	hit	hit	hit
burst	burst	burst	hold	held	held
buy	bought	bought	hurt	hurt	hurt
cast	cast	cast	keep	kept	kept
catch	caught	caught	know	knew	known
choose	chose	chosen	lay	laid	laid
cling	clung	clung	lead	led	led
come	came	come	leap	leapt	leapt
cost	cost	cost	leave	left	left
creep	crept	crept	lend	lent	lent
cut	cut	cut	let	let	let
deal	dealt	dealt	lie	lay	lain
dig	dug	dug	light	lit/lighted	lit/lighted
do	did	done	lose	lost	lost
draw	drew	drawn	make	made	made
dream	dreamed/dreamt	dreamed/dreamt	mean	meant	meant
drink	drank	drunk	meet	met	met
drive	drove	driven	overcome	overcame	overcome
eat	ate	eaten	pay	paid	paid
fall	fell	fallen	prove	proved	proved/proven*
feed	fed	fed	put	put	put
feel	felt	felt	quit	quit	quit
fight	fought	fought	read	read	read

Irregular Verbs

Simple Form	Past	Past Participle	Simple Form	Past	Past Participle
ride	road	ridden	steal	stole	stolen
ring	rang	rung	stick	stuck	stuck
rise	rose	risen	sting	stung	stung
run	ran	run	strike	struck	struck/stricken*
say	said	said	strive	strove	striven
see	saw	seen	swear	swore	sworn
seek	sought	sought	sweep	swept	swept
sell	sold	sold	swim	swam	swum
send	sent	sent	swing	swung	swung
set	set	set	take	took	taken
shake	shook	shaken	teach	taught	taught
shoot	shot	shot	tear	tore	torn
show	showed	showed/shown*	tell	told	told
shut	shut	shut	think	thought	thought
sing	sang	sung	throw	threw	thrown
sink	sank	sunk	thrust	thrust	thrust
sit	sat	sat	understand	understood	understood
sleep	slept	slept	upset	upset	upset
slide	slid	slid	wake	woke/waked	woken/waked
slit	slit	slit	wear	wore	worn
speak	spoke	spoken	weave	wove	woven
spend	spent	spent	wet	wet/wetted	wet/wetted
spin	spun	spun	win	won	won
split	split	split	wind	wound	wound
spread	spread	spread	withdraw	withdrew	withdrawn
spring	sprang	sprung	write	wrote	written
stand	stood	stood			

*These participles are most often used with the passive voice.

Appendix 2

Spelling Rules and Irregular Noun Plurals

Spelling Rules for -s, -ed, -er, -est, and -ing Endings

This chart summarizes the basic spelling rules for endings with verbs, nouns, adjectives, and adverbs.

Rule	Word	-s	-ed	-er	-est	-ing
For most words, simply add -s, -ed, -er, -est, or -ing without making any other changes.	clean cool	cleans cools	cleaned cooled	cleaner cooler	cleanest coolest	cleaning cooling

Rules for Spelling Changes

Rule	Word	-s	-ed	-er	-est	-ing
For words ending in a consonant + *y*, change the *y* to *i* before adding -s, -ed, -er, or -est. Do *not* change or drop the *y* before adding -ing.	carry happy lonely study worry	carries studies worries	carried studied worried	carrier happier lonelier worrier	happiest loneliest	carrying studying worrying
For most words ending in *e*, drop the e before adding -ed, -er, -est, or -ing. *Exceptions:*	dance late nice save write agree canoe		danced saved	dancer later nicer saver writer	latest nicest	dancing saving writing agreeing canoeing
For many words ending in one vowel and one consonant, double the final consonant before adding -ed, -er, -est, or -ing. These include one syllable words and words with stress on the final syllable.	begin hot mad plan occur refer run shop win		planned occurred referred shopped	beginner hotter madder planner runner shopper winner	hottest maddest	beginning planning occurring referring running shopping winning

Rules for Spelling Changes

Rule	Word	-s	-ed	-er	-est	-ing
In words ending in one vowel and one consonant, do *not* double the final consonant if the last syllable is not stressed. *Exceptions:* including words ending in *w*, *x*, or *y*	enter happen open travel visit bus fix play sew	buses	entered happened opened traveled visited bused fixed played sewed	opener traveler fixer player sewer		entering happening opening traveling visiting busing fixing playing sewing
For most words ending in *f* or *lf*, change the *f* to *v* and add *-es*. *Exceptions*	half loaf shelf belief chief proof roof safe	halves loaves shelves beliefs chiefs proofs roofs safes	halved shelved	shelver		halving shelving
For words ending in *ch*, *sh*, *s*, *x*, *z*, and sometimes *o*, add *-es*. *Exceptions*	church wash class fix quiz tomato zero dynamo ghetto monarch piano portfolio radio studio	churches washes classes fixes quizzes tomatoes zeroes dynamos ghettos monarchs pianos portfolios radios studios				

Irregular Noun Plurals

person	people	foot	feet	deer	deer	series	series
child	children	tooth	teeth	fish	fish	species	species
man	men			goose	geese		
woman	women			ox	oxen		

Irregular Noun Plurals with Foreign Origins

alumnus	alumni	analysis	analyses	basis	bases	crisis	crises
criterion	criteria	curriculum	curricula	hypothesis	hypotheses	oasis	oases
memorandum	memoranda	synthesis	syntheses	thesis	theses	radius	radii
phenomenon	phenomena	nucleus	nuclei	stimulus	stimuli		
syllabus	syllabi or syllabuses						
index	indices or indexes						

Appendix 3

The with Proper Nouns

The has specific uses with proper nouns, especially with geographical locations. Because proper nouns identify specific places, *the* is often used. There are few exceptions to the rules. Study the following chart and use it for reference.

With *the*		Without *the*	
Rules	**Examples**	**Rules**	**Examples**
The is used when the class of noun (continent, country, etc.) comes before the name: *the* + class + *of* + name. *The* is used with most names of regions. *Exceptions*	the continent of Asia the United States of America the U.S.A. the West the Midwest the equator New England southern (northern, etc.)	*The* is not used with names of planets, continents, countries, states, provinces, cities, and streets. *Exceptions*	Mars Africa Antarctica Russia Ohio Quebec Austin State Street (the) earth the world the Netherlands
The is used with plural islands, lakes, and mountains. *The* is used with oceans, seas, rivers, canals, deserts, jungles, forests, and bridges.*	the Hawaiian Islands the Great Lakes the Alps the Pacific Ocean the Persian Gulf the Mississippi River the Suez Canal the Sahara Desert the Black Forest the Golden Gate Bridge	*The* is not used with singular islands, lakes, and mountains. *Exceptions*	Oahu Fiji Lake Superior Mt. Whitney the Isle of Wight the Matterhorn (and other mountains with German names that are used in English)
The is generally used when the word *college*, *university*, or *school* comes before the name: *the* + ... + *of* + name.	the University of California the Rhode Island School of Design	*The* is not used when the name of a college or university comes before the word *college* or *university*. *Exception*	Boston University Amherst College the Sorbonne

* The class name is often omitted with well-known oceans, deserts, and rivers: *the Atlantic, the Nile*.

With *the*		Without *the*	
Rules	**Examples**	**Rules**	**Examples**
The is used with adjectives of nationality and other adjectives that function as nouns.	the Germans the Japanese the rich the poor the strong	*The* is not used with names of languages. *Note: The* is used with the word *language: the German language.*	German Japanese
The is used in dates when the number comes before the month.	the twenty-eighth of March	*The* is not used in dates when the month begins the phrase.	March 28
The is used with decades, centuries, and eras.	the 1990s the 1800s the Dark Ages	*The* is not used with specific years.	1951 1890
The is used with names of museums and libraries.	the Museum of Modern Art the Chicago Public Library		

Appendix 4

Formation of Statements and Questions

The Simple Present and Past Tenses and *Have* as a Main Verb*

	Question Word	Auxiliary Verb	Subject	Auxiliary Verb (and Negative)	Main Verb	Auxiliary Verb	Pronoun
Affirmative Statement			You (I, We, They) Ted (He, She, It) She (We, They, etc.)		study. studies. studied.		
Negative Statements			You Ted	don't (didn't) doesn't (didn't)	study. study.		
Tag Questions			You You Ted Ted	don't doesn't	study, study, studies, study,	don't do doesn't does	you? you? he? he?
Yes/No Questions		Do(n't) Does(n't) Did(n't)	you Ted she		study? study? study?		
Short Responses		Yes, No, Yes, No,	I I he he	do (did). don't (didn't). does (did). doesn't (didn't).			
Information Questions	Where When Who	do does	you Ted		study? study? studied?		

* *Have* as a main verb forms statements and questions in the same way as other simple present and past tense verbs.

The Continuous and Perfect Tenses, the Modal Auxiliaries, and *Be* as a Main Verb*

	Question Word	Auxiliary Verb	Subject	Auxiliary Verb (and Negative)	Main Verb	Auxiliary Verb	Pronoun
Affirmative and Negative Statements			Ted Ted Ted	is (was)(not) should (may, etc.) (not) has (had) (not)	studying. study. studied.		
Tag Questions			Ted Ted Ted Ted Ted Ted	is isn't should shouldn't has hasn't	studying, studying, study, study, studied, studied,	isn't is shouldn't should hasn't has	he? he? he? he? he? he?
Yes/No Questions		Is(n't) Should(n't) Has(n't)	Ted Ted Ted		studying? study? studied?		
Short Responses		Yes, Yes, Yes,	he is. he should. he has.	No, he isn't. No, he shouldn't. No, he hasn't.			
Information Questions	Where What How long Who	is should has	Ted Ted Ted	 is	studying? study? studied? studying?		

*Be as a main verb forms statements and questions in the same way as the auxiliary *be* does.

Appendix 5

Modal Auxiliaries and Related Structures

Present/Future Time Frame		
Modal Auxiliary	**Function**	**Examples**
can	ability informal request	**Can** you touch your toes without bending your knees? **Can** you teach me to swim?
could	request possibility	**Could** I make an appointment with Dr. Horiuchi? Perhaps Noriko **could** take you to the dentist.
may	request permission possibility	**May** I leave now? Yes, you **may**. Sulaiman **may** be sick.
might	possibility	He **might** have the flu.
must	probability need	He **must** be at the doctor's because he isn't at home. You **must** take this medicine on an empty stomach.
must not	strong need not to do something	You **must not** drive while you are taking this medicine.
ought to	advice expectation	She **ought to** get more rest. The doctor **ought to** be here soon.
shall	request intention	**Shall** I get a bandage? We **shall** probably go to the hospital later today.
should	advice expectation	He **should** give up smoking. The swelling **should** go down in a few hours.
will	intention	I **will** get more exercise from now on!
would	request preference	**Would** you get me a bandage, please? **Would** you mind getting me a bandage? **Would** you like soda pop? I **would rather** have juice than soda pop.
be able to	ability	**Are** you **able to** swim three miles?
had better have to (have got to) don't/doesn't have to	advice need lack of need	You **had better** not swim so soon after lunch. I **have to** (**have got to**) lose weight. We **don't have to** get X rays.

Past Time Frame

Modal Auxiliary	Function	Examples
could	ability	I **could not** swim until last year.
could have	possibility	I **could have** taken lessons sooner.
may have	possibility	They **may** already **have** gone to the hospital.
might have	possibility	Juan **might have** injured his back when he fell.
must have	probability	He **must have** been in a lot of pain.
ought to have	advice not taken expectation	He **ought to have** been more careful. The doctor **ought to have** called us by now.
should have	advice not taken expectation	**Should** we **have** waited for help? Someone **should have** arrived by now.
would	habits	When I was younger, I **would** always faint at the sight of blood.
would have	preference intention not completed	**Should** we **have** waited for help? She **would rather not have** visited the hospital. Under other circumstances, **would** you **have** had that operation?
be able to	ability	Nadia **was able to** run two miles.
didn't have to	lack of need	We **didn't have to** practice on Monday because of the rain.
had to	need	We **had to** practice twice as long yesterday because we missed practice on Monday.
used to	habits	We **used to** eat a lot of sugar, but we don't anymore.

Appendix 6

Summary of Gerunds and Infinitives

Verbs Often Followed by Gerunds

admit	She **admitted** stealing the money.	involve	This job **involves** meeting a lot of people.
anticipate	We **anticipate** arriving late	keep (on)	**Keep on** working until I tell you to stop.
appreciate	I really **appreciated** getting your card.		
avoid	She **avoids** stepping on cracks—a superstition.	mention	Did she **mention** quitting her job?
be worth	I am sure it **is worth** waiting.	miss	I **miss** hearing your voice.
can't help	He **can't help** getting upset about that.	postpone	Will they **postpone** calling a meeting?
consider	Have you **considered** moving?	practice	A good tennis player has to **practice** serving.
delay	They **delayed** starting the game because of the rain.	recommend	I **recommend** taking some aspirin.
deny	He **denied** speeding.	regret	I **regret** saying that.
dislike	He really **dislikes** getting up early.	risk	She **risked** losing all her money in that deal.
dread	She **dreads** going to the dentist.		
enjoy	We always **enjoy** traveling.	spend (time)	Do you **spend** much **time** doing your homework?
escape	We narrowly **escaped** hitting the other car.	suggest	They **suggested** having a picnic.
finish	Have you **finished** writing that paper?	tolerate	I can't **tolerate** listening to rock music.
forgive	I can **forgive** his cheating, but I can't forgive his lying.		
imagine	Can you **imagine** living in Bogotá?	understand	Do you **understand** his not calling?

Verbs Often Followed by Infinitives

afford	We can't **afford** to go.	know how	Do you **know how** to play squash?
agree	They **agreed** to help.	learn	She is **learning** to play tennis.
appear	She **appeared** to be calm.	manage	Somehow he **managed** to finish the race.
be	We **were** to do the homework in Chapter 3.	offer	They **offered** to help us.
be able	**Were** you **able** to finish the work?	plan	We **planned** to leave earlier.
be supposed	You **were supposed** to do it yesterday.	prepare	They **prepared** to get on board the plane.
care	I don't **care** to go.		
decide	He **decided** to stay.	pretend	He **pretended** not to notice us.
deserve	She **deserves** to get a high grade.	refuse	I **refuse** to get up at 5:00 A.M.!
fail	They **failed** to make the deadline.	seem	He **seems** to be upset.
forget	I **forgot** to buy eggs.	tend	She **tends** to forget things.
happen	Did he **happen** to stop by?	threaten	The employee **threatened** to quit.
have	I **have** to leave.	volunteer	She **volunteered** to help us.
hesitate	Don't **hesitate** to call!	wait	She **waited** for the letter carrier to come.
hope	We **hope** to visit Rome next spring.		
intend	I **intend** to stop there for several days.	wish	We **wished** to go, but we couldn't.

Subject + verb + (optional noun or pronoun) + infinitive

ask	We **asked** to come. We **asked** them to come.	promise	She **promised** to help. She **promised** her mother to help.
beg	He **begged** to go. He **begged** us to go.	want	They **want** to leave. They **want** us to leave.
dare	I **dare** to go. I **dared** him to go.	would like	He **would like** to stay. He **would like** you to stay.
expect	I **expect** to finish soon. I **expect** them to finish soon.	use	They **used** to live there. (habitual past) They **used** a hammer to fix the table. (method)
need	I **need** to go. I **need** you to go.		

Subject + verb + noun or pronoun + infinitive

advise*	The doctor **advised** me to rest.	permit*	Will they **permit** us to camp here?
allow*	He won't **allow** you to swim.	persuade	Perhaps we can **persuade** them to let us go.
cause*	The accident **caused** me to faint.	remind	Did you **remind** her to buy milk?
convince	She **convinced** us to try again.	require	The school **required** us to wear uniforms.
encourage*	I **encourage** you to study languages.		
force	The hijacker **forced** them to land the plane.	teach*	He **taught** me to play tennis.
get	He **got** them to pay ransom.	tell	I **told** him not to come.
hire	We **hired** you to do the job.	urge	We **urge** you to change your mind.
invite	They **invited** us to come.	warn	I am **warning** you to stop!
order	I am **ordering** you to stop!		

* These verbs are followed by gerunds if no noun or pronoun object is used after the main verb.

Verb + gerund or infinitive (same meaning)

begin	She **began** to work (working) on the project.	hate	He **hates** to play (playing) golf.
		like	I **like** to play (playing) tennis.
can't bear	I **can't bear** to see (seeing) her work so much.	love	Mary **loves** to read (reading) novels.
		neglect	We **neglected** to tell (telling) her about that.
can't stand	She **can't stand** to stay (staying) alone at night.	prefer	I **prefer** to go (going) alone.
continue	They'll **continue** to practice (practicing) several days more.	start	We **started** to worry (worrying) about the situation.

Verb + gerund or infinitive (different meanings)

mean	I **meant** to finish the project sooner. This **means** delaying the project.	remember	Did you **remember** to tell her? I **remember** telling her about it, but she forgot.
quit (stop)	He **quit** (**stopped**) to take a long break. We **quit** (**stopped**) taking breaks in order to leave work.	try	We **tried** to call you, but the phone was out of order. I **tried** calling, and then I decided to write you a note.

Photo Credits

Page 3: © SW Productions/Brand X Pictures/Getty Images; 5: © Via Productions/Brand X Pictures/Jupiterimages; 17: © McDaniel Woolf/Getty Images; 21: © Jack Prelutsky/ Stock Boston; 39: © Royalty-Free/CORBIS; 40: © SW Productions/Brand X Pictures/ Getty Images; 42 (both): © image100 Ltd; 44: © The McGraw-Hill Companies Inc./Ken Cavanagh Photographer; 54: © image100 Ltd; 58 (left): © Ryan McVay/Getty Images; 58 (right): © PhotoLink/Getty Images; 61: © The Mc-Graw-Hill Companies Inc./Ken Cavanagh Photographer; 65: © PhotoLink/Getty Images; 85: Courtesy Patricia Werner; 87: © Getty Images; 92, 93: Courtesy Patricia Werner; 100: © H. Dratch/The Images Works; 112: © CORBIS; 118: © Brand X Pictures/PunchStock; 131: © image100/ PunchStock; 140 (left): © BananaStock/PictureQuest; 140 (right): © Digital Vision/ PunchStock; 145: © Neil Beer/Getty Images; 146: © Hoby Finn/Getty Images; 147: © Stockbyte/Punchstock; 149: © Royalty-Free/CORBIS; 160: © PhotoLink/Getty Images; 162: © Dynamic Graphics/JupiterImages; 163 (left): © PhotoLink/Getty Images; 163 (right): © Karl Weatherly/Getty Images; 170: © Ryan McVay/Getty Images; 173: © Getty Images; 181: © BananaStock/PictureQuest; 183: © Ryan McVay/Getty Images; 186: © Jules Frazier/Getty Images; 200: © Ted Soqui/CORBIS; 205: © Time & Life Pictures/Getty Image; 207: © PhotoLink/Getty Images; 212 (left): © G.K. & Vikki Hart/Getty Images; 212 (right): © Stockbyte/PunchStock; 213: © George Silk/Time Life Pictures/Getty Images; 216: © Bruno Herdt/Getty Images; 217: © Jim Arbogast/Getty Images; © Digital Vision/Getty Images; 247 (bottom): © Digital Vision/PunchStock; 256: © Bettmann/CORBIS; 269: © Tina Manley/Alamy; 275: © PhotoLink/Getty Images; 278: AP/Wide World Photos; 286: Courtesy of Bill Johnson; 291: © Ryan McVay/Getty Images; 295: AP/Wide World Photos; 297, 302: © Adriana Romero; 307: © Getty Images; 313, 316: AP/Wide World Photos; 325: © Kent Knudson/PhotoLink/ Getty Images; 331: © Liquidlibrary/Dynamic Graphics/Jupiterimages; 333 (top left): © Brand X Pictures/PunchStock; 333 (top right): © Corbis/PictureQuest; 333 (bottom): © Digital Vision/Getty Images; 339: © Brand X Pictures/Punch-Stock; 340 (left): © Stern/ Black Star; 340 (right): AP/Wide World Photos; 341: © Bettmann/CORBIS; 346 (top): © Doug Menuez/Getty Images; 346 (middle): © Brand X Pictures/PunchStock; 346 (bottom): © Dynamic Graphics/JupiterImages; 351, 356: © Bettmann/CORBIS; 358 (left); Courtesy Patricia Werner; 358 (right): AP/Wide World Photos; 359 (all): © Bettmann/CORBIS; 360: Library of Congress; 369: © Annie Reynolds/ PhotoLink/Getty Images; 383: © Royalty-Free/CORBIS; 385 (top left): © T. O'Keefe/ PhotoLink/Getty Images; 385 (top right): © C. Borland/PhotoLink/Getty Images; 385 (bottom left): © H. Wiesenhofer/PhotoLink/Getty Images; 385 (bottom right): © Dynamic Graphics/ JupiterImages; 388: © Photo Researchers; 390: © Royalty-Free/CORBIS; 394: © Digital Vision/Punchstock; 408: © Ryan McVay/Getty Images; 413: © M. Freeman/PhotoLink/Getty Images; 417: © Glen Allison/Getty Images; 423: © David Hiller/Getty Images; 425: © Royalty-Free/CORBIS; 436: © Bryan Mullennix/Getty Images; 442: © Steve Cole/Getty Images; 446: © PhotoDisc/Gettty Images; 447: © BananaStock/ JupiterImages; 450: Library of Congress, Prints and Photographs Division [LC-USZ62-117124]; 453: © PhotoLink/Getty Images.

Text Credits

Page 13 "New Cultures" from *The Silent Language* by Edward T. Hall. © 1990 New York: Anchor Books. **Page 18** "What is Culture?" from *Beyond Culture* by Edward T. Hall. © 1989 New York: Anchor Books. **Page 26** "Time" from *The Dance of Life* by Edward T. Hall. © 1983 New York: Anchor Books. **Page 26** Frank and Ernest cartoon "Knowing two tenses is enough reality for me." Used with permission of Tom Thaves. **Page 43** Graph, "Competitive and Cooperative Learning Index in OECD Member Countries," from *Knowledge and Skills for Life*. © 2001, OECD. Reprinted with permission. **Page 53** Real Life Adventures cartoon by Gary Wise and Lance Aldrich. January 12, 1994. **Page 99** The Family Circus cartoon. © Bil Keane, Inc. King Features Syndicate. Reprinted by permission. **Page 196** Committed cartoon. © United Features Syndicate, Inc. Reprinted by permission. **Page 210** Graph "Online Language Populations, September 2004," www.glreach.com, accessed 9/6/06. **Page 247** Cathy cartoon. © Cathy Guisewite. Reprinted with permission of Universal Press Syndicate. All rights reserved. **Page 377** Cartoon "Weekly Invention" from Side Show by Rube Goldberg. Reprinted with permission of Rube Goldberg. Rube Goldberg is the ® and © of Rube Goldberg, Inc.

Skills Index

a, 232
ability, expressing, 134
abstract nouns, 228
active voice, 184. *See also* passive voice
adjective clauses
    and appositive phrases, 414
    introduction to, 387
    and past participial phrases, 415
    and present participial phrases, 416
    restrictive vs. nonrestrictive, 397–398, 399, 407
    shortening to phrases, 414, 415, 416, 418
    and subject/verb agreement, 418
    with *that,* 387, 390–391, 392, 398, 399, 407
    with *when* and *where,* 387, 393
    with *whom* or *which,* 407
    with *who* or *which,* 399
    with *whose,* 387, 402, 409
adjective phrases, 414, 415, 416, 418
adjectives
    demonstrative, 121
    of emotion, 289
    indefinite, 238–239, 240
    infinitives following, 289
    participles as, 322
    as parts of speech, 6
    possessive, 14
    in reported speech, 121
    word order, 31
admit, 297
adverb clauses, 393
adverbials
    adjective clauses replacing, 393
    in reported speech, 121
    word order, 33
adverbs
    infinitives following, 290
    as parts of speech, 6
    with present perfect tense, 102–103
    in reported speech, 121
    of time, 32
    with time clauses, 352
    word order, 32
    See also adverbs of frequency
adverbs of frequency
    introduction to, 62
    in passive voice, 185, 196, 201, 206
    in simple past tense, 88
    with time clauses, 352
    word order, 32, 62, 88, 185, 201
advice, expressing, 155, 158, 439
advise, 172, 300, 308
a few, 240, 242
a few minutes/moments ago, 94
afford, 298
after, 11, 344, 352, 353, 369
after that, 338
agree, 298
a little, 240, 242
all, 265–266
all morning (day/week), 77
allow, 300, 308
all the time, 62
almost always, 32, 62
almost never, 62
a lot (of), 238, 242
already, 102–103, 352
although, 334
always, 32, 62
amaze, 322
an, 232
and, 11, 334, 336–337
anger, showing, 46
annoy, 322
another, 243
anticipate, 297
anticipatory *it,* 192, 287
any, 238
any-, words beginning with, 265–266
anyone, 238
appear, 9, 297, 298
appositives, 414
appreciate, 297
articles
    definite, 248, 249
    indefinite, 232
    as parts of speech, 6
as, 344, 361, 369
as a rule, 62
ask, 300
as soon as, 352, 369
astonish, 322
at that time, 94
at times, 62

auxiliary verbs
    adverbs following, 32
    with adverbs of frequency, 62
    in information questions, 47
    with *nor,* 337
avoid, 297

barely, 352
be
    adverbs following, 32
    with adverbs of frequency, 62
    gerunds following, 297
    infinitives following, 298
    as linking verb, 9
    with *nor,* 337
    with present participles, 19
    and sentence structure, 44
    in subjunctive mood, 426, 433
    See also passive voice
be able to, 134, 297, 298
because, 11, 334
become, 9
before, 344, 352, 353, 369
beg, 172, 300
begin, 292
be going to, 71, 371
be having, 66
being, 279
believe, 192
be supposed to, 297, 298
be worth, 297, 308
bore, 322
but, 11, 334, 336–337
by
    omitted with gerunds, 279
    in passive voice, 189, 190, 196, 201, 206
    in time clauses, 353
    by and large, 62
    by the time (that), 352

can
    in passive voice, 206
    pronunciation of, 134
    in reported speech, 171
    for requests, 141, 142
    in time clauses, 369
can (not) afford, 292
can't, 134
can't bear, 292
can't stand, 292
care, 298
causative verbs, 317–318

cause, 300, 308
clauses
    adverb, 393
    appositive, 414
    in complex sentences, 334
    of condition, 347, 361, 371
    coordinate, 335
    identifying, 249
    restrictive vs. nonrestrictive, 397–398, 399, 407, 414
    as subjects, 8
    subordinate, 335
    of time, 344, 352–353, 361, 369
    See also adjective clauses
collective nouns, 263–264
command, 172
commands
    in reported speech, 172
    and sentence structure, 7
    and simple verb form, 19
commas
    with appositive phrases, 414
    comma splices, 374
    in compound sentences, 11
    with coordinate clauses, 335
    with coordinating conjunctions, 336
    with restrictive vs. nonrestrictive clauses, 398, 407
    with transition words/phrases, 335
comma splices, 374
commonly, 62
complements, 9, 278, 286
complex sentences
    introduction to, 11
    past perfect continuous tense in, 115, 352
    past perfect tense in, 113
    review, 334
compound/complex sentences, 334
compound sentences, 11, 113, 334
compound subjects, 11
compound verbs, 11
concrete nouns, 228
condition, clauses of, 347, 361, 371
conditionals, imaginary, 433, 443, 444
confirm, with anticipatory *it,* 192
confuse, 322
conjunctions
    in compound sentences, 11, 334, 335
    coordinating, 11, 334, 336–337
    as parts of speech, 6
    subordinating, 353

connecting words
    and comma splices, 374
    in complex sentences, 11, 334
    as time expressions, 96
    when and *while,* 96
consider, 66, 79, 297
continue, 292
continuous tenses, 19
    future, 72, 201
    future perfect, 116
    with passive voice, 201
    past, 94, 96, 361
    past perfect, 115, 201, 352
    present, 64, 71, 344, 369
    present perfect, 76–77, 201, 344
    and sentence structure, 44
    verbs rarely used in, 66, 79
contractions
    for expressing advice, 155
    for expressing preference, 144
    in negative yes/no questions, 46
contrast, showing, 338
convince, 300
coordinate clauses, 335
coordinating conjunctions, 11, 334, 336–337
could
    for expressing ability, 134
    with imaginary conditionals, 433
    with *otherwise,* 432
    in passive voice, 206
    as perfect modal auxiliary, 437
    in reported speech, 171
    for requests, 141, 142
    in subjunctive mood, 426
could (have), 161
count/noncount nouns, 263–264
    with definite article, 248, 249, 250
    groups of, 229
    with indefinite adjectives/pronouns,
    238–239, 240
    with indefinite articles, 232
    introduction to, 228
    with modifiers, 242
    nouns that can be both, 230
    unspecified/unidentified, 232–233

dare, 297, 300
decide, 297, 298
definite article (*the*)
    with count nouns, 249
    introduction to, 248
    with noncount nouns, 250

    with proper nouns, 251
delay, 297
demonstrative adjectives, 121
deny, 192
dependent clauses. *See* adjective clauses
deserve, 298
didn't have to, 154
direct, 172
direction, adverbials of, 33
direct objects, 9, 33, 187
disappoint, 322
dislike, 297
do, 43, 44
do/does not have to, 151

each, 265–266
earlier, 338
-*ed* forms
    in past tense, 19
    in present perfect tense, 101
    pronunciation, 20, 89
    spelling rules, 88
embedded questions, 55, 56, 175
emotion, adjectives of, 289
emphasis, expressing, 338
enable, 300
encourage, 172, 300, 308
enjoy, 297
enough, 290
escape, 297
estimate, 192
ever, 102–103
every-, words beginning with, 265–266
every now and again, 62
every now and then, 62
examples, providing, 338
excite, 322
exclamations, 7
expect, 300
expectation, expressing, 137

facts, expressing, 59
fail, 298
fascinate, 322
fear, 192
feel, 9
feelings/thoughts, verbs for, 66
few, 240, 242
finally, 338
finish, 297
first, 338

for
in compound sentences, 11, 334, 336–337
with infinitives, 287
with present perfect continuous tense, 77
force, 300
for example, 338
forget, 298
forgive, 297
for instance, 338
fragments, 374
frequency, adverbials of, 33
frequency, adverbs of. *See* adverbs of frequency
frequently, 62
frighten, 322
from, 33
from time to time, 62
future, reference to, 70–71
clauses of condition, 371
present continuous tense for, 64, 71
simple present tense for, 59, 71, 369
and subjunctive mood, 426, 427
time clauses, 369
was/were going to, 108
future continuous tense, 72, 201
future perfect continuous tense, 116
future perfect tense, 19, 116
future tense
continuous, 72, 201
perfect, 19, 116
perfect continuous, 116
simple, 19, 70, 185

generally, 62
gerund phrases, 8
gerunds
following prepositions, 281–282
following verbs, 292, 297, 308, 311–312
forms of, 279
functions of, 278
and parallelism, 293
with *used to,* 107
with *would you mind,* 141
get, 9, 300, 318
going to, 71

habits/routines, expressing, 59, 347
habitual past tense, 107
had better, 155
had to, 154
happen, 298
hardly, 352
hardly ever, 62

hate, 292
have
as causative verb, 318
with continuous tenses, 66, 201
gerunds following, 297
infinitives following, 298
in passive voice, 196
with perfect modal auxiliaries, 437
and sentence structure, 44
have to, 151, 172
have trouble, 297
help, 317
here, 121
hesitate, 298
hire, 300
hope, 192, 297, 298, 426
how, 48, 240, 290
however, 338
how far, 48
how like, 48
how long, 48
how long... ?, 77
how many, 48
how much, 48
how often, 48

identifying clauses, 249
identifying phrases, 249
if
in clauses of condition, 347, 361, 371
in complex sentences, 334
in embedded questions, 55
with imaginary conditionals, 433, 443, 444
if... not, 347, 371
imaginary conditionals, 433, 443, 444
imagine, 297
in addition, 338
indefinite adjectives, 238–239, 240
indefinite articles, 232
indefinite pronouns, 238–239, 240, 265–266
indirect objects, 9, 172, 187
indirect questions. *See* embedded questions
in fact, 338
infinitive phrases, 8, 172, 174, 175
infinitives
following adjectives and nouns, 289
following adverbs, 290
following verbs, 292, 298, 300, 308, 311–312
forms of, 287
functions of, 286
gerunds following, 281
introduction to, 19

and parallelism, 293

phrases, 8, 172, 174, 175

information, providing, 338

information questions

changing to embedded questions, 56, 175

forms of, 47

question words in, 47, 48, 50

in general, 62

-ing forms, 64, 94, 320. *See also* gerunds

in order, 286

inspire, 322

intend, 298

intentions, expressing, 70, 108

interest, 322

intransitive verbs, 9

intrigue, 322

invite, 300

involve, 297

irregular verbs, 22

it

anticipatory, 192, 287

with infinitives, 289

just

with count/noncount nouns, 242

with past continuous tense, 94

with present perfect tense, 102–103

with time clauses, 352

keep (on), 297

know (how), 297, 298

lack of need, expressing, 151, 154

lately, 77

later, 338

learn (how), 297, 298

let, 317

like, 292

linking verbs, 9

little, 238, 240, 242

look, 9

lots (of), 238

love, 292

-ly forms, 32

make, 317

manage, 298

manner, adverbials of, 33

many, 238, 240, 242

may

in clauses of condition, 371

in passive voice, 206

as perfect modal auxiliary, 437

in reported speech, 171

for requests, 142

may (have), 161

mean, 79, 312

measurement, units of, 256

mention, 192

metric/British units of measurement, 258

might

in clauses of condition, 371

with imaginary conditionals, 433

with *otherwise,* 432

in passive voice, 206

as perfect modal auxiliary, 437

in reported speech, 171

might (have), 161

mind, 297

miss, 297

modal auxiliaries

in clauses of condition, 371

for expressing advice, 155, 158

for expressing expectation, 137

for expressing need/lack of need, 151, 154, 171

for expressing possibility, 161

for expressing probability, 164, 171

with imaginary conditionals, 443, 444

introduction to, 134

with passive voice, 206

perfect, 437, 439, 443

for preference, 144

in reported speech, 171, 172, 174, 175

for requests, 141, 142–143, 174

and sentence forms, 43–44

and sentence structure, 44

and simple verb form, 19

in time clauses, 369

modifiers, 242, 386. *See also* adjective clauses

much, 240, 242

must

for expressing need, 151, 154

for expressing probability, 164

in passive voice, 206

as perfect modal auxiliary, 437

in reported speech, 171

must have, 164

need, 300, 318

need, expressing, 151, 154, 171

negatives

with adverbs of frequency, 62

for expressing advice, 155

for expressing lack of need, 151, 154
with gerunds, 279
with indefinite adjectives/pronouns, 240
with infinitives, 287, 290
with *nor,* 337
in present perfect tense, 103
questions, 46, 137
with *should* and *ought to,* 137
with *would you mind,* 143
neglect, 292
never, 32, 62, 102–103
next, 338
no, 238
no-, words beginning with, 265–266
none, 238, 239, 265–266
nonrestrictive clauses, 397–398, 399, 407, 414
nonspecific nouns, 249, 250
nor, 11, 334, 336–337
normally, 62
no sooner, 352
not, 279, 287
not enough, 290
not ever, 102–103
not many, 240
not much, 240
not yet, 102–103
noun clauses, 175
nouns
    gerunds as, 278
    infinitives following, 289
    as parts of speech, 6
    proper, 251
    as subjects, 8
now, 121, 338
now and again, 62
now and then, 62
number
    and indefinite pronouns, 265–266
    subject/verb agreement, 262–263, 418
numbers, ordinal, 249, 289, 338

object pronouns, 14
objects
    adjective clauses replacing, 392
    and adverb word order, 32
    following verbs with infinitives or gerunds, 300, 308
    gerunds as, 278
    infinitives as, 286
    and passive voice, 187
    in reported speech, 172
    with transitive verbs, 9

whom or *which* replacing, 407, 409
occasionally, 62
of, 256, 289
off and on, 62
offer, 298
offers/promises, expressing, 70
often, 62
on a regular basis, 62
once, 352, 369
once in a (great) while, 62
one, 243
only, 242
on the other hand, 338
opinions, expressing, 59
or, 11, 334, 336–337
order, 172, 300
ordinal numbers, 249, 289, 338
others, 243
otherwise, 432
ought (not) to have, 158, 439
ought to
    for expressing advice, 155
    for expressing expectation, 137
    in passive voice, 206
    as perfect modal auxiliary, 437, 439
    pronunciation, 137, 155
    in reported speech, 171

parallelism, 293
participles. *See* past participles; present participles
parts of speech, 6. *See also* adjectives; adverbs; nouns; pronouns; verbs
passive voice
    anticipatory *it* in, 192
    by in, 189, 190, 196, 201, 206
    causative verbs in, 318
    common verbs for, 190–191
    with continuous tenses, 201
    gerunds in, 279
    and indirect objects, 187
    infinitives in, 287
    introduction to, 184
    with modal auxiliaries, 206
    past participles in, 19, 185, 196, 201, 206, 287
    with perfect tenses, 196
    and reported speech, 192
    with simple tenses, 185
past continuous tense, 94, 96, 361
past participial phrases, 415
past participles
    as adjectives, 322

for expressing advice, 158
for expressing possibility, 161
for expressing probability, 164
introduction to, 19
in passive voice, 19, 185, 196, 201, 206, 287
in past perfect tense, 113
with perfect modal auxiliaries, 439
in phrases, 415
in present perfect tense, 103
in subjunctive mood, 427
past perfect continuous tense, 115, 201, 352
past perfect tense
    with adverbs of frequency, 61
    introduction to, 19
    with passive voice, 196
    vs. simple past, 113–114
    with time clauses, 352
past tense
    continuous, 94, 96, 361
    habitual, 107
    introduction to, 19
    perfect, 19, 61, 113–114, 196, 352
    perfect continuous, 115, 201, 352
    for reported speech, 119, 120, 192
    with *was/were going to,* 108
    with *would you mind,* 143
    See also simple past tense
pauses, 398
perception, verbs of, 66, 320
perfect modal auxiliaries, 437, 439, 443
perfect tenses
    with adverbs of frequency, 61
    future, 19, 116
    future continuous, 116
    with passive voice, 196
    past, 19, 61, 113–114, 196, 352
    past continuous, 115, 201, 352
    present continuous, 76–77, 201, 344
    and sentence structure, 44
    and verb forms, 19
    See also present perfect tense
permission, requesting, 142–143
permit, 300, 308
person, 14
persuade, 300
phrases
    appositive, 414
    identifying, 249
    infinitive, 8, 172, 174, 175
    past participial, 415
    present participial, 416
    as subjects, 8

subordinate, 335
place, adverbials of, 33, 393
plan, 298
please, 322
plenty (of), 238
plurals. *See* number
possessives
    adjectives vs. pronouns, 14
    and gerunds, 279
    verbs, 66
    whose replacing, 402
possibility, expressing, 161
postpone, 297
practice, 297
predictions, 70
prefer, 292
preference, expressing, 144
prepare, 298
prepositions
    and adjective clauses, 409
    gerunds following, 281–282
    with participles used as adjectives, 322
    as parts of speech, 6
    in passive voice, 190, 191
    in time clauses, 353
present continuous tense, 64, 71, 344, 369
present participial phrases, 416
present participles
    as adjectives, 322
    introduction to, 19
    in phrases, 416
    and verbs of perception, 320
    verbs of perception, 320
present perfect continuous tense, 76–77, 201, 344
present perfect tense
    adverbs of frequency with, 61
    adverbs with, 102–103
    for continuing actions, 79
    introduction to, 19, 101
    with passive voice, 196
    in time clauses, 344, 369
present tense
    continuous, 64, 71, 344, 369
    perfect continuous, 76–77, 201, 344
    See also present perfect tense; simple present tense
pretend, 298
probability, expressing, 164, 171
promise, 300
pronouns
    indefinite, 238–239, 240, 265–266

as parts of speech, 6
possessive, 14
reflexive, 14
in reported speech, 121
as subjects, 8, 14
pronunciation
can, 141
can/can't, 134
could, 141
could have, 161
-ed forms, 20, 89
going to, 71
had better, 155
have/has to, 151
may have, 161
might have, 161
must have, 164
ought to, 137, 155
ought to have, 158
pauses in, 398
-s forms, 20
should have, 158
will, 141
would, 141
proper nouns, 251
punctuation
and sentence problems, 374
and sentence types, 11, 334, 335
See also commas; semicolons
purpose, expressing, 286, 289

questions
with adverbs of frequency, 62
and adverb word order, 32
embedded, 55, 56, 175
for expressing advice, 155
with indefinite adjectives/pronouns, 240
information, 47, 48, 50, 56, 175
with modal auxiliaries, 43–44
negative, 46, 137
in present perfect tense, 103
and sentence structure, 7
yes/no, 43, 44, 46, 55, 175
See also yes/no questions
question words
in embedded questions, 56
in information questions, 47, 48, 50
quit, 312
quite, 242
quotations
commands in, 172
embedded questions in, 175

vs. reported speech, 119
requests in, 174
tense in, 120
rarely, 62
reasons, providing, 338
recently, 77, 102–103
recommend, 297
reflexive pronouns, 14
refuse, 298
regret, 297
relative clauses. *See* dependent clauses
relax, 322
remember, 311, 312
remind, 300
repeated nouns, 249
report, 192
reported speech, 119–120
commands in, 172
embedded questions in, 175
infinitive phrases in, 172, 174, 175
modal auxiliaries in, 171, 172, 174, 175
and passive voice, 192
pronoun/adjective/adverbial changes in, 121
vs. quotations, 119
requests in, 174
requests, 70, 141, 142–143, 174
require, 300
restrictive clauses, 397–398, 399, 407
results, providing, 338
risk, 297
run-on sentences, 374

satisfy, 322
say, 123, 192
scarcely, 352
second, 338
seem, 9, 298
seldom, 32, 62
semicolons, 334, 335, 432
sentences
complex, 11, 113, 115, 334, 352
compound, 11, 113, 334
compound/complex, 334
problems with, 374
simple, 11, 334
structures of, 6–7, 9
types of, 6–7, 11, 324
sequence, showing, 338
sequence expressions, 88
-s forms
in noncount nouns, 228
pronunciation, 20

and subject-verb agreement, 262

shall, 206

short responses, 43–44

should
in clauses of condition, 371
in commands, 172
for expressing advice, 155
for expressing expectation, 137
in passive voice, 206
as perfect modal auxiliary, 437, 439
in reported speech, 171, 172
in time clauses, 369

should (not) have, 158, 439

simple future tense, 19, 69–70, 185

simple past tense
with clauses of time and condition, 361
introduction to, 19, 88
with passive voice, 185
vs. past perfect, 113–114
pronunciation, 89
with *when* or *while,* 96

simple present tense
with adverbs of frequency, 62
introduction to, 19
with passive voice, 185
for reference to future, 59, 71, 369
in time clauses, 344, 369
uses of, 59

simple sentences, 11, 334

simple verb form
for expressing need, 151, 154
for expressing possibility, 161
for expressing probability, 164
introduction to, 19

since, 77, 344

smell, 9

so, 11, 334, 336–337

some, 238

some-, words beginning with, 265–266

someone, 238

sometimes, 62

sound, 9

specific nouns, 249, 250

spelling rules for *-ed* forms, 88

spend time, 297

start, 292

statements
with adverbs of frequency, 62
with modal auxiliaries, 43–44
in present perfect tense, 103
and sentence structure, 7

still, 94, 102–103

stop, 312

subject pronouns, 8, 14

subjects
adjective clauses replacing, 390–391
and adverb word order, 32
gerunds as, 278
infinitives as, 286
pronouns as, 8, 14
and sentence structure, 7, 8
in simple sentences, 11
understood, 8
who or *which* replacing, 399
See also subject/verb agreement

subject/verb agreement, 262–264, 418

subjunctive mood, 426–427, 433, 443, 444

subordinate phrases/clauses, 335

subordinating conjunctions, 353

suggest, 297

superlatives, 249

surprise, 322

surprise, showing, 46

tag questions, 44

take, 289

taste, 9

teach, 300, 308

tell, 123, 172, 300

tend, 298

tenses
formation of, 19, 22
in passive voice, 184
system of, 26
See also specific tenses

testing practice, 82–83, 127–128, 177–178, 220–222, 271–273, 328–329, 379–380, 420–421, 457–459

that
in adjective clauses, 387, 390–391, 392, 398, 399, 407
with anticipatory *it,* 192
in complex sentences, 11, 334
omitted, 392
in present participial phrases, 416
in reported speech, 119, 120, 121
in restrictive vs. nonrestrictive clauses, 398, 399, 407

the (definite article), 248, 249, 250, 251

then, 94, 121, 338

the other, 243

the others, 243

there, 121

there + be, 289

therefore, 338
these, 121
think, 66, 79, 192
this, 121
those, 121
threaten, 298
thrill, 322
time clauses, 344, 352–353, 361, 369
time expressions
    adverbials of time, 33, 393
    adverbs of time, 32
    connecting words, 96
    with past continuous tense, 94
    with present perfect continuous tense, 76, 77
    with present perfect tense, 79, 369
    in reported speech, 121
    time clauses, 344, 352–353, 361, 369
    as transitions, 338
    See also adverbs of frequency
tire, 322
to, 33, 282, 293
today, 32, 121
tolerate, 297
tomorrow, 32, 121
too, 242, 290
transition words/phrases, 334, 335, 338, 432
transitive verbs, 9
try, 312
typically, 62

understand, 297
unique nouns, 249
units of measurement, 256
unless, 347, 361, 371
unspecified/unidentified count/noncount nouns, 232–233
until, 344, 352, 353, 369
until now, 77
up to now, 77
urge, 172, 300
use, 300
used to, 107
usually, 32, 62

verbs
    and adverb word order, 32
    causative, 317–318
    gerunds following, 292, 297, 308, 311–312
    infinitives following, 292, 298, 300, 308, 311–312
    irregular, 22

    objects following, 300, 308
    as parts of speech, 6
    for passive voice, 190–191
    of perception, 66, 321
    principal parts of, 19
    for reported speech, 119–120, 192
    and sentence structure, 7, 9
    in simple sentences, 11
    transitive vs. intransitive, 9
    See also auxiliary verbs; modal auxiliaries; simple verb form; subject/verb agreement; tenses
very, 242
volunteer, 298

wait, 298
want, 79, 300
warn, 172, 300
was, 426
was/were going to, 108
we, 8
were, 426, 433
what
    in embedded questions, 56
    with infinitives, 290
    in information questions, 50
    as question word, 48
what... be (look) like, 48
what color (size, shape), 48
what time, 48
when
    in adjective clauses, 387, 393
    in complex sentences, 334
    as connecting word, 96
    in embedded questions, 56
    with infinitives, 290
    in information questions, 47
    in past perfect tense, 113–114
    as question word, 48
    in time clauses, 344, 352, 361, 369
whenever, 344
where
    in adjective clauses, 387, 393
    with infinitives, 290
    in information questions, 47
    as question word, 48
whether, 55
which
    in adjective clauses, 387, 399, 407, 409
    with infinitives, 290
    in information questions, 50
    in present participial phrases, 416

as question word, 48

while
    in complex sentences, 11
    as connecting word, 96
    in time clauses, 344, 361, 369

who
    in adjective clauses, 387, 391, 399
    in complex sentences, 11, 334
    in embedded questions, 56
    in information questions, 50
    in present participial phrases, 416
    as question word, 48

whom
    in adjective clauses, 387, 407, 409
    in embedded questions, 56
    as question word, 48

whose
    in adjective clauses, 387, 402, 409
    in information questions, 50
    as question word, 48

why, 47, 48, 56
why... not, 47, 48

will
    in clauses of condition, 371
    vs. *going to,* 71
    in passive voice, 206
    in reported speech, 171
    for requests, 141

will be, 185, 201
wish, 298, 426
without fail, 62

word order
    in adjective clauses, 409
    adjectives, 31
    adverbials, 33
    adverbs, 32
    adverbs of frequency, 32, 62, 88, 185, 201
    in appositive phrases, 414
    in information questions, 47, 50
    in passive voice, 185, 196
    in present participial phrases, 416
    in present perfect tense, 103
    sequence expressions, 88

worry, 322

would
    in habitual past tense, 107
    with imaginary conditionals, 433
    with *otherwise,* 432
    in passive voice, 206
    as perfect modal auxiliary, 437
    pronunciation, 141
    in reported speech, 171
    for requests, 141
    in subjunctive mood, 426

would like, 144, 292, 298, 300
would love, 292, 298
would rather, 437
would rather (not), 144
would you mind, 141, 143

yes/no questions
    changing to embedded questions, 55, 175
    forms of, 43, 44
    negative, 46

yesterday, 33, 121

yet
    in compound sentences, 11, 334, 336–337
    with present perfect tense, 102–103

you, 8